EVANGELIZING (the) CHOSEN PEOPLE

Missions to the
Jews in America,
1880–2000
by Yaakov Ariel

The University of North Carolina Press

Chapel Hill and London

Set in Minion and Castellar
by Keystone Typesetting, Inc.
Manufactured in the United States of America
The paper in this book meets the guidelines for permanence and
durability of the Committee on Production Guidelines for Book
Longevity of the Council on Library Resources.
Parts of Chapter 4 have appeared in revised form in "The Evangelist
at Our Door: The American Jewish Response to Christian
Missionaries, 1880–1920," American Jewish Archives 48 (Fall–Winter
1996): 139–60.
Parts of Chapter 12 have appeared in revised form in "Eschatology,
Evangelism, and Dialogue: The Presbyterian Mission to the Jews,
1920–1960," Journal of Presbyterian History 75, no. 1 (Spring 1997):
29–41.
Parts of Chapter 14 have appeared in revised form in "Evangelists in
a Strange Land: American Missionaries in Israel, 1948–1967," in
Studies in Contemporary Jewry, vol. 14, Coping with Life and Death:
Jewish Families in the Twentieth Century, edited by Peter Y. Medding
(New York: Oxford University Press, 1998). Used by permission of
Oxford University Press, Inc.
The first part of Chapter 19 uses material previously published in
"Counterculture and Mission: Jews for Jesus and the Vietnam Era
Missionary Campaigns, 1970–1975," Religion and American Culture
9, no. 2 (Summer 1999): 233–57.
Library of Congress Cataloging-in-Publication Data
Ariel, Yaakov S. (Yaakov Shalom), 1954–
Evangelizing the chosen people: missions to the Jews in America,
1880–2000/Yaakov Ariel.
     p. cm.
Includes bibliographical references and index.
ISBN 0-8078-2566-2 (cloth: alk. paper)—
ISBN 0-8078-4880-8 (pbk.: alk. paper)
1. Missions to Jews—United States—History.   I. Title.
BV2620 .A72   2000
266'.0088'296—dc21   00-023447

04   03   02   01   00   5   4   3   2   1

This book was published with the assistance of the H. Eugene and
Lillian Youngs Lehman Fund of the University of North Carolina
Press. A complete list of books published with the assistance of
the Lehman Fund appears at the end of the book.

To my parents,

Batya and Aharon Ariel

Contents

Acknowledgments

I decided to write about the history of missions to the Jews sometime after I had completed a dissertation on American fundamentalist attitudes toward the Jewish people and Zionism. Martin Marty, my adviser at the University of Chicago, deserves special thanks for his interest in my work and his encouragement all along the way. I owe a debt of gratitude to the Louisville Institute, a Lilly Endowment Program for the study of American religion based at Louisville Seminary, which provided me with a generous grant that enabled me to carry out my research. Its director, James W. Lewis, has been particularly helpful. I am thankful to the Blumenthal Foundation for its support and to the University of North Carolina at Chapel Hill for a semester of leave, which enabled me to advance on my writing. I also owe thanks to the American Jewish Archives in Cincinnati for the fruitful time I spent at the archives.

I was fortunate in having received much help in my search for sources from a number of people who provided valuable data and insight into the missionary scene. William A. Currie shared his experiences as director of the American Messianic Fellowship. I also benefited greatly from talks with Harold A. Sevener, former president of the Chosen People Ministries. Wes Taber allowed me access to archival material at AMF-International, offered kind hospitality, and discussed issues relating to the current missionary scene. Rich Robinson provided helpful guidance while I was doing research at the archives of Jews for Jesus in San Francisco. I owe special thanks to Louis Goldberg, former director of the Jewish program at the Moody Bible Institute in Chicago, for his constant help. Robert I. Winer, M.D., shared documents with me that he had collected on the early history of the Hebrew Christian movement in America and introduced me to leaders in the Messianic Jewish community, among them Johanna, David, and Joel Chernoff, Joe Finkelstein, and Michael and Rachel Wolf, all of whose testimonies on the early beginnings of Messianic Judaism have been particularly illuminating. Arnold G. Fruchtenbaum, John Fischer, and Elwood McQuaid, veterans of the missionary and Messianic Jewish movement, sent me copies of their books or discussed issues relating to their work with me. Ray Ganon sent me a collection of documents on the history of Pentecostal efforts at evangelizing Jews. Gabi Zeldin, whose Ph.D. dissertation I had the privilege of guiding, directed me to a number of sources relating to the history of American missions in Israel. Michele Rosenthal very generously sent me her collection of books and articles on Messianic Judaism. Michael Zuckerman and Shan Holt were immensely kind to me while I was doing my research in Philadelphia.

A number of colleagues and friends read the manuscript in part or in its entirety and provided valuable comments and editorial advice: R. Scott Appleby, Ruth Blum, Paul Cohen, Gershon Greenberg, Richard Polenberg, Alifa Saadya, and Jonathan Sarna. Their suggestions have helped improve the manuscript immensely. Others discussed issues with me that came about during my writing or gave me copies of their work, among them Catherine L. Albanese, Benjamin Beit-Hallahmi, Menahem Benhayim, David Halperin, Carol Harris-Shapiro, Samuel Heilman, Dana Kaplan, Ruth Kark, Benny Kraut, Paul Merkley, Gershon Nerel, Leonard Prager, Louis Rambo, Jack Sasson, and John Van Seters. Research assistants at the University of North Carolina have helped me with the manuscript: Michele Easter, Mary Frances Kerr, Amy Lorion, and Jennifer Wojcikowski. So did Katherine Monahan, who showed an unusual amount of goodwill and patience. Grace Buonocore, Elaine Maisner, and Pamela Upton of the University of North Carolina Press have also been very helpful.

Last, but not least, are members of my close family: my wife, Rachel, and my children, Yael, Nadav, and Tamar, who tolerated my dedication of time and energy to the exploration of missions and offered love and support, as did my parents, Batya and Aharon, to whom this book is dedicated.

EVANGELIZING the CHOSEN PEOPLE

Introduction

It was August 1993. I was doing research at the archives of Jews for Jesus, the best-known and most visible mission to the Jews in America. I tried to make the most of my stay and remained in the archives, which were located in the Haight-Ashbury section of San Francisco, until it was time for me to go to the airport, at which point I ordered a cab. The cabbie, noticing the sign on the door of the building, began cursing. When we introduced ourselves, I learned that he was Jewish, secular, and unaffiliated with any form of Jewish religious life. He knew very little about missions to the Jews, their character and motivation. Nevertheless, for him, Jews for Jesus was an enemy group, out to capture Jewish souls and destroy the Jewish people. The cabbie's reaction was typical of Jewish attitudes toward the attempts to evangelize Jews. Not only cab drivers but also community leaders and scholars have depicted missionaries in unfavorable terms. Jews have tended to look upon the modern missionary movement as a continuation of the centuries-long intolerant stand of the non-Jewish world and its attempts to do away with the Jews: assimilate or annihilate them.[1] The movement signified a delegitimization of Judaism as a vital religious community alongside Christianity. Discussing the issue with the cabbie, I explained that I was not a member of the missionary organization but had come as a scholar to research it and that, in my opinion, the only way to understand it was to treat it seriously and respectfully, studying and judging it on its own terms.

My interest in missions began in early childhood when I encountered American missionaries in the neighborhood of Jerusalem in which I grew up: a poor section on the dividing line between the Israeli and Jordanian parts of the city, inhabited by newly arrived immigrants from North Africa and the Middle East. One unforgettable missionary was Uga ("Cake" in Hebrew), who earned her name by offering the neighborhood children "cakes" (in actuality, cookies) as a means of approaching them and gaining their trust. Uga was an unusual person; an independent missionary, she lived in a room she sublet from a poor North African family and rode bicycles—an unusual habit that no other elderly female ventured to do in Jerusalem in those days. Another visible missionary presence in the neighborhood was that of the A. N. Dugger's Church of God, which organized activities for children. The mission handed out pamphlets on street corners, some of which I still keep. My interest in the topic was aroused again years later, when I examined American Protestant attitudes toward the Jewish people. I came to the realization that the biblical, premillennialist messianic image of the Jews and the zeal to convert that people were strongly connected—one motivating the other.

Missions to the Jews have played an important role in American religious history and stood high on the agenda of conservative Protestants who sponsored the missionary activity and of the Jewish community that defended against it. The missionizing efforts stirred strong emotions in both religious communities and stood at the center of the encounter between Christians and Jews in America. By the late twentieth century, the movement had even formed a new subdivision in American Christianity: Messianic Judaism, which aims to combine the Christian faith with Jewish ethnic loyalties.

Curiously, virtually no academic books have been published on the history of missions to the Jews in America. Most works on the subject have been hagiographic accounts by members of the missionary community, or antagonistic Jewish ones that vehemently attacked the missions' work.[2] Neither genre does justice to the complex history of the movement. In this book, I offer a different point of view. I wish neither to canonize nor to condemn. Rather, the book explores the history of the movement to evangelize the Jews, aiming, in the words of a leading historian of American missions, to cut a balance between appreciation and criticism.[3] I endeavored to study the missions and the missionaries on their own ground, trying to reconstruct their world and understand their motivation. Similarly, the book analyzes other participants in the missionary drama—the converts, as well as the Jewish leadership and laypersons who reacted to the missionary activity—on their own terms, without praising or condemning.

American Protestants first began to evangelize Jews in 1816. During the middle decades of the nineteenth century, Protestants continued their attempts to convert American Jews; this shaped Jewish-Christian relations, provoking Jewish resentment, and left its mark on the Jewish social agenda.[4] Until the 1880s, however, the missionary enterprises were small and sporadic.[5] Before that time, mainline Protestant churches had not yet embraced the premillennialist messianic belief, which usually brought with it an increased interest in the Jews and the prospect of their conversion and national restoration. The premillennialist movements of antebellum America—such as the Mormons or Millerites—operated outside the mainstream of American Christianity.[6] Only after the Civil War did large numbers of mainline Protestants endorse the belief in the Second Coming of Jesus and his reign on earth for a thousand years.

The driving force for a strong movement of American Christians laboring at missionizing the Jews has been a new school of premillennialist hope: dispensationalism. This conviction focused much attention on the Jews and has served as the most decisive motivation for those who have evangelized Jews in the United States. John Darby and the Plymouth Brethren crystallized this school of Christian eschatology in Britain in the 1830s.[7] Dispensationalists have seen the Jews as heirs of historical Israel and the object of the biblical prophecies about a restored Davidic kingdom in the Land of Israel, which they identified with the messianic commonwealth. According to the dispensationalist eschatological narrative, the Jews would return to Palestine to build an independent political state, thereby preparing the way for the arrival of the Messiah. By the time Jesus came to establish his righteous kingdom, the Jews would welcome him and recognize him as their Savior. From the widespread acceptance of this belief in America during the 1870s, its adherents took great interest in the Jewish people, the prospect of their national restoration, and religious conversion. Dispensationalist literature has highlighted the Jews and their central role in the eschatological events.[8] And in the late nineteenth century, American Protestants influenced by premillennialist ideas had come up with initiatives that aimed at restoring the Jews to the Land of Israel.

In the late 1870s, only one mission labored among the Jews in America. By the 1910s, dozens had sprung up, employing hundreds of missionaries in a wide and aggressive movement of evangelism directed specifically at Jews. The messianic hope also shaped the missions' character. The names of the missions, their mottoes, the literature they distributed among supporters and prospective converts, and the reasoning they used in propagating the Christian gospel among the Jews were all marked by a dispensationalist messianic understanding of history's course and the Jewish role in it. The Protestant missionary efforts, motivated by the dispensationalist messianic understanding of that nation and its role in history, have continued uninterrupted throughout the twentieth century.

The theological motivation for evangelizing the Jews remained the same, whereas the techniques used to approach them changed from one generation to another. The movement to evangelize the Jews proved resourceful, adapting skillfully to prospective converts' changing interests and needs. As the Jewish community and its cultural context shifted, so did the missions. During the first period of the premillennialist missions to the Jews, from the 1880s to the 1910s, Jewish immigrants from eastern Europe crowded into poor neighborhoods in major American cities. Missions operated in the immigrants' quarters, concentrating on newly arrived young people who were trying to build homes and find work in America. Missions offered immigrants a variety of social services in an attempt to gain trust and open doors.

A second phase began in the 1920s. Jewish life in America changed considerably: the 1924 legal restrictions put a stop to the large influx of Jewish immigrants, and the proportion of American-born Jews grew considerably. Accordingly, missions began directing their attention to the second generation, the sons and daughters of immigrants. Those young Jews had attended American schools and were much more at home in American society and culture than their parents were. Many missionary agencies moved from storefront missions in the immigrant quarters to the middle-class Jewish neighborhoods to which many Jews had moved. Missions adapted their techniques to the hopes and aspirations of the new generation. In the late 1960s and the early 1970s, missions faced new social realities: the coming of age of the third generation of American Jewish immigrants, the Jewish baby boomers, who were mostly raised in middle-class families. This generation was fully at home in America and strongly influenced by the turmoil of the Vietnam War era. Again, the movement to evangelize the Jews altered its techniques in accordance with the values and tastes of the new generation. This period witnessed the rise of Jews for Jesus, a missionary group that split from an older established mission. Adopting the young people's style in dress, hair, and music, the new mission proved successful with the new generation. Messianic Judaism also emerged during that era as a movement of Jewish converts to evangelical Christianity who wished to retain their Jewish identity while they practiced the Christian faith. The Messianic Jewish movement, which arose out of the missionary efforts, became a major arm of the movement to evangelize the Jews. Messianic Jews established their own congregations, which then became centers for propagating the Christian gospel among unconverted Jews.

Ironically, missions have become part of Jewish life in America. Jews were bound to encounter missionaries, very often on sidewalks as the latter were distributing their tracts and inviting people to prayer meetings or as the former were passing by mission houses. Many visited these centers either out of curiosity or as recipients of various services. In later years, Jews encountered missions through ads in newspapers and magazines and on the World Wide Web.

At any given time during the twentieth century, dozens of American missions employing hundreds of missionaries focused on Jews. Whereas almost all missions shared the same theology and sense of purpose, they still competed with one another for support, power, and prestige. Rivalries and disagreements broke out, factions arose and schisms took place, and the status of different missionary agencies that constituted the wider movement changed throughout the years. New ascending missions often introduced new methods and sparked enthusiasm, becoming leaders of the movement.

The decision to evangelize the Jews, or to condemn such activity, expressed dramatically different Christian beliefs and values. The missions' base of support shifted throughout the years. Some mainline denominations that supported missionary activity in the earlier periods abandoned it by the 1960s. The more conservative evangelical churches, however, pursued Jewish evangelization wholeheartedly. Unimpressed by the new trends of interfaith dialogue, conservative Christians have continued to view evangelism as a manifestation of goodwill and positive intentions. Influenced by a biblical premillennialist outlook, many in this camp have continued to view the Jews as God's covenant nation, who, while blinded to their true destiny in our age, were still destined to return to their former glory in the messianic age. As viewers of such televangelists as Pat Robertson know, evangelizing the Jews has remained high on the evangelical agenda. As it did a hundred years before, missions continue to arouse heated reactions in the Jewish community.

The missionary movement, I suggest, played an important role in the history of Christian-Jewish relations in America. Understandably, the missionary agenda of large segments of American Christianity influenced the relations between the two religious communities. Jewish leaders protested the missionary presence and described it as an obstacle to a good relationship based on mutual respect. Amazingly, the Jewish reaction has influenced the missionary enterprise. Missionaries took notice of Jewish complaints and accusations and anticipated those objections in their own apologetic tracts and evangelization strategy.

The book is divided into three sections, corresponding to the three main periods in the history of the missions to the Jews in America. Although the sections are organized chronologically, chapters within them are arranged thematically, dealing with the theology and activity of the missions, as well as with the converts and the reaction of the Jewish community. The chapters pay special attention to institutions, organizations, conferences, publications, and individuals that shape the missionary agenda or respond to it.

Missions to the Jews have become more relevant toward the end of the twentieth century than ever before, as the number of converts swells to perhaps the largest voluntary movement of Jewish converts to Christianity in the history of Jewish-Christian contact. It serves as a striking demonstration of the success of the missionary movement to convert large numbers of Jews and its ongoing vitality. It also points to the need to explore the rich and lively history of the missions, which stands in the background to the rise of the current movement of converts.

I

The Rise of
the Movement
to Evangelize the
Jews, 1880–1920

1

Eschatology and Mission

In the 1890s, an unusual religious group convened on the Lower East Side of New York: immigrant Jews who had accepted the Christian faith yet continued to retain Jewish rites and customs. Established by Methodist missionaries, the "Hope of Israel" mission aimed at propagating the Christian gospel among the Jews, while promoting the idea that Jewish converts should not abandon their cultural and religious heritage. This attempt to create a congregation of Jewish converts to Christianity was one manifestation of a larger movement that came to evangelize the Jews in America at that time. It advocated a premillennialist messianic theology and emphasized the central role of the Jews in the divine program for the End Times. The messianic belief shaped the character of the missionary movement, its rhetoric, symbols, the publications it produced, and its appeals to supporters as well as to potential converts.

The movement to evangelize the Jews in America had its precedent in Europe. European pietists had established missions to the Jews in the seventeenth and eighteenth centuries, which served as early models and inspiration for future Protestant evangelization enterprises. The early nineteenth century saw a dramatic rise in attempts to convert Jews in Britain, which was witnessing a strong evangelical and premillennialist resurgence, including hope for the national rejuvenation of the Jews.[1]

Missions to the Jews began in America in the early years of the nineteenth century.[2] But although Jewish leaders reacted with anger and alarm to the attempts to evangelize their people, only one missionary enterprise, the American Society for Meliorating the Condition of the Jews, lasted long enough to receive much visibility in the Protestant community.[3] Prior to the 1880s, evangelizing the Jews was not a high priority for American Protestants, especially when compared with the support they gave this work from that time onward; nor do early-nineteenth-century evangelization efforts compare to work carried out in Britain during the earlier parts of the nineteenth century.[4] During an era labeled "a century of missions," in which American Protestants spent much energy, personnel, and resources bringing the gospel to the unchurched, both at home and abroad, the realm of Jewish missions was relatively neglected. Unlike in Britain, where there was an ardent interest in the early and middle decades of the nineteenth century in converting the Jews, American Protestants lacked the necessary motivation, namely, an intensive messianic, premillennialist hope that viewed the Jews as the chosen people and emphasized the role of the Jews in God's plans for the End Times.

There were groups in America in the earlier parts of the nineteenth century that advocated the idea of the Second Coming of Jesus to earth, such as the Millerites and the Mormons. These groups, however, were ostracized by mainstream American Protestants.[5] The Millerites, who stirred an unprecedented movement of messianic expectation in America in the 1830s and early 1840s, assigned no particular role in their messianic scheme to the Jews.[6] The belief in the Second Coming of Jesus and his reign on earth for a thousand years began capturing the hearts of members of major Protestant churches in America only in the decades after the Civil War, when a new messianic belief known as dispensationalism was accepted by millions of American Protestants.

Dispensationalism was crystallized in Britain in the 1830s by John Darby and the group he led, the Plymouth Brethren.[7] For Darby and his disciples, the Jews were historical Israel and the object of the biblical prophecies about the restored Davidic kingdom in the Land of Israel. According to the dispensationalist messianic hope, the Jews will return to their land "in unbelief," that is, without having accepted Jesus as their Savior, and will establish a sovereign state there. The actual apocalyptic events will begin with the "rapture of the church," when the true believers will be raptured from earth, meet Jesus in the air, and stay with him there for seven years (according to some variations, three and a half years). The earth will undergo a period of turmoil known as the "Great Tribulation." This will include a series of natural disasters: earthquakes, floods, and plagues as well as social and political unrest, including wars, revolutions, and a series of invasions of the Land of Israel. Eventually, about two-thirds of humanity will perish.[8] For the Jews, that tumultuous period will be the "Time of Jacob's Trouble" (Jeremiah 30:7). Antichrist, a Jewish ruler and an impostor of the Messiah, will reestablish the Temple, reinstate sacrifices, and inflict a reign of terror. During this reign the Jews will gradually recognize Jesus as their Savior and will receive him gladly when he comes to earth with his saints, the true believers, crushing Antichrist and establishing his righteous kingdom. During the messianic period the Jews will be restored to their position as the chosen people and will serve as Christ's lieutenants—the administrators and evangelists of the millennial era.

This messianic belief gained ground in the last decades of the nineteenth century among members of evangelical Protestant churches in America, such as Methodists, Presbyterians, and Baptists. In the late nineteenth and early twentieth centuries, dispensationalism became an important component of the worldview of the conservative camp within American Protestantism. It meshed well with the fundamentalist view, which criticized the prevailing cultural trend in society, and offered an alternative philosophy of history to the liberal postmillennialist notions that prevailed in American Christianity at the time.[9] In contrast to the liberal belief that human beings could work toward the building of a better, even perfect, world, dispensationalists insisted that only divine intervention—the appearance of the Messiah—could remedy the problems of the human race. The growing prominence of the messianic belief among conservative Protestants was demonstrated by the popularity of dispensationalist premillennialist literature. Books advocating the messianic belief, such as James H. Brookes's *Maranatha*, were sold by the hundreds of thousands. Brookes, a Presbyterian minister from St. Louis, first published his book in 1874. In the following decades, the book appeared in numerous editions, becoming a best-seller. *Maranatha* elaborated on the role of the Jewish people in the events of the End Times and in the millennial kingdom. Like other advocates of the belief in the Second Coming of Christ and the centrality of the Jewish people for the advancement of the messianic age, Brookes strongly supported missions to the Jews. Another popular publication that enhanced the spread of the dispensationalist belief and the idea that the Jews were God's chosen nation was *The Scofield Reference Bible*. Published in 1909, the book sold a few million copies and helped strengthen the bond between fundamentalism and the dispensationalist school of messianic faith.

Dispensationalism had a decisive influence on the way the American evangelical Protestant community viewed the Jewish people. The 1870s, 1880s, and 1890s witnessed the beginning of a keen interest of members of this camp in the Jews, whom they saw as the chosen people, destined to play a dominant role in God's plans for humanity. Since the 1870s, almost all popular books intended to promote the dispensationalist premillennialist creed have emphasized the role of the Jews in the advancement of the messianic age.[10] The interest premillennialist evangelicals took in the Jewish people manifested itself in initiatives intended to advance the return of the Jews to the Land of Israel, a prerequisite, from a dispensationalist point of view, to the arrival of the Messiah.[11] One such outstanding example was that of William Blackstone, founder of the Chicago Hebrew Mission. In 1891, Blackstone organized a petition to the president of the United States, Benjamin Harrison, urging him to take steps in the international arena to secure the return of Palestine to the Jews.[12]

The more usual vehicle through which Protestants influenced by the premillennialist belief expressed their interest in the Jews was, however, the mission. The missionary impetus proved extremely strong. In the 1870s there was almost no missionary activity aimed specifically at converting Jews, but by the outbreak of World War I America could claim a large and vivid network aimed at evangelizing the Jews, which included dozens of missionary posts and hundreds of missionaries.[13] Missions operated in virtually all Jewish communities with a few thousand Jews or more. Some cities, such as Chicago or Philadelphia, could claim a number of mission houses. New York had more than a dozen. The scope of the missionary involvement was large and represented a wide spectrum of conservative Protestantism in America, including missions sponsored by denominational bodies such as the Methodists, Baptists, Presbyterians, Episcopalians, and Lutherans, as well as a number of interdenominational efforts, such as the Chicago Hebrew Mission, and independent missionary enterprises.[14]

The majority of Protestants in America at the turn of the century were not premillennialists. Yet dispensationalist premillennialists were very influential in setting the missionary agenda of Protestantism in America, and even denominations that on the whole could not be described as premillennialist aided the cause of propagating Christianity among the Jews.[15] Liberal members of mainline Protestant churches usually did not put the same emphasis on evangelizing the Jewish people. In later years many among the liberals would come to doubt the legitimacy of evangelizing the Jews altogether. Yet at the turn of the century premillennialists could still muster support from nonconservative and nonpremillennialist Protestants for their goal of missionizing the Jews.

The same years that saw the growing impetus to evangelize the Jews in America also saw large streams of Jewish immigrants coming to America from eastern Europe. The missions directed much of their effort to evangelizing the new immigrants. This has made some historians speculate that the missions' aim was actually the absorption of the immigrants into American Protestant society and culture.[16] Such an interpretation, however, shows insufficient awareness of the missions' ideology and character. It would not explain the outburst of desire to evangelize the Jews in early-nineteenth-century Britain, where there was a very small Jewish population and no significant immigration into the country. Nor does it explain the complete failure of Americans in the decades prior to 1880, which witnessed the large Jewish emigration from Germany, to establish a large and durable missionary network. The difference between the two periods lies unmistakably in the rise of dispensationalism as a vital force in American religious life in the post–Civil War era, its impact on the evangelical community, and the new interest it inspired in the Jews and the prospect of their conversion to Christianity. The missions' extensive publications—books, journals, tracts, biblical exegeses, and prophetic expositions—clearly delineate their motivations. It is undeniably true, however, that the missions during that period were institutions operating among the newly arrived immigrants who were taking their first steps into American society.

The rise of the movement to evangelize the Jews in America also coincided with the rise of Zionism, the Jewish national movement that aimed at rebuilding Palestine as a Jewish center. The missionary community, like American dispensationalists in general, took a great deal of interest in the developments among the Jewish people. As believers in the imminent Second Coming of Jesus, missionaries, like other dispensationalists, were fascinated and encouraged by the Jewish national revival that began in the last decades of the nineteenth century. The missions' journals paid special attention to the emergence of the Zionist movement and the new Jewish settlements in Palestine.[17] Such developments were interpreted as "signs of the times" (based on Matthew 16:3), which indicated that the present era was ending and the eschatological drama was beginning to unfold.[18] They were seen as proof that the premillennialists' biblical exegesis on which the missions were built ideologically were correct and that prophecy was being fulfilled. These signs encouraged the missionaries, who felt that they were working to evangelize a nation that was in the process of recovering its position as God's chosen people and that had a great future before it. No cause could be more worthy. When World War I took place, many evangelists interpreted it as a watershed event. The unprecedented magnitude of the war and the killing and destruction it brought with it caused believers in the Second Coming of Christ to speculate that the war—with all its horrors—was part of a divine purpose and the arrival of the Messiah was at hand.[19] Similarly, they saw the Balfour Declaration and the British takeover of Palestine as clear indications that the current era was ending and the events of the End Times were to begin very soon.[20] Such developments validated, in dispensationalist premillennialist eyes, their interpretation of Scriptures and history. Leaders in the movement to evangelize the Jews were particularly enthusiastic and saw the prospect of the Jewish conversion to Christianity as nearer than ever before.[21] Their attitude served to solidify and intensify the missionary impetus.

Perhaps not surprisingly, missionaries to the Jews were among the major propagators of the dispensationalist premillennialist belief. William Blackstone, founder of the Chicago Hebrew Mission, for example, was the author of the premillennialist best-seller *Jesus Is Coming* (1878) as well as other books and pamphlets that promoted belief in the imminent return of Jesus.[22] The Jews and their role in God's redemptive plans occupied a major place in his writings.[23] Arno C. Gaebelein, the founder of the Hope of Israel mission in New York, also published many books that enjoyed great popularity. Like Blackstone, he too promoted the dispensationalist belief and put special emphasis on the role the Jews were to play in the End Times.[24] Gaebelein became one of the major fundamentalist leaders in America in the 1900s to 1930s and the mission's journal, *Our Hope*, one of the important organs of the fledgling fundamentalist movement.

Missionaries to the Jews played a dominant role in the Bible and prophecy conferences, which took place in America between the 1870s and 1910s and served as a meeting ground for American fundamentalist theologians and leaders and as a means to promote their ideas. In these gatherings, missionaries as well as other prominent figures in the conservative evangelical camp expressed their opinion that the Jews were still to be considered God's chosen people and were destined to occupy a central place in the coming kingdom.[25] They called on the evangelical community to look favorably on the Jews, stressing the importance of evangelization work among them.[26] In their addresses and writings, missionaries maintained that lack of support for Jewish evangelization indicated indifference, ingratitude, and even malice toward Jesus' nation.[27] Well aware of anti-Jewish prejudices, missionaries emphasized the importance of the Jews in God's plans for humanity.[28] They condemned anti-Semitism and discrimination against Jews worldwide.[29] Some of them made a particular effort to combat such anti-Semitic accusations as the blood libel of ritual murder, which was still alive at the turn of the century.[30] Missionaries were vocal in separating themselves from the long and unhappy history of Christian-Jewish encounters. They made the claim that Christian wrongdoings toward Jews throughout the ages were done by Roman Catholic or Orthodox Christians, whose beliefs and practices they considered to be distorted, false forms of Christianity.[31] In their view such Christians were not Christians at all. Evangelical Christians who had undergone a genuine act of conversion, they asserted, treated Jews with kindness and appreciation. Protestant evangelical missionaries thus justified the Jewish unwillingness to embrace Christianity in its Roman Catholic or Orthodox interpretations.[32]

This is not to say that missionaries, like others in the conservative evangelical camp, did not at times hold stereotypical images of Jews, such as the belief that Jews were unusually successful businesspeople and held "a large and rapidly increasing portion of the wealth of the land."[33] Some missionaries expressed such prejudice at the same time that they were fighting anti-Semitism and preaching the centrality of the Jewish people in God's plans for humanity. In 1895, in a speech given at the prophecy conference in Allegheny, Pennsylvania, Ernest F. Stroeter of the Hope of Israel mission in New York, while promoting the dispensationalist idea of the Jewish role in history and calling for a more positive attitude toward the Jews, also accused the Jews of killing Jesus—"[God's] own Son, whom, like all God's messengers, they rejected and killed"—and remarked about modern Jews: "A few decades of emancipation and equal rights and behold the unbearably proud and loud and obnoxious modern Jew."[34] Yet missionaries such as Stroeter were, from their own point of view, ardent friends of the Jews. Their commitment to evangelize that people was, they believed, a sign of dedication and love. Stroeter would have been taken aback had someone accused him of anti-Semitism, since he did not, in any way, advocate discrimination against the Jews but rather the opposite.

The new dispensationalist understanding of the role of the Jewish people in God's plans for humanity demonstrated itself in the way the missions presented the Christian belief to the Jews. They promoted the idea that the acceptance of the Christian faith was compatible with the Jewish faith and heritage. Throughout the centuries, Christians expected Jews who had embraced Christianity to turn their back on their Jewish heritage and identity. Their Jewishness had been looked upon as a deficiency, an obstacle to be overcome. In the Roman Catholic Church there had been a special prayer in the conversion ceremonies of Jews in which the converts renounced their old ways and thanked God for leading them from darkness into light. The new evangelical missions, on the other hand, presented the acceptance of Christianity as a fulfillment of one's Jewish destiny. By accepting Jesus as Lord and Savior, they claimed, Jews were becoming truer to their Jewish selves, for they were at long last recognizing the Messiah of whom the biblical prophecies spoke.[35] This approach, which reflected the dispensationalist understanding of the Jews and their place in history, was also meant to persuade Jewish converts that they were not betraying their people or faith.

Missionaries maintained that they were reaching out to the Jews in order to open their eyes to their true destiny. They held that Judaism could not offer salvation to its adherents, and with the arrival of Jesus, the observance of the Law had become futile. The Jews were keeping unnecessary laws, instead of recognizing their Savior. Still, the laws, customs, and rites of Judaism had kept the Jewish people alive and also had kept the Jews in readiness to fulfill their heroic mission in the days to come.[36] Orthodox Jews, the missionaries discovered, were more open to the evangelical message than other Jewish groups.[37] There was common ground for discussion and persuasion as both groups viewed the Bible as the revealed word of God. And it was the new immigrants from eastern Europe, all of whom came from traditional Jewish homes, who were exploring their new surroundings, looking for new moral and communal frameworks that would enable them to settle down and build their lives in a new homeland. The better-established Reform Jews or those among the immigrants who had already found comfort and meaning in secular movements did not take much interest in the missionary's message. The disenchantment was mutual. With the exception of Zionists, whose work and achievements they admired, the missionaries had little patience for either Reform or secular Jews.[38] Liberal Jews, they contended, had turned their backs on their role and duty in history; unlike their Orthodox brethren, they had abandoned hope for the appearance of the Messiah and the reestablishment of a Davidic kingdom in the Land of Israel. Since they had turned away from traditional Jewish values and practices but had not embraced Christianity, they were left with no moral principles to guide them; in the missionaries' eyes, nothing good could be expected from them; they had gone astray and unintentionally had become instruments of Satan.[39]

Influenced by their dispensationalist understanding of the Jews and their role in history, missionaries often portrayed Orthodox Jews and the Jewish tradition in favorable terms. Such journals as *Our Hope*, the *Jewish Era*, *Prayer and Work for Israel*, the *Chosen People*, the *Glory of Israel*, and *Immanuel's Witness* regularly published articles on Jewish religious themes, describing holidays, rites, and customs manifesting respect for the Jewish heritage. Mission houses often refrained from using outright Christian symbols such as the cross on their buildings.[40] Instead, almost all of them made use of Jewish symbols in decorating the mission houses and in their publications. Many of the missions' books and journals were illustrated with scenes from traditional Jewish life, such as women lighting candles, a *melamed* (teacher) teaching young children the Torah, a Bar Mitzvah celebration, and the like.[41] Missionaries often preached on Saturday, so as to give Jews the feeling that they were not neglecting to fulfill their religious obligations in coming to hear a Christian sermon. Missionaries referred to Jewish religious holidays in their services and sermons,[42] often conveying a Christian interpretation and meaning of the events commemorated. Passover, for example, served to present Jesus as the Passover lamb, whose sacrifice offered humanity salvation.[43] Arno Gaebelein's Hope of Israel mission in New York even distributed *matzot* (unleavened bread) to needy Jews on Passover.[44] Similarly, missionaries often built their arguments on passages from the Hebrew Bible, with which traditional Jews were acquainted, to prove that the appearance of Jesus and his deeds had been discussed in the Jewish Holy Scriptures and that he is the Messiah of whom the prophets spoke.[45] One missionary reminisced, "We held three services during Rosh Hashonoh (New Year). . . . The story of Isaac's birth and the intended sacrifice on Moriah was being read in the synagogues. I read the same lessons. I took as a text a sentence from the Jewish orthodox prayer book—'Look upon the Lamb of Morijah' meaning, of course, the substitute ram which Abraham offered instead of Isaac. I spoke of the true Lamb, our gracious substitute."[46]

The names of missions and their journals, and even the missions' emblems and mottoes, clearly coincided with the dispensationalist belief and its understanding of the role of Jews in history. The Chicago Hebrew Mission called its journal the *Jewish Era*, revealing its understanding that history is divided into eras and that the one to come is expected to be a period of glory for the Jews. The subtitle reads: *A Christian Magazine on Behalf of Israel*, which, in addition to signaling the friendly intention of the mission, implied that the mission saw the Jews as the historical Israel—a nation with a role and purpose in God's plans for humanity. The Magen David, the six-pointed Star of David, appeared on the front cover, with the motto "Izkor LeOlam Brito" "He will ever be mindful of his covenant [with Israel] (Isaiah V, John XV) [sic]." The Williamsburg Mission to the Jews published the *Chosen People*, indicating its understanding of the Jewish position in God's eyes. Its mottoes read: "And the Lord hath chosen thee to be a peculiar people unto himself" (Deuteronomy 14:2) and "Jacob whom I have chosen, the seed of Abraham my friend. I have chosen thee, and not cast thee away" (Isaiah 41:8–9). Arno Gaebelein chose the name "Hope of Israel" for his mission to express the idea that the Jews had a future history embodied in Jesus Christ. Accepting Jesus as their Savior, they would be able to reach not only personal salvation but national restoration as well. The New Covenant Mission, in Pittsburgh, called its journal the *Glory of Israel* and chose as mottoes "A Light to lighten the Gentiles and the Glory of the People Israel (Luke 2:32)," and "Israel shall blossom and bud, and fill the face of the world with fruit (Isaiah 27:6)," which referred to the glorified future promised to the Jews according to the dispensationalist belief.

That a messianic belief that places the Jews at the center of its drama stirs its proponents to evangelize the Jews can also be seen from the history of the European and British missionary movements. These forerunners of the American missions included German pietist societies aimed at converting the Jews, as well as British missions to the Jews, which were also evangelical and premillennialist in nature.[47] Motivated by a biblical-messianic understanding of the Jewish people and their role in history, the movement to evangelize the Jews in Britain started at the beginning of the nineteenth century with much strength and enthusiasm. Until the end of the nineteenth century it was larger than the one in America, with greater financial resources and more missionaries at its disposal, carrying out extensive missionary work among Jews in Britain and in many other parts of the world. The situation was to change during the twentieth century as interest in evangelizing the Jews decreased in Britain but grew stronger in America. After World War I and even more so after World War II, the American movement would become far larger and more influential than the one in Britain; in fact, most international activity to evangelize the Jews would be sponsored in the latter decades of the twentieth century by Americans.

Although many European pietist and British evangelical missionaries adhered to a school of eschatological belief known as "historical" and not to dispensationalism, they shared with the American missions a similar understanding of the role of the Jews in the millennial kingdom.[48] The latter often made use of British published material, particularly that produced by dispensationalist missions such as the London-headquartered Mildmay Mission to the Jews. They circulated books and tracts written by British missionaries and reprinted their articles in their journals.[49] British missionaries such as David Baron and John Wilkinson traveled to America on lecture tours and participated in Bible and prophecy conferences.

Yet an apparent contradiction seemed to exist between the vision of the place of the Jews in the millennial age and the strong impetus to evangelize them that that vision inspired. If the Jewish nation was destined, as the missionaries believed, to recognize Jesus as its Savior by the end of the Great Tribulation and the beginning of the millennial age, why put so much effort into bringing them the Christian message? The answer to that paradox can be found in the missionaries' articles and tracts. The growing effort to evangelize the Jews derived from the dispensationalist messianic belief. According to this eschatological scheme, those

Jews who die without accepting Jesus as their Savior are doomed for eternity. Moreover, only part of the Jewish people (about a third) will survive the turmoils of the Time of Jacob's Trouble, which will take place during the Great Tribulation. Jews who accept Jesus as their Savior before the events of the End Times begin, on the other hand, will be raptured with the true Christian believers and thus be spared the misery of that unhappy time, and they will be guaranteed their personal salvation.[50] Should they die before the great events take place, they will rise from the dead. So the goal of the missionaries was to save individual Jews from eternal death and suffering.

In addition to this consideration, missionary zeal was strengthened by another assumption derived from the messianic theory. According to the dispensationalist eschatological scheme, 144,000 Jews, 12,000 from each tribe, will accept Jesus as their Lord and Savior at the beginning of the Great Tribulation and the apocalyptic events of the End Times. They will serve as evangelists to their brethren, spreading among them the knowledge of the true Messiah. They will be persecuted, and some will be martyred. Gradually, however, more and more Jews will be persuaded to accept Jesus. When the Great Tribulation ends and Jesus arrives on earth, the remnant of the Jewish people that survives this period of turmoil will be fully converted, will welcome Jesus as their Messiah, and will be ready to fulfill their glorious role in the millennial kingdom.[51] For this scheme to be fulfilled it was essential that there would be 144,000 Jewish persons who would possess the knowledge of the Christian gospel—even though they did not accept it—so that they could fulfill their role after the rapture and the beginning of the Great Tribulation. These Jews would recognize the events of the End Times as correlating with the Christian teachings they had learned but did not accept. They would realize the truth of the Christian message, accept Jesus as their Savior, and serve as evangelists to their brethren.

So preaching the Christian gospel to the Jews in its dispensationalist interpretation was a goal in itself, even if it did not result in large numbers of immediate conversions. The premillennialist missionary attempt was based on the realistic assumption that only a small part of the Jewish people would accept Jesus as their Savior in the present age. Unconverted Jews would include a sufficient number to fulfill their part in God's plan. That some Jews did accept Christianity was an encouraging sign that eventually all would come to accept the Christian gospel and become ardent followers of the true Messiah.[52] In addition, the missionary zeal should also be understood as an impulse that resulted from the new appreciation for the Jews that the messianic hopes brought about. For dispensationalists, "witnessing" to the Jews was a manifestation of love and concern. Jews, as might have been expected, viewed the matter differently.

An outstanding example of the influence of dispensationalist thinking on implementing a missionary policy can be found in the history of the Hope of

Israel mission and its attempt to build a Jewish Christian congregation in the 1890s on the Lower East Side of New York. Its founder, Arno Gaebelein, was a German Methodist with scholarly inclinations who eventually became a noted theoretician and polemicist of the fundamentalist movement.[53] Established in the 1880s, the mission had in its early years a conventional premillennialist character in line with that of the majority of missions to the Jews in America at the period. Gaebelein preached on Saturdays and Jewish holidays, decorated the mission with Jewish symbols, and emphasized the special destiny of the Jews in history. But, like other missionaries, he expected Jews who converted to Christianity to join ordinary Protestant churches.

In the early 1890s Gaebelein was joined in running the mission by Ernest Stroeter, also a German-born Methodist, who served previously as a professor at the University of Denver. Like Gaebelein, Stroeter was an ardent premillennialist and a believer in the glorified future of the Jews in the millennial kingdom. Gaebelein and Stroeter developed an innovative and daring missionary theory. The new principle of the mission was that Jews who accepted Jesus as their Lord and Savior did not have to turn their back on their Jewish heritage or cut their ties with the Jewish community, and they could continue to keep observing Jewish rites and customs. "And all that was divinely given him through Moses he has full liberty to retain and uphold as far as possible when he becomes a believer in Jesus Christ," declared the Methodist missionaries.[54] The leaders of the mission further held that converted Jews were not obliged to join any particular denomination but could form a congregation of their own in which they could retain their Jewish identity.[55]

Gaebelein and Stroeter's attempt to create a congregation of Jewish Christians was one of the earliest of its kind in the modern era. In Kishinev, Russia, Joseph Rabinowitz presided over a Jewish Christian congregation called Israelites of the New Covenant.[56] Gaebelein, like other dispensationalist leaders in the United States, was acquainted with Rabinowitz and had even visited his congregation in 1895. He further translated into English Rabinowitz's book *Jesus of Nazareth, King of the Jews* and published and distributed it as part of the missionary literature the Hope of Israel was using to promote the Christian faith.[57] A few years later another mission in New York, the Williamsburg Mission to the Jews, would also try to build a congregation of Jewish converts to Christianity. This was a bold policy at the time. The history of missions in America was marked by an ongoing debate between those who wished to propagate the Christian tenets of faith per se and those who saw the American Anglo-Saxon norms and manners as part and parcel of the religion they wished to promote.[58] The Hope of Israel choice reflected the advocacy of a "Christ not culture" line: "From the very start of my work among the Jewish people, I felt that they should not be Gentilized and that the attempt to make Methodists, Baptists, Lutherans or Presbyterians out of them would be a mistake," Gaebelein wrote.[59] The leaders of the Hope of Israel were, in many ways, more daring than, for example, those who worked toward the establishment of a Chinese Protestant church. The term "Jewish" designated not merely a different people and culture but a different religious tradition altogether, one that Christianity had come to replace and one with which it historically had been at odds. Moreover, in the eschatological belief to which the missionaries adhered and which motivated their evangelization efforts, Jews and Christians were assigned different roles. According to that messianic hope, Christians who accepted Jesus as their personal Savior were expected to be raptured from earth when the apocalyptic events began and to meet Jesus in the air. The Jews on the other end were expected to remain on earth and build a national polity in the Land of Israel.

It is no wonder, therefore, that the new principles of the Hope of Israel mission were controversial and attracted both praise and criticism in the conservative Protestant camp. Some of America's major premillennialist leaders looked favorably on Gaebelein and Stroeter's work.[60] James H. Brookes, for example, the author of the best-seller *Maranatha* and one of the outstanding leaders of the early fundamentalist movement, was delighted with the mission's character and work.[61] He offered his praise and encouragement. Others were not so enthusiastic. Those who objected to the principles of the Hope of Israel movement rejected the idea that Jews who had converted to Christianity could continue to be part of the Jewish people and observe the Jewish rites. The critics considered Jews who accepted Jesus as their Savior to have joined the church and therefore considered the Hope of Israel attitude misleading and confusing.[62] The different reactions to Gaebelein and Stroeter's experiment reflected, among other things, the premillennialist nature of the missionary movement that shaped its discourse.

In 1899, Gaebelein abandoned his hope in the possibility of amalgamating the belief in Christ with the Jewish religion. He based this change of views on his understanding of the dispensationalist hermeneutical system. Gaebelein continued to hold the idea, so he wrote, that Jews did not have to join any particular Christian denomination when they accepted Jesus as their Lord and Savior. Yet he became convinced that in this dispensation those converted Jews were no longer under the Law but rather under Grace and should not practice Jewish rites.[63] Gaebelein thus joined the majority in the dispensationalist camp in America at the time.

The development of the movement to evangelize the Jews in America between the 1880s and the 1910s serves as an important example of the power of messianic belief to stir evangelization efforts. Virtually nonexistent in the 1870s, missionary work among the Jews grew throughout the 1880s to 1910s into one of the largest networks of evangelization among any of the ethnic groups in America. Influenced by messianic faith, which emphasized the centrality of the nation of Israel for the events of the End Times, the "need to evangelize the Jews" stood very high on the Protestant missionary agenda. The messianic belief also shaped the character of the missions, their symbols and their rhetoric, which carried a distinct dispensationalist premillennialist understanding of the Jews and their role in history. The premillennialist nature of the missionary impetus also expressed itself in the attempts to create congregations of Jewish converts and the dilemmas such experiments caused the missionary community.

2

The Missionary Work

Motivated by a premillennialist belief that has viewed Jews as the chosen people, the movement to evangelize the Jews grew impressively. By the 1910s there were forty-five missionary societies in America aimed specifically at evangelizing Jews (in comparison with only one in the early 1880s).[1] Some missions operated more than one station. More than two hundred full-time paid missionaries served as evangelists to the Jews in America at the time. Missions also employed volunteers from the evangelical community who devoted time and energy to what they saw as an important cause. Similarly, missionaries' wives, even if not officially on the payroll, were, in actuality, part- or full-time workers. The field of missions to the Jews became one of the largest in America and was of a considerable size in personnel, missionary stations, and publications. By that time, missions had been established in New York City; Buffalo; Rochester; Paterson, New Jersey; Philadelphia; Chicago; Boston; Minneapolis; Pittsburgh; St. Louis; Washington, D.C.; Baltimore; Cincinnati; Cleveland; Atlanta; Louisville; Memphis; Los Angeles; and San Francisco. A number of these cities had more than one such mission. New York City had a dozen, Philadelphia six, and Chicago five.[2]

This very large missionary network, which sprang up in America within a relatively short period of time, had to struggle with patterns of work ranging from the recruitment of employees and the location of missions to methods of approaching Jews and the literature that the missions were producing. The missionary movement drew partially on the rich experience of evangelical missions in general and on the experience of evangelical and pietist missions to the Jews in Britain and Europe, which provided examples of methods employed specifically in evangelizing Jews, and to a large degree on trial and error. The period between 1880 and 1920 was certainly a period of infancy in the history of missions to the Jews in America, and the movement was still struggling to establish its norms and working methods.

Some missionaries, such as Leopold Cohn, who studied in Scotland, or Samuel Freuder, who graduated from the Chicago Theological Seminary, had received some theological education and ministerial training before entering their vocation. Many, however, particularly the Jewish converts who became missionaries, had no previous training. They relied on their evangelistic zeal to spread the Christian faith among the Jews and on their personal knowledge of the Jewish religion and way of life. Only later on would the movement to evangelize the Jews establish training programs for prospective missionaries to the Jews, screen candidates, and set norms and regulations. In this early period, the field of evangelism among the Jews was relatively open; but although there were no strict, or even defined, criteria for the recruitment of missionaries, the population the missions targeted was well defined.

The era that marked the rise of the movement to evangelize the Jews in America also saw the beginning of a mass Jewish immigration to America from eastern Europe. From the early 1880s onward, hundreds of thousands of Jews arrived, often penniless. They inhabited the poorer quarters of major American cities, many of them working in sweatshops to earn their living.[3] The missions directed their attention and energy to this group in the Jewish population. Consequently, the socioeconomic, cultural, and demographic realities of the immigrants' community shaped much of the missions' work, character, means of approaching prospective converts, the languages used, and the way the missions chose to present their messages.

One means the missions used to reach the immigrant community was to offer them medical, educational, and relief services. The missions were attempting to reach a community of poor working-class immigrants that was undoubtedly in need of assistance of that sort. An impressive program of immigrant aid was carried out by the well-established German Jewish community, but there was room for additional help, and the missions often filled some of the gap. They distributed packages of food and clothing and opened dispensaries in which Jewish patients received treatment and medications free of charge or for a minimal fee. The missions organized various activities for Jewish children including summer camps and Sunday-school classes. They offered evening English lessons to the new immigrants and provided other services as well.[4] Such relief and educational and medical assistance were common features of Protestant missionary work worldwide.[5] These activities were intended to demonstrate the quality of Christian charity and served to bring Jews to hear the Christian message. The hope was that many Jews who would not otherwise listen to a missionary preaching and would refuse to read missionary tracts would approach the mission out of need. Then, being impressed by the kindness that was bestowed on them, and thankful, they would be more willing to hear the Christian message. "It is easier to reach the Jews while the heart is softened by suffering and while the good work which they see done for poor Israel is breaking down their prejudice," wrote Bernhard Angel of the Chicago Hebrew Mission.[6] The philanthropic work strengthened the missionaries' view that their efforts were a manifestation of goodwill and charity toward the Jews.[7] Their appeal to the evangelical community "to show kindness to Israel" included both the spiritual and material spheres.

Another means of approaching Jews was through written material: leaflets and brochures that missionaries distributed on street corners or through home visitations. Such literature, much of it in Yiddish, was also made available to Jews in missions' dispensaries and educational projects. A major tool in the missions' operations was the missions' journals. These periodicals were not merely for the propagation of the gospel among prospective converts. They functioned more like organs of a religious ideological movement and were intended primarily for supporters within the evangelical community. They gave expression to the missions' beliefs and priorities and conveyed appeals for financial support. The journals promoted the increasing interest of the evangelical community in the Jews, their national rejuvenation, and their potential conversion. Some missions, such as the Hope of Israel mission and the American Board of Missions to the Jews, published separate journals for evangelical supporters and Jewish readers.

Although motivated by the same dispensationalist premillennialist theology and employing similar rhetoric in approaching prospective converts, different missions had unique characteristics. Some of the variations were caused by the different personalities of the missions' directors. But other differences also played a part in shaping the characteristics of the missions: their geographical location, whether the missionaries were Jews or non-Jews, and the missions' standing in the Protestant community.

Much of the growing missionary activity was sponsored directly or indirectly by Protestant denominational bodies. A few missionary enterprises operated independently but received help from churches, which often lent their names and provided partial financial support. Leopold Cohn, for example, operated officially under the auspices of the American Baptist Home Mission Society, which also assisted him financially. His mission, however, proved to be an independent enterprise rather than an agency of the Baptist Church, a situation that at times created tensions between the Home Mission Society and Cohn.[8] A similar, though calmer, relationship existed between Arno Gaebelein's Hope of Israel mission and the Methodist Episcopal Church.[9] The churches gave these missions a sense of legitimacy and respectability, both of which were needed in their first years of operation. In the case of both these missions, the connection with the sponsoring bodies was severed once they were well established and had acquired reputations of their own.

The Chicago Hebrew Mission listed a number of Protestant churches as its sponsors. In actuality, the mission was nondenominational in its operation and character and had a distinct premillennialist ideology. Although some sponsoring churches did not necessarily share its messianic conviction, they nevertheless approved of the mission's character and methods, realizing that the messianic vigor and the specific understanding of Israel's role in history were instrumental in appealing to the Jewish population. The Christian and Missionary Alliance began its activity not as a denomination but rather as an organization aimed at evangelizing the entire world in the current generation. Established by ardent premillennialists, it took special interest in evangelizing the Jews both in America and in Palestine. The histories of these three missions—the interdenominational Chicago Hebrew Mission, the Williamsburg Mission to the Jews, independent under a denomination's auspices, and the third one established by the Christian and Missionary Alliance, an American organization for international evangelism with denominational tendencies—can shed light on the nature of the movement to evangelize the Jews, its different agencies, and the different means of operation it took.

The largest mission to the Jews in America during the 1880s to 1910s was the Chicago Hebrew Mission. Founded in 1887, it has continued to operate without interruption ever since. The mission served for decades as an inspiration for a number of other missionary organizations that were established in other cities following its example.[10] Its history throughout more than a century reflects the changes and developments that took place in the movement to evangelize the Jews.

The impetus for the establishment of the mission and its explicit theology was the dispensationalist messianic belief and its understanding of the Jewish people and their role in history. This was unmistakably revealed in the mission's publications and its journal, the *Jewish Era*. The magazine regularly published articles on the emerging Zionist movement and the development of the Jewish settlement in Palestine, which it interpreted as "signs of the time" indicating that the present era was ending and the messianic age was at hand.[11] The living spirit in founding the mission and leading it in its first generation was William Blackstone, one of the outstanding propagators of the dispensationalist hope in America and an ardent supporter of Zionism because of this messianic hope.[12] Blackstone served for a number of years as the mission's secretary-treasurer. For some time he served as superintendent and for a while edited its journal. The missionaries and staff shared his messianic convictions. Nonetheless, the church bodies that lent their support to the mission in its first decades, including the Presbyterians, Methodists, and Episcopalians, were not all ardent premillennialists. The leaders of the mission, who were ardent dispensationalist premillennialists, were able to muster support among many liberal and moderate Protestants who, during this era, saw the cause of propagating Christianity among the Jews as a worthy one.

One noted liberal who supported the mission was Jane Addams, a famous urban reformer who was influenced by liberal Christian social thought.[13] Addams did not attribute a special role to the Jews in any End Times scheme. For her, they were not a chosen people destined to a glorious future in a messianic kingdom but masses of new immigrants: deprived and poor, living in devastating conditions, and very much in need of the social services the missions were offering and, perhaps, of the ameliorating help of the Christian message as well. Her

Christian views were very different from those of the directors of the mission, and she was an unlikely—indeed, an amazing—supporter of the mission. Nonetheless, in 1891 Addams became a member of the mission's executive committee, which acted like an advisory committee or a board of trustees. Symbolically, the mission was located for a while in Hull House, which served some time later as Addams's center of activity in Chicago. Addams's association with the mission did not last very long, as her set of beliefs differed so greatly from those of the mission's leaders and workers. Her case was representative. Support by liberals for those missions to the Jews that were directed by premillennialists and carried the latter's creeds would not last long. As the division within the Protestant camp deepened in years to come and as liberals began entering into dialogue with Jews, they withdrew their support, and the missions' proponents would be found almost exclusively in the conservative camp.

A remarkable feature of the Chicago Hebrew Mission in its early years was the prominent role women played in the work of the mission. Women sat on the executive committee, served as editors of the mission's magazine, and, in one case, actually superintended the mission for more than two decades. In retrospect this was remarkable; women would not hold such positions of authority in the mission in the coming generations. In some ways the situation in that mission correlated with the larger reality of the position of women in the emerging fundamentalist camp. In the first generation of the movement, women often played a vital role, helping to build its early institutions and holding positions they would generally be denied a generation later when the movement became more established.[14] C. F. Howe served as the editor of the mission's journal, the *Jewish Era*, in its first years. This was an influential position because the journal expressed the mission's views and served as a major avenue to reach supporters. Her role in the mission was, however, overshadowed by a much more predominant figure, that of Tryphena C. Rounds (1842–1939). "Sister Rounds," as her friends called her, or "Mother Rounds," as the employees of the mission later came to refer to her, was a longtime evangelist active in Chicago in the later decades of nineteenth century. A friend of such leading evangelists as Dwight Moody and William Blackstone, she was among the founders of the mission, and in 1888, when Blackstone went abroad, Rounds replaced him as secretary-treasurer of the mission and editor of the *Jewish Era*. In 1897 the board of trustees appointed the female evangelist superintendent of the mission pro tem. The board was evidently reluctant to grant her the full title of director, which would have designated her real standing in the mission. As a "temporary" superintendent, Rounds served as director for more than twenty years. Authoritative, tough, and, at times, confrontational, she certainly did not lack any of the qualities typical for an American boss at the turn of the century. Rounds proved to be an able organizer and fund-raiser; the scope of the mission's activity grew considerably during her tenure.

It was during Rounds's tenure as director of the mission that a change took place in the position of Jews in the mission. Jewish converts fulfilled an important role in the mission's operations in its first decade and a half. Most of the mission's field evangelists were Jewish; converted Jewish physicians worked in the mission's medical clinic, and two of the mission's early superintendents, J. R. Marcusson and Bernhard Angel, were Jewish. Marcusson was among the founders of the mission and sat on its executive board. After Angel left the mission in 1894 and Rounds replaced Marcusson as superintendent in 1897, no Jew served as director, the number of Jews within the body of missionaries decreased steadily, and the mission became more and more a "gentile" evangelization agency. Throughout the 1880s and 1890s, missions found that non-Jewish missionaries and directors had a more solid reputation in both the Jewish and Christian communities. Some, like the leaders of the Chicago Hebrew mission, eventually concluded that non-Jews should serve as missionaries and evangelize Jews.[15] Ironically, one of the people who promoted the idea that Jews should not become directors of missions was the Jewish missionary Bernhard Angel. He gave public expression to his views a short while after he left the Chicago Hebrew mission, where he had served as superintendent, to become the director of a mission to the Jews in New York.[16] In stating his opinion, Angel, a converted Jew who enjoyed the trust of Christians, repeated many of the prejudices that existed against people like himself: "It is a mistake to put in any Jewish convert as a leader without adequate training. If anyone needs to be watched carefully, instructed systematically, and disabused of many of his former ideas, it is that Jew who leaves the religion of his ancestors and comes within the bounds of Christianity. Much evil has been done to the cause at large by entrusting its leadership to the hands of glib-tongued, smart, aggressive converts."[17] Angel's words can explain why the Chicago Hebrew Mission adopted the policy it did. There was definitely prejudice and suspicion toward converted Jews, those "glib-tongued, smart, aggressive converts." In casting doubt in general over the character of a "Jew who leaves the religion of his ancestors," Angel also conveyed the guilt of a Jewish convert.

The Chicago Hebrew Mission succeeded in establishing itself as a respectable fundamentalist evangelical institution and managed to escape many of the scandals and accusations and much of the slander in which a number of missions found themselves caught, a fact that even Jewish antagonists noticed.[18] The mission was in many ways better protected from such situations. The Chicago Hebrew Mission was established and directed by persons who came from the heart of evangelical Protestantism. Its leaders in its early years came from the circle of

Chicago evangelists associated with Dwight Moody, and the mission enjoyed the public sponsorship of major Protestant churches. Its directors were, needless to say, familiar with the norms and manners of the Protestant establishment. Acquainted with middle-class American norms, the Chicago Hebrew Mission acknowledged from the very beginning every donation it received and published a list of donors and amounts in its journal. From its inception, the mission thrived on Protestant respectability and propriety, associating itself with the mainstream of conservative Protestantism of its day. Some of the mission's founders, including William Blackstone and Tryphena Rounds, were active in the founding of the Bible Institute that Moody and his circle established in Chicago in 1887, and the mission kept close ties with the Moody Bible Institute over the years. Its history, like that of the Bible Institute, has reflected, in some ways, the developments that took place in evangelical Christianity in America. As the division between liberals and conservatives in American Protestantism became more pronounced, the mission, being an institution with a premillennialist worldview, associated itself more and more with the conservative camp.

In contrast to the Chicago Hebrew Mission, which was backed from inception by a group of churches and respectable evangelists, the Williamsburg Mission to the Jews had to struggle for support and recognition. One of the most noted independent missions during that period, it had eventually grown into both a national and an international organization. Its history has reflected the changing character of both the Jewish community and the missionary movement. Similarly, the controversies surrounding the mission, which have been particularly noticeable, are symptomatic of the reputation and problems of the evangelization of the Jews.

The founder of the mission, Leopold Cohn, became one of the most noted and at the same time most controversial figures in the field of Jewish evangelism, provoking heated reaction from all sides. For the mission's people and its supporters, he was nothing short of a saint. For his antagonists, both Jewish and Christian, he was practically the devil incarnate.[19] The controversy manifested itself even in relation to Cohn's elementary biographical details. There has been little agreement, for example, as to the events of his early life. Even his real name has been in dispute. The founder of the mission was born in 1862 in Berezna, Hungary. According to his autobiographical account, which has become the accepted history for his mission, he spent his early years studying with the Hasidic rabbi Zalman Leib Teitelbaum. He then pursued his studies at the prestigious non-Hasidic Hatam Sofer's Yeshiva in Presburg, currently Bratislava, the Slovak capital. According to his account, he was ordained as a rabbi when he was eighteen. He then married, moved to live with his wife's family, and practiced as a rabbi in three small Jewish communities. Reading the Scriptures, he was intrigued by the question of the identity of the Messiah.[20] He discussed the matter with a fellow rabbi in a nearby town and the latter advised him to go to America, where it would be easier for him to search for an answer to that question. According to his account, he did not go back home to tell his wife, lest she try to persuade him not to take this course of action, and he set sail for America. In New York he came upon Herman Warszawiak, a Polish-born Jewish convert who had studied theology in Scotland and was a particularly successful missionary preacher. It was Warszawiak who introduced Cohn to Christianity and obtained a scholarship for him to study theology in Edinburgh, Scotland. His wife and children joined him there and later converted too.[21]

The mission's antagonists drew a different biographical sketch. Cohn's real name, they argued, was Itsak Leib Joszovics. Orphaned at an early age, he received little education, and, upon marriage and settling in his wife's hometown, he became an inn- or saloon keeper rather than a rabbi. The Hungarian authorities, the alternative biography says, charged him and his brother-in-law with forging the deed of a dead peasant's farm. Joszovics (alias Cohn) fled.[22] Thereafter, one's assertion of Cohn's true identity and the biographical account one chooses to adopt have typically reflected one's standing not only toward Cohn the person but also toward his mission as a whole and, at times, toward the movement to evangelize the Jews at large. For his supporters, he was the former rabbi he claimed to have been. For Jewish antagonists, and at times non-Jews, he symbolized all that was wrong with the movement to evangelize the Jews.[23]

If Cohn was not the former rabbi he claimed to have been, then he must have been a particularly gifted person. His knowledge, intelligence, and writing ability were much superior to those that could be expected from an uneducated saloon keeper. Cohn had an undeniably strong scholarly inclination that manifested itself in his missionary tracts and the "Questions and Answers" column he published in his mission's journal, the *Chosen People*. He demonstrated a remarkable knowledge of the Scriptures, Jewish rabbinical tradition, and Christian theology, which he followed in its evangelical dispensationalist version.[24] His English, which he studied when he was in his thirties, was good. If he was indeed the runaway saloon keeper his enemies claimed him to be, he had found a more fulfilling vocation in his second career as a missionary.

One of the reasons for Cohn's remarkable success as a missionary was his ability to establish contact with and gain the trust of influential persons in the Protestant community such as Ralph Cuttler, an affluent lay Presbyterian, or Thomas Whitaker, a Baptist minister in Brooklyn. Both became convinced of the importance of evangelizing the Jews and of Cohn's potential as a missionary. The Brooklyn Extension Society of the Baptist Church assisted his mission for a while. Through that body Cohn encountered the Brooklyn Chapter of the American Baptist Home Mission Society, which took upon itself to sponsor his work on a more permanent basis. In actuality, the Williamsburg Mission to the Jews was independent, and Cohn was his own boss. The relationship with the Mission Society lasted for a number of years and was not without its difficulties. The Baptist sponsorship granted Cohn a degree of legitimacy, yet the Baptist missionary society expected him to be much more subservient than he was willing to be. In 1907, the relationship reached a crisis when the Mission Society objected to Cohn's receiving a large donation from Frances J. Huntley, a woman whose trust Cohn obtained and who became one of the mission's most generous supporters.[25] The Baptist officials felt that they should be the ones to handle such a gift and rejected Cohn's independent spirit of expansionism and large-scale fundraising. The Baptist agency turned from patron to enemy, denouncing Cohn and calling upon potential donors to refrain from supporting the mission. At this stage, however, the mission was standing on its own feet and was not in need of Baptist sponsorship. Cohn had built long-lasting and, from the mission's point of view, fruitful relationships with generous benefactors.

Although Jewish activists despised him, Cohn undoubtedly possessed a personality that impressed both Christian supporters and prospective converts. It is an ironic fact that this very controversial evangelist laid the foundation for what would later become the largest mission to the Jews in America and made many more converts than any other missionary during the 1890s to 1910s. This included persons who later made a name for themselves and enjoyed a great amount of respectability in the evangelical community, such as Samuel Needleman, who became a minister in Maine.[26]

In his memoirs, Joseph Hoffman Cohn, Leopold's son, described the mission in its early years as a small, struggling institution, fighting to receive support and recognition from conservative Protestants, countering attacks from Jews as well as antagonists within the missionary movement, and fearful of both economic ruin and public loss of trust. At the same time, the Cohns demonstrated perseverance, ambition, and an ability to adapt themselves to the norms, manners, and expectations of the evangelical Protestant community. The pages of the *Chosen People*, the mission's journal, burst with energy and plans for expansion.[27] Among other things Leopold Cohn asked interested evangelicals to work as volunteers for the mission. Realizing the importance of mustering grassroots support in the evangelical Protestant community, he took it upon himself to lecture in churches. There Cohn promoted the cause of evangelizing the Jews and often took a collection for the mission after his speech.[28] Church members thus became familiar with the mission and would, at times, become regular contributors. In addition to speaking in churches, Cohn appealed in writing to potential donors. The mission's journal served as a public relations medium, offering a means of communicating with supporters and sharing the mission's work and ideology with them.

Like the Chicago Hebrew Mission, the Williamsburg Mission to the Jews published the names of the donors and the amounts they gave in the pages of its journal. Careful to keep donors happy, Cohn also sent acknowledgment letters, but the addresses of contributors were kept secret. The Cohns were afraid that antagonists would use the list to send discouraging letters to supporters or that competing or aspiring missionaries would use the list for their own purposes and would thus take potential donors away from the mission.[29] This fear reflected, among other things, the feelings of suspicion, mistrust, and competition that existed at times between different missionaries.

In making his appeals to supporters, Cohn referred to the dispensationalist messianic belief that attributed a central place to the Jews in the messianic age. But, like others, he thought that although this belief motivated many Protestants to support the movement to evangelize the Jews, other reasons were needed to convince more in the Protestant community to support it.[30] The Christians, he claimed, owe a debt to the Jews: Jesus was a Jew who preached to Jews; the first Christians including the apostles were Jewish, and the Bible was a Jewish book. The way to repay the Jews for their contribution to Christianity would be to open their eyes and hearts to the truth of the Christian faith. The current generation of Jews, he asserted, were ready to hear the Christian message. Living Jews had never heard the Christian gospel and were not given a chance to accept it; they were not the generation that had rejected Christ. Jews, he further claimed, were abandoning their religion, which they saw as dead wood, and the options that confronted them were either destructive heathenism or Christianity. So there was a sense of urgency in evangelizing that nation. "Judaism has become bankrupt. . . . This is little short of calamity. . . . A nation which has lost its grip on God . . . sinks to a low plane of morality. . . . We tremble," he declared.[31] Such a warning would become typical of missionaries calling upon the Christian community to promote the evangelization of Jews. But Cohn did not attempt merely to scare the evangelical community into supporting the mission. Engaging in the evangelization of Jews had its rewards, the missionary patriarch promised. The Jews were a literary people; they were highly capable and, when converted, would serve as ideal evangelists and leaders in the Christian community.[32]

Mary C. Sherburne, a non-Jewish volunteer, offers a description of the day-to-day operations of the Brownsville Mission in the 1890s.[33] The mission was located on Rockaway Avenue not far from the center of the Jewish neighborhood. The building included an auditorium for 160 people where Cohn preached. There was a reading room and evening schools for newly arrived immigrants, which included classes in English and preparation for citizenship. They also offered sewing classes for women, which were particularly popular. Many of the newly arrived Jews found their livelihood in the needle industry, for which sewing proved a useful skill. Cohn preached on Saturday afternoons and Thursday nights. Volunteers taught English on Monday, Tuesday, and Wednesday evenings and sewing classes on Thursday afternoons. The mission also conducted door-to-door visitations in Jewish homes and distributed tracts. In these activities Cohn's children also took part, including Joseph, who began distributing tracts when he was nine years old and encountered some of the resentment Jews felt toward missionaries.[34]

Joseph began at a relatively young age to take upon himself central responsibilities in the mission. In his autobiography, he describes his lecturing in churches with great vividness.[35] Joseph's English and his oratorical abilities were better than his father's, and he soon replaced the latter as the mission's itinerant representative and speaker, going on cross-country tours to churches as far away as Los Angeles. At the end of such talks, he would organize a "collection." How vital the collections were for keeping the mission and his family going is evident from Joseph's description of buying food for himself after successful talks in churches.[36]

Not the sort to be satisfied with being just an ordinary missionary among the many, Leopold Cohn set about expanding his mission. In 1896 the mission opened a second branch, also in Brooklyn, moved its headquarters to Williamsburg, and changed its name in 1897 to the Williamsburg Mission to the Jews. Its new headquarters was much larger and included, among other things, a medical clinic that offered needy Jews free medical services. Contrary to a prevailing myth, Jews did not boycott missions, and the physicians working at the clinic were nonconverted Jews who worked for pay. Like the patients who patronized the clinic, they did not consider the mission to be a danger.[37] The mission's program included "Gospel services" on Sunday and Monday nights and sewing and English classes on other nights. The establishment of a boys' club and a Girl Scout troop indicated a growing attempt to evangelize youth. Remarkably, some volunteers in the mission studied Yiddish in order to be able to approach prospective converts who spoke that language. In the early 1900s, the mission hired its first employees and began a course of expansion that eventually would turn it into a national organization. This process intensified after 1908 when Joseph Cohn, who studied at the Moody Bible Institute in Chicago, joined his father in directing the mission.

The Cohns showed a great amount of energy in promoting different evangelization initiatives. The mission produced a large variety of tracts intended to persuade Jews that Jesus was indeed the Messiah prophesied in the Bible.[38] It set out to approach Jews not only in New York City but also in sea resorts that New York Jews frequented such as Coney Island, where the mission established a regular missionary station a few years later. The mission operated a mail evangelization program, urging Christians who were acquainted with Jews to send the latter's names and a small donation. The mission then sent those Jews tracts, offered to send them the New Testament, if they so wished, and invited them to approach the mission with further inquiries. If they showed interest and responded, further communication would take place.

In his own way, which for almost all Jews at the time was unacceptable, Leopold Cohn was a proud Jew. He advocated the controversial position that Jews who accepted Christianity had the right to retain Jewish customs and ethnic attributes. There was no reason for them, he argued, not to celebrate the Sabbath on Saturday.[39] He himself retained Jewish practices in his own household and openly declared that he did not wish for converted Jews to assimilate and disintegrate into the general Christian society.[40] Unlike the Chicago Hebrew Mission, which promoted the idea that non-Jews should evangelize Jews, Cohn believed that only people like himself, born and raised Jewish, could understand their brethren and possess the knowledge necessary to approach Jews, reason with them, and persuade them of the truth of the Christian message.[41] Cohn tried a number of times throughout his ministry to establish a congregation of Jewish Christians in Brooklyn, but his efforts failed. It took some courage on the part of a missionary who depended on Christian support to express such views. It also took an exceptional talent to articulate such ideas and still build and retain a working relationship with Protestant individuals and church bodies that trusted him and continued to assist his mission. Perhaps the secret of the success of the Williamsburg Mission was indeed the ability of its leaders to be connected to both worlds: the community of Jewish immigrants with its beliefs, language, customs, and aspirations, and the manners and priorities of the Protestant milieu that supported their cause. The expansion and growth of missions to the Jews over the years would depend on the missionaries' ability to understand the two communities and adopt means to approach them effectively, either as supporters of the missionary cause or as potential converts.

As was already mentioned, Cohn was the most controversial figure in the realm of missions to the Jews, facing accusations that included an alleged criminal past and the falsifying of his true identity. In 1916 James Gray, a prominent conservative Protestant who later became dean and president of the Moody Bible Institute, formed a committee of investigation into the accusations against the missionary. The group, which was composed of evangelical activists, became convinced that Cohn's activities were honest. Gray published the committee's resolution in the *Christian Worker's Magazine*, which he edited, and called upon his readers to support the mission's efforts.[42] This acquittal was symptomatic of the position of the Brooklyn-based mission in the evangelical community. It attracted much suspicion and accusation, yet its leaders succeeded in gaining sufficient trust and support to carry out their work and even expand it. Leopold Cohn, whom some Jews and Christians almost demonized, received an honorary doctorate degree in 1930 from Wheaton College, one of the most prestigious evangelical institutions in America. That event symbolized recognition and triumph for Cohn and his agenda. By that time he was no longer the director of the mission; his son took over in 1920, and the mission was no longer the local Brooklyn evangelization agency it had once been.

The efforts of the Christian and Missionary Alliance (CMA) at evangelizing the Jews had a different character than that of either the Chicago Hebrew Mission or the Williamsburg Mission to the Jews. The alliance was not a mission created for the sole purpose of missionizing the Jews; yet, motivated by the dispensationalist messianic belief, it gave the evangelization of Jews a very high priority. The CMA began its course in the late 1880s with the initial aim of becoming an interdenominational organization for world evangelism. Its founders, many of them associated with Dwight Moody and his circle, adhered both to dispensationalist premillennialism and to Holiness teachings, which emphasized the human ability to attain sanctification and divine healing. One of its founding fathers was William Blackstone, who wanted to see the entire world evangelized in the current generation and was upset that no missionaries propagated the Christian gospel in Tibet.[43] The official goal of the new organization was thus "to carry the Gospel to Tibet and other parts of the world."[44] Its first director, Albert B. Simpson (1843–1919), was a Canadian Presbyterian minister who, like Blackstone, adhered to a dispensationalist worldview and promoted Holiness teachings in his organization. Simpson, like Blackstone, saw evangelization as "the Lord's own appointed way of hastening his speedy coming."[45] He summarized the theological principles of the CMA as the "Four-Fold Gospel": salvation, sanctification, divine healing, and the Second Coming of Christ.[46]

For Simpson, as for all dispensationalists, the Jews were the chosen people, heirs to the biblical promises about a restored kingdom in the Land of Israel.[47] In Simpson's view, evangelizing that nation was of special importance. Even if only few Jews accepted Christianity in the current generation, he argued, their conversion prefigured the eventual conversion of all the Jewish people.[48] The evangelization of the Jews was connected closely in Simpson's view with the arrival of Jesus. When evangelized successfully, those Jews who accepted Christ before the events of the End Times began would be saved and serve as a nucleus of the converted Jewish nation of the millennial era.[49] He identified that group with the 144,000 Jews mentioned in Revelation 7:4. Once converted and restored to their ancient glory, the Jews would serve as the most perfect evangelists: "Israel will soon be entrusted with this glorious task and then 'all flesh shall see the salvation of God,' and 'the knowledge of the Lord shall cover the earth as the waters cover the sea.' "[50]

With such a messianic theological impetus, it was no wonder that the evangelization of the Jews received a high priority in the CMA's early years. The international missionary organization set out to evangelize Jews both in America and in

Palestine. Aiming at the same time to propagate Christianity among the Jews and be present in the holy city, the CMA evangelization efforts in Jerusalem began three years after the missionary organization was established. The first missionaries were two single women, Lucy Dunn and Eliza J. Robertson, who had come to Jerusalem on their own initiative after attending the newly created CMA training school in Nyack, New York. That the two women went to work on their own in Jerusalem should not be surprising. Dozens of women missionaries worked in Jerusalem at that time, often directing missions on their own. Missionary work at the turn of the century was a means for women to pursue careers that were both fulfilling and respectable;[51] indeed, women would constitute the majority of CMA missionaries in the country.[52] Between 1890 and 1914 two-thirds of the CMA workers in Palestine were women. It was ironic, perhaps, that a daring woman evangelist such as Lucy Dunn shared the conventional belief that men were the natural candidates to direct missionary posts with women serving only as aides and auxiliaries to them. She repeatedly asked the headquarters in New York to send a man to assume responsibility for the leadership of the mission.[53]

The alliance tried to comply with Dunn's requests. In its leader's mind, a missionary station not run by a man ranked second, and the CMA wanted to promote its Jerusalem operations. In April 1894 James Cruickshank arrived in Jerusalem with his wife to assume leadership of the CMA work in Palestine. Cruickshank did not live to leave a strong mark on the work of the mission. A few months after his arrival he died of sunstroke; his two young daughters died of a fever a few weeks later. Robertson also became ill and died at the same time. Their deaths demonstrated some of the harsh realities of life in turn-of-the-century Palestine that missionaries faced and that shaped the nature of their activities. There were no paved roads, no running water or sewage system, and, needless to say, no electricity. Missions were the main providers of medical treatment in the country, sending doctors and nurses and building hospitals and clinics. The CMA itself had built a hospital in Hebron. Many Protestants who came to Jerusalem full of religious fervor found themselves burying their dear ones.[54]

The CMA sent four new missionaries to replace its dead evangelists. Eight women missionaries arrived between 1895 and 1903. By that time the mission had expanded its work to Hebron and Jaffa. Whereas women could not always influence the spiritual choices of men in this part of the world, they had much easier access to women and to homes. It was unheard of in the Muslim-dominated society that men would attempt to evangelize women.[55] The number of missionaries and the scope of missionary activity grew considerably as the alliance recruited local converts as "Bible Women," that is, women missionary-practitioners. The CMA's activity in the country received a further boost with the arrival of Albert E. Thompson (1903–14). An ardent premillennialist and advocate of the cause of missions to the Jews, Thompson enjoyed the trust and respect of the CMA leadership. During his tenure he purchased property and began building ventures, including two church compounds on the Prophets Street in the center of the new city of Jerusalem.

Buildings, however, as impressive as they may be, were not the goal of the CMA. The missionaries initially went to evangelize Jews but faced problems in that area. To begin with, the Jewish population of Jerusalem and Palestine in general was not really neglected as far as evangelization efforts were concerned. A number of missionary agencies—among them English, Scottish, and German Protestant, as well as Roman Catholic—were busy propagating Christianity among the Jews, offering the local Jewish population a variety of educational opportunities and medical help.[56] Thus, the CMA people were facing serious competition and did not make real progress in their efforts at Christianizing Jews. There was only one report of a Jewish convert to Christianity through the work of the Christian and Missionary Alliance in its first generation.[57] The CMA people soon discovered something that other, more veteran missions had known for quite a while: the easiest and most fruitful field of evangelization in the Middle East was the local Christian populations who were affiliated with non-Protestant churches, including Greek Orthodox, Roman Catholic, Uniate (mainly Greek Catholic and Armenian Catholic), Monophisite churches such as the Armenian, and a number of other Middle Eastern churches.

The CMA evangelized successfully among Christians and soon ventured into a new field: missionary work among Muslims. It opened branches in Hebron and Beer-Sheva, which had exclusive Muslim populations, as well as among Bedouins in Transjordan. The Ottoman authorities had put a ban on Muslim conversions to other religions, and the CMA's work was therefore more daring than that of most other Western missions, which usually concentrated their efforts in the major cities where there were large Jewish and Christian populations. The CMA work in Palestine was to continue for decades to come, particularly after the British replaced the Turks as rulers of the country and installed a missionary-friendly policy. Although the CMA did not give up on evangelizing the Jews, that nation would not rank first on its Holy Land missionary agenda.

The Christian and Missionary Alliance also carried on missionary work among Jews in America. The alliance's evangelization efforts were concentrated in New York during the 1890s to 1900s, including the Lower East Side.[58] Its work in this field, as reflected in the annual reports, was not different from evangelization work done by other missions: it included home visitations, distributions of tracts, and activities for children.[59] Although the CMA's work among Jews in America was not distinctive, the fledgling missionary organization used this work to promote its activity at large. Evangelizing the Jews ranked high in the eyes of the evangelical public, which supported the CMA's missionary work, and so the CMA highlighted its work among Jews in its fund-raising events.[60]

All three missions were motivated by the same premillennialist messianic belief, held the same view of the Jews and their role in history, and produced similar literature. Yet they developed different characteristics. The Williamsburg Mission developed into a "Jewish mission": its leaders and most of its workers were Jewish, and the mission adopted an ideology that allowed for Jews to retain their Jewish heritage and even attempted to establish a Jewish congregation. The other two missions, as with most societies aimed at evangelizing the Jews, did not share that course.

The different characteristics of the three missions point to some of the crucial elements in the successful development of missions to the Jews during the era. It was essential for missionary organizations to establish strong bases of support in the evangelical community, either through denominational backing or independently. Those missions that were established or directed by churches had a much easier time as far as their public standing was concerned. The Chicago Hebrew Mission initially had an advantage over other missions. It had a very large base of support because of the many churches and distinguished Protestant individuals that backed its work. Independent missions, such as the Williamsburg Mission to the Jews, faced more difficulties in that respect and were exposed to more anger and defamation. Yet, paradoxically, it would be the Williamsburg Mission that would enlarge and prosper more than the others. Independent organizations also had an advantage: they were aimed specifically at evangelizing Jews and could disregard denominational priorities. Cohn, for example, collected more money on his own than the Baptists could or were willing to give him. He had to struggle harder than the denominational missions to survive, but his mission endured and eventually thrived. Some missions that began their activity during the period would grow and prosper; others would decline and, at times, would shut down completely. The field would remain dynamic, responding to changes in both the community that sponsored the missions and the community that was the object of evangelization. An important aspect for the missions' survival and vitality would become their ability to adapt to the social and cultural developments of both the Christian and the Jewish communities at hand. Another important aspect of the missionary activity and its relative success or failure was the converts.

3

The Converts

The large and energetic movement to evangelize the Jews did make some modest gains during the period 1880–1920 as far as conversions were concerned. The number of converts, their demography, their social and cultural struggles after conversion, and their inner turmoil were indistinguishable parts of the history of the movement to evangelize the Jews, helping to shape its character and priorities.

The Jewish converts to evangelical Christianity in America at the time fit into clear demographical patterns. Most of the newly converted were young, male immigrants who came from traditional eastern European Jewish backgrounds. It was among this group that the missions invested most of their efforts between 1880 and 1920. There were Jews who converted to other, nonevangelical forms of Christianity during the period such as Christian Science or Unitarianism. As a rule, however, they did not come from the immigrant community, and their conversions were not related to missionary activity.[1]

Although many in the Jewish community reacted negatively to the attempt to evangelize Jews, there was no effective boycott of the missions, and the latter had no difficulty in making their voices heard and in approaching potential converts.[2] As one member of the Jewish community wrote: "A young man who was a friend of our lodgers used to . . . visit them. Of course, he was out of work. It was six months now since he had earned anything. He looked like the rest of us, shabby, despondent, half-starved. . . . He would sit and argue that it was no sin to accept food from missionaries when one was almost starving."[3] The missions interacted with many segments of the Jewish immigrant population through their social services, but it was unmistakably the young who showed interest in the missionaries' messages and appreciated their attentions beyond the immediate material help they could receive. Some of the young Jews undoubtedly made their first (and at times the last) contact with the missionaries out of need: they were lonely and impoverished, seeking help, shelter, or work from a mission.[4] Yet some were also interested in hearing what the missionaries had to say. Many of those who came in contact with the missions were not necessarily attracted to the Christian belief, with which they were usually completely unfamiliar. They were, rather, curious about it.[5] By the beginning of the twentieth century, there were missions to the Jews in virtually every city in America that had a community of a few thousand or more Jews. The missions became, to a certain extent, part of the surrounding scenery of Jewish neighborhoods in American cities.[6] Coming to hear missionaries preach or entering missions' reading rooms was part of exploring that environment and its possibilities. In large Jewish areas such as Brooklyn or the Lower East Side of New York, as many as several hundred came to hear a missionary preach.[7] Most of the immigrants came from areas in which the prevailing forms of Christianity were Roman or Greek Catholicism or Russian or Romanian Orthodoxy, which Jews often perceived as hostile and offensive. Most of them would not even have considered entering Christian houses of prayer in their old countries. Many of them were brought up to utter *shaketz teshaktzeno* ("thou shalt despise it") on passing a church. In the New World, things were different. Many of those who came to hear the Christian message had come to America on their own, their parents remaining in Europe. Even when parents and children arrived together, a vast generation gap developed, and parents lost much of their authority. Life in the large American cities, where most Jewish immigrants congregated, offered greater opportunities and freedoms to young Jews than they had ever experienced in the small Jewish towns of eastern Europe from which they had come.[8]

Most young Jews encountered the missionaries as part of their explorations of their new environment, seeking to make sense of it and find means to accommodate themselves in a new society. Conversion to Christianity should be seen as one of the means or options the newly arrived immigrants encountered in their quest to find a set of beliefs and values that made sense in their new country and helped them to build a new life for themselves in America. There are no definitive, agreed-on statistics concerning Jewish converts to evangelical Christianity during the period. In the early 1900s Louis Meyer, whom remarkably both Christians and Jews esteemed as a reliable recorder of missionary activity, placed the number of Jews who had converted in America and who joined Protestant evangelical churches at 4,033.[9] Meyer consulted the figures presented by different church bodies, and his evaluation seems reasonable. If Meyer's estimation is indeed correct, then the number of Jews who converted to evangelical Christianity in America between the years 1880 and 1900 was in the range of 150–200 per year. These are not numbers that can be overlooked. From the missionaries' point of view, they were certainly an achievement. Yet they represented only a small fraction of the Jewish population at large. In those years, Jewish immigration reached its peak with tens of thousands of Jews (and at times more) arriving every year. One might conclude that only a small percentage of the Jews who came to America at the time chose the option of conversion.

Jewish immigrants from eastern Europe usually lived in poor neighborhoods in the major American cities, often working in sweatshops and dwelling in crowded tenement houses. Their environment offered them, however, vital social, political, and cultural lives. Most of them abandoned traditional Orthodox Judaism in favor of other options that seemed more appropriate for America. It was in those years that the Conservative movement in American Judaism had its origins, attracting many among the second generation of eastern European immigrants. There was a vast movement toward secularization and the discarding of Jewish rites. Many joined socialist parties or Zionist groups or became active in labor unions.[10] Conversion was an option few chose. Examining evangelical Christianity was one thing; accepting it was another. Many Jews came to hear the missionaries present the Christian message, but once their curiosity was satisfied, most would leave, rejecting conversion as an option that suited neither their identity as Jews nor their personal quests.[11]

Conversion was a radical move that conflicted with many of the values Jews were brought up to hold; it was in many ways taboo. Becoming American and choosing new lifestyles were changes that put many young Jews of that era in conflict with their parents, particularly if the latter resided in America themselves. But conversion would have put them in even greater conflict with themselves. It was a self-transformation that only a few Jews of the period were willing to make. They had been brought up to regard conversion as an act of betrayal of one's people and heritage, as joining the enemy camp. Conversion generally evoked guilt, inner turmoil, and pain.[12] "I tried to find a way through the confusion of ideas and the mixture of motives. . . . It was . . . mental and physical torture," wrote Edward Steiner of his feelings. "At the one end of it the mother who bore me in bodily and mental agony; at the other end this homeless and useless self. . . . Should I cut myself loose from a race and its traditions, and in doing so wound all those who were flesh of my flesh?"[13] Henry Hellyer, in describing the inner turmoil he had experienced before his conversion, wrote, "I could see my mother and my sister and brother looking at me in terror, and my town people pointing their fingers at me in their rage; I could hear the entire Jewish race shouting at me in true fury."[14] The image of converted Jews on which Jews were brought up played a part. "Then too, I had a harrow of the so-called converted Jew, who often changes his faith for convenience," wrote Steiner.[15] With such strong inhibitions and inner turmoil it was no wonder that even young Jews who found themselves attracted to the missions' atmosphere and message were in the end reluctant to convert.[16] Many of those considering the option of conversion to Christianity were also not ready for the long-range social implications of the act of choosing a new faith. At the turn of the century, there was a strong social separation between Jews and non-Jews, and conversion usually meant leaving the Jewish community and moving into a completely different environment.

"Conversion," wrote Lewis Rambo, "is a process of religious change that takes place in a dynamic set of force fields involving people, institutions, events, ideas, and experiences," and the study of conversion has to take into account a variety of factors.[17] The evidence that converts from the era have left indeed suggests a number of factors that led to conversion. Some of those who did become Christian gave evidence in their writings of their quest for spirituality and meaning in their lives, a quest that not all young Jews necessarily shared. "Deep down in my life . . . was a spiritual hunger, of which I was then becoming conscious, and which my Jewish friends did not and could not satisfy," wrote one convert in describing his spiritual quest before encountering Christianity.[18] The general trend toward secularization and away from religious observance eliminated traditional Judaism as a possible answer. To many young Jews the religion of their parents seemed irrelevant to the needs and challenges of the time and place. It was an anachronistic religion identified with "the old country" and outdated values and modes of living. Enter the missionaries. Evangelical Christianity had agents approaching such young people and advocating the Christian belief, something advocates of Jewish tradition during the period did not do.

Individual personalities and experiences had undoubtedly played a role in people's inclination to convert. Studies of the conversion phenomenon have pointed out that many converts come from families in which there were either no fathers or fathers who were weak or abusive.[19] But such studies were done decades later and in a different cultural environment. There is no way of proving or disproving in any definite way this hypothesis regarding the converts of this early period because they cannot be interviewed. Autobiographical accounts of converts of this era tend, however, to support such a theory. Edward Steiner did not have a father and grew up with a widowed mother.[20] Elias Bernstein, who converted in Europe, was also an orphan who grew up with his mother.[21] So was the case with Henry Hellyer.[22] John Goldstein, who also converted in Europe, grew up with an abusive stepfather; the missionary couple who preached the gospel impressed him as an exemplary family and wonderful human beings.[23] Hilda Koser, who converted in America, offered a similar description of an abusive father and of missionaries who offered a sense of guidance and home.[24] Esther Bronstein's conversion, which followed that of her fiancé, took place when she was thousands of miles away from her parents.[25] Samuel Freuder left home when he was twelve years old. He converted years later in America, also thousands of miles away from his parents.[26] In all the different autobiographical accounts and the many testimonies in missionary magazines of that period, I have not found one that described a person who converted while living with a warm and supportive two-parent family.

A central element that brought young Jews to the mission and enhanced their willingness to consider conversion was the personal attention missionaries offered. The latter often served as father figures to the young men who approached them. Similarly, women missionaries and missionaries' wives served as mother figures to young Jewish women and, at times, to some of the young men, too. In their memoirs, converts portray the missionaries who evangelized them in warm, idealistic terms.[27] Scholars investigating the conversion phenomenon note that a crucial element in the process is a personal contact between the convert and an individual who advocates the belief system and serves as a model and a source of inspiration.[28] At times this relationship becomes the center and the driving force of the process.[29] Such a motif was labeled by John Lofland and Rodney Stark as "affectional" and was definitely identifiable in the process of conversion of Jews in America.[30] During the period from 1880 to 1920, it was often the interest, love, and nurturing bestowed by missionaries that affected the converts. This would change during the century as groups of peer converts would become, in the latter decades of the twentieth century, the means of effective evangelization of Jews.

Converting was, among other things, a way Jewish youngsters could pay their missionary benefactors back for all the attention and goodwill the latter bestowed upon them. It was also the means to obtain their ultimate approval. Conversion was, however, a gesture many prospective converts felt they could not make. Missionaries describe many potential converts who showed interest, hung around, and enjoyed the attention and the feeling of home the missionaries offered but stopped short of the actual conversion. They eventually left and searched for other options and ways to go on with their lives.[31]

With the missionaries serving as father figures to prospective converts, the young Jews who did convert often wished to remain close to their spiritual parents. Missionaries, on the other hand, often preferred to send the newly converted out into the evangelical society so that they could be free to devote their time and energy to new spiritual foster children who had not yet converted.[32] Letters from converts that were published in missions' magazines reveal the personal attachment of the recently converted to the missionaries. They often read like letters of children who reside out of town to their beloved parents. Converts saw a need to share their love and longing, seeking reassurance that their adoptive, spiritual parents were still interested and concerned. "I desire to let you know that I arrived safely in New York, and I am[,] thank God, well," wrote a recent convert to J. R. Lewek of the Chicago Hebrew Mission. "Excuse me that I have not written before," he apologized. "I waited until I had something worth while to write. God has been very good to me. He has answered your prayers and mine. I found work almost as soon as I arrived here. Our God does nothing in halves. I have good work and am earning $19 a week."[33]

Pointing out the social and emotional characteristics of the converts does not mean, of course, that conversions served only social, cultural, or emotional needs. One should not overlook the spiritual aspects of conversions, including the genuine quest for spiritual meaning and fulfillment. The converts often explained their conversions in religious terms and emphasized the spiritual transformation their conversions brought about.[34] Similarly, theological and exegetical questions—such as "Was Jesus the Messiah prophesied in the Old Testament?"—were lively issues in the discourse between missionaries and prospective converts as is evident from missionary tracts.[35] Yet the converts' autobiographical accounts convey the social and emotional realities and dilemmas of those who contemplated or actually underwent a conversion to Christianity. That converts to evangelical Christianity came, for the most part, from a well-defined social group and that those who described their lives and experiences had shared similar personal situations in their families suggest that conversions indeed occurred within certain social and emotional contexts at the same time that they embodied a genuine spiritual quest.

Did economic needs or expectations play a part in the conversion process, as the Jewish popular image and the Jewish antimissionary crusaders sometimes claimed? The missions operated social services, which were intended to demonstrate Christian virtues and charity and to help establish contact with the Jewish immigrant population, but not in return for conversions. No deals were made. At one time accusations that a missionary was promising financial benefits in exchange for coming to hear him preach the Christian message were cause for scandal and indignation within the missionary community.[36] Missions offered help and hospitality to prospective converts, but in these cases, too, although the generosity of their hosts enhanced feelings of gratitude and obligation on the part of prospective converts, such help, as a rule, was not done in exchange for conversions. Even had some missionaries been so unprincipled as to tempt prospective converts with economic rewards, the financial situation of the missions would not have allowed them to offer any financial benefits that could have made a difference in the standard of living of the newly converted. Most missions struggled to maintain themselves financially; their budgets covered salaries, publications, and operating costs. There were no extra funds for "buying converts." But the truth was that, contrary to a common Jewish perception, missionaries were interested in sincere, truly converted people and not in bought ones.[37] Moreover, missionaries expected converts to become economically independent and provide for themselves.[38] The Protestant missionary assumption has been that the truly converted were, as a matter of course, diligent, conscientious people, exemplary members of the community. They expected the conversion experience to have positive effects on all spheres of the convert's life, including the development of economic independence. Converts, on their part, felt a need to demonstrate their sincerity and genuine conversion by proving themselves to be good, hardworking citizens. There were, of course, Jews who approached the missions expecting prizes in exchange for conversion. Arno Gaebelein reported that some young Jewish men would occasionally stop by the mission on the Lower East Side of New York and inquire as to the benefits the mission could offer them. Would the mission, for example, finance their studies?[39] Needless to say, he neither could nor wished to accept converts on such terms. Another missionary pointed out that the relief services the missions offered attracted—as welfare agencies often do—persons who become something of professional receivers of help.[40]

Not only did the missions refrain as a rule from offering economic rewards to the newly converted, there were no prizes waiting for Jews who embraced Christianity and entered Protestant society. Some faced economic hardships. Many immigrant Jews found their first jobs within the Jewish community, and their new interest in Christianity had often put them in an uncomfortable position. At times they lost their jobs.[41] Missionaries complained that economic considerations worked against converting to Christianity. "Alas! While they own it in their hearts . . . they dare not confess it openly. . . . They fear for their daily bread."[42] Another remarked: "Here lies the great burden upon the missionary's heart. . . . Sincere seekers after the Lord . . . must turn back because ruin stares them in the face should they be known as Christians."[43] Leopold Cohn proposed to build an industrial plant "to give employment to these inquirers who [were] denied work among their blind brethren on account of their allegiance to the mission."[44] Some Jews who converted, like Maurice Reuben, who owned a department store, were economically secure and even wealthy. One could hardly accuse him of converting in order to improve his economic situation. Upon his conversion, however, his family placed him in a mental hospital, as did Samuel Needleman's family.[45] Samuel Freuder, a Jew who converted to Christianity and later retracted and went back to Judaism, wrote a book describing his experience as a Christian.[46] In it he complained bitterly about missionary conduct and standards. Yet he insists that he was not offered any financial rewards and did not offer such rewards in his work as a missionary.[47] He faced financial difficulties during his years as a Christian. Freuder, who published his book under Jewish antimissionary sponsorship, attacked the missionary enterprises endlessly. His testimony, as antagonistic to missionaries as it may have been, should lay to rest any claims that financial benefits were given in exchange for conversions.

Converts often felt themselves to be on the defensive in their new environment and felt at times that they had to make a special effort to prove their sincerity to the evangelical community.[48] They felt that not only Jews questioned their motives and sincerity and looked upon them as dubious persons but at times also Christians. "We had to watch our steps. If we wanted to eat a Jewish corned beef sandwich we were considered as Judaisers," wrote one convert.[49] This notion, a very natural one for people who have chosen to live in a new environment, might have been more a reflection of their own insecurity and their struggle to be accepted by the larger evangelical community than a response to animosity and suspicion.

Some negative feelings certainly existed in the new environment in which the converts tried to build their lives. Many Protestants in America maintained their prejudices against Jews, and converts encountered sometimes unfavorable remarks about Jewish characteristics or outright rejection.[50] One leading evangelist who expressed suspicion of converted Jews was Dwight Moody, who nevertheless promoted the evangelization of the Jews and invited Jewish converts to preach in his campaigns.[51] Despite some amount of suspicion and prejudice, it would be a mistake to conclude that most Jews who embraced Christianity were rejected or treated as second-class citizens by the Protestant community at large. Evidence shows otherwise. There were many in that community who, even while holding stereotypical images of Jews, welcomed Jewish converts. There certainly did not seem to be discrimination against converts in the evangelical camp. By the beginning of the twentieth century, for example, 120 Jewish converts served, according to one source, as ministers of Protestant congregations.[52] Ministers had been respectable members, indeed leaders within their communities. Many congregations evidently trusted and appreciated the Jewish candidates whom they chose as their pastors. "I had no reason to complain. My church . . . gave me an important place in the life of the community. It gave me a social position of no mean degree. . . . I was . . . becoming hardened by respectability and softened by the solid comforts," wrote Edward Steiner of his experience as a minister.[53] Jews were occasionally entrusted with prestigious and influential positions within the conservative Protestant framework. Louis Meyer became, toward the end of his short life, editor of the *Fundamentals*, a widely circulated and influential organ of conservative American evangelicalism at the time, one that helped shape the emerging fundamentalist movement.[54] In addition to ministers many converts chose to become missionaries. By World War I there were more than two hundred converts participating as evangelists in the efforts to proselytize the Jews, as well as dozens of others who joined missions that directed their attention at non-Jews. The conversion experience and joining a new religious community engendered a great deal of enthusiasm and a wish to share their faith with others, particularly fellow Jews.[55] As Steiner described his desire to evangelize, "I had an unquenchable ardor, a burning passion, an apostolic zeal."[56]

Most converts, as previously noted, were young single men. There are no accurate surveys or list of converts, but both missionaries and observers note that men overwhelmingly constituted the most interested inquirers and converts. This was not necessarily just a result of greater numbers of men than women immigrating to America during that period.[57] In an era long before women's liberation, more men than women crossed the Atlantic on their own and tried their luck in a new land. Sometimes men came first, their fiancées or wives staying behind in Europe and joining them at a later time. Some young men left their wives behind and never called upon them to come to America.[58] There was another major reason and a more important one for the disproportionate number of men who converted. Although America offered women more freedoms and opportunities than the old country, women still tended to be less independent than men. Unlike men, women were less likely than men to emigrate on their own; parents did not allow such freedom for their daughters. Devastating stories about the fate of unaccompanied young women in the New World, which spread around eastern European Jewish communities, added to the discouragement of such ventures. Unmarried women usually accompanied their parents or other relatives en route to America. Upon arrival, women were more likely than men to remain with parents, be greeted by husbands or fiancés, or go to live with relatives. There were often parents, aunts, or uncles to whom they were accountable, a reality that limited their choices and freedoms considerably. They were less likely than men to explore their surroundings and make choices for themselves. It was a daring act to break taboos and cross the community boundaries from Judaism to Christianity, and at that time men were more likely to do so than women.[59] Jewish men were also more inclined than Jewish women to intermarry during the period.[60]

The fact that it was mostly men who converted shaped the character of the converts' lives after conversion. With few marriageable Jewish women in their new community, many converts married non-Jews. Intermarried and feeling not altogether welcome at the Jewish quarters of the major cities, they moved away into non-Jewish towns and neighborhoods.[61] They joined Protestant churches and built their homes and lives in the non-Jewish environment. Both Arno Gaebelein and Leopold Cohn attempted in the early years of the twentieth century to establish congregations of Jews whom they had converted to the Christian faith. Their attempts failed, since the young men who the two missionaries had hoped would serve as the constituency of the unusual congregations they were trying to build preferred to move out of the Jewish neighborhoods.[62]

A common Jewish myth about converts to Christianity has been that their families ostracized them.[63] Memoirs of converts reveal that this picture is very much exaggerated and that Jews who embraced Christianity, for the most part, were able to retain their family ties.[64] Very often, there were periods of tension and conflict between converts and their parents and siblings; in some cases, ties were broken for a while but were usually reestablished.[65] Parents of the young converts, many of whom were still living in Europe, were often saddened and even shocked at their sons' or daughters' decision to embrace a new faith; some of them did "sit shivah" (mourned their children as if they were dead), but most eventually came to terms with their children's conversion. Nor is it true that converted Jews were completely ostracized by the Jewish community. As a rule, Jews did not look favorably on *meshumadim* (apostates), and many of the converts felt the resentment and kept at a distance. Yet those converts who wished to retain ties with the Jewish community managed to do so, as converts' memoirs suggest.[66] The writer Amos Dushaw, for one, even chose to reside among the masses of Jews on the Lower East Side of New York and felt at home there.

The most difficult thing for converted Jews was not the reserved, suspicious, or outright resentful attitudes in the Jewish or Christian communities but their own uneasiness. Some converts carried within them the Jewish opinion expressed by Bernhard Angel of "a Jew that leaves the religion of his ancestors and comes within the bounds of Christianity."[67] The major dilemma that faced converted Jews was how to have peace of mind with a choice and an action that they had been brought up to regard as a betrayal of their people and heritage. Jews who embraced evangelical Christianity in the last decades of the nineteenth century and the early decades of the twentieth were often seeking a new set of beliefs and meaning in their lives. Their conversion did not necessarily mean that they renounced their Jewish ethnic identity. Many of them saw themselves as Jews and, as such, were struggling with feelings of remorse, doubt, and guilt that resulted from their conversion. The dispensationalist belief, which recognized the Jews to be the historical Israel and emphasized the centrality of that people in God's plans for humanity, was helpful in that respect, since it offered a sense of purpose to the converts who had accepted that faith as well as giving them a sense that their new community was appreciative of the Jews and their role in history. But it could not eliminate the uneasy emotional reality in which many Jewish Christians lived and their feeling of not being completely at home in either world.[68]

Although hardly acceptable to the larger Jewish community and living their lives in a non-Jewish milieu, many of the converts were in their own way proud Jews. Many continued to present themselves as Jewish and retained their Jewish names. Some converts continued to take interest in the developments that were taking place among the Jewish people. Converts established an organization of Jewish Christians thus declaring themselves to be a group with special interests and characteristics within the larger conservative Protestant milieu.[69] Within that context, they often represented the Jewish cause as they saw it. In addition to fighting anti-Jewish prejudices, they called for recognition of the centrality of the Jewish people in God's plans for humanity and for more support for the cause of the evangelization of the Jews.[70]

The particular situation in which Jewish converts found themselves, struggling for recognition within the Protestant evangelical framework on the one hand and yearning to retain some sort of Jewish identity on the other, created dilemmas for many of the newly converted. Could they maintain their Jewish identity and still be accepted by the Protestant community? What parts of their Jewish identity and heritage could be retained and in what forms? One way to help ease the situation was for converts to gather together to discuss various options for accepted Jewish expressions in the Christian community. Conferences of Jewish Christians started in the beginning of the twentieth century. They led eventually to the creation of the Hebrew Christian Alliance of America in 1915, a national organization of Jewish converts to evangelical Christianity.[71] In Britain, where a strong premillennialist missionary movement to evangelize the Jews began decades before that of America, a similar organization had been created almost fifty years earlier.

The first meeting of Jewish converts to Christianity in America to discuss the possibility of forming a permanent organization took place in July 1903 in Mountain Lake Park, Maryland. Only a relatively small number of converts attended the early gatherings. Most of them were ministers and missionaries, a constituency that was to characterize such meetings for many decades and influence their agenda. A central concern for this group of converts was the wish, among other things, to promote the cause of evangelizing the Jews. Activists of the organization even justified the creation of their alliance by claiming that it was intended to promote such an agenda. A. R. Kuldell, a Lutheran pastor from Allegheny, Pennsylvania, who chaired the conference, claimed in his opening address that Jewish Christians had a special role and mission within the body of the believers in Christ: to serve as mediators between the church, the Christian faith, and the Jews. It was their duty, he declared, to arouse awareness in the church of the need to evangelize the Jews: "We, the men of Israel, who were once blind, but now see . . . we must point the nation, and the church to the fountain of healing and life even for Israel and its troubles. . . . We do not stand as members of denominations here, but as members of one nation . . . wandering and bleeding, Christless and dying. Let us cry . . . to Him: 'Come Lord Jesus and save thine inheritance,' and to His . . . Church: 'Come to the rescue of our perishing brethren. They need your sympathy, your prayers, your love, your testimony. In blessing them ye shall be blessed.' "[72] Kuldell clearly stated the opinion in this passage that converted Jews, "men of Israel," were still part of the Jewish nation and that they had a responsibility toward their brethren: to help bring them to believe in Christ. The converts had an additional duty to be the voice of Israel in the Protestant world, to struggle for a more favorable attitude toward Jews identified with increased efforts at their evangelization.

In demanding that evangelization of the Jews receive a higher priority in the Protestant world, Kuldell was thinking of what he considered to be the good not only of the Jewish people at large but also of himself and his friends. Recognizing the importance of missionary work among the Jews in the evangelical community would legitimize and validate the path the converts had chosen as well as give them a higher status in their new Christian milieu. Kuldell's view was to represent the attitude of organized Jewish Christians for decades to come. It would find its expression in speeches and articles, as well as in statements of purpose of the Hebrew Christian Alliance.[73]

The issue of the relation of Jewish Christians to Jewish religious rites had already been raised in the first years of the alliance.[74] Mark Levy, a Jewish convert who served as an Episcopalian priest, advocated the idea that Jews who accepted Christianity could, if they wished to, retain Jewish rites and practices. Few supported his suggestion. Levy's official proposal at the alliance meeting was turned down by an overwhelming majority of the participants. Although some converted Jews wanted to retain Jewish rites, it was evident that the majority of converts in those years did not approve of an attempt to amalgamate Christian belief with Jewish religious life. Most of them felt that Jews should neither establish congregations of their own nor retain their previous religious tradition.[75] It was one thing to establish an organization that came to offer a meeting ground for converts to discuss mutual problems and concerns and to promote the cause of Jewish evangelism in the Protestant camp. It was another thing altogether to create a "Jewish church" or to observe the Law. Some of those who objected took their view from Paul, who considered it futile to observe the Law in the period of Grace, after Jesus' atonement for human sins. But it also seems that the idea of retaining Jewish rites frightened some converts. They felt that they had to demonstrate the sincerity of their belief and that adherence to their former religion would cause resentment and even rejection on the part of the evangelical community. Most of those who took part in the conferences were already committed to a specific denomination, many serving as ministers. They continued to identify themselves as Jews, but they had already made choices that did not allow them even to consider observing Jewish rites and practices.

Remarkably, there were a number of non-Jewish evangelical activists, such as Arno Gaebelein and Ernest Stroeter, who endorsed the idea that Jews should retain their distinct ethnic and liturgical Jewish heritage and not integrate into the general "gentile" environment.[76] Similarly, Mark Levy had more success in advocating his cause with the leadership of his Episcopalian church, which approved of Jews retaining their ethnic and cultural distinctiveness while practicing the Christian faith.[77] Their standing at this point was academic, for there were no Jewish Episcopalians building their own congregations or practicing Jewish rites.

It was in these early stages that the term "Messianic Jews" came into being, although it was not used very often.[78] Messianic Jews came to designate the very small minority of converts who advocated observance of Jewish rites and the establishment of Jewish congregations. The majority of converts referred to themselves as Hebrew Christians; they identified themselves as Jews and were often concerned with Jewish matters but joined regular churches, were socially part of Protestant communities, were married to non-Jewish wives, and rejected the Messianic Jewish notions. The difference between the two opinions mirrors a wider struggle that took place in the missionary community. For many Protestant missionaries their cultural norms were part and parcel of the Christian message. Others, a minority at the time, wished to propagate the basic tenets of Christianity but were willing to leave room for converts to practice their new faith in their own cultural form.[79] Jewish converts were, however, in an even more delicate and defensive position in this matter than many other groups who had accepted Christianity. "Jewish" denoted for many people not only a unique people and culture but a different religious tradition altogether. Jews were more reluctant to retain features of their tradition or to build their own congregations than, for example, Chinese who had accepted the Christian faith in its Protestant evangelical form. They were afraid that their new religious community might question the sincerity of their conversions or, worse still, suspect them of being agents of a different religious tradition and practicing a distorted form of Christianity.[80]

It was therefore not surprising that Jewish converts to Christianity in the early years of the twentieth century were reluctant to create their own churches or to grant legitimacy to attempts by Jewish fellow converts to observe the Law while holding Christian beliefs. It was perhaps surprising, considering their inhibitions and sense of vulnerability, that converted Jews were openly building an organization whose aim was to give expression to their special needs, dilemmas, and priorities. It was no less amazing that the Hebrew Christian Alliance could carry out its work and be accepted in Protestant circles. Such a development was due to the influence of the dispensationalist belief in evangelical Protestant America, which brought about a new attitude toward Jews and their role in history and gave a special status to Jewish converts.

The Hebrew Christian Alliance proved to be a solid institution and gained the trust of the Protestant evangelical camp. Its gatherings took place in central Protestant churches; its financial supporters included non-Jews, and it promoted the cause of giving a high priority to evangelization of the Jews in the Protestant missionary agenda.[81] Among other things, it succeeded in creating a program for training missionaries to the Jews in one of the leading evangelical schools of higher learning in America, the Moody Bible Institute. The alliance helped finance the program and select its professors.

When a more vigorous and assertive Messianic Jewish movement came along in America in the 1970s and 1980s, its proponents tended to look upon the early members of the Hebrew Christian Alliance as Jews who had no national pride and had compromised their distinct Jewish characteristics in order to be accepted by the larger evangelical network.[82] Such a view tends to ignore the vulnerabilities of Jewish converts during those early years and the circumstances they faced. There were converts who did not care very much about retaining their Jewish roots, but there were others who allowed themselves as much self-assertion as they felt they could afford without losing credibility in their new environment. The remarkable thing about the attitudes of the Jewish Christian activists of the early twentieth century was not their unwillingness to build new modes of Jewish Christian life but rather that they did get together and find the courage to build an organization of their own in which they gave expression to their mutual concerns. Such a development would have been unheard of for converted Jews throughout most of Christian history. The differences between the Jewish Christian activists of the early decades of the century and those of half a century later should not therefore be understood in revolutionary terms but rather as stages in an evolutionary process. The foundations of Messianic Judaism of later years were laid in this early period.

The alliance's publications reflect the priorities of this group of Jewish Christians. Its journal endorsed the Zionist plan for the Jewish restoration in the Land of Israel.[83] This was a unique form of Zionism. It combined the Jewish national hope with the Christian messianic belief and looked to the realization of the Jewish dream only within the realm of the Second Coming of Jesus. A striking example of this special version of Zionism was provided in one of the early volumes of the *Hebrew Christian Alliance Quarterly*, which published a Hebrew Christian version of the Zionist national anthem, "Hatikva" (the Hope). The Hebrew Christian version followed the structure, rhythm, music, and general atmosphere of the anthem, but, in contrast to the original Zionist version, it advocated the acceptance of Jesus as its goal instead of the national restoration of Jews in their ancient homeland.

> We have not yet lost our hope
> the hope of prophets who expressed the word of God
> that our nation shall seek
> the face of its Messiah and God.[84]

Support of Zionism was one component of Jewish nationality that Jewish Christians felt free to express, knowing that it was warmly accepted by the evangelical premillennialist camp.

Some converts retracted their conversions and pointed to their sense of guilt, inner conflict, and turmoil as reasons for their unhappiness and restlessness in their new community and their decision to return to their old religion.[85] But it was not only those who returned to Judaism who pointed to the complicated and at times tormented life of the convert. Some who remained convinced Christians made this same point, as well. One such person was Amos Dushaw, who gave voice in his novels to the struggles and dilemmas of converted Jews.[86] Like the heroes of his books, the Jewish Christian writer came to America at the turn of the century and settled in New York. He studied at Union Theological Seminary, a liberal Protestant institution, and was influenced by the ideas of the Social Gospel movement. In his writings he criticized American Protestants both for their conservative standing on social issues and for their unwelcoming attitude toward Jews. Through his novels *Proselytes of the Ghetto*, *The Rivals*, and *When Mr. Thompson Got to Heaven*, he expressed a disappointment with the church establishment and the characteristics and values of the middle-class Anglo-Saxon church environment. In *When Mr. Thompson Got to Heaven*, the Jewish convert minister launched an acidic attack on American Protestant norms and characteristics: "Mr. Thompson was quite satisfied with himself and proud of his success in business, of his social standing, of his church of which he was an officer, of his race, of his politics, and of his prejudices. . . . In the concern of which he was president there was a standing rule that no man or woman of the Jewish race should be given employment."[87] A committed convert nonetheless, Dushaw differentiated between institutional Christianity and the true teachings of Jesus. "Calvinism, Lutheranism, Wesleyanism . . . stand out so conspicuously that Jesus is practicably concealed underneath these 'isms,' " he complained.[88] "There is strictly speaking no religion of Jesus except as it is practiced by individuals," he declared.[89] It will be up to converted Jews, he hoped, to serve as an avant-garde that will revive Christianity and bring it back to its true values. In his writings, he refers to Jesus as the Nazarene and not Christ, which to him signified an alien Hellenic churchly form.[90] Dushaw in this respect resembles a number of Jewish writers, scholars, and novelists who began in the late nineteenth century and early twentieth to "reclaim" Jesus as a teacher in Judaea instead of the god of the gentiles.[91] Dushaw, the Jewish Christian writer, differed from them in that, for him, Jesus was indeed the Savior and God's one begotten son. His writings criticized Protestant Christianity bitterly for identifying its rituals and hierarchy with the true teachings of Jesus but in no way sought to undermine the latter.

Dushaw's writings resemble those of Abraham Cahan, the famous Yiddish writer of turn-of-the-century America, whose *The Rise of David Levinsky* became a best-seller. Like Cahan, Dushaw wrote about the eastern European Jewish immigrant community in New York, concentrating on personal and domestic dramas caused by the move to the New World. Where he differs from Cahan is in his concentration on conversion as a central element of the crisis that confronts the immigrants in their new environment. In Dushaw's books *The Rivals* and *Proselytes of the Ghetto*, the problems of families or of a romantic relationship are stirred or intensified by the decision of one of the heroes to embrace Christianity, a move that is not shared by family members or sweethearts. The fictions offered the Jewish Christian writer an opportunity to promote his own opinions on Christianity, Christian attitudes toward Jews, social justice, the Jewish situation in the modern world, and what he considered to be the solution to the Jewish problem as a persecuted minority. Convinced that his own religious outlook embodied social justice, he wished to create "a synthesis of progressive Judaism and New Testament Christianity."[92] Converted Jews, he believed, would "stand between the synagogue and church." Jews could never amalgamate into Christian churches and feel at home there. "We know Russia and its Christian Church; we feel a little better about the American Church; but as to becoming members of it, we could not do so."[93] The American church also advocated a social and economic agenda that was unacceptable to the socially oriented immigrant Jews. "We want freedom," says one of the heroes in his play. "The church, if it does not stand for slavery, nevertheless does not stand for freedom . . . for economic and industrial freedom."[94] Dushaw took a positive, warm attitude toward Zionism. The future for the Jews lay, he believed, in Jews turning to Jesus' true teachings on the one hand and to Zionism on the other. "Zionism will do it, from a political point of view, and the gospel from a spiritual point of view; and the intelligent Jews are turning to Zionism for political freedom, and to the gospel for spiritual freedom."[95]

Dushaw was part of a small literary circle of Jewish converts to Christianity that concentrated around the journal *The Land, the People, the Book*. The journal's name reflected a dispensationalist messianic understanding of the Jewish people, the Land of Israel, and the Bible. Ironically, "The Land, the People, the Book" was also the motto of the Orthodox Jewish Zionist party Mizrachi, which was formed during those years. Dushaw's journal was published for two decades but had little influence on the attitudes of the community of converts, most of whom did not even know that it existed. Similarly, although Dushaw gave expression in his writings to the fate and issues of Jews who embraced Christianity, he was a rare bird in their circles and was mostly ignored. He participated in the early gatherings of Jewish Christians at the beginning of the century, yet he was a marginal figure at these conferences. His ideas were radically different from those of other delegates, who during that period followed the conservative evangelical "orthodox" line. Almost needless to say, his ideas carried little weight. Even though Dushaw was not a typical convert and did not speak in the name of the majority of the converts, he did give expression to what many of them felt. Although few concerned themselves with social justice, showed sympathy to socialism, or openly endorsed Dushaw's rejection of post–New Testament Christian theologies and his crude criticism of the church, many Jewish Christians had a favorable attitude toward the Zionist ideal and hoped that Jewish national restoration would come hand in hand with a greater acceptance of Jesus on the part of Jews. Some yearned for the amalgamation of the Jewish nationality and the Christian faith.

Although hardly an influential figure in the converts' circles and certainly not voicing conventional views, Dushaw convinced the Hebrew Christian Alliance in 1920 to send him to Palestine as its representative. As a missionary in the Land of

Israel, the Jewish Christian writer could combine his Christian Zionist stance with his desire to propagate the Christian gospel among his brethren, free from church affiliation, "representing Messiah and not any particular Christian sect."[96] Dushaw did not hold a position of leadership in the HCA and his views were not necessarily shared, and certainly not endorsed, by the members of the alliance, but the organization was evidently inclusive and open enough to accommodate the writer and allow him to evangelize overseas.

In sum, during the period of the 1880s to the 1910s, only a small minority of American Jews converted to Christianity. Their attraction to their new faith resulted from a genuine quest for meaning in their lives, but they belonged for the most part to a well-defined group within the Jewish community and demonstrated some common emotional trends. Most converts found their place in the non-Jewish middle-class Protestant environment. Many, however, showed interest in Jewish issues and continued to identify themselves as Jews. The converts during the period overwhelmingly rejected ideas of separateness from the Christian society. They wished neither to build congregations of their own nor to retain Jewish religious customs. Yet the period saw the early beginnings of and first attempts at creating a community of Jewish Christians: indeed, some activists convened and established an organization of their own. Being part of the movement to evangelize the Jews, that society became an interest group within the evangelical community for the cause of missions to the Jews, promoting the idea that the Christian community should concentrate its efforts on evangelizing Jews. Jews, however, did not necessarily welcome such efforts.

4

The Jewish Reaction

During the period of the 1880s to the 1910s, the Jewish community in America was preoccupied with the growing Christian missionary activity. Community activists, scholars, journalists, and laypersons reacted strongly to the Christian missionary efforts, and the alleged missionary threat ranked high on the Jewish public agenda. The Jewish responses to the presence of missionaries reflected the concerns, insecurities, and sensitivities of the Jewish community. The Jewish reaction to the evangelization efforts further shed light on Jewish attitudes toward Christianity and American society at large. The Jewish responses were, however, far from being unanimous or consistent. The various reactions serve as an indication of the feelings, values, and aspirations of different groups within the Jewish population. They reflected not only the indignation and insecurity of a minority group but also class differences, self-interest, and inner divisions.

The group that encountered the missionaries on a day-to-day basis more than others consisted of the masses of immigrants in the poor neighborhoods. Arriving from eastern Europe, those Jews were often predisposed against Christianity. Many immigrants came from czarist Russia, where Jews were restricted in settlement, education, and occupation and at times victims of pogroms. The vision of the Christian faith, usually Greek Orthodox, Greek Catholic, or Roman Catholic in such areas, was often that of a hostile oppressive religion. Yet, for all its initial hostility and suspicion, the immigrant community was far from unanimous in opposing the missionaries. Its reaction was rather ambivalent, reflecting a great amount of self-interest as well as curiosity.

Needy immigrants often approached the missions as consumers of the various relief services the evangelizers provided. This included medical clinics, English lessons for the newly arrived, sewing classes for women, and a variety of activities for children. Taking advantage of the help the missions offered did not necessarily imply any commitment or a desire to consider conversion. Many poor Jews believed that they could receive the help and remain immune to the missions' messages.[1] Many of the newly arrived immigrants also came to hear missionaries preach or to visit the missions' reading rooms. Both missionary and Jewish sources as well as the general press report that young Jews would go by the hundreds to hear Christian missionaries preach.[2] "One Saturday afternoon, father came home and said that he had just passed the missionary store on Grand Street. 'They are doing good business these days,' he said, 'as I passed, the door opened and I saw the place crowded with people.' "[3] The missions were part of the scenery of the Jewish neighborhoods, and many of the newly arrived explored the missions and their messages as part of their encounter with their new environment and its opportunities. Once their curiosity was satisfied, they usually ceased visiting the auditoriums where the preaching took place. The general trend for the younger generation of immigrants was to Americanize as Jews. Very few chose to convert. Accepting Christianity was an unappealing option for most Jews of that generation.

Perhaps unexpectedly, members of the Jewish elite were most troubled by the missionary presence. The German Jewish community was, by the turn of the century, well established socially and economically, and its members were much more at home in America than their eastern European brethren. It was precisely because of that reality that the Protestant evangelization attempts alarmed that prosperous group of Jews. The Jewish elite saw evangelization as a threat to their status as equal American citizens, with the right to retain their religious persuasion and yet be accepted as respected members of the American community.[4] Jewish leaders and activists who came from that group resisted the missionaries' work, seeing their struggle as a fight for Jewish dignity and equality. Jewish American leaders regarded the missions' activity as an indication that Christians did not respect the Jewish religion or believe it could offer spiritual meaning and moral guidance to its adherents. It was further an indication, in their eyes, that Christians did not recognize the right of the Jewish nation to exist. Missionary enterprises, they contended, were consistent with the traditional Christian view that Jews were a people who should long ago have realized the supremacy of the church over the synagogue and dissolved into the Christian nations. Largely unaware of the missions' more appreciative attitudes toward the Jews, they regarded the attempt to evangelize them as the result of centuries-old hatred and rejection. Rabbi Abraham Simon of Sacramento, in relating to the growing missionary presence felt in virtually all Jewish communities, wrote: "He employs different methods from the open anti-Semite, though he too is a persecutor."[5]

It was therefore not surprising that leading opponents of the missionary movement came from the ranks of the well-established German Jewish elite, often members or leaders of the Reform movement in American Judaism. It was Jacob Schiff, the noted financier and philanthropist from New York, a German Jew and member of a Reform synagogue, who helped finance Adolph Benjamin, a lifetime activist against the missionaries.[6] Schiff and his social circle were almost never exposed to missionary propaganda, but he obviously considered the antimissionary activity a worthy cause.

The Reform leadership was particularly sensitive to the evangelization efforts.

Perhaps the most noted and aggressive antimissionary spokesman during the late nineteenth century was Isaac M. Wise (1819–1900), an architect of Reform Judaism in America. Wise's activity in this area began before the resurgence of the movement to evangelize the Jews in the 1880s. The scope of the missionary activity from the 1850s through the 1870s was much smaller, and Wise gave personal attention to almost every missionary and every Jewish convert who became engaged in Christian activity. He continued his vigorous antimissionary campaign well into the 1890s. His sarcastic style found full expression in his attacks on missionaries and converts.[7] "The proselytizing fury is an outrage on religion, is a blasphemy on the Most High, a curse to the cause of humanity, hence the reverse, the direct opposite, of true religion," he bitterly complained.[8]

Some Reform leaders, including Wise, looked down on evangelical Christianity, considering it much inferior to their own enlightened form of pure, rational monotheism. Reform Judaism in the late nineteenth century and early twentieth had built a triumphalistic Jewish theology, which presented Judaism as the leading moral force in the building of the modern world and as the religion of the utopian future toward which the world was progressing.[9] For these Reform leaders, the missionary endeavor was particularly irritating. An attempt to evangelize the Jews cast doubt on their self-image as an elite class, the "Brahmins" of the new age. In addition, they believed that Reform Judaism provided Jews with a theology that allowed them to retain their Jewish identity and also participate in the American commonwealth as full citizens. The evangelical message asserted that good citizens and constructive members of society were only those who had undergone a conversion experience and accepted Jesus as their personal Savior. Reform Jews felt that evangelical missionary efforts were a challenge to their secure position in society and their status as middle-class Americans.

Perhaps not surprisingly, missionaries for their part took a very negative attitude toward Reform Judaism. They recognized that this group of Jews had become comfortable, well to do, and influential, more so even than most Protestants. They were living proof that Jews could find their way into American society and be accepted without embracing Christianity. Missionaries sometimes pointed to the unfortunate situation of the Jewish people throughout the ages, ascribing it to their stubborn refusal to accept Christ.[10] But the German Jewish community in America was doing extremely well, a reality that touched on a sensitive evangelical nerve, since it exposed the inability of conservative Protestants to impose their values on the entire society and turn America into a "righteous kingdom."[11] Reform Jews, like their progressive Christian counterparts, and like many liberal Jews and non-Jews, demonstrated by their successes that evangelical Christianity, with all its vigor, had not won the day. In addition, many evangelicals found the concept of "Reform Judaism" strange and even irritating. Judaism for them was monolithic and static; it could not reform without the acceptance of Jesus as Lord and Savior. The Reform movement was a hollow pretense, they thought, a rebellious attempt on the part of obnoxious people. Some missionaries labeled Reform Judaism "deformed."[12] Evangelicals portrayed Reform Jews as fallen people who walked in the darkness of Satan. Since God did not seem to have punished these Jews in this era, he was undoubtedly going to do so in the next one. Reform Jews had no chance of survival.[13]

In addition to their resentment over missionary activity, Reform Jews found themselves on the defensive, facing attacks by Orthodox Jews who blamed the Reform movement for Jewish apostasy and conversions out of the faith. One such attack came from Britain's chief rabbi, Joseph Hertz, who pointed to the conversion of three graduates of the Hebrew Union College as a proof that the Reform ideology led to apostasy.[14] Reform leaders found it necessary to defend themselves. Gerhard Deutsch, a professor at the Hebrew Union College, wrote to repudiate Hertz's claims. The three Reform Jews who converted to Christianity, he claimed, came from Orthodox homes and had Orthodox upbringing. Deutsch went on to list names of prominent Orthodox converts to Christianity. Attempting to place the blame at the Orthodox door, Deutsch then claimed that it was the inability of Orthodoxy to provide answers and meaning that turned Jews away from the faith. "If Orthodoxy cannot prevent the next generation from being non-observant Jews or Reformers—and it evidently cannot—is not Orthodoxy responsible for the apostasy of the next generation, if such occurs?" he asked.[15]

Orthodox and Reform Judaism would have been on less than agreeable terms without the missionary presence, but the latter added to the ill feelings and mistrust. Rabbi Hertz's opinion was not unique; Orthodox Jews blamed conversion to Christianity on the turning away from "observing Torah and Mitzvot [commandments]." If Jews adhered to their old religion, they would be immune to the seductions of other religions. Strengthening the Orthodox educational system was their proposed remedy to the missionary threat.[16] "The only way to counteract the pernicious influences of the hypocritical missionaries," claimed Rabbi Mordecai Aaron Kaplar of the Lower East Side, was by "the establishment of Talmud Torahs (religious schools for children) and Synagogues."[17]

At times, spokesmen for the Jewish elite made an effort to persuade the Christian community on moral grounds that proselytizing Jews was inherently wrong.[18] Jews could not understand why otherwise honest, intelligent Christians should support and, worse, still be involved in evangelizing Jews. The Jews, who had been noted in the New Testament to be a proselytizing people (Matthew 23:15), had ceased evangelizing altogether in the early Middle Ages as a precondition for living as a tolerated minority in Christian and Muslim lands.[19] Conversions to Judaism were reduced to a minimum, as they often posed danger to both converts and community and were reserved to extraordinary cases of people who knocked hard on the door and proved their sincerity beyond all doubt. Necessity turned into virtue, and nonproselytizing became a characteristic of the Jewish religion. Jews, who considered their religious heritage a part of their ethnic and cultural identity, could not understand why Christians could not leave them alone and evangelize in their own quarters only. Most were ignorant of the characteristics and motivation of evangelical Christianity. "When will they learn that one cannot 'get religion.' Religion cannot be put on the market. You can no more change a man's religion than you can his color. We are what are parents are," wrote Rabbi Abraham Simon of Sacramento.[20] Simon expressed the standard Jewish opinion on people's affiliation with religious communities. Jews have looked upon being Jewish as an inherited obligation and privilege. They did not call on people from the outside to join in but expected those inside the fold to remain there.

Jewish leaders did not object to evangelists working to bring Christianity to the down and out in the non-Jewish population, but Jews, they stated, were not in need of the Christian message. They had their own religious tradition that offered them all they needed spiritually and morally. The missionary endeavor was thus an insult and a cause for indignation. "I can understand and I can appreciate it when you and those like you go among the drunkards, the thieves, the harlots, and the lost classes of our population and try to redeem them. I cannot understand it that you should think the Jews of Chicago to be not better than thieves. We 'damned Jews,' we thank you for your good opinion of us," wrote Rabbi Bernhard Felsenthal of Zion congregation in Chicago to William Blackstone, founder and superintendent of the Chicago Hebrew Mission in 1891.[21] Needless to say, when Christians who supported or were involved in evangelizing Jews were confronted with the Jewish arguments against missionizing, they were not persuaded. They had known ahead of time that Jews would resent the attempts to evangelize them and would misinterpret their meaning. They were determined to evangelize Jews whether the Jewish community liked it or not.[22] From their perspective, evangelism was legitimate, and propagating Christianity among the Jews was an act of goodwill and kindness.

The most common method Jewish leaders used in their struggle was to try to discredit the missionaries and converts on moral grounds. Jewish opinion of both missionaries and converts was indeed very poor. Just as decent people did not set out to induce Jews to abandon their fathers' faith, so sane and loyal Jews would never convert to Christianity. Deceit, they assumed, was the only means by which missionaries could make their way into the Jewish community.[23] "He would convert the Jew by inducements and enticements that a low, vulgar Jew would not fail to seize. He prefers tricks of speech, wicked persuasion, twisting Scripture, falsifying religion, throwing mud at another faith, but always in the name of love and peace," wrote Rabbi Abraham Simon, expressing again a common Jewish view.[24] The antimissionary crusaders wanted to share their impressions with the general public and stir public ire against the missionaries. Remarkably, Jewish antimissionary activists approached the Christian evangelical community and shared their accusations against missionaries. In some cases they succeeded in convincing Christian supporters and cast doubt over the integrity of some missionaries.[25] But these cases were rare. More often than not, little attention was given to such accusations. Supporters of the missions expected Jews to blame the evangelists, and the converts they made, and ascribe bad qualities to them.

Jewish antimissionary writers often described missionaries as swindlers and impostors. They accused missionaries of fabricating their personal histories, providing exaggerated accounts of their successes, using dishonest methods to bring Jews to hear the gospel, buying off converts, and embezzling the missions' assets and giving false financial statements.[26] Some of the accusations sound almost unbelievable. If one was to accept Jewish reports as noted above, then Leopold Cohn, founder and director of a Baptist-sponsored mission in Brooklyn, was not the former rabbi that he claimed to be but rather a runaway saloon keeper; when he posed as penniless and appealed for financial support, he actually held considerable property and was using for personal gain donations that had been given to him for the mission.[27] Jewish critics of mission activity were quick to point out that prominent converts were often presented as former rabbis, even if they had never been officially ordained.[28] The conversion of rabbis obviously filled missionaries with great satisfaction, and they boasted of such incidents with pride.[29] Jews, for their part, were terribly embarrassed when rabbis converted, and they contended that many who claimed to be rabbis were not fully ordained. There were, of course, a few cases of fully ordained rabbis converting to Christianity. Others had served, prior to their conversions, as *hazan-shochet* (cantor–ritual slaughterer) or *shatz-matz* (cantor-teacher), which meant that they held semirabbinical positions in small Jewish communities. Although Jews often accused them of being impostors, their claim to the rabbinate was not completely unfounded.[30]

Jews rarely questioned the personal integrity of non-Jewish missionaries; they mostly directed complaints at Jewish converts who had become engaged in evangelization work. Jews reacted much more negatively toward Jewish converts involved in evangelization of Jews than toward non-Jewish missionaries. Gentiles could be expected to evangelize Jews, but Jewish missionaries were conceived of as traitors twice over. Not only had they defected from the Jewish camp; they had also joined the enemies in their struggle to destroy the Jewish faith and Jewish national existence. They were bound to be villains.

There was a certain irony in the attitude of Jewish opponents of missionary activity toward the propagation of Christianity among Jews. On the one hand, Jewish leaders such as Wise rejected the evangelical impulse on the grounds that it implied intolerance of Judaism and endangered the social and political status of Jews in the American commonwealth. On the other hand, they were unwilling to recognize the right of missionaries to preach their message among Jews or the freedom of Jews to choose their religious belief. Reform Judaism differed on many issues with traditional Jewish attitudes, but in this realm Reform rabbis manifested the traditional Jewish response, asserting that Jews had an inherited, indelible commitment to their religion. They could not walk away from it; their Jewishness was not a matter of choice. America was a free country in the sense that Jews were granted full civil liberties and had an equal status in the community, but not in the sense that they could choose their religious affiliation. Non-Jews were free to do so but not Jews.

It was not only members of the German Jewish elite who tried to fight missionaries; some initiatives also took place in the immigrant neighborhoods, where reaction to the missionaries was far from unanimous. A glimpse into conflicting Jewish attitudes is provided by an article in the *American Hebrew*, the writer of which described the following:

> The missionaries have been active for some years in the neighborhood of Park avenue and 102nd street. A church there devoted to their uses is well lit up with electric lights and kept warm in winter, and with lectures and entertainment the children of the neighborhood are inveigled into attendance. Even a Jewish religious school has been maintained by them at times. Self-respecting people of the neighborhood have at different times taken the matter in their own hands and threatened to withdraw their trade from the Jewish butcher, baker, etc., who permitted their children to attend and take advantage of their outings, vacations, parties and treats. These tradesmen pleaded that no harm could come to their children, who needed the clothing and gifts they got, that the place kept them off the street, etc. It developed later unfortunately that the butcher, baker, etc., were held in the grasp of the missionaries by being allowed to hold services on the holidays for their own private use, which netted quite a penny to them and the pity is that they could not see the sinfulness of utilizing the missionaries' church with its crosses upon the seats and elsewhere, for petty gain.[31]

This passage betrays an elitist, condescending tone toward "butchers, bakers, etc." Yet it reveals clearly the realities of Jewish cooperation with and resentment toward the missions. It explains why working-class Jews, themselves attached to Jewish tradition, allowed their children to attend activities sponsored by missionaries. The report suggests that their parents did care about Jewish tradition and were in fact observant Jews. But they did not think that the missionary message could affect their children very much, and they felt that the services the mission was offering their children outweighed the danger of their becoming Christian.

The article in the *American Hebrew* demonstrated the fact that the mission offered much of what children could not always obtain elsewhere. It reveals differences of class and opinion in the immigrant community. "Self-respecting people of the neighborhood" resented the approach of those who were willing to accept benefits from the missions under the assumption that "no harm could come to their children." Part of the Jewish reaction to the missionary activity was an attempt to address the lack of sufficient facilities for Jewish youth.[32]

Jonathan Sarna, who examined the Jewish reaction to Christian missionaries in the early and middle decades of the nineteenth century, has argued convincingly that missionary activity spurred American Jews to organize and build educational, cultural, medical, and charitable enterprises that were intended, among other things, to neutralize similar services the missionaries offered the Jewish population.[33] Jewish leaders and benefactors were both embarrassed and worried by the help provided by missionaries. This was undeniably the case in the earlier period of missionary activity in America (1820s to 1870s) with which Sarna deals. By the 1880s and 1890s American Jewry had developed a network of educational, medical, and charitable organizations that were reinforced in order to offer help to the Jewish immigrants from eastern Europe who were pouring into American cities in unprecedented numbers.[34] In addition to having an earnest desire to help their needy brethren, the more established Jewish elite that sponsored the philanthropic initiatives was also motivated by the desire to help the newly arrived integrate into American society. The need to "do something," lest the missionaries use the unfortunate conditions of poor Jews to capture their souls, was a secondary consideration during that period.[35] During the 1880–1920 period, one might point to a number of educational initiatives that were intended to serve as an antidote to the missionary presence, many of which were occasional and on a small scale. This included such ventures as an Orthodox group raising money to complete the establishment of a Talmud Torah by proclaiming its effectiveness in combating missionary efforts, or a group of Jews on New York's West Side deciding to become involved in educational work among the area's children in order to counterbalance missionary work among poor Jewish youth.[36]

That many in the immigrant community came to hear missionaries and use their services did not mean that missions did not encounter opposition in the poor neighborhoods. On the popular level, immigrant Jews whom missionaries evangelized occasionally harassed missionaries, called them names, interrupted their services, and tore up their tracts.[37] These were, for the most part, spontaneous outbursts. Such actions, however, had little success in stopping the missionaries from carrying out their work. Missionaries knew that some amount of animosity on the part of individual Jews was inevitable, and they were ready to face it.[38] They saw such unpleasant occurrences as a manifestation of ingratitude and evidence of the spiritual blindness that afflicted Jews. Yet they were certainly not discouraged. For some missionaries such negative reaction gave more meaning to their work. It proved that their work made a strong impact in the Jewish community, so much so that it aroused anger and opposition. They advertised the incidents in the missions' journals. The reaction served as proof of their dedication and evidence of the difficulties they faced. If anything, such harassment served to boost missionary morale and strengthen the missionary cause in the evangelical community.

A particularly sensitive issue for both the masses of Jewish immigrants and the Jewish elite was the evangelism of children, an area in which Jews felt particularly vulnerable because they considered children to be more susceptible to influence by missionaries. In this case, too, the heated Jewish reaction could be misleading. Evidently, many in the immigrant community allowed their children to attend educational and recreational activities sponsored by missionaries, overlooking the evangelization agenda of such enterprises. For many Jewish children, using the missionary facilities meant merely that—using them, with no lasting effects on their religious persuasion and communal loyalties. Yet the Jewish community as a whole saw the evangelization of children and teenagers as an almost monstrous scheme. "Stealing Jewish Children," ran the title of an article on missionary work among Jewish children in the usually calm *American Hebrew*.[39] Jewish public opinion was stirred to action whenever a missionary attempt to convert teenage children was crowned with success and rumors of pressures put on Jewish children to convert were spread.

Such was the case when Esther Yachnin, a fifteen-year-old girl from New York, converted to Christianity in 1911, an event that became a cause célèbre.[40] Yachnin was baptized, without her parents' consent, at the Eighteenth Street Methodist Church, in Brooklyn. Her baptism stirred so much antagonism on both the popular and organizational levels that the Brooklyn Federation of Jewish Organizations called a protest meeting. Participants at the gathering demanded that the state of New York declare it illegal to evangelize children. A Jewish attempt to introduce a bill that would have made the proselytization of minors without parental consent a misdemeanor proved unsuccessful. Even in New York, where the Jewish population had considerable political influence, the legislature was not persuaded to pass such a law. Protestant influences were stronger, and the freedom to propagate the gospel took precedence over the Jewish community's fear that its youth would be converted.[41]

The inconsistent relationship with missionaries characterized not only the immigrant community but also the elite. Despite their resentment at attempts to evangelize their people, Jewish leaders did not refrain from cooperating with missionaries when they felt that it would serve the Jewish cause. Such an approach was evident in the relationship between the American Zionist leadership and William Blackstone. The hope that a Jewish national home would be built in the Land of Israel was held by both evangelical premillennialists such as Blackstone and the Zionists. In 1891, Blackstone organized a petition to the president of the United States, Benjamin Harrison, urging him to convene an international conference of world powers that would decide to give Palestine back to the Jews. In 1916, at the urging of the leaders of the Zionist Federation in America, Blackstone renewed his petition. Zionists such as Supreme Court justice Louis Brandeis, Rabbi Stephen S. Wise, and businessman Nathan Straus considered Blackstone's efforts advantageous to the Zionist cause. They regarded him as a friend and overlooked his missionary intentions.[42]

Their resentment of the missionary enterprise notwithstanding, Jews looked cynically on conversions, regarding them as inherently insincere and most likely motivated by social and economic gains. Spiritual meaning or religious persuasion had nothing to do with it, they asserted.[43] Jews, according to that view, converted either to escape their unfortunate condition and enjoy the security and privileges that the non-Jewish community could offer or else to raise their social status, gain acceptance by circles that had been closed to them, and win new economic opportunities.[44] Jews believed that, in many cases, converts had merely been "bought out" by financial promises made by propagators of the Christian faith. "The majority of Hebrew Christians that fill the churches of the missionaries of this city are mostly subventioned legionnaires. . . . These renegade Jews are not worth the notice of self-respecting men," wrote M. Ellinger, the editor of *Menorah*, the organ of the B'nai B'rith order.[45] Jews have often looked upon converts as the scum of the earth, the rotten fruit on the Jewish tree, picked by the enemies of Judaism, who were unable to reach any of the good fruit.[46] The idea that some converts might have been persuaded by the Christian message and had embraced Christianity after much thought and inner struggle was a possibility their fellow Jews were often unable to countenance. That the missionaries perceived themselves as sincere friends of the Jews and that they saw their work as a manifestation of goodwill were concepts many Jews could not understand.

The aggressive missionary enterprises left their mark on Jewish perceptions of Christian attitudes toward Jews. Many in the Jewish immigrant community became suspicious of Christian charitable, welfare, or educational enterprises and at times were convinced that any Christian willingness to show goodwill toward the Jews was motivated by a hidden missionary agenda.[47] Such was the case with Jacob Riis, a journalist, photographer, and urban reformer who wrote about the immigrant Jewish community of New York. Riis's photographs, which reveal the poverty and deprivation on the Lower East Side of New York, can well explain why so many in the community were willing to use the services the missions were offering.[48] Yet his attempt at carrying out urban reform work in the poor Jewish neighborhood did not always meet with approval.[49] Riis was not a missionary and did not hold to a dispensationalist premillennialist worldview. His perspective was that of a progressive elitist, patronizing perhaps, but not conversionist. Indeed, he expressed appreciative opinions of Jews and stated that they did not need to abandon their religion.[50] The urban reformer befriended Stephen Wise, a Reform rabbi and an active opponent of missionaries, and invited him to speak in the tenement center he operated in the Lower East Side. Yet poor Jews, newcomers to American society who rarely encountered members of America's Christian elite, could not figure Riis out. After all, what was a Christian do-gooder doing in a Jewish neighborhood? Unfamiliar with Riis's social and cultural background, they could not grasp his motivation. Considering the resentment that Christian missionary "intruders" aroused among many Jews, it was not surprising that Riis encountered suspicion.[51]

Some Jewish activists published guidebooks for Jews, offering answers to some of the arguments used by the missionaries.[52] One such book was Lewis A. Hart's *Jewish Response to Christian Evangelists*. Hart wished to provide his readers with the Jewish interpretations of passages from the Hebrew Bible with messianic overtones that missionaries used to persuade Jews that Jesus was the prophesied Messiah and to provide Jews with arguments of their own to counter the Christian claims. The author was aware that many of the young Jews who were approached by missionaries were puzzled by the Christian interpretation of certain biblical passages. He believed that acquainting them with traditional Jewish interpretations that could be used as counterarguments would strengthen their resistance to the Christian message. Hart's book, which included extensive quotations from the Hebrew Scriptures, is reminiscent, at times, of the medieval Jewish-Christian debates in which the Jewish spokesmen responded to and tried to repudiate the Christian typological reading of the Bible as a prelude to the New Testament. *A Jewish Response to Christian Evangelists*, as well as similar guidebooks for Jews, was based on the rather naive assumption that young Jewish men and women would read the book even before they encountered missionaries and heard their message or immediately after such a meeting took place. It was further based on the idea, just as naive, that missionaries convinced Jews to embrace Christianity by concentrating on biblical exegesis. Discussing key biblical passages and their meaning occupied undoubtedly an important part in the dialogue between missionaries and prospective converts. It was, however, only one aspect and not necessarily the central one in a much more complicated process of interaction between evangelists and would-be converts. Other factors played an important role, including the converts' quest for meaning and community in their lives.[53] It is doubtful, therefore, whether a decision for or against the acceptance of Christianity depended on reading the counterarguments that guides such as this offered.

Hart was not alone in writing books to combat missionaries. A number of other community leaders wrote tracts that were intended to give expression to the Jewish opinion on the Christian missionary enterprise. Such publications did not necessarily provide a guide to Jews considering the missionary biblical exegesis, but they often served as an apologia for Judaism, listed Jewish objections to missionary activity, and offered an opportunity for the authors to let off steam. It is doubtful whether such books had any influence on Jews considering conversion. Missionaries definitely did not reverse their policy and cease evangelizing on account of reading such expositions. Yet such books give evidence of the Jewish perception of the Jews' own tradition. They also demonstrate the pain the missionary offensive caused. Remarkably, the authors of such apologies came from the leadership of the Reform movement. Louis Weiss, a rabbi in Columbus, Ohio, published *Some Burning Questions: An Exegetical Treatise on the Christianizing of Judaism*. In the same year another rabbi in the Midwest, Bernhard Felsenthal of Chicago, published *Why Do the Jews Not Accept Jesus as Their Messiah?*

The turn of the century witnessed a large Reform apologetic and polemic literature that was intended to defend Judaism.[54] Much of that literature did not relate to evangelical Christianity and missionaries. Rather, it reacted to non-proselytizing liberal forms of Christianity and came to explain to Jews who were attracted to such religious communities why Christianity was not in any way superior to Judaism. Weiss and Felsenthal echoed some of these arguments, yet their books were not part of the genre because they were designed to counterattack missionaries and not Unitarians or Quakers.

Defending the right of Judaism to exist alongside Christianity, both Weiss and Felsenthal expressed the standard Jewish perception regarding religious affiliation. In their view, those raised as Christians should be Christian, whereas those raised as Jews should remain Jewish and not be exposed to Christian evangelism, which both rabbis saw as a destructive intrusion.[55] The midwestern rabbis demonstrated some of the misunderstanding between Christians and Jews over the issue of evangelism. For Jews, religious affiliation was intertwined with their ethnic identity and was determined at birth. For evangelical Christians, the definition of a Christian was a person who had undergone a conversion experience and accepted Jesus as his or her personal Savior. They were unwilling to restrict the work of propagating Christianity exclusively to people who grew up in Christian homes. Moreover, as has been noted, as far as they were concerned, evangelizing the Jews had particular merit and stood high on their agenda. Leaders and activists of the two communities therefore failed to understand each other's values and motivation. What was right in one tradition was wrong in the other, and what was offensive for one community was a virtue in another.

A rather unusual literary treatment of converts to Christianity was provided by Abraham Cahan, the prominent Jewish journalist whose writings dealt with the new realities and dilemmas of Jewish immigrants in America. In "The Apostate of Chego-Chegg" (1899) Cahan describes the travails of Rivka, alias Rebecca, alias Michalina, a *meshumadeste*, a convert to Christianity and a new immigrant to America, who joins a new agricultural village in Long Island. Rivka's conversion in Cahan's story has nothing to do with religious beliefs; she embraces Christianity in order to marry a man she loves. But her relationship with her husband does not replace the close family ties she was privileged to have had before her marriage. She becomes lonely and isolated and yearns for the warmth and support her former Jewish environment had provided her before her conversion. She begins an emotional, social, and geographical journey home to her family and religion. But her love for her husband does not allow her to settle back down with her family. She is again on the road, miserable, restless, and devastated. Although Cahan portrayed his fictional heroine with sympathy and compassion, he nonetheless describes her as a torn, tormented person, a lost soul. Cahan, a secular socialist, followed the traditional Jewish view of the *meshumadim* as "the destroyed." In his description, which well reflected the popular Jewish outlook of the time, joining Christianity was merely a social decision, devoid of spiritual or theological persuasion. It was an unfortunate decision based on miscalculation, for the new environment could not offer the warmth, security, and clear sense of identity the Jewish community offered. Converts were wandering souls rejected in one community and strangers in the other. Cahan's short story, originally published in a general American literary magazine, clearly revealed that resentment of Jews, including secular ones, toward apostates was just as strong in America as in Europe. Jews in Cahan's story could neither understand the heroine's choice nor tolerate it and refused to relate to her again, unless she recanted. In their world, a *meshumadeste* was what it literally meant: she was someone who had destroyed herself.

The Jewish response to the growing missionary activity was truly paradoxical. On the one hand, Jews portrayed the attempts to evangelize them as a complete failure. "We are no longer indignant. We have gone beyond that; we smile, pitying your fruitless efforts," wrote a Jewish activist in an open letter to a Christian leader whose church engaged in missionary work.[56] Unacquainted with the theology that motivated the missionaries, Jews assumed that the extensive missionary network and the enormous zeal it displayed were aimed at the conversion of the entire Jewish population. As such, they viewed the missions as a failure because only a relatively small number of Jews converted. At the same time, Jews vociferously condemned the missions' activities and carried out a propaganda campaign against them. If the missionaries were having such poor results, why give them so much attention and why bother to mobilize public opinion against them? The answer is that even though Jews sincerely believed that Christian evangelization attempts were failing miserably, these efforts had nevertheless clearly touched sensitive Jewish nerves. As noted above, Jews perceived the fact that American Protestants saw a need to Christianize them as a signal of delegitimization, a denial of the legitimacy of Judaism as a separate religion and of the right of Jews to exist as a people with their own religion and culture. Missionary activity obviously stirred up old fears and frustrations, which resulted in a reaction that was disproportionate to the loss they believed the missionary activity had caused them.

In the final analysis, it was more than anything else the belief that missionary activity posed a threat to Jews' status in the American polity that stirred the heated reaction to evangelization efforts. The Jewish elite and the newly arrived immigrants reacted differently; yet both groups of Jews shared similar feelings about the missionaries. The elite felt that the missionary agenda and the beliefs it represented questioned the standing of Jews who had built a home for themselves in America and considered themselves to be among its proudest citizens. Many in the immigrant community sensed that missionaries represented an attitude that could stand in the way of their building such a home and attaining solid, respectable standing in the community. It was perhaps no wonder, therefore, that the Jewish attitude toward missionaries relaxed considerably in the 1920s and 1930s, when the Jewish community reached the conclusion that missions did not affect the position of Jews in the American polity and that the greatest dangers to their standing in that society came from other quarters.

Although Jews did not always realize it, the missionary community did not remain indifferent to the Jewish opinion. Many among the missions' supporters and leaders became increasingly aware of the bad reputation the missionary endeavors acquired in Jewish quarters and were afraid that it could affect their evangelization work among the Jews. Missionaries took notice of the Jewish accusations, and their awareness of them often shaped the missions' rhetoric and agenda.[57]

5

The Reputation of the Missions

Jewish antimissionary activists could not stop the missions from pursuing their work, but they had some success in casting doubt on the conduct and character of missionaries. On their own, such accusations would be insufficient to harm the missionary cause and injure its reputation. That Jews hated missionaries and would portray them in the worst terms was taken for granted. In this campaign, Jews received, however, help from an unexpected camp: the missionaries themselves. Missionaries at times attacked fellow evangelists and repudiated their conduct. Some of them were sincerely concerned about the reputation of missions and the proper handling of missionary affairs. But there was another side to missionaries casting doubts on one another: rivalry, inspired by competition for Protestant support and predominance of the field. Missionaries promoted themselves and accused one another of improper behavior. Arno Gaebelein, founding head of the Hope of Israel mission, for example, attacked Herman Warszawiak, a missionary in New York, for offering bonuses to Jews who came to hear him preach. Gaebelein declared such methods unethical. To offer another example, in his memoirs, Joseph Cohn asserted that his mission, in contrast to others, really carried out the activities it advertised and could account for every penny it received, leading the reader to understand that other missions' accounts might be dubious.[1]

It was perhaps significant that most complaints were directed toward missionaries of Jewish decent who were working in New York.[2] The geographical element strengthens the assumption that some of the accusations derived from the competition that existed between missions that were located in the same district. Such missions were struggling to maintain themselves, competing for financial support from the Protestant community. By the beginning of the twentieth century, a dozen different missions to the Jews operated in New York. By that time, there were about a million Jews in the city, which meant that there was plenty of work for missionaries, yet resources were limited, and some obviously felt threatened by the competition. One of the reasons Leopold Cohn had been particularly targeted for attacks was clearly his success. By the late 1890s, his mission operated in two sections of New York and was producing numerous publications. The mission went from better to best. In later decades, it would become the largest mission to the Jews in America, with branches all over the

United States and abroad. Consequently he became the missionary whom both Jews and fellow evangelists chose to blame and attack.

With accusations, slander, and scandal hanging over the heads of missions, Protestant Christian supporters, for their part, were sometimes uncertain of the integrity of missionaries to the Jews. Contrary to the prevailing impression in the Jewish community, the movement to evangelize the Jews demonstrated concern for professional ethics and morality. Ethical issues were discussed in missionary conferences.[3] Participants asked themselves, for example, when does legitimate charitable help end and a bonus to attract converts begin?[4] That the supporters of the missions did concern themselves with missionary norms and behavior was evident from a number of inquiries made into the conduct of missionaries and the instances in which the careers of missionaries were brought to an end because of accusations and scandals. In some cases, church bodies took it upon themselves to inquire into the methods and management of missions, and, on a few occasions, the careers of missionaries were brought to an end by their findings. Herman Warszawiak, a gifted and popular missionary preacher, was one example of a Jewish missionary who had to give up his career in the field owing to Protestant disapproval.[5]

Warszawiak was born in Warsaw, Poland, in 1865. At the age of twenty-two he emigrated from his homeland, leaving his wife and two daughters behind. In Hamburg, on his way to America, he converted to Christianity and proceeded to Edinburgh, Scotland, to obtain theological education. In 1890, he arrived in New York and began his missionary work under the auspices of the New York Mission and Tract Society. The newly arrived immigrant proved an able orator; hundreds of Lower East Side Jewish immigrants came to hear his sermons. In 1892, Warszawiak brought his wife from Europe. He could not bring over his daughters, of whom his wife's parents claimed custody, on account of the parents' conversion. It was only a few years later that the daughters joined their parents. In his early years as a missionary in New York, the handsome and successful preacher became a darling of the missionary community. His former sponsors in Scotland published a small book trumpeting his success. *Herman Warszawiak "The Little Messianic Prophet"* or *Two Years of Labour among the Refugee Jews of New York* described the young missionary achievements in hagiographic terms: "A wonderful sight—one indeed unexampled since the early days of the Christian era—is now to be seen in New York City every Saturday afternoon, viz., a congregation of from three hundred to eight hundred adult Jews with a small proportion of women, assembled in a Christian church! And what is the attraction? to hear one of their brethren, quite a young man, prove out of the Scriptures that Jesus is the Christ."[6]

Accusations against Warszawiak began early on in his career, with Adolph Benjamin, a Jewish antimissionary crusader taking a particular interest in defaming the successful young missionary. It was not, however, the Jewish accusations that destroyed Warszawiak's reputation in evangelical eyes. A comparison between his career and that of other fellow missionaries, such as his friend Leopold Cohn, brings one to speculate that his career might have continued successfully had it not been for the resentment he aroused among his Christian supporters and associates.

In 1895 Warszawiak established his own independent mission, the American Mission to the Jews, and began weekly preaching on Saturday afternoons at the Presbyterian church at Henry and Market Streets. To attract crowds to hear his sermons, he distributed leaflets in Yiddish announcing: "Whoever comes this Sabbath afternoon to our meeting at 19 Market Street will receive a free ticket to a wonderful electric picture exhibition. Come and secure free tickets. The collection of pictures is highly interesting. The tickets to be purchased will cost 50¢." The bonus offered to Jews aroused a scandal. Notably, it was other missionaries to the Jews who denounced him. Warszawiak's downfall began when he sought ordination in 1896 from the New York presbytery. The request was turned down, stirring a debate over the missionary's personal integrity, which resulted in the Fifth Presbyterian Church suspending him from membership. The charges were not related to his work as a missionary but to his personal morality. Anthony Comstock, a famous "antivice crusader" at the time, gave testimony that he saw Warszawiak visit a "house of vice" in Weehawken, New Jersey, where gambling and drinking took place. Although the decision to expel him from the church was later reversed, his reputation received an irrevocable blow; donations to the mission stopped, members of the board resigned, and Warszawiak had to quit his profession.[7] His was not the only case in which evangelical disapproval brought a missionary's career to an end. Jacob Freshman, one of the early activists of the movement to evangelize the Jews in the 1880s, was also expelled from the missionary field in disgrace on account of suspicion of misconduct.[8]

These incidents left their mark on the community of missionaries, which viewed the downfall of some of its members with mixed feelings. Notably, some Jewish missionaries were supportive of their fellow missionaries who lost favor and had to resign the field. Leopold Cohn, for example, remained a close friend throughout Warszawiak's long years of travail. Cohn might have been convinced of Warszawiak's innocence, but his sympathy was very much that of a colleague. He was also a Jewish missionary, an immigrant from eastern Europe who was evangelizing Jews in the crowded Jewish neighborhoods of New York. His loyal friendship, which demanded courage, reflected his sense of vulnerability in the face of evangelical church authorities. Cohn was also under attack and had his enemies in the Christian Protestant community. He sensed that he could easily have fallen just as his friend did.[9]

Some Jewish missionaries, surprisingly, shared the unfavorable image most

Jews had of Jewish converts turned missionaries. Bernhard Angel, in an article titled "Mistakes," listed what he considered to be setbacks in the operation of the movement to evangelize the Jews: "It is a mistake to put in any Jewish convert as a leader without adequate training. . . . If any one needs to be watched carefully, instructed systematically, and disabused of many of his former ideas, it is that Jew who leaves the religion of his ancestors and comes within the bounds of Christianity. Much evil has been done to the cause at large by entrusting its leadership to the hands of glib tongued, smart, aggressive converts."[10] Angel, a missionary leader himself, adopted wholeheartedly the negative stereotype of Jewish missionaries. He might have been strongly influenced by the scandals that erupted in the missionary community, particularly the Warszawiak case. It is still surprising to read such words from a missionary convert. They reflect something deeper than disappointment in and hence suspicion toward fellow missionaries. The Jewish missionary expressed negative feelings, indeed contempt, toward converts like himself. One had to be, he claimed, particularly careful and skeptical, indeed mistrustful, in relation to them. Was he projecting his own ambivalence and discomfort over his conversion on the community of people like himself? Between the prejudices of Christians, the antagonism of the Jewish community, and the Jewish missionaries' own uneasiness with the choices they made, it was perhaps no wonder that views such as those expressed by Angel circulated in the missionary community. Jewish missionaries felt insecure and feared that discoveries of wrongdoings and scandal would undermine their cause. Some missions indeed concluded that hiring non-Jews as evangelists would serve their cause better because the reputation of Jewish ones was at times questionable.

The Jewish missionaries were particularly vulnerable. They were newly arrived immigrants from eastern Europe used to an eastern European shtetl (small town) style of administration and finance. In the shtetlach, Jewish enterprises were often run with no systematic bookkeeping and with no accounting to a governing body or to outside inspectors. The prevailing attitude was that supporters trusted the managers and their deeds; as for outsiders, they did not deserve an accounting. As a matter of fact, keeping outsiders in the dark was considered to be the best policy, so that they would not be able to use the information to undermine the enterprise. Jewish associations in eastern Europe and in the New World at that time were run on a casual basis, as far as bookkeeping was concerned.[11] Similarly, many Jewish organizations in the immigrant community in America did not keep accurate books or published financial reports and governed their affairs through a nonelected directorship. In pointing to "mismanagement" of missions, Jewish antagonists of evangelization were demanding that the missions hold to standards that were perhaps prevalent among middle-class Americans but certainly not among newly arrived immigrants.

Protestants who supported the missions were in turn demanding that the latter operate according to middle-class Protestant standards rather than those of the immigrant community and that they be accountable to their benefactors. In order to survive, the missionaries had to retain the trust of the evangelical Protestant community that supported them. They therefore began to adapt to the demands and norms of American middle-class society, which included accurate bookkeeping, providing receipts for donations, and establishing boards of directors. This was a long and painful process, for, as Melvin Urofsky pointed out, it did not come easily to eastern European Jews, who often felt that their word or handshake was their bond. Asking for records appeared to indicate a lack of trust in their work and was considered an insult.[12]

That there sometimes were discrepancies in some of the missionaries' practices is more than likely. Indeed, at times missionary publications circulated inaccurate accounts of the kind that sustained the Jewish impressions that missionaries were falsifying information. Biographical sketches of missionaries and converts were popular in missionary publications, and, while much of the information they conveyed was certainly reliable, they tended toward hagiography.[13] In a manner typical of that literary genre, they described persons and situations in idealized tones. The aim of such sketches was evidently not to provide accurate historical information but rather to furnish readers with exemplary models of Christian life. This is particularly evident in descriptions of the conversion experience of missionaries and prominent converts.[14]

Although the practices of certain missionaries were questionable, they were by no means the rule. The missions' tracts and journals and minutes of converts' conferences, as well as autobiographical accounts, reveal a great deal of sincerity on the part of both the missionaries and the converts. Missionaries were often characterized, appropriately, by their sense of mission—a call to carry out their work among the nation of Israel—and showed great dedication to their work. Their interest in their task was, as a rule, keen and earnest. The evangelical Protestant community, on the whole, appreciated the missionaries' work, seeing it as fulfilling an important evangelical premillennialist task. For the most part, Protestant supporters dismissed accusations against missionaries as slander and expressed confidence in them. As noted earlier, Leopold Cohn, whom Jews and, sometimes, Christians attacked endlessly, received an honorary doctorate of divinity in 1930 from Wheaton College, one of the most respectable and prestigious evangelical schools of higher learning in America. This gesture reflected the opinion of evangelicals not only of Cohn personally, whom they obviously appreciated, but also of the importance of his work. They continued to support missionary work of the kind Cohn carried out, overlooking the accusations against him and the doubt cast over his and other missionaries' character.

Jewish activists and historians have tended not only to question the integrity of missionaries but also to portray the efforts to evangelize the Jews as a failure. The movement to evangelize the Jews, they contended, had generated enormous hope and enthusiasm, but only a small percentage of the entire Jewish population converted.[15] The missionaries took the opposite point of view: for them, there were many reasons to declare it a success.[16] Their work was an aim in and of itself and derived from their premillennialist theology. Moreover, they knew from the start that they were not going to convert *all* the Jews and had no illusions during that period that such a scenario would take place. That missions did manage to operate in the midst of the Jewish community and to make an impact there was, in their eyes, an impressive achievement. They could point to the large number of Jews who came to hear their sermons, to many more who took advantage of the missions' services, to the children attending classes and summer camps, and to the extensive distribution among the Jews of books, pamphlets, and journals, many of them in Yiddish or Hebrew.

Jews who evaluated the success of missions to the Jews have commonly perceived that Christian missions among other groups were successful in converting masses of people over short periods of time. The same successes could not be repeated among Jews, who were largely immune to the Christian message. The Jews, according to this view, were the least open to accepting the Christian message. Consequently, there were only a few conversions among them.[17] Proponents of the cause of evangelizing the Jews, on the other hand, pointed out that missions active among other nations in the nineteenth century did not necessarily enjoy greater success than those among the Jews. The movement to evangelize the Jews was, perhaps surprisingly, somewhat more successful than movements to evangelize other people. The results of evangelization efforts among Jews should not be contrasted with those among Americans of Protestant descent who were induced, through revival campaigns, to join the church.[18] Their type of conversion, scholars of the conversion experience point out, was the intensification of a faith with which the converts had previous affiliation, formal or informal.[19] Propagating the gospel among the Jews should be compared with evangelization efforts among other non-Christian people, those with an established religious tradition that also served as a focus of cultural and ethnic identity. Such groups would typically have viewed Christianity as an alien religious tradition. This type of conversion involves a move from one major religious tradition with its distinct ritual system, symbols, collective memories, and lifestyle to another.[20] The missionary zeal to Christianize the Indian nation, for example, was also great; India in the nineteenth century attracted large amounts of personnel, financial investment, and energy from the worldwide missionary movement.[21] But the number of Indians who had converted to Christianity relative to the country's total population was much smaller than the percentage of Jews in America who had converted. According to one source, after seventy years of ardent Protestant activity in India, by the end of the nineteenth century there were 30,000 Protestant Christians who were indigenous Indians, of all denominations and trends, in a population of more than 200 million. In America, there were at that time about 4,000 Jewish converts to evangelical Protestant Christianity in a population of less than 2 million Jews.[22] A few thousand more Jews had joined non-Protestant or nonevangelical churches, such as Roman Catholicism or the Unitarian Church.

In evaluating the success or failure of missions to the Jews, one should not overlook their demographic aspect. As noted, Jewish converts to Christianity in that period were young people, usually in their early twenties, in the prime of life, full of plans and hopes for the future. Their conversions filled the missionaries with pride and satisfaction. Although the average missionary might manage to convert, in a lifetime of work, no more than a few dozen Jews, he or she would typically be perfectly content with his or her achievements.[23]

Questions over their numerical successes or integrity were not the only criticism missions had to face. Some critics pointed to the lack of professional training and adequate and respectable evangelization literature as deficiencies that signified low quality of work. Most of the heat in this case came not from antagonists but from within the missionary community or from converts themselves.[24] At times, Jews would also ridicule low-quality Yiddish or Hebrew translations.[25] A number of missionaries began calling for the recruitment of missionaries who were specially trained for the field of evangelizing the Jews and for the production of missionary literature, such as a good, respectable, Yiddish translation of the New Testament.[26]

Haunted by the effects of the attacks and slander in the formative years of the movement to evangelize the Jews, leaders and activists of missions to the Jews would see the building of a good reputation as an important task. Middle-class respectability would become one of their goals and would characterize them for decades to come. They would follow middle-class Protestant mores and standards, striving for the approval of conservative Protestants. Similarly, they would set out to upgrade their professional standards, training their workers for the job they were doing and taking pride in more solid, accurate published material.

The years 1880–1920 were formative for the movement to evangelize the Jews in America. The period witnessed a remarkable growth in the field of missions to the Jews. From almost no missionary activity among Jews in the beginning of the period, the movement developed into a large and vigorous one, consisting of dozens of missions and hundreds of missionaries and attracting a great deal of attention in both the Jewish and the Protestant communities. The movement's theology and zeal and many of its methods of propagation were laid down at that time. Some missionary societies that were established during the period would eventually close down, while others would expand, open new branches, and become national organizations. Techniques of evangelization would also change throughout the years; but the basic evangelical and, more specifically, dispensationalist theological claims would remain the same.

II

Years of
Quiet Growth,
1920–1965

Choosing Sides

The period 1920–65 in the history of missions to the Jews in America can be described as the years of quiet growth. In those years, the movement to evangelize the Jews grew in activity yet avoided most of the confrontations and scandals of the earlier period. From the perspective of the missions, the period was marked by maturation, learning, and systematization. The missionary movement progressed toward a more systematic and professional effort to evangelize the Jews. Missions became larger and initiated training programs aimed specifically at preparing personnel for the field of Jewish evangelization. The period witnessed the rise of national organizations of missionaries to the Jews as well as the convening of conferences on Jewish evangelization at the national and international level. It was in this period that the missionary movement established the first enduring congregations of Hebrew Christians in America.

During the same period, major changes, both social and demographic, took place in the American Jewish community. Missions adapted their techniques and working methods accordingly, attempting to make their work as effective as possible. The missionary community responded strongly to major events in the life of the Jewish people that took place during the era, central among them the birth of the state of Israel, and directed much personnel and energy to evangelization work in the new country. One of the major tasks of the movement to evangelize the Jews in America during the 1920s and 1930s was choosing sides and defining its position vis-à-vis the growing division between the liberal "modernists" and the conservative "fundamentalists" in American Protestantism.

During the period from the 1920s to the early 1960s, the movement became increasingly associated with the conservative elements of American Protestantism. The missionaries defined their stand and self-identity as conservatives in relation to the modernist-fundamentalist controversy in American Protestantism that had led to a growing gap between conservatives and liberals in American religious life.

While the movement to evangelize the Jews in America began in the 1880s, motivated by a dispensationalist premillennialist understanding of the course of human history and the role of the nation of Israel, American Protestantism as a whole was undergoing major changes. The 1880s and 1890s saw the beginnings of a division within the ranks of the Protestant churches, between liberal modernists and conservative fundamentalists.[1] The modernists accepted the Higher Criticism of the Bible—which developed in German universities in the nineteenth century and examines the Bible as a historical and literary text—as a valid means of interpreting the Scriptures. In their eyes, Christianity had to accept modern science, that is, the findings of academic disciplines, if it wanted to sustain itself as a leading force in society.[2] They abandoned the evangelical claim that individuals should undergo a conversion experience in order to be saved, placing their emphasis instead on social reform. In addition, modernist Protestants were willing to cooperate with Protestants of nonevangelical backgrounds, as well as with non-Protestant Christians, and initiated a movement toward Christian unity. In 1906, liberal Christians established the Federal Council of the Churches of Christ in America, an organization whose participants included Protestants of both evangelical backgrounds, such as the Methodists and Presbyterians, and non-evangelical backgrounds, such as the Quakers and Mennonites.

Many conservative Protestants reacted with alarm to the new liberal trends. It seemed sacrilegious that Protestant groups that had emerged from the American revivalist tradition were willing to abandon the evangelical credo that a personal experience of conversion was essential for salvation. These conservative anti-modernists, who by the 1920s were called fundamentalists, rejected as equally abhorrent the liberal willingness to enter dialogue on equal terms with non-Protestants and considered the liberal acceptance of the Higher Criticism of the Bible unforgivable.[3] For them, the Bible was the foundation of Christian life and was inerrant. Since the 1880s, many conservatives had adopted the dispensationalist hope not only as a messianic conviction but also as a system of biblical hermeneutics and a philosophy of history. Dispensationalist teachings meshed with the conservative defense of the Scriptures as God-given and inerrant. The conservative outlook denied any human ability to overcome major social problems and bring about God's kingdom on earth and insisted that only the arrival of the Messiah could solve the earth's problems and redeem humanity.[4] These dispensationalist messianic teachings recognized the Jews as the Children of Israel and expected them to play a central role in the coming eschatological events. Interest in the fate of the Jewish people, in the prospect of Jewish national rejuvenation and expected Jewish acceptance of Christianity, was therefore much stronger among conservatives than in other segments in Christianity; it turned more and more into an almost exclusively conservative stand.[5]

In a number of cases, meanwhile, such as the American Baptists or the Presbyterian Church in the U.S.A., liberals and conservatives were struggling over the very character of the denominations. The conservatives did not necessarily win the battle.[6] Yet conservatives could carry out some of their agenda within the major denominations, including the operation of missions to the Jews based on a dispensationalist premillennialist theology, and could muster their churches' support for efforts directed toward that purpose.[7]

Siding with the conservatives became more and more the norm for missionaries to the Jews. Their outlook on the Bible and on the unfolding of the divine plane for humanity was conservative to begin with. It was their biblical-messianic understanding of the role of the nation of Israel in history that motivated their missionary efforts. The dispensationalist premillennialist rhetoric expounding the historical-biblical-prophetic destiny of the Jews was expressed time and again in mission publications, in approaching prospective converts, and, at times, in appeals to potential converts. Missions to the Jews thus depended for their survival on a strong Protestant interest in the Jews derived from a more literal reading of the Bible and a belief that the Jewish nation was destined to play a role in the arrival of the Messiah and the establishment of the kingdom of Christ on earth. The liberals, on the other hand, did not share the premillennialist messianic hope. In their eyes, the Jews were not the chosen people and were not destined to play a role in the events of the End Times (the coming of which they did not believe in), so there was no particular calling in evangelizing them. Moreover, liberals entered into interfaith dialogue that eventually led to a new evaluation of the Jews and their role in history. Many liberals would decide in due course that there was no theological basis for evangelizing Jews because Judaism could offer its adherents moral guidance and spiritual meaning as much as Christianity. Missionaries felt that the liberal approach undermined their cause. Jewish missionaries in particular reacted negatively to the liberal views. They considered the liberal-modernist view, which did not accept the premillennialist belief and did not emphasize the need to evangelize the Jews, as a rejection of the Jews and the idea of their special role in history, as undermining their agenda as missionaries, and as an insult to them and their personal choices as Jews who had converted to Christianity.

There were, of course, Jews who converted to liberal forms of Protestant Christianity during those years; but they were likely to assimilate into the Christian milieu they had joined. They did not as a rule take part in the Hebrew Christian Alliance of America, nor did they take interest in evangelizing their Jewish brethren. Jewish converts, who were active in missions or in the efforts to build a network of support and self-assertion for Jewish converts, were almost by definition on the conservative side. They appreciated the conservative attitude, which emphasized the special role of the Jewish people in history. The emphasis on missions to the Jews, which resulted from this attitude, gave Jewish converts a sense of affirmation for their path and cause.

Joseph Cohn, director of the American Board of Missions to the Jews, the largest mission to the Jews in America during the period, published a number of articles and tracts denouncing the liberal stand.[8] For him, liberal Protestantism became a nonexistent segment of Christianity as far as mustering support for his mission was concerned. When appealing for endorsement of the missionary agenda and for donations, he directed his efforts exclusively to the fundamentalist-premillennialist camp.[9] Elias Newman, a Jewish convert, who for many years served as a missionary for the conservative Lutheran Zion Society for Israel in Minneapolis, complained bitterly in his autobiography, published in 1933, about the new liberal trends. It meant, he claimed, the abandonment of missionary work among the Jews, which for him was an expression of basic Christian principles.[10] Jacob Peltz, general secretary of the Hebrew Christian Alliance of America, wrote an editorial in the *Hebrew Christian Alliance Quarterly* entitled "Christian Modernism and Reform Judaism in League against Jewish Evangelization." Peltz took issue with the new liberal Christian trends that began in the 1920s and 1930s whereby liberal Christians expressed themselves in the establishment of organizations and committees intended to promote dialogue, mutual respect, and cooperation between representatives of the two religions. Such a climate, Peltz complained, was undermining the cause of missions as well the raison d'être of Jews who had converted to Christianity. He was particularly enraged by the willingness of liberal Protestants to engage in dialogue with liberal Jews, thus granting the latter's creed legitimacy, rather than attempting to bring such Jews to accept Christianity. He complained: "And the sad fact is that these misguided leaders of Israel are aided in their attacks on Jewish missions by no less a body than the Federal Council of Churches of Christ in America. In the Good-Will meetings and seminars, conducted by the Secretary of the Good Will Committee of the Federal Council of Churches, Hebrew Christians and their missionary activities have been misrepresented and slandered."[11]

One might conclude that both the missionaries and the community of active converts did not have much choice but to side with the conservatives. Liberal Protestants became, during the period, less and less interested in converting Jews. By the end of the period, the missionary endeavor was completely located on the conservative side. It was the conservatives who supported the missions, and it was their interest and funding on which missions had to rely (and at times compete) for their endurance and growth. The location of the missionary movement in the conservative camp had a profound effect on the character and messages of the missions. The missions had always advocated such tenets of Christian belief as the virgin birth of Jesus as well as the need to undergo a personal experience of conversion and accept Jesus as a personal Savior. Their messages from the 1920s onward reflected conservative views not only on matters of theology and doctrine but at times on cultural and even social and political matters as well. From dress to drinking habits to political views, the missions would reflect the values and views of conservative Protestantism.

At the same time that missions defined their standing within American Protestantism, they were undergoing other changes and reforms including a more systematic study of the Jews and the means to approach them.

7

Getting Acquainted with the Jews

In the previous generation of missions to the Jews in America (1880–1920), missionaries approached the Jewish community holding an evangelical premillennialist image of the Jews and their role in history. These early missionaries, for example, were often taken aback when they encountered secular and Reform Jews, whose liberal thinking and way of life contrasted with their preconceptions of what Jews were like and how they were supposed to behave and react.

In the second phase (1920–1965), missionaries began to take a more realistic view of the Jews. They set themselves the goal of bringing the Christian message to real Jews and not to imaginary or idealized ones and therefore made an attempt to learn more about the Jews, including their divisions and characteristics, so they could develop better methods of evangelizing them. Striking features of the period are books, manuals, and articles written by more experienced missionaries to inform a new generation of prospective evangelists of demographic, social, and cultural aspects of Jewish life, Jewish religious practice, and national aspirations. Missionaries in earlier periods had published informative articles on the Jewish religion, but these had dealt mostly with traditional Judaism, which the writers had considered the normative form of Jewish religious life, if not the only one. In the newer publications, writers were determined to acquaint their readers with the realities of Jewish practices. They pointed to various Jewish subgroups and inner divisions, described their different modes of life and backgrounds, and made suggestions on how to approach different groups with the Christian message. Reform and Conservative Judaism, which missionaries either ignored in earlier publications or looked upon as an aberration, were described in great detail during this period. Although missionaries did not necessarily admire such expressions of Jewish life, they no longer presented these groups as lapsed Jews who had abandoned traditional Jewish life but as groups within Judaism that needed to be explored in order to be approached successfully. Such manuals also offered advice on techniques of evangelization and the organization of mission houses and listed biblical passages that could be used to persuade Jews of the Christian message.

Wishing to convey their experience to others, some missionaries who had spent a lifetime evangelizing Jews wrote guides on missions to Jews. The Lutheran missionary Albert Huisjen, from the American Lutheran Church Ministry to the Jewish People, for example, published *The Home Front of Jewish Missions* after thirty-eight years in the field. It is an impressive book, reflecting a thorough knowledge of Jewish life and heritage and demonstrating a professional attitude toward the field of Jewish missions. Huisjen also wrote a second book, *Talking about Jesus to a Jewish Neighbor*, which was directed toward laypersons interested in evangelizing Jewish neighbors and acquaintances.

A number of guides and studies on this topic were published by the American Board of Missions to the Jews, the largest mission to the Jews in America at the time. One of them, *Studies in Jewish Evangelism*, was written by Henry J. Heydt, president of the Lancaster School of the Bible and School of Theology, in Lancaster, Pennsylvania. Published in 1951, the book emphasized that prospective missionaries were expected to acquire a thorough knowledge of the Jews before attempting to approach them. Heydt began with a chapter entitled "Types of Hebrew People," in which he presented demographic information on the Jewish community and characteristics of its various subgroups. Much of his information, like that of other such books, ironically came from Jewish studies on the demographics, dispersion, and characteristics of different groups of Jews. Heydt described both Jewish religious literature and the theology of anti-Semitism. Missionaries to the Jews, including non-Jewish ones, concerned themselves with the phenomenon of anti-Semitism and expressed their disapproval of it. This element in the missionaries' self-perception and rhetoric was due in part to a natural empathy with the people they were trying to reach. In addition, they shared the general dispensationalist premillennialist outlook, which condemned anti-Semitism. Although Jews were offended by missionary activity, at times viewing the missionaries as outright enemies, and although missionaries were not always devoid of prejudice against Jews, the missionaries themselves considered their work an expression of goodwill, friendship, and appreciation toward the Jews. There was also a practical dimension to the missionary concern with anti-Semitism. Missionaries had to relate to the phenomenon when approaching Jews. For many Jews, even those who were not fully acquainted with the history of the Jewish-Christian relationship, Christianity was associated with anti-Semitism, and Jews saw in the Christian faith a source of much of the hatred of non-Jews against them. Such an attitude did not help the missionary cause. In their training guides, veteran missionaries advised against making any remarks that might be interpreted in any way as anti-Semitic and that might hurt the feelings of prospective Jewish converts, such as "Jew boy."[1] An important aspect of the evangelical message to Jews was that evangelical Christianity had nothing to do with Christian maltreatment of Jews throughout the ages. Such injustice, they claimed, had been carried out by what they held to be distorted forms of the Christian religion, such as Roman Catholicism and Greek Orthodoxy.

Heydt, like others, wrote about the Written Law and the Oral Law, the Jewish calendar, feasts and holidays, and the customs, rites, and foods associated with them. He mentioned in detail a variety of Jewish groups and trends of thought and elaborated on such issues as Jewish messianism. In other chapters he made suggestions on how to approach the Jews, what arguments could be persuasive, and the scriptural passages that were applicable in such circumstances.

Heydt, who had worked for many years at the American Board of Missions to the Jews, also published a second book to promote the missionary work among the Jews, *The Chosen People: Question Box II*, based on a column he wrote for many years in the board's journal, the *Chosen People*. The book's foreword was written by Schuyler English, the prestigious editor of the revised edition of the widely circulated *Scofield Reference Bible*. English endorsed the theological correctness of the book, thus giving it an aura of legitimacy as far as the Protestant evangelical community was concerned.

Another employee of the American Board of Missions to the Jews who wrote a guide on Jewish evangelism was Daniel Fuchs, who later became the director of the mission. His book *How to Reach the Jew for Christ* was published in 1943 and was intended for the instruction of laypersons who were interested in approaching Jewish neighbors with the Christian message. In line with the general approach adopted in that era, the book was not merely a set of practical instructions on how to evangelize Jews but rather intended to acquaint Christians with the Jewish people. Much of the book is an exposition of Jewish history, the idea being that a better knowledge of Jewish history and life would lead to more effective evangelism.

One of the outstanding missionaries to the Jews in America during the period from the 1930s to the 1950s was Jacob Gartenhaus. Born in Austria and converted in his native country, Gartenhaus immigrated to America prior to World War I and enrolled as a student at the Moody Bible Institute. He then proceeded to the Southern Baptist Theological Seminary in Louisville, Kentucky, where he studied for the ministry and was subsequently appointed as a missionary of the Southern Baptist Convention. Under his guidance, its department for Jewish evangelism grew to employ more than twenty missionaries in a number of cities in America. After many years in the field, Gartenhaus wrote *Winning Jews to Christ*, which begins by presenting the Jews, their history, demography, subdivisions, religious conviction, and practices. The book demonstrated a particularly thorough knowledge of Judaism, its tenets of faith, and subgroups. Gartenhaus described the Jewish attitude toward Christianity and Jesus of Nazareth. He pointed out that, in the twentieth century, there had been a change in attitude in some Jewish circles toward Jesus Christ. For secular Zionist writers, for example, Jesus was no longer perceived as the god of their persecutors but as a sincere and charismatic Jewish teacher of the Second Temple period. A Jewish "reclamation" of Jesus was taking place.[2]

Gartenhaus also wrote a pamphlet, based on his larger book, *How to Win the Jews*, which enjoyed great popularity and was printed in many editions. Gartenhaus's books gained prestige among missionaries and converted Jews; *Winning Jews to Christ* was published in London by the International Board of Jewish Missions under the name *Unto His Own* and was circulated in Britain, Canada, South Africa, Australia, and America.

Another missionary who published a systematic study of the Jews, their religious beliefs, their position in society, and the means to approach them was C. M. Hanson, a Lutheran from Minneapolis. Unlike the attitude among missionaries in the earlier period, Hanson treated liberal forms of Judaism respectfully. The correct term for liberal Jews was "Reform" and not "Reformed," he cautioned his readers.[3] The book also expresses empathy for Jewish suffering throughout history and takes a very different attitude than the standard missionary claim that real Christianity had nothing to do with mistreatment of Jews. Unless Christians were willing to take responsibility and express regret for the wrongdoing that Christians inflicted upon the Jews throughout the ages, Hanson warned, they would fail to bring the gospel to the Jews. He proclaimed:

> The name of Christ . . . will most certainly draw [the Jewish person's] mind . . . to experiences which have left a bitter reaction to anything Christian. The . . . first reaction [of missionaries] is going to be an inclination to . . . justify the Christian side of the historic past. It might be far better to simply confess the errors, and even deep wrongs of the Church in its historic contact with the Jews. . . . The failure to rise up and be counted in the various crises which have involved the Jew has denied the vital qualities of the Gospel and Christian Living. Confusion is not only good for the soul. It can break down some rather formidable walls of resistance to the message of God.[4]

Another patriarch of Jewish evangelization was Aaron J. Kligerman, who worked on behalf of the Presbyterian Church in the U.S.A. in Baltimore from 1922 until 1952. The Russian-born Kligerman studied at the Moody Bible Institute, was active in the Hebrew Christian Alliance of America, and published a number of tracts in which he shared his knowledge of Jews and Judaism and his suggestions about how to convert them.[5] His major book, *The Gospel and the Jew*, took a somewhat different approach than other similar books written by his colleagues. The Presbyterian missionary devoted large parts of his book to persuading his readers of the dispensationalist premillennialist understanding of the unique and central role of the Jews in history. They had an obligation as Christians toward the Jews, he claimed, which should demonstrate itself in sharing the gospel with them. Kligerman then moved on to describe the Jewish nation and its religious beliefs. He wrote with much appreciation and warmth about the Jews, whom he regarded as his own people.

To sum up, missionaries made an effort to familiarize themselves with the Jews and their characteristics. They shared their knowledge and experiences with one another, attempting to make the field more professional and effective. They also put their new attitude into practice in the literature they prepared for distribution among potential converts.

The Yiddish Translation of the New Testament

One feature of the new, more professional attitude toward the evangelization of the Jews, and an attempt to produce effective missionary literature, was the translation of the New Testament into Yiddish. Until the turn of the century, Yiddish New Testaments were reprints of sixteenth- and seventeenth-century publications with slight editorial touches. These were basically Yiddishized versions of German translations going back as far as Martin Luther's major translation of the New Testament. Missionaries who knew Yiddish well considered them, in fact, to be an embarrassment to the missionary cause, particularly when read by educated Jews. Inaccuracies in the Yiddish text were cited by Jewish antagonists to missionary activity as a sign of the illegitimacy of the gospel message.[1]

It was during this period that a Jewish missionary, Henry Einspruch, took it upon himself to translate the New Testament into modern literary Yiddish. Einspruch was born in 1892 in Tarnow, Galicia, a section of Poland that was then under Austro-Hungarian rule. He was raised in a Yiddish-speaking home and studied Yiddish in the Jewish school in his hometown. In 1911 he went to Palestine as a *halutz* (a Zionist pioneer) and worked for a few weeks on a newly founded Zionist agricultural farm where he contracted malaria and decided to leave. On his return to Poland he met a missionary, Hayim Lucky, a Polish Jew who had graduated from Union Theological Seminary in New York and went back to Galatz, Poland, to evangelize Jews. Einspruch was attracted to the company of the knowledgeable Lucky and, under his guidance, accepted Christianity. He then left Poland for America, where he could practice his new faith more openly, far from the intimidating presence of family and friends. He decided to become a missionary and took a position with the Cleveland Hebrew Mission.[2] Like other missionaries of his generation, he felt a need for a more thorough education in Christianity and ministry and, in 1917, enrolled at McCormick Theological Seminary in Chicago. During these years, he began writing missionary tracts in Yiddish and English, which were published by the Chicago Tract Society. It was also during this period that Einspruch began translating the New Testament into Yiddish. His translation of the Book of Matthew was published by the American Bible Society, which sponsored the publications of many Bible translations. Upon his graduation from the seminary in 1920, Einspruch began working with the

United Lutheran Church in America, which sponsored his Salem Hebrew Mission in Baltimore, Maryland, giving him a large amount of autonomy.[3]

Intellectually inclined, Einspruch devoted much time to teaching and writing. "There was an emphasis on a literary ministry," wrote Einspruch in describing his work.[4] He also saw a need to advocate the cause of evangelizing the Jews in the Christian community.[5] Like others of his generation who were educated and trained for work in Jewish missions, Einspruch was concerned with promoting a responsible professional attitude. Missionaries had often, he complained, dealt with their Jewish audience without adequate, deep knowledge of Jews and Judaism, a deficiency that affected both their presentation of Jews to the Christian community and their outreach to the Jews.[6] He particularly complained about the Yiddish texts the missions provided: "Most Jewish missionaries are familiar with the derisive appellation 'missionary Yiddish.' To say that the greater part of our Yiddish tracts are a horrible mutilation of a people's language (and in this I include the Yiddish Old and New Testaments) is to put it very mildly."[7]

Attempting to set the record straight, Einspruch established his own missionary journal, the *Mediator*, in 1928. The name was symbolic, as it demonstrated the mission's purpose as a mediator between the beliefs and values of Protestant Christian America and the immigrant Jewish community. This Yiddish and English quarterly enjoyed a circulation of more than fifty thousand copies at its peak. The journal functioned for thirty-five years; its closing down in the mid-1960s marked the end of an era, as Yiddish ceased to be a vital language for American Jews.

Einspruch's magnum opus, a Yiddish translation of the complete New Testament, was motivated by his desire to provide prospective Jewish converts with an accurate, modern edition of the Christian gospel. It also reflected Einspruch's literary inclinations as a Yiddish writer and gave him an opportunity to express his gifts. In this respect, Einspruch was not unique; the task of translating the Bible often gave missionaries with scholarly and literary inclinations an opportunity to express themselves and their creativity while serving missionary needs and without stepping out of line doctrinally.[8]

Unlike his earlier translations, this enterprise was not carried out through the American Bible Society but rather as his mission's independent enterprise. This demanded taking care of all stages of production. In order to produce the book, Einspruch had to acquire his own printing equipment, since none of the very few Yiddish printing presses in America at the time would print it. The cost of this project, as well as Einspruch's other literary ventures, was considerable, much more than the local Lutheran church in Baltimore was willing to spend on literary enterprises related to Jewish evangelism. Einspruch approached private donors and was successful in gaining the support of Harriett Lederer to sponsor the mission and its publications. Lederer's assistance gave Einspruch's mission financial security and greater independence. As the United Lutheran Church lost interest later on in Jewish evangelism, the mission became an independent organization and assumed the name the Lederer Foundation.

Einspruch's New Testament in Yiddish came out in 1941 in a 590-page edition. It was revised in 1959 and has served since then as the standard Yiddish version of the New Testament, distributed to the dwindling Yiddish-reading population in North America. Translations involve theological and cultural choices, and, in the course of his work, Einspruch made some major ones.[9] It was important for him to write in good Yiddish prose, yet he was also a missionary and tried to choose words and expressions that would promote the Christian evangelical message and would make the text more acceptable to Jews. Einspruch, for example, chose for his translated New Testament the title *Der Bris Chadosha* instead of *Der Neu Testament*, which had served as the title of New Testament translations until then.[10] Literally, Bris Chadosha does not mean the New Testament but rather the New Covenant. The new title was probably borrowed from Franz Delitzsch's late-nineteenth-century translation of the New Testament into Hebrew. Einspruch thus conveyed through the title of his translation a message that emphasized the dispensationalist premillennialist missionary interpretation of history, namely, that there is a new covenant between God and his people.

The translation is accompanied by a number of illustrations that created a pleasant, familiar atmosphere meant to make the New Testament more acceptable and legitimate for Jews. The first page of the text, which begins with the Gospel of Matthew, shows an old Jewish man with a long white beard, dressed with a yarmulke and *talit* (a prayer shawl), surrounded by burning candles, and reading from a book. The scene clearly suggests that the New Testament is an old Jewish book that should be read and studied like a sacred Jewish text. The message of the illustration correlates with the opening verse of Matthew in Einspruch's translation, "Das is das sefer fon dem yichus fun Yeshua hamasiach, dem zon fun Daviden, dem zon fun Avrahamen," which familiarizes Jesus as a descendant of David and Abraham.

His missionary intentions notwithstanding, Einspruch's translation aroused the interest and appreciation of the Yiddish literary community. Melech Ravitsh, one of the noted Yiddish writers of the day, published a *ratsenzia*, a Yiddish review of the book. Ravitsh was residing at that time in Mexico City and wrote for the Yiddish daily *Der Weg*. He was not a Jewish Christian but rather a non-Zionist Jewish nationalist (a common trend among Yiddish-speaking Jews before World War II). He did not care for Einspruch's dispensationalist understanding of history and missionary aims, but he appreciated the translation. In his review article, Ravitsh explained to his readers why he thought it necessary for Jews to read the New Testament: "For well known reasons, the New Testament has remained for many of us Jews as a book sealed with seven seals. And that is truly a pity, for to some seven hundred million people it is a sacred book. A cultured person should know such a work; I myself have read it and recommend it to every intelligent Jew. . . . The New Testament [is] one of the most important books in the world. How then can we Jews afford to ignore it?"

Ravitsh welcomed the new translation, which he felt was the first decent one, and remarked, "The Einspruch translation of the New Testament is unquestionably beautiful. One feels that the translator is familiar with modern Yiddish literature and that he is master of the finest nuances of the language. In comparison with previous translations, this is truly an outstanding work."[11] Ravitsh's appreciative outlook, which filled Einspruch with joy, reflected a common trend among Yiddish writers. Although they were not really enthusiastic about missionary work among their brethren, they did not ostracize Jewish Christian Yiddish writers, not even those who made their livelihood by missionizing fellow Jews. Contrary to a prevailing Jewish myth, the dislike of *shmad*, or Jewish conversions to Christianity, did not necessarily bring about a termination of the convert's connections with Jews and Jewish life. It only made these connections more difficult and complicated. Einspruch's literary achievements gave him an entry into Yiddish literary circles, which had opened its doors to other converted Jewish Yiddish writers as well.

At the same time that Einspruch was working on his translation, a few thousand miles away, another Jewish convert to Christianity was preparing a translation of the New Testament into Yiddish. Aaron Krelenbaum had also been born in Poland, converted to Christianity in the early 1920s, and moved to England, where he received a thorough Christian education as a minister. Krelenbaum became a missionary with the Mildmay Mission to the Jews, an institution with a distinctly dispensationalist outlook, and worked among the Jewish immigrants of the East End of London.[12] Like Einspruch, he pursued his studies and obtained a doctorate degree; a scholar by inclination, he learned Greek and Hebrew and took upon himself the task of translating the New Testament into Yiddish. Like his American fellow missionary, Krelenbaum wanted to present his readers with an accurate, respectable version of the New Testament. He, too, saw it as a personal challenge and an expression of his scholarly and literary abilities. It might well be that when the two missionaries began pursuing their great literary tasks they did not realize that they were working against competition. But they both possessed an almost passionate determination to translate the New Testament nonetheless. One can imagine how alarmed Einspruch was when, in 1949, just a few years after the triumphant appearance of his own translation, another one appeared in England to even greater acclaim. Paul P. Levertoff, the patriarch of Jewish Christian writers, wrote an introduction to Krelenbaum's translation and praised it as an excellent literary achievement, calling it the best translation of the New Testament into Yiddish. To add insult to injury, Einspruch learned that the Million Testaments Campaign, a mission to the Jews headed by George T. B. Davis, headquartered in Philadelphia, decided to publish and distribute Krelenbaum's translation when it appeared in 1949. This, however, was an exception; most American missions distributed Einspruch's translation.[13]

The relationship between the two missionaries became one of open animosity. Einspruch accused Krelenbaum of plagiarism; Krelenbaum in his turn dismissed Einspruch's work as second-rate and claimed that Einspruch had not really translated from the original Greek.[14] For these rivals, then, Christian tolerance and love were commandments they adhered to in principle but found difficult to carry out in practice. The clash between Einspruch and Krelenbaum showed them to be typical Yiddish writers of their day—jealous, grudging, and self-centered. The Yiddish literary community of the time perceived that it was producing works for a dwindling readership. A large percentage of Yiddish readers perished in the Holocaust; this, together with the integration of second-generation immigrants into New World cultures and the emphasis by Zionists on learning modern Hebrew, led to a greater decline in the use of Yiddish. That situation made Yiddish writers feel insecure and bitter. Generosity and indulgence were qualities one could hardly hope to find in their relationships with one another.[15]

It was indeed ironic and even somewhat tragic that the publication of an accurate and respectable translation of the New Testament into Yiddish came out just when Yiddish was in the process of dying out. Einspruch's was the last generation that could make use of it. Even when it was published, most American Jews were already reading English. In the 1980s, about a decade after Einspruch's death, when Yiddish was virtually a dead language and the Yiddish New Testament ceased being distributed, the directors of the Lederer Foundation donated the Yiddish printing set and equipment that Einspruch had acquired to the Yiddish Book Center in Amherst, Massachusetts.

The translation of the New Testament into Yiddish was one step in the more systematic attitude the missions were taking. Another such step was the creation of a professional academic program in a leading evangelical school, the Moody Bible Institute, for the training of missionaries to the Jews.

The Moody Bible Institute and the Training of Missionaries to the Jews

Since its early days, the Moody Bible Institute has taken an interest in Jewish evangelization. The Bible Institute was established in the 1880s as an evangelical school for training ministers, missionaries, and Sunday school teachers in line with the values and aspiration of the emerging fundamentalist movement in American Christianity. From its inception, its teachers and administrators held to a dispensationalist premillennialist understanding of the Bible and the course of human history. Strong advocates of this school of biblical exegesis and philosophy of history, they considered the Jews to be the biblical nation of Israel and heir to the covenant with God and saw a special mission in propagating the gospel among that nation. Dwight Moody himself mentioned the duty of Christians to bring the gospel to the Jews in many of his sermons.[1] In the evangelization campaign he launched in connection with the World's Columbian Exposition in 1893, he invited a Jewish Christian, Joseph Rabinowitz from Russia, to conduct revival meetings among Jews. Some Jewish converts came to the Moody Bible Institute in its early decades to acquire training as missionaries. In its publications, the Bible Institute emphasized that it trained Jews, as well as members of a number of other nationalities, for missionary work among their people.[2] By the early 1920s there were a number of missionaries to the Jews in America who had received their training at the institute.[3] Joseph Cohn, who directed the American Board of Missions to the Jews from the 1920s to the 1950s, studied at the Moody Bible Institute in 1907–8. Jacob Gartenhaus and David Bronstein, also noted missionaries during the 1920s to 1950s, studied there in 1915–17.

The Moody Bible Institute's positive stance toward the field of Jewish evangelization manifested itself in the many notices found on the pages of the *Moody Monthly*, the institute's journal, in which, beginning in 1930, a large number of missions to the Jews had placed advertisements asking for financial support. The institute's president, deans, and professors often served on boards of trustees for Jewish missions, helping to legitimize and promote missions in the evangelical public's eyes. In 1923, the Moody Bible Institute opened a special department for training missionaries for Jewish evangelization. This was in line with the general trend in the movement to evangelize the Jews in America, which worked toward professionalizing and solidifying its work. Evangelizing among the Jews was no longer conceived as something that any dedicated Christian worker could do. Directors and activists of the missions realized that even Jewish missionaries, as acquainted as they often had been with Jewish life, had to be trained for the job. Workers in the field recognized that a better knowledge of the Jews and their culture and the appropriate means to approach them would help a great deal and would make for more effective and respectable missions. In addition, missions felt a need to be more selective in the recruitment of missionaries. Graduates of the prestigious and demanding Moody Bible Institute, they believed, would make for a solid, respectable cadre of workers. Significantly, the program to train missionaries at the Bible Institute was not solely the institute's own initiative. The community of missionaries and converted Jews saw it in its interest to see such a program established within the realm of a prestigious conservative institution. The Hebrew Christian Alliance of America, which had come into being just a few years earlier, acted as an interest group within the conservative evangelical community for the establishment of such a course of study. The program in Jewish evangelization at the Moody Bible Institute in its early years was also financed in part by money collected by the alliance, which saw special merit in the success of such a program.[4]

Although the program in Jewish studies had the pragmatic purpose of training missionaries to the Jews, and although the Jewish religion was not studied from an intrinsically Jewish perspective, the fact that the Moody Bible Institute offered a special program in Jewish studies in its curriculum was in some ways remarkable. It was certainly unique among Christian institutions of higher education in America at the time. Ironically, it was a conservative institute that was the first to introduce a course of Jewish studies rather than a liberal one. Half a century later it would become fashionable for liberal Christian seminaries and divinity schools to include Jewish studies in their curriculum. The establishment and continuation of the program throughout the years could not be explained merely on pragmatic grounds. It reflected the dispensationalist understanding of the Jews and their role in history that prevailed in that conservative Protestant institution. It is not surprising, therefore, that the program for training Jewish missionaries continued at the institute long after the Hebrew Christian Alliance ceased supporting it financially in the early 1930s.

The Moody Bible Institute's first choice of a professor for the department of Jewish evangelism was Joel Levy. Born in Lithuania in 1877 and educated in a yeshiva (a rabbinical academy), he immigrated to England, where he had converted to Christianity in 1905 through the efforts of the Mildmay Mission to the Jews. He studied at a Bible college in Glasgow and in 1914 came to America and worked in a number of missions to the Jews, including the New Covenant Mission in Pittsburgh. On the recommendation of the Hebrew Christian Alliance, the Moody Bible Institute appointed Levy to be its professor of Jewish studies, but he died suddenly a short time after the appointment was made.[5] The institute, again on the recommendation of the Hebrew Christian Alliance, hired Solomon Birnbaum, a Jewish Christian scholar, to serve as the expert on Jewish studies, entrusted with the wide-ranging teaching load of Hebrew, Yiddish, Jewish history, and Jewish religion ("Rabbinics"), as well as Jewish evangelization. Born in 1890 in Galicia, Poland, Birnbaum had converted to Christianity at the age of eighteen. He then moved to England, where he studied at the University of London, concentrating on Semitic languages, and completed his ministerial training at the seminary of the Church of England, St. John's Hall in Highbury.[6] In 1921, Birnbaum moved to America, where he worked for the Presbyterian Church in the U.S.A. in Baltimore, Maryland. The founders of the program at the Moody Bible Institute were obviously looking for a jack-of-all-trades in Jewish missions who could teach a variety of subjects, as well as instructing students in practical missionary work among the Jews. Birnbaum did not, however, teach the Hebrew Bible (or Old Testament, as it was called at the MBI), since those topics were part of the basic curriculum and were therefore taught by other teachers at the institute. In 1923, with Birnbaum taking up the position of Jewish studies professor at the Moody Bible Institute, the program began.

The course at the Moody Bible Institute consisted of two years of studies and fifteen weeks of fieldwork. In addition to the general requirements, which included such courses as an introduction to the Bible, public speaking, teacher training, pedagogy, and Sunday school organization and administration, the Jewish missions course required the study of Hebrew, Yiddish, messianic prophecy, rabbinics, Jewish history, and Jewish feasts and customs.[7] The program reflected the understanding of the missionary community that knowledge was essential in order to approach the Jews more effectively. In describing the course in Jewish history, the bulletin stated:

> This subject, which comes in the Jewish Missions course, embraces the outstanding facts and movements in Jewish history from the time of the Maccabees to our day. It is these facts which have vitally contributed to making the Jew what he is today and an acquaintance with them helps the Gentile, in the course of his mission work, the better to reach and present the Gospel to the Jew. With the instruction in Jewish history is combined that in Jewish feasts and customs, together with a study of the Jewish prayer books and the books of rules for daily life with their religious and symbolic import.[8]

This statement clearly reflected the new policy adopted in the field of Jewish missions in America in the years following World War I: namely, that a thorough knowledge of the Jewish people, their history, thinking, tradition, customs, and languages was needed in order to approach them successfully. The choice of languages is instructive. Jewish evangelists were required to study Hebrew so that they could become familiar with the Hebrew Bible and other Jewish sources. It was assumed that knowledge of the Bible in English alone would be insufficient when approaching those Jews who were well acquainted with their Scriptures. Similarly, although most Jewish immigrants to America soon learned English, Yiddish was still spoken in many homes. For many in the older generation, Yiddish was their mother tongue. Many daily expressions, even among those Jews who became fluent in English or those who had been born or raised in America, were in Yiddish. Missionaries were expected to handle the language in order to gain credibility with their prospective Jewish converts. Knowledge of Yiddish demonstrated a familiarity with Jews and their culture. Yiddish continued to be a required part of the curriculum in Jewish studies at the Moody Bible Institute for a number of decades and was removed only in 1965, when the directors of the institute concluded that Yiddish was no longer the common language of American Jews.

Birnbaum devoted time and energy not only to the academic instruction of his students in the various aspects of Judaism and Jewish life but also to the practical side of Jewish evangelism. During the summer, for example, he took his students to Atlantic City, a resort popular among East Coast Jews, to conduct evangelization campaigns.[9] A large part of the practical training offered to the students in the program was, of course, carried out in Chicago, often in conjunction with the work of established missions to the Jews. One such mission was the Chicago Hebrew Mission, another the American Board of Missions to the Jews. Such collaboration helped both parties. It offered the students at the institute an opportunity to practice and gain expertise in actual evangelism with no cost to the program, since tracts, for example, were supplied by the missions. The missions in their turn received volunteer field-workers, supervised by their professor. Birnbaum was declared an honorary missionary by the American Board of Missions to the Jews.[10] The fieldwork that the students carried out in the Jewish neighborhoods in Chicago brought them in contact with Jewish life in Chicago and with Jewish reactions toward attempts to evangelize them, which were not always favorable.[11]

Birnbaum, who moved on to become a full-time missionary with the American Board of Missions to the Jews, was succeeded in 1940 by Max Reich. Born in Germany in 1867 and raised in England, where he converted to Christianity, Reich settled in America in 1915 and became an active member of the Hebrew Christian Alliance, the organization of Jews who accepted Christianity in its conservative evangelical form, which had just organized that year.[12] He served as its president from 1921 until 1926 and again from 1935 until 1945. A Quaker by denominational affiliation, Reich nonetheless considered himself Jewish and took a strong interest in Jewish and Zionist affairs. He wrote poems that were published in the *Hebrew Christian Alliance Quarterly* and other organs of missions to the Jews, such as the *Jewish Era*.[13] In his poetry, Reich expressed a Jewish Christian messianic hope and interpreted the rise of the Zionist movement as a significant event in the messianic time table. His dispensationalist Jewish Christian outlook was also expressed in his biblical exegesis, as well as in a book dedicated to exploring the expected Jewish future within the messianic hope.[14] In polemical articles, he expressed a view that was not shared by all in the conservative Protestant evangelical community, namely, that converted Jews should not disappear into the gentile society but rather retain their separate Jewish identity.

> Recently while at an open discussion of the book of Romans . . . I asked the question, "When a Jew becomes a Christian does he cease to be a part of Israel?" The whole company almost shouted with one voice, "Yes." I then pointed out that it was the unbelieving branches who were cut off of their own olive tree. The believing branches remain where they had their origin. The olive tree represents the spiritual Israel rooted in the soil of the natural Israel. . . . Gentiles . . . must not crowd out the branches that have never been broken off. . . . God has always recognized an inner and outer Israel. The effective Israel was never more than a remnant at any time. And the inner was the salt of the outer, preserving it from decay. Hebrew Christians cannot fulfill their mission to their people unless they remain a part of Israel. The salt cannot do its work unless it mixes with that which is to be salted.[15]

In this passage, Reich justified the existence of Hebrew Christians as a separate entity within the Christian community by emphasizing the obligation this group had to evangelize its brethren. The role of Hebrew Christianity was thus presented to the larger evangelical community in missionary terms. Equipped with this ideology and sense of mission, Reich was a natural candidate for the position of professor of Jewish evangelization at the Moody Bible Institute. That a major conservative Protestant institution of higher learning had hired Reich—a propagator of the uniqueness of Jewish Christianity and a writer of poems on the restoration of the Jews to Zion—to teach in the department of missions was in many ways remarkable and should be understood in the light of the institute's distinctive dispensationalist theology.

For the institute leaders during this period, such as James Gray, the institute's president during Birnbaum's tenure at the Moody Bible Institute, the Jewish people were indeed the chosen people destined to play a dominant role in God's plans for humanity.[16] Similarly, Gray shared Birnbaum's and Reich's positive attitude toward the Zionist movement and the prospect of the Jewish restoration to Zion.[17] Although not as outspoken as Gray on biblical and theological matters, William Culbertson, Gray's heir who served as president of the Moody Bible

Institute during the 1940s, shared the same views on the role of Israel in history and gave his support to Jewish evangelism. Culbertson served as a sponsor and member of the board of directors of the American Association for Jewish Evangelism in the 1940s and 1950s, offering the association an aura of legitimacy and acceptance in conservative evangelical eyes.

The Moody Bible Institute considered the program of Jewish evangelism to be an integral part of its mission and took pride in it. In the early 1930s, the institute advertised the program proudly in its bulletin, featuring a photo of Solomon Birnbaum, the professor of Jewish evangelization, with the twenty students who were enrolled in the department at the time. The photograph was accompanied by a short paragraph entitled "Debt to the Jew": "The Jewish nation gave to the world the Messiah, and yet that nation remains blind to the glorious fact that Jesus of Nazareth is indeed He of whom the prophets wrote. The Moody Bible Institute has formally recognized, by the maintenance of a Jewish Missions Course, the debt that the Christian world owes to the Jewish race. Christian Jews, and such Gentile Christians as desire training for introducing Christ to the 'lost sheep of the house of Israel,' are in the course instructed in a number of subjects additional to the regular subjects of the General Course."[18] A plea for donations to the institute was placed just below the article. The Jewish missions program continued at the MBI throughout the 1930s, 1940s, and 1950s with little change.[19] In addition to the general course (the basic curriculum for all students) and Jewish studies, the school added an additional course of studies of English for newly arrived immigrant students.[20]

The studies at the Moody Bible Institute not only gave prospective missionaries a good preparation for a career of spreading the Christian message among the Jews but also enabled them to become acquainted with the evangelical world. Throughout the period, the MBI was an institution representing the values, norms, and doctrines of the mainstream of the evangelical-fundamentalist camp. The students in the program for Jewish evangelism studied with future ministers, missionaries, and leaders of the evangelical camp. They learned at first hand the evangelical mores, customs, and regulations. The connections they made often served them throughout their lifetime careers as missionaries. Curiously, the life and studies at the MBI often brought Jewish students to realize the enormous gap between them and their evangelical friends, and they sometimes experienced the loneliness of being a Jewish student in a "gentile" environment.[21] Jewish students, for example, often could not stand the American food served in the institute's dining room, which to them was completely tasteless. Being used to Jewish bread, they could not eat the white "cotton" bread the dining room served. At one time they even protested against what they considered to be the lack of adequate food. Similarly, Jews at the MBI had a hard time with the many regulations governing the details of everyday life at the institute. Coming from a culture very different from that of evangelical Protestant Americans and accepting Jesus as their Savior, they could not always comprehend why a rigid lifestyle was considered a Christian way of life.

Perhaps not surprisingly, many of the graduates of the Jewish program during that period became active in the Hebrew Christian Alliance, which conformed to the evangelical spirit of the day yet provided converted Jews with their own organization, representative body, and support group. It is perhaps also significant that although Jewish immigrants to Palestine from America during the 1920s to 1950s were a rare phenomenon, a number of graduates of the Jewish evangelization program at the Moody Bible Institute, such as Moshe Ben Meir, immigrated there as Jewish Christian Zionists, choosing to live among their fellow Jews and take part in the national Jewish revival.

Reich, who died in 1946, was replaced as director of the Jewish mission program by Nathan Stone, a graduate in 1925 of the first class in Jewish missions at the Moody Bible Institute. Born in England and raised in Canada, Stone, a veteran of World War I, came to study at the MBI a short time after his conversion to Christianity. After graduation, he went on to receive a degree in ministry from the Louisville Presbyterian Seminary and worked for a few years as a missionary on behalf of the Presbyterian Church among the Jews.[22] Like other teachers of Jewish evangelism at the institute throughout the years, Stone not only taught at the Bible school but was active on the boards of a number of missions to the Jews, as well as in the Hebrew Christian Alliance. In 1944, a few years after he started his work in the program of Jewish evangelism at the MBI, Stone published a book that received some notice in evangelical circles at the time, *Names of God in the Old Testament*. Based on a course he gave at the institute and demonstrating a good knowledge of biblical Hebrew, Stone explored the names of God in the Hebrew Bible. Viewing the matter from a Christological and Trinitarian perspective, Stone, perhaps not surprisingly, concluded that the different attributes of God in the Old Testament find their counterparts in the person of Jesus Christ (and the Holy Spirit) as expressed in the New Testament. Stone, an ardent dispensationalist, also used the occasion to promote the idea of God's continuing covenant with Israel and of the expected arrival of the Messiah. After Stone's death in 1965, Louis Goldberg took over as the professor of Jewish evangelization at the MBI. A California-born engineer, Goldberg converted to Christianity in the 1940s and spent a number of years studying Christian theology at Northern Baptist Theological Seminary and Grace Theological Seminary, where he received a doctor of theology degree. He thereafter served as a minister of Baptist congregations in Iowa, Illinois, and Tennessee. A scholar by inclination and active in the circle of Jewish converts to evangelical Christianity, the Jewish Baptist minister was happy to accept a position as a professor at the Moody Bible Institute.

This change of guard correlated with the end of an era in the history of the movement to evangelize the Jews in America. The new professor convinced the dean to introduce changes in the program, such as abandoning the teaching of Yiddish, which he no longer considered to be a necessary tool for approaching Jews in America. The curriculum was to change further in the late 1960s and would include yearly evangelization tours in Israel by the students, where they would evangelize young Israelis. The underlying theology, then, of the MBI, as well as the premillennialist hope that emphasizes the role of the Jewish people in God's plan for the messianic age, would remain as strong as when the program was founded and would continue to serve as the impetus and raison d'être of the department.

The attempts at building a selective and well-trained cadre of missionaries to the Jews were reflected not only in the program at the MBI but in the actual operation of missions during the period, such as those of the American Board of Missions to the Jews.

10

The Rise of the American Board of
Missions to the Jews

The history of the Williamsburg Mission to the Jews best reflects the changes in the organization, working methods, and character of missions to the Jews in America that took place between the 1920s and 1960s. Like other missions of the earlier period (1880s to 1910s), it had begun as a small, one-person establishment, under the formal auspices of a Protestant denomination (the Baptists), and concentrated its activities in a single urban area (Brooklyn, New York). During the 1920s to the 1940s, it grew to become a nationwide institution, administered like a large corporation using techniques of mass salesmanship, such as radio broadcasting and advertisements in daily newspapers, and operated by personnel who were often specifically trained for the evangelization of Jews.

The person responsible for this transformation was the founder's son, Joseph Cohn. Joseph was a small boy when his father converted, immigrated to America, and began his career as a missionary in the Brownsville section of Brooklyn, New York. Joseph grew up in Brooklyn and worked in his father's mission.[1] After completing high school in 1907, he spent a year at the Moody Bible Institute in Chicago, at that time the central and most influential evangelical institution of ministry and missionary training in America. His studies at the institute gave young Joseph a firsthand acquaintance with evangelical life, as well as enabling him to build long-lasting friendships with future ministers and evangelical activists. On his return to New York, he immediately began to take an active part in running his father's mission. He showed enormous energy and zeal and set out on fund-raising campaigns in various parts of the United States, lecturing in churches and collecting funds thereafter. His father, Leopold, had relied at first on the support of the Brooklyn chapter of the Baptist Church. Later on, an affluent beneficiary, Frances Huntley, took the fledgling mission under her auspices and poured tens of thousands of dollars into its operations in the early years of the century.

Although Jews doubted Leopold Cohn's claim that he had actually been an ordained rabbi before his conversion to Christianity, there could be little doubt that he was well read in rabbinical literature and had acquired, after his conversion to Christianity, a good knowledge of Christian theology as well.[2] Joseph, on the other hand, had neither the theological knowledge of his father nor the desire to deal with theological matters; he was much more interested in the practical day-to-day administration of the mission and worked on its expansion. Thus, a division of labor developed between father and son: Leopold concentrated on theological writing, and Joseph assumed the administrative and financial duties. The difference between father and son reflected not only the change of generation within the Cohn family but also a move toward a larger and more professional operation within the mission.

A major change in American Jewish demography had taken place in the 1920s and 1930s, and the mission now aimed to reach a new generation of Jews whose needs were different from those of their parents. Leopold Cohn had established the mission in the early 1890s in Brooklyn, addressing himself to the newly arrived immigrants from eastern Europe. Between 1880 and 1920, more than two million Jews from eastern Europe settled in America's large cities. By the early 1920s, the influx of Jewish immigrants from eastern Europe had slowed considerably, partly as a result of new restrictive immigration laws. The percentage of second-generation, American-born or American-raised Jews grew considerably, and the missions had to alter their work and evangelization techniques accordingly. Himself a child of Jewish immigrants and well acquainted with the needs and wishes of his generation, Joseph Cohn led the mission from concentrating on evangelizing immigrants to approaching their children. A look at the development of missions to the Jews in America shows that those missions that took notice of the demographic and cultural changes and adapted themselves accordingly were those that grew and prospered. There were missions during the period that continued to operate in the same manner as before, but they did not grow to become national organizations.

In the 1920s, the board of directors decided officially to appoint Joseph as the director of the mission. Leopold Cohn, his father, was named superintendent emeritus.[3] In 1923 Joseph Cohn persuaded the board to approve a name change that was to reflect the new directions and aspirations the mission was taking. The new name, the American Board of Missions to the Jews, reflected Cohn's and the mission's ambition to become not just the largest and most powerful agency of Jewish evangelization in America but the only one, administering branches all over the nation. The name also implied a change in the management of the mission, which was no longer a family enterprise (although the Cohns continued to administer it for many years) but rather a corporation governed by a board of directors. Joseph Cohn utilized his connections with prestigious conservative evangelical leaders such as Keith L. Brooks and Lewis S. Chafer, recruiting them to enter into mutual ventures with the mission or to sit on the mission's board of directors and lend their names to the promotion of the mission's cause.

The mission produced a number of publications, including a series of tracts in

Yiddish and English, for missionary purposes. These dealt with various theological issues, such as the meaning of Jesus and his death, and confronted standard Jewish reactions or challenges to the Christian message. Many of these tracts were written by Leopold Cohn, whose works the mission printed and distributed long after he ceased to direct the organization.[4] Cohn tried to persuade potential converts that basic Christian tenets of faith such as the Trinity or the virgin birth of Jesus were compatible with Jewish religious concepts and were actually discussed in the Hebrew Bible.[5] The mission also published a number of journals both to propagate its cause and to muster support for its activities among Protestant evangelical supporters and potential converts.

The *Chosen People* served as the mission's journal and newsletter. As it announced various plans, opinions, and exchanges of letters and events, it reveals, among other things, the development of the mission. The journal tried to promote its cause by emphasizing a dispensationalist premillennialist interpretation of historical events and propagating the idea that the Jews were destined to play a central role in the events of the End Times. The journal took a pro-Zionist stance and reported on events in the life of the Jewish people. Such championing of the idea that the Jews were still the chosen people was essential, the directors of the mission believed, in order to recruit Christian support. The *Shepherd of Israel* was published simultaneously in English and Yiddish and was meant to convey the mission's message to interested Jews and potential converts. The *Chosen People* and the *Shepherd of Israel* both represented the mission's theological standing, which was conservative evangelical and premillennialist. Yet they were written in different styles because they were meant for two different audiences. In the *Shepherd of Israel*, Cohn voiced his opinion more as a Jew among Jews, using (particularly when writing in Yiddish) idiomatic terms and expressions, language that Jews spoke only among themselves, such as "mishmash." The different names of the journals were suggestive. The *Shepherd of Israel* refers, of course, to Jesus; the journal was accompanied by Hebrew quotations from Ezekiel 34:23 ("and I shall place upon them one shepherd") and John 10:11 ("I am the good shepherd"). This dual quotation from the Hebrew Bible and the New Testament was in line with the Christian understanding of Scriptures, according to which prophecies in the Old Testament were fulfilled in the new one. The name of the journal and the quotations were in line with the mission's attempt to persuade Jews that Jesus was the Messiah of Israel. The name the *Chosen People*, on the other hand, was in line with the mission's attempt to persuade its supporters that the Jews were historical Israel, the chosen nation, destined to play a dominant role in the great events of the End Times, and that its evangelization was therefore a worthy cause.

The magazine carried a "Questions and Answers" column that was of particular importance because it presented the mission's stand on biblical and theological issues and reflected its position vis-à-vis American Christianity in general. It also presented the mission's ideology concerning Jewish acceptance of Christianity, clearly revealing a conservative evangelical premillennialist outlook, very much in line with that of the *Scofield Reference Bible*. Many of the questions dealt with theological matters, expressing the mission's understanding of the role of Jews in history. The column gave expression to the mission's declared view that Jews who converted to Christianity fulfilled their destiny and became complete, "true" Jews.[6]

A look at the articles in the *Shepherd of Israel* reveals something about the mission's character and agenda. Naturally, the journal was promoting the Christian tenets of faith, but at the same time it was also advocating the conservative worldview of evangelical Protestants in America at the time on political and social issues. An ongoing debate in the missionary community was whether missions should advocate their particular cultural and social norms or concentrate on merely advocating the belief in the messiahship of Christ.[7] The latter approach of "Christ not culture" did not appeal to the leaders of the mission. For the directors of the American Board, as well as those of other missions to the Jews in America, accepting the Christian faith meant adopting the opinions and ways of the evangelical Christian community. They were, in a way, not only missionizing Jews but educating them as well. They wanted Jews to accept their conservative social and political worldview. One striking example was the issue of communism. Coming from a conservative Protestant point of view, Cohn and his successor, Fuchs, took great exception to communism and to the Soviet Union. Both missionaries published articles and tracts in Yiddish and English to combat pro-Communist trends among Jews.[8] In 1948, when the state of Israel was established, the director of the mission, who held a pro-Zionist stance, rejoiced in the establishment of the state that he considered to play a prominent role in the events of the End Times. He was, however, taken aback when he discovered that the new country had established a friendly relationship with the Soviet Union. Cohn used his editorial position in the *Shepherd of Israel* and devoted half an issue to attacking the Russian-Israeli relationship vehemently: "What a mess! Russian Anthem, Zionist Hatikvah . . . What a mess!"[9]

The American Board of Missions to the Jews allied itself with the conservative segment of American Protestantism, which was influenced by premillennialist thinking. In particular, the mission followed what could be described as respectable, mainline fundamentalist evangelicalism in America at the time. It disassociated itself completely from the Pentecostal movement, for example, which in those years did not enjoy much prestige and was snubbed by the leading forces in American evangelicalism. The American Board sought acceptance, respectability, and support. It successfully courted evangelical premillennialist leaders: known pastors or professors and deans of leading Bible schools and theological seminaries. The mission's conservative and conformist character manifested itself also in matters of style and dress, which were in line with conservative middle-class propriety.[10] Similarly, the services conducted in the mission's center followed those of conservative, middle-class, noncharismatic Protestant congregations.

The American Board of Missions to the Jews, more than any other mission to the Jews during the period, was successful in building avenues into the evangelical community and gaining its support. One means the mission used to establish its reputation as a respectable and central evangelical premillennialist mission was organizing Bible and prophecy conferences.[11] Biblical and prophecy conferences had been a known institution in American Christianity since the late nineteenth century. Such conferences served as a means for the conservative wing of the evangelical community to express its opposition to modernist trends in American Protestantism and to convey its messianic reading of the Scriptures and its critique of history and culture. The conferences were instrumental in solidifying and shaping the fundamentalist movement at the end of the nineteenth century and the beginning of the twentieth.[12] By organizing such conferences, the American Board of Missions to the Jews not only associated itself with the conservative premillennialist wing of American Protestantism but attempted to place itself at the center of this movement in American Christianity.

The first conference took place in Winona Lake, Indiana; presentations concentrated on premillennialist views of the Jews and their place in history and included such topics as "The Day of Jacob's Trouble" and "They that did the King's Business helped the Jews."[13] Some of the topics related to the fundamentalist critique of the current world situation and culture. In 1942, the American Board organized a "National Conference of Prophecy" in New York. The list of speakers in this conference reads like a who's who in the evangelical-fundamentalist camp, including such leaders, writers, ideologues, and spokesmen as Lewis Chafer, an evangelical theologian and president of Dallas Theological Seminary; Keith Brooks, premillennialist writer and editor of *Prophecy* magazine; Harry Ironside, pastor of Moody Memorial Church in Chicago; John Walvoord, who later became president of Dallas Theological Seminary; Louis Talbot, president of the Bible Institute of Los Angeles (BIOLA); and Charles Feinberg, originally a missionary with the American Board, who had built a career as a leading evangelical academician, first at Dallas Theological Seminary and later on as dean of Talbot Seminary in Los Angeles. The participation of such persons in a congress organized by the mission helped to promote its status as a solid conservative evangelical institution. The presentations at the conference followed the dispensationalist interpretation of history, which included an emphasis on the role of the Jews in God's plans for humanity.[14] From the mission's point of view, such an understanding served as a charter for the mission's operation.

Lewis Chafer gave a speech entitled "The Coming Destruction of Ecclesiastical

and Political Babylon." Although World War II was at its peak, Chafer was not referring to Nazi Germany or Japan. For him, political and ecclesiastical "Babylon"
meant the culture of the day, which he perceived to be non-Christian. The conservative theologian took strong exception to the nonevangelical ecclesiastical establishment.[15] Some speakers elaborated specifically on the relationship between
the evangelical community and the Jews. Albert Lindsey, a Presbyterian pastor
from Detroit, spoke on the topic "What the Church Will Have to Do for the Jew
in the Post War Period."[16] In Lindsey's opinion, the missions to the Jews, although
representing only part of Christendom, had been successful. He argued that, in
proportion to the number of Jews, there had been more Jewish converts than
converts from other nations. Yet the church as a whole, he claimed, was far from
treating the Jews fairly. "Spiritually speaking, we are what we are and have what
we have largely because of the Jew," he argued. Yet "within the fold of the Church
there is today an unusual amount of ignorance, misunderstanding and actual
hate of the Jew."[17] The church, he claimed, should support the building of a
Jewish national home in Palestine and educate the Christian population about
"the Jew as he truly is in his proper light, and the all-important role he plays in the
divine program of God's Word, including our own responsibility to him."[18] Lindsey's words reveal the unmistakable connection between building a favorable
image of the Jews—that is, convincing Christians that Jews fulfill a positive role in
history—and mustering Christian support for evangelizing the Jews. Speakers
such as Chafer and Lindsey also explained clearly why the American Board of
Missions to the Jews, as well as the movement to evangelize the Jews in general,
aligned itself with the conservative wing in American Christianity, whose theology favored the promotion of missions. The conservative championing of the
importance of the Jews came as part and parcel of a larger worldview. Speakers in
the conference presented a fundamentalist worldview and condemned the prevailing cultural trends of their era. As the participants of this large gathering saw
it, their view on social and cultural matters was related to their messianic beliefs,
which in turn inspired their understanding of the role of Jews in history and their
commitment to evangelizing the Jews. By organizing the conference, the mission
not only strengthened its position as a credible evangelical-fundamentalist organization but helped to promote the worldview that sustained its activities.

The American Board's campaigning for acceptance and building a strong
network of support as well as its insistence on professionalizing the mission and
running it as a large corporation proved successful. By the early 1940s, the mission fulfilled its aspirations and operated throughout the United States in virtually all large Jewish communities. It employed more than sixty field missionaries in addition to the staff in its large New York headquarters, moved from
Brooklyn to Manhattan. The headquarters, in addition to administration, supervision of fieldwork, and fund-raising, played a central role in the evangelization

efforts, including the publication of the mission's journals, the production of booklets and tracts, and the launching of radio programs. The last included radio advertisement "spot announcements," which cost the mission, in the early 1940s, sixty dollars for fifty words. The radio became a popular form of propagating the Christian gospel in the 1930s and 1940s. Cohn thus adapted his mission to the means and possibilities of evangelism in his day. The radio programs also signified the mission's prosperous situation and its leading role in the field of Jewish evangelization. Most other missions did not show the same initiative and innovation at the time. The mission broadcasting program in the post–World War II years and its messages were well noticed by members of the Jewish community, who reacted with particular anger.[19] The bitter Jewish reaction testified, in some ways, to the power and significance of radio broadcasting in the 1940s, before the rise of television. Whereas Jews tended during the period to dismiss missionaries and their messages as eccentric and futile, the radio program clearly alarmed them.

The American Board of Missions to the Jews was a patriarchal, hierarchical enterprise, typical of American organizations of the period; yet the mission did hire and train women as missionaries. As a matter of fact, women constituted a large percentage of the missionaries, not to mention the administrative staff. Numbers differ from one decade to another; by the 1950s, women actually outnumbered men.[20] The mission relied heavily on its women missionaries' dedication and competence. Yet most of the heads of the branches of the mission were men, and only men served as the mission's directors and on the board of directors. A few women did stand out as pillars and leaders in the mission. One noted evangelist was Hilda Koser, who operated the mission branch in Coney Island for a number of decades. A formidable, determined, and energetic person, Koser gained the trust and appreciation of the mission's director. Although she and Cohn clashed at times, they respected each other, and Koser remained one of the mission's more senior and trusted field evangelists and director of the mission's branch.

In addition to its successful attempts at opening mission branches in major American cities, the American Board of Missions to the Jews under Joseph Cohn's leadership operated in Palestine, Europe, and South America. Its approach was not based on sending a well-trained employee from America to open a missionary station abroad. Rather, the mission contacted a local Jewish Christian whom it trusted and whose views and beliefs were compatible with those of the mission and hired him to work on its behalf in propagating the gospel among the Jews. Whereas in America the mission operated branches for decades and would close one down only if major demographic changes took place and the Jewish community in the area dwindled, its missionary stations opened and then shut down rather frequently in the different overseas areas where the mission operated. This was due in no small part to political instability in some of those countries. Although many of the stations did not operate for long periods of time, the mission's involvement with overseas work continued. It is perhaps a remarkable fact that during the 1930s, in the arduous years of the depression, the operations of the American Board overseas actually grew.

The first foreign branch of the mission opened in the early 1920s in Kovno, Lithuania, where the work of the mission was carried out by a local Jewish Christian named Simon Aszur.[21] The American Board of Missions to the Jews was not the only mission working to evangelize Jews in this part of the world. There were a number of societies working toward that goal. Evangelical missions among Jews in eastern Europe were almost always western European or North American and represented religious communities and a culture different from that of the area, the local population being mostly Roman Catholic, Greek Catholic, or Greek Orthodox. German, Norwegian, and British missionary societies such as the Norwegian Zion Mission to the Jews, the London Society for Promoting Christianity amongst the Jews, or the Mildmay Mission to the Jews, had been working among Jews in eastern Europe since the early and mid-nineteenth century. Only toward the end of the century, with the rise of dispensationalism as a central theological component of American evangelicalism, did the first American missions to the Jews begin working in Europe. After World War II, the overseas American missionary efforts would overshadow that of the European (mainly British and Scandinavian) missions.

Working in eastern European countries where there were long-established state churches was not an easy task. In some countries, such as czarist Russia, permits were required from various legal or ecclesiastical authorities,[22] but in the 1920s, with the Soviet regime taking over in Russia, the situation became even more difficult. The Soviets cared little for missions, particularly when they were sponsored by societies located in Western countries; missionaries fled, and missionary societies had to close down their work in Russia. In the late 1920s, Joseph Cohn and the American Board decided to take over the work of the Mildmay Mission to the Jews in Ekaterinaslav, a town in the Ukraine, which the Soviets renamed Dnepropetrovsk. It was an almost incredible undertaking, considering the suspicion and hostility of the regime. Indeed, the mission work was eventually shut down by the government; in January 1930, Gregory Guberman, the missionary whose work the American Board was sponsoring, sent the headquarters in New York his last report. The mission assumed that the missionary was then arrested and either killed or exiled.[23]

In 1934 the American Board took it upon itself to operate in Poland and hired Moses Gitlin to carry out evangelization work there. A graduate of the Moody Bible Institute who went back to eastern Europe, Gitlin was already working in Poland when he was hired by the mission.

In the early 1920s the American Board began cosponsoring missionary work in Palestine on a partial basis, in conjunction with a British mission. The board, like many other evangelical missions during the period, was eager to be represented in the Land of Israel. Dispensationalists understood the developments that took place in the Holy Land in eschatological messianic terms. Their interest in the country was enhanced by the Balfour Declaration and the British takeover of Palestine. A number of American churches and missionary organizations opened branches in the country, taking advantage of the fact that the British were much more friendly and welcoming to missions than the former rulers of the land had been. In the early 1930s, the American Board opened its own branch in Palestine for the first time. It hired a former missionary of the British Foreign Missionary Society, Frank Boothby, who already resided in the country. The American Board also cooperated with the British Jews' Society in supporting a missionary at Haifa. The standard salary the mission paid its workers overseas was fifty dollars a month. In Palestine of those days this was a generous salary, much larger than that of a schoolteacher, for example. In 1935 Cohn, the director of the mission, came on a visit. He complained that it was difficult to recruit dedicated reliable missionaries in the country. He also commented on the particularly unwelcoming attitude of the Jewish population in Palestine to missionaries and the difficulty of preaching the Christian gospel to the Jews.

In 1935, following his visit to Palestine and Europe, Cohn persuaded the board of directors to carry on missionary work among Jewish refugees in Europe. Jews were fleeing Germany, many of them to France, and were, he claimed, in need of both material and spiritual assistance. The mission opened a branch in Paris where they hired a Jewish convert, André Frankel, as their main full-time missionary. Among other ventures, Frankel and others translated the mission's journal, the *Shepherd of Israel*, into French. The mission could not afford to produce genuine French literature for its mission branch in France. But the translation of the magazine also signified the priorities of the mission and what it considered to be appropriate missionary literature. The *Shepherd of Israel*, the magazine it published and distributed among potential converts in America, seemed to the mission directors to be the obvious choice for distribution among prospective converts in France. It was the literature they produced and therefore trusted; its content fully reflected the mission's views on all matters. From their perspective it advocated the right Christian message. Similarly, from the point of view of prospective converts they were not merely taking interest in the Christian message in the abstract but rather were responding to missionaries who advocated a message and worldview that reflected a particular culture—that of American evangelical Christianity. The mission's magazines were also translated into German and Spanish. The mission opened more branches overseas. Among others, it established a branch in Vienna in 1936.

During the late 1930s, as the situation in Europe and particularly in Vienna became very difficult for Jews, the mission helped its own missionaries to escape Nazi persecution. This included Herbert Singer and Moses Gitlin, who came to America. Emmanuel Lichtenstein, the mission's representative in Vienna, fled with his family in 1941 to Sweden before proceeding to Argentina. There the mission employed him in a joint venture with the Lutheran Church. Helping their own workers to escape and relocate in safe havens was the norm for British, Scandinavian, and American missions. Some tried to rescue converts as well. With its European missionaries relocated elsewhere, and with the coming of World War II, the missionary work of the American Board in Europe came virtually to an end. The mission tried to revive its work in France after the war and continued its international activity in other parts of the world, especially in South America and Israel.

One issue that worried the mission's directors endlessly was the quality and integrity of its missionaries overseas. Throughout the entire period, the American Board, still traumatized by the accusations and controversies of its early period, put enormous emphasis on a well-trained, professional, accountable, and supervised missionary staff. Cohn and his successors were therefore ambivalent at times regarding the operation of mission branches abroad. They wanted the mission to be represented in Europe, Palestine, and, later on, in Latin America, yet they felt uneasy. Operating before the age of jet planes, fax, e-mail, and direct-dial telephones, they felt that they could not supervise their overseas branches effectively. They tried to overcome the difficulty by paying visits to the different stations or by asking respectable local church people whom they trusted to visit, inspect, and report. In Paris, for example, Cohn asked a local Huguenot pastor, Henri Vincent, to supervise the work of the mission and its distribution of funds. But even with all these difficulties, the mission's directors were eager to expand their work and spread the mission's message around the globe, and the board of directors approved the allocation of what were then relatively large sums of money for evangelizing Jews in countries other than America. The funds allocated for work overseas can indicate something about the scope of the activity there. In 1936 the mission's budget for overseas work was $14,000. By 1948 it had increased to $127,000. Naturally the buying power of the dollar in those days was much higher than today, and the sums meant much more than in the 1990s.[24] The missions' operations overseas helped its work at home. Its publications boosted the activities abroad, particularly when they were asking for funds. It was a proof of the global scope and, therefore, importance of the mission's work. It validated and legitimized its missionary agenda as a whole.

The American Board of Missions to the Jews should be viewed as part of the conservative fundamentalist-premillennialist network in America during this period. Its history during that period was that of growth and expansion. The mission was not unique in this respect. Following the Scopes trial in 1925, the image of the fundamentalist movement, at least in liberal eyes, was one of defeat and descent. But a large conservative Protestant evangelical network of educational and evangelistic institutions thrived and expanded, among them missions to the Jews.

The expansive character of the American Board reflected its leader's ambitious personality. Joseph Cohn was not, however, an easygoing, indulgent person, and like his father, he eventually became a controversial figure. Determined, vigorous, opinionated, energetic, and, at times, intimidating, he was every inch the pre–World War II domineering "boss" of urban America and was often accused of tyrannical practices. He ran the missionary organization, which he had expanded so successfully, as an efficient and centralized commercial enterprise. Reactions in Christian evangelical circles to Cohn and the American Board of Missions to the Jews were mixed. Many approved of the mission and praised its leader.[25] The growth and success of the mission proved Cohn's ability to gain the trust of Protestant evangelical supporters. Some, however, criticized Cohn's personality and tactics and resented the American Board's rise to prominence.[26] Many of the workers whom Cohn recruited to the mission and trained felt that Cohn's leadership left little room for them to develop, express their abilities, or gain prominence in the larger organization. Some of them resigned and established their own missionary organizations. Most newly established missions to the Jews in America between the 1920s and 1960s were offshoots of the American Board of Missions to the Jews and were founded by former employees of the board such as Jacob Gartenhaus, Victor Bucksbazen, and Abraham Machlin. The American Board viewed such missions for the most part as unwanted, illegitimate offspring. Paradoxically, it was precisely Cohn's choice of personnel for his mission that invited such disagreements, factions, and resignations. He recruited gifted, energetic, and ambitious young men and women and allowed them a great deal of freedom up to the point at which he felt his authority challenged. Some of the more able and ambitious persons in the mission sensed that they could advance no further in the organization or else clashed with Cohn over issues of authority. The parting of the ways was rarely happy, with bitterness and rivalry on both sides.

Although many Jews viewed Cohn's activities as a potential threat to Jewish survival, from his point of view he was a proud Jew, fighting for the Jewish cause within the ranks of evangelical Christianity. In his autobiography, *I Have Fought a Good Fight*, which he completed just before his death in 1953, Cohn recounted his lifelong struggle to muster support for his mission. He also described numerous incidents in which he fought prejudices against the Jews. During the 1930s and 1940s he caused a scandal when he accused a number of fundamentalist leaders, notably William B. Riley, of anti-Semitism.[27] Riley was one of the outstanding activists of American fundamentalism during the 1920s to 1940s and the founder of the Northwestern School of the Bible in Minneapolis.[28] Clashing with prominent leaders of the conservative camp was not in the best interests of Cohn's mission, but that did not stop the stubborn, confrontational missionary from attacking a prestigious fundamentalist leader whom he believed to be prejudiced and antagonistic toward Jews.

From Cohn's point of view, not only did he act as a proud Jew when he denounced Riley (whose attitude toward the Jewish people was much more ambivalent and complicated than Cohn presumed)[29] and other persons whose remarks he considered anti-Semitic, but he was also fulfilling his duty, as he understood it, as the director of the largest mission to the Jews in America. The mission was presenting the Christian evangelical message and promoting the Christian way of life and values to the Jews, and Cohn considered it essential, therefore, to protest any manifestation of anti-Semitism within the conservative evangelical camp, thus making a point that the outlook he was denouncing was not an inherent part of evangelical theology. Missionaries such as Cohn assured prospective Jewish converts that true Christians treated Jews with kindness and that evangelical Christianity had nothing to do with the long, painful history of Christian persecution. Besides Cohn, other Jewish missionaries denounced what they considered to be anti-Semitic remarks by evangelical leaders. David Bronstein, for example, also attacked Riley, and Elias Newman published a special tract to denounce the spread of anti-Semitic convictions in the conservative Protestant camp during the 1930s.[30]

Cohn's sudden death in 1953 at first created a vacuum in the leadership of the mission. Cohn relied heavily on his secretaries in his day-to-day work but had no deputy or heir apparent. "Joseph's need for control—his insistence on placing his stamp of approval on every worker, every project, and every program of the mission—had left the mission with no one groomed to be his successor," wrote the American Board's official historian.[31] Some in the mission felt that Cohn's death put the very survival of the mission in danger, but the organization proved strong enough to survive the death of its authoritarian director. The board of directors of the mission decided that the executive committee would run the mission's affairs. The executive committee originally consisted of three members. One of them, Joseph Cohn, was dead. The other two were Frank Davis, vice president and treasurer of the board, and Harold Pretlove, a businessman who acted as secretary of the board of directors. In actuality, Pretlove took over the superintendence of the mission, and the board of directors chose him to become the executive secretary of the mission.

Pretlove's ascendance to the position of directing the mission caused resentment among its workforce. Pretlove was not a missionary; in addition, he was a gentile, whereas the field missionaries of the American Board were Jews. When he was alive, Cohn served as the link between the board of directors, which was composed of non-Jewish evangelical ministers and businessmen, and the missionaries, who were Jewish, mostly of eastern European background. Cohn felt at home in both worlds and was trusted and respected by both groups. But after his death, many missionaries felt that the board of directors was imposing a director on them who was not one of their own. The board of director's choice, they believed, demonstrated that the board members did not trust the missionaries. They also felt that Pretlove did not possess the vision and leadership of Joseph Cohn and that the new director knew very little about the fieldwork of evangelizing Jews. Aware that the missionaries were unhappy with Pretlove's position and the tension this appointment created, the board of directors decided to restrict Pretlove's responsibilities to administrative and financial duties. In March 1955, the board appointed a veteran Jewish missionary, Daniel Fuchs, as director of missionary activity and Emil Gruen as responsible for organizing conferences. The new system created something of a "troika," yet Daniel Fuchs emerged by the late 1950s as the leader of the mission, gaining the trust of both the workers and the board of directors, although he never exercised the same kind of authority as Joseph Cohn. He proved to be a more amiable person than his predecessor, a quality he had probably had to nurture in order to survive under Cohn's domineering personality.

Fuchs's tenure as the director of the American Board of Missions to the Jews stands at the end of an era in the history of the mission and the movement to evangelize the Jews in America at large. Fuchs did not develop new approaches or strategies. The mission's approach to Jewish evangelism, as shaped by Cohn between the 1920s and the 1950s, continued to concentrate thereafter on the second-generation American Jews. When the mission was confronted in the late 1960s with new developments in American social and cultural life and a new generation of prospective converts, it would have a hard time adjusting.

11

Tension and Rivalry

After 1920, the reputation of Jewish missions and missionaries improved. Some of the former accusations, for example, that some missionaries were phony and had faked their biographies—common in the earlier period—disappeared. To be sure, Jewish community leaders continued to be distrustful and contemptuous toward missions, but they no longer portrayed missionaries as no better than fugitive criminals.[1] Scandals, such as those surrounding Jacob Freshman and Herman Warszawiak, who had lost the trust of the evangelical community and were subsequently ostracized and cast out of office in shame, did not recur. One reason for the change was the professionalization of the missions. The old paradigm, whereby converts who had just emigrated from eastern Europe, with no screening, training and experience, opened their own small missions, died out.

Although many of the Jewish missionaries between the 1920s and the 1960s were immigrants from eastern and central Europe, some of whom opened new missions, they often had received special training at the Moody Bible Institute or similar programs and then gained experience in one of the established missions, usually the American Board of Missions to the Jews. Many of them enrolled as students and graduated from theological seminaries. The extensive preparation served as a screening mechanism that ensured that stable and reliable persons entered the field. It also gave future missionaries an opportunity to become acquainted with the norms and standards of Protestant missions. Missions to the Jews during that period adopted standard business practices such as supervision by boards of directors, keeping accurate financial records, publishing the mission's income and expenses in detail, and payment of fixed salaries to personnel.

More careful recruitment, better organization, and improved financial accountability did not, however, eliminate the possibility of competition and rivalry among the various mission bodies. There were occasional episodes of mistrust, accusations of wrongdoing, and the development of factions. The relationship between the two major missionary enterprises of the 1920s to 1940s, the American Board of Missions to the Jews and the Presbyterian Board of Home Missions, for example, was one of mistrust and anger.[2]

Joseph Cohn was particularly targeted for accusations, perhaps because his power and success aroused resentment and made him a natural candidate for attacks of all sorts. His father's antagonists had described Leopold Cohn as a phony, but this particular charge was never leveled at Joseph. Rather, his enemies, most of whom were within the missionary community, pointed to his large salary: by 1944 Cohn was earning ten thousand dollars a year, which some people considered excessive. He also had to worry about potential allegations regarding his private life and marital problems. According to his own testimony, his wife did not share his evangelistic aspirations, and her dissent brought the marriage to a severe crisis, eventually leading to a separation. Cohn, who openly complained about his wife, became attached, in the early 1940s, to his administrative assistant and toyed with the idea of divorcing his wife and marrying the woman he loved. However, a divorce was not something a director of a conservative evangelical institution could afford. It was virtually unaccepted in the circles of the mission's supporters and would have cast a dark shadow on him and on the American Board in general. The divorce did not occur, and the young woman accepted a marriage proposal from another man, though Cohn begged her to wait until he was free. This private odyssey was unknown to the general public, but his enemies within his organization tried to use it against him.[3]

In 1944, a crisis developed in the American Board of Missions to the Jews involving the resignation of Abraham Machlin, an employee of the mission who decided to establish a new mission. Several members of the board of directors resigned as well, accusing Cohn of tyrannical practices and of harassing Machlin. Among other things, they pointed to Cohn's private life in an effort to discredit him.[4] Machlin was not a young man when he and Cohn clashed in the early 1940s. Trained at the Moody Bible Institute, Machlin began his career in Buffalo, New York, as a missionary of the Buffalo Hebrew Christian Mission under the auspices of the American (Northern) Baptist Church. During his years of work in Buffalo, he established connections and gained the trust of some influential conservative Protestant leaders there and in Chicago. Some of them, such as J. Palmer Muntz, a Baptist pastor in Buffalo at the time, later backed him in his fight against Cohn. The zeal of Northern Baptists to evangelize Jews cooled during the 1930s. The denomination had undergone an inner struggle in the 1920s and 1930s between conservatives and liberals over the character of the church, and the latter eventually gained the upper hand. Adopting a more liberal line, devoid of premillennialist influence, the church soon abandoned its interest in the conversion of Jews. Struggling to sustain the mission and the local Baptist group that backed him, Machlin approached the American Board of Missions to the Jews and asked for support, later suggesting that the board take over the work.[5]

A veteran missionary, however, Machlin was too independent and assertive to work under Cohn, and after a relatively short time in his new position, he quit. Building on his connections with former students and professors at the Moody Bible Institute, he soon established his own mission in Chicago. Muntz, who resigned his position as a board member of the American Board of Missions to the Jews, became president of the executive board of the new mission. It eventually acquired the name "American Association for Jewish Evangelism" and developed into a national organization with a number of branches in the United States and Canada as well as in Israel. The new mission acquired a solid reputation and position in the conservative evangelical camp. Prestigious evangelical leaders lent their names to it.[6] The more prominent among them were William Culbertson, president of the Moody Bible Institute in Chicago, and Louis Talbot, president of the Bible Institute of Los Angeles (BIOLA). John Bradbury, editor of the *Watchman-Examiner*, a Baptist weekly with conservative premillennialist leanings, also lent his support.

Following the example of the American Board, the American Association for Jewish Evangelism also organized Bible and prophecy conferences at Winona Lake as a means to make a name for itself, earn recognition, and build connections. The new mission virtually took over the Winona Lake Bible conferences from its parent organization. Bradbury, who edited the collection of essays based on the prophecy conference organized by the American Board, also edited *Israel's Restoration*, a collection of essays based on lectures given by participants in prophecy conferences organized by the American Association for Jewish Evangelism. The essays in *Israel's Restoration* reflect the close connection between the dispensationalist premillennialist hope and the interest it inspired in the Jewish people and their conversion.[7] One of the speakers at the conferences was Lewis Chafer, the prestigious president of Dallas Theological Seminary, who presented "an introduction to eschatology," making a case for the legitimacy, authenticity, and antiquity of the Christian dispensationalist eschatological creed.[8]

Harry Ironside, pastor of Moody Church in Chicago, also defended the dispensationalist messianic scheme and the role assigned to the Jews in this creed.[9] Ironside was only too aware that many Christians resented the idea that the Jewish people were God's chosen people and were destined to play a leading role in history. In his opinion, this negative attitude even kept some gentiles from accepting the dispensationalist faith. The Chicago clergyman pointed to what he considered to be "fulfilled prophecy" as a proof of the validity of the eschatological hope he was trying to promote. In a similar manner, John Bradbury pointed to the newly created state of Israel as a proof of the truth of the dispensationalist eschatological hope.[10] Promoting the dispensationalist school of messianic expectation was a first step in an appeal to Christians to support missions to the Jews, as it justified and gave meaning to the evangelization efforts. A second step was taken by other speakers who elaborated on the Jewish people and their role in history.

Hyman Appelman, for example, a veteran missionary who joined the staff of the American Association for Jewish Evangelism, gave a lecture entitled "A Suffering People." "I am speaking as a Christian to Christians," exclaimed the Jewish Christian. "I plead with you do not hurt the Jew. . . . I warn you that the promise of God still stands, 'I will bless them that bless you, and curse them that curse you.' "[11] In asking Christians to treat Jews fairly, Appelman was promoting the cause of evangelizing the Jews. It has been a long-argued theme in the missions' appeal to the Christian community that a positive attitude toward the Jewish people should manifest itself in support for evangelizing the Jews. But there were other reasons in Appelman's eyes to support the cause of Jewish evangelism: "You must remember, the possibilities in the Jews for evil, for great evil. They are in high places. . . . Many of them have control over radio stations and radio programs. These can be used by Satan or by God. . . . It is in our hands in which direction the ambitions, the powers of the Jews will be challenged. . . . The Jews are a brilliant people, energetic, ambitious. If these are not directed in the way of Christ and Christianity, they are extremely dangerous. We have to Christianize them or they will paganize us."[12] This again has been a long-repeated claim in the argument in favor of extensive missionary efforts among the Jews. As Jews were secularizing and walking away from the faith of their fathers, they were going astray. Christianity, the advocates of evangelizing the Jews claimed, was the Jews' best remedy and could set them once again on a constructive path. J. Palmer Muntz offered another pledge for Christian support for Jewish missions. The Buffalo minister narrated the history of the Jewish people and their place in God's plans for humanity.[13] Muntz declared that Christians should not blame the Jews for not accepting Christ but rather themselves. "Are we not, in the measure that we have not presented the gospel to him, to blame for his present rejection?"[14]

The new mission held the same ideology and perception of the Jews and their role in history as did its parent organization; the reason for the parting of ways, after all, was certainly not over theological matters. In a manner typical of missionary publications the cover of the new mission's monthly journal *Salvation* carried the motto "Salvation is of the Jews." The journal published articles on Jewish affairs and a regular column offered news from Israel. However, it eventually took a different character than that of its parent mission. It became, following the death of Machlin and a change of guard, a "gentile" mission, that is, the director, the members of the executive board, and the field missionaries it hired to carry on its work were non-Jews.[15] In contrast to the policy of the American Board of Missions to the Jews and the Department of Jewish Evangelization of the Presbyterian Church in the U.S.A., the directors of the American Association for Jewish Evangelism concluded that the gospel was best preached to the Jews by gentiles. Jews, they believed, had more respect and tolerance for non-Jews who tried to evangelize them than for Jews. A noted exception was the mission's representative in Israel for more than three decades, Haim Haimoff-Bar David, who was Jewish. The mission's leaders, particularly Ralph Gade, who replaced Machlin as its director, also adopted the view, not unlike that of many other missions, that Jews who have accepted Christianity joined the body of Christian believers and should therefore join a general "gentile" church. The only exception to that rule was again in Israel, where the mission approved of the establishment of Jewish-Israeli congregations, as they were the indigenous churches.

Although the new organization earned itself a respectable place in the framework of missions to the Jews, it never reached the size and importance of the American Board of Missions to the Jews. The American Board faced a major crisis with the resignation of experienced missionaries and major supporters as well as the establishment of a new rival and competing organization, not to mention the attacks on its director. Yet it survived the crisis, recruited new supporters, and retained its position as the leading mission to the Jews in America.

The American Board attracted occasional antagonism not only from disappointed employees or former members of its own board of directors but in the evangelical camp as well. A noted case was the animosity that developed between Joseph Cohn and William Riley, the formidable Baptist minister and fundamentalist leader from Minneapolis. Riley was initially an ardent supporter of the mission and a member of its board of directors. Having built something of a conservative fundamentalist empire, including a Bible school, a network of publications, radio programs, and missionary agencies, Riley wished to enlarge the scope of his activity and include the evangelization of Jews in his ministry. It was over this issue that Cohn and the midwestern fundamentalist leader clashed. Riley reports having expected Cohn and the American Board to cooperate with him in establishing a mission to the Jews in Minneapolis.[16] One can believe Riley's complaint that Cohn was less than helpful. Cohn's vision of his mission was that of a general all-encompassing mission to the Jews in America, ideally the only one. He saw no reason for other individuals and agencies to engage in missionizing the Jews except under his authority and his mission's jurisdiction. In his eyes, his was the one mission that operated in a professional, responsible, and accountable manner; the rest were in one way or another dilettantish, inexperienced, or irresponsible. Cohn was interested in recruiting Riley and his like to support his work but did not wish to share territory with them in the realm of evangelizing Jews or to help them to create their own agencies. Riley, who was hurt by Cohn's unwillingness to cooperate with him, severed his connections with the American Board and turned against Cohn and the mission. The two parties exchanged accusations, both verbal and written. Riley attacked Cohn vehemently. An evangelical supporter of the American Board, on the other hand, published a booklet repudiating Riley's attacks.[17]

Cohn openly accused Riley of anti-Semitism. Riley, for his part, indeed admitted his negative attitude toward Jews but claimed that it was his bad experience with Cohn that turned him against that people. "My feelings on this matter have been entirely influenced by my own experience. . . . I was also on two committees trying to put over Jewish work in Minneapolis and in each case, the Jew missionary did us up and deserted us."[18] Riley remained a staunch premillennialist who believed that the Jews were the heirs to the covenant between God and Israel and the object of the biblical prophecies that spoke about the return of the Jews to Zion, the arrival of the Messiah, and the reestablishment of a Davidic kingdom in Jerusalem.[19] Yet Riley's messianic outlook did not guarantee an admiring view of the Jews. He shared a notion common among some fundamentalist thinkers during the period that, since the Jews had not accepted Jesus as their Savior, they were spiritually and morally depraved and thus were susceptible to distorted ideologies such as socialism. Riley's accusations against Cohn, and the latter's busy denunciation of Riley's bigotry, did not bring about an abandonment of conservative evangelical support for the mission, which continued to flourish. From Cohn's point of view, it was just one of many incidents or obstacles that evangelicals had placed in the way of his building a vital and independent mission. That Cohn retained his position amid opposition, attacks, and doubts concerning both his private life and his leadership of the mission was due not only to his formidable and determined character but also to his successful management of the mission, which had grown considerably during his administration.

Another missionary who was targeted for attacks and accusations was Arthur Michelson, the founding head of the First Hebrew Christian Synagogue and the Hebrew Evangelization Society. Michelson recounts his background in two autobiographical accounts significantly entitled *Out of Darkness into Light* and *From Judaism and Law to Christ and Grace*. In these memoirs, he describes an imposing father who domineered him as a child, a youth, and a young man. Following his father's instructions, he studied law and became an attorney. He obeyed his father and fulfilled his expectations up to a certain point, when he rebelled, married a Roman Catholic woman, converted to Roman Catholicism, and left for America. Michelson then underwent a second conversion, this time to evangelical Christianity, and accepted Jesus Christ as his personal Savior. He decided to become an evangelist to his Jewish brethren. He first worked as a missionary in New York and then moved to Los Angeles, where he established his own mission.

Michelson's missionary venture proved successful. His was not an ordinary small mom-and-pop mission but quickly developed into a medium-size enterprise. The mission put out a series of publications and used the radio as a means of evangelism and raising support. After World War II, the mission grew even larger as it opened a number of branches outside America. In those years, its budget grew to five hundred thousand dollars a year. In addition to evangelism, Michelson organized a congregation of Jewish converts to Christianity. In his books, tracts, and leaflets Michelson proudly advertised his Hebrew Christian church, one of the early ones in America.[20] He accompanied the texts of his publications with photographs of himself presiding over prayers in his congregation. In them, he is depicted surrounded by traditional artifacts of the Jewish religion, an indication of an attempt on his part to retain Jewish symbols and some features of Jewish identity.[21] Although the theological and liturgical agenda of the church was conservative evangelical, the emphasis on Jewish symbols was nonetheless daring. Michelson should be viewed, in that respect, as a forerunner of a movement of Jewish Christian self-assertion, which became much larger and stronger in years to come.

Like several other patriarchs of the movement to evangelize the Jews during this period, Michelson was a rather bossy and assuming man. The publications of his mission boasted of his successes, ventures, and knowledge. The photographs accompanying the text regularly depicted him in the center of all events.[22] His enterprise relied heavily on his charisma and authority, and although it was successful during his lifetime, it collapsed after his death.

That Michelson acquired bad press in the missionary community should come as no surprise. He was both successful and assuming. In addition, Michelson did not have the usual curriculum vitae of a Jewish missionary. He came from Germany, whereas most other Jewish missionaries were from eastern Europe. He did not receive the same education and training that other leaders in the missionary movement obtained and did not graduate from the Moody Bible Institute or an equivalent program of evangelical higher education or missionary training. Rather, he held a doctorate degree from a prestigious German university. The German Jewish missionary became something of a white raven, an outsider in the community of missionaries and active converts.[23] He had little interaction with other missions or with the organized community of Jewish converts. He was active in neither the Hebrew Christian Alliance of America nor the Committee on the Christian Approach to the Jews. Some accused him of conducting some of his affairs in a manner that was not above question. In the mid-1940s the American Prophetic League, a non-Pentecostal premillennialist organization that was involved in sponsoring missionary activity among the Jews, circulated a letter to Jewish national and metropolitan organizations in which it listed its complaints against Michelson.[24] The director of the Prophetic League was Keith Brooks, a staunch supporter of the American Board of Missions to the Jews.

It is evident that antagonists within the missionary camp were willing—not for the first time—to approach the Jewish community in an attempt to discredit a missionary to whom they took great exception. Jewish activists took such accusations at face value, assuming that evangelical Christians would not defame one of their own in vain.[25] In viewing the accusations, one must note that they were not quite like those directed against missionaries in the earlier period. Michelson, according to Brooks, was indeed the lawyer he claimed to have been prior to his immigration to America and held a valid J.D. degree. Yet the latter questioned the former's claim to have been a court assessor in Prussia. Brooks had relied, however, on an official document supplied by the German government in June 1940, not a very good time to ask and obtain accurate information from the German government about a Jewish former lawyer.

Cohn and Michelson were certainly not the only Jewish evangelists who could be difficult to work with. The files of the Department of Jewish Evangelization of the Presbyterian Church, for example, contain a number of letters from Jewish missionaries, working under the auspices of the department, complaining and accusing one another of various misdeeds.[26] Christian charity and forbearance were values with which missionaries agreed in principle but found very difficult to practice. The directors of the various missions, as well as the different branches and centers, between the 1920s and the 1950s were mostly Jewish immigrants of eastern and central European origin. They underwent long and painful cultural and spiritual odysseys, as well as endless struggles during their careers as missionaries, and were strong willed, determined, and vigorous—qualities they had to nurture in order to endure the difficulties they experienced and to obtain and maintain the positions they reached. However, these characteristics made it difficult for them to cooperate with their fellow Jewish missionaries, to compromise, and to be tolerant of one another. Louis Goldberg, who was active in Jewish Christian organizational enterprises from the 1940s, recalls meetings of the leaders of the Hebrew Christian Alliance in the 1940s and 1950s. He remembered them as a group of strong, imposing, difficult patriarchs who could not, and would not, share power or prestige or yield to one another. It was almost an impossible mission for them to work together constructively.[27]

Did the rivalries between the different missions and missionaries hurt the cause of evangelizing the Jews or slow it down? The missions were, after all, aimed at promoting the same cause, or, in commercial terms, selling the same merchandise. Remarkably, the rivalries, successions, and opening of new missions did not damage the growth, expansion, or reputation of the missions during the period. It was a surprising fact that the establishment of the American Association for Jewish Evangelism, which tore workers and supporters from the American Board of Missions to the Jews, did not really harm the latter. Nor did the establishment of the succeeding mission come at the expense of any other mission, such as the Chicago Hebrew Mission, which was also headquartered in Chicago and continued to maintain its position as a large and vital mission. There was obviously room, as far as the resources of the evangelical community were concerned, for new missionary enterprises. The competition and rivalry often forced missions to search more energetically and dig more deeply to recruit supporters and obtain funding. Each mission established its own niche with its supporters, often in different areas or circles. The American Association for Jewish Evangelism, for example, found its base of support in Chicago, as did the Chicago Hebrew Mission. Michelson found his base of support in Los Angeles. It is a remarkable fact that, with all their petty rivalries, missions to the Jews not only endured but even enlarged the scope of their activities during the period that included the difficult years of the depression and World War II. One missionary enterprise in particular that thrived during the period from the 1920s to the 1950s was that of the Presbyterian Church in the U.S.A.

12

The Rise and Fall of the Presbyterian Mission to the Jews

Between the 1920s and the 1950s, the Presbyterian Church in the U.S.A. conducted the most extensive denominational efforts at evangelizing the Jews. The Presbyterian missionary enterprise left its mark on the Jewish-Christian relationship and on the emergence of Jewish Christian communities in America. Its history reflects some of the developments the Presbyterian Church (as well as other mainline churches) underwent during the period and the changes in its agenda. The history of the Presbyterian missions to the Jews further testifies to the developments that took place in the denomination's relationship with the Jewish people and the inner conflicts and the paths on which the denomination at large decided.

The Presbyterian efforts at converting Jews began as early as 1820, when the General Assembly of the Presbyterian Church accepted a trust that was to be used for the conversion of the Jews. From 1845 until 1908, the Board of Foreign Missions of the Presbyterian Church directed various attempts at evangelizing Jews, but most efforts in that early period were sporadic, short lived, and frustrating.[1] In 1908, influenced by premillennialist messianic views of the Jews and their role in history, the General Assembly of the Presbyterian Church in the U.S.A. instructed the Board of Home Missions to organize evangelization work on a national basis. It was only in 1920, however, when the Board of Home Missions of the Presbyterian Church organized the Department of Jewish Evangelization, that the Presbyterians began making a serious impact on the field of Jewish evangelism. The Presbyterian Church as a whole during the 1920s did not hold to a premillennialist messianic hope. This conviction was held by only a fraction of the members. Yet this premillennialist minority had a strong influence in shaping the missionary agenda of the denomination.[2] The character and ideology of the mission were undeniably premillennialist, emphasizing the central role of the Jews in the events that would lead to the messianic age. This view manifested itself in the writings of the directors of the department, in the journal the department published, and in its appeal to prospective converts.[3]

In the last decades of the nineteenth century and the first of the twentieth, the Presbyterian Church was torn between two conflicting points of view that struggled over hegemony in the denomination and over shaping its agenda and priorities. On one side stood the liberal modernists, who advocated a postmillennial view of history, accepted the Higher Criticism of the Bible, and advocated social reform; on the other stood the conservatives, who objected to the new academic theories of biblical exegesis, insisted on the need to be born again in order to be saved, and advocated a premillennialist understanding of the course of human history. Many Presbyterians were neither ardent modernists nor fundamentalists, yet the struggles between the liberals and the conservatives would strongly influence the Presbyterian missionary agenda and its evangelization enterprise among the Jews. The premillennialist belief that many conservative Presbyterians adopted during the last decades of the nineteenth century strongly affected their attitude toward the Jewish people. They tried to influence their denomination's agenda to include both pro-Zionist and missionary work aimed specifically at Jews. In May 1916, the General Conference of the Presbyterian Church adopted a statement calling upon the American government to use its power to promote in the international arena the building of a Jewish state in Palestine.[4] Another avenue for premillennialists to express their interest in the Jews and take an active part in their lives was through missionary work.

The department's first director, John S. Conning, was well aware that the premillennialist hope and its distinct view of the Jews would not suffice to make a case for a strong commitment from most members of his denomination to the field of Jewish evangelism. The motivation for nonpremillennialists to support missionary work among the Jews, he believed, had to be derived from social and cultural considerations. He therefore pointed to the social and intellectual realities of the Jews in America at the time as a good reason to support missionary work among them.[5] American Jewry was still essentially an immigrant community, he observed. Seeking to Americanize, Jews often abandoned their old way of life and turned their back on the observance of the Jewish religion.[6] Abandoning their old faith but not accepting Christianity, the Jews were, he cautioned, turning to all sorts of dangerous secular teachings such as socialism. This situation, the director of the mission believed, provided an enormous potential for missionary work among them.

In Conning's view, propagating Christianity among the Jews was every Christian's duty. He also wanted the members of his denomination to support the work of his department, but at the same time, he asked them to act as evangelists on a small scale. Many Presbyterians, he claimed, had Jewish neighbors or acquaintances whom they could evangelize. He presented his case in a book entitled *Our Jewish Neighbors*. It included a strong confirmation of premillennialist belief in the glorified future of the Jews in the messianic kingdom.

In his yearly reports to the General Assembly, Conning again emphasized "the state of crisis," as he understood it, in American Jewish religious life. Missionaries, he contended, had to be acquainted with Jews, their mentality and aspirations, and relate to them accordingly. The Department of Jewish Evangelization also had to educate Christians concerning their duty toward the Jews just as much as it had to concentrate on evangelizing Jews. He summarized the mission's task as follows: "The education of the church to an appreciation of the need and urgency of a Christian ministry among the Jews. The enlistment of Churches in every Synod and Presbytery in some form of definite service for their Jewish neighbors. The establishment of neighborhood Centers of Evangelism in large Jewish communities now unoccupied by any denomination. The enlisting and training of workers to understand the peculiar needs of the Jews and effectively reach them with the Gospel."[7] This statement reveals the mission's priorities and agenda. Wishing to expand as much as possible the scope of Jewish evangelism within the Presbyterian Church, and at the same time being aware of the limited resources of his department, Conning called upon Presbyterian churches and synods to lend a hand in evangelizing Jews. Pastors and congregants, he repeatedly asserted, should approach Jews and invite them to their churches.[8]

The statement also revealed the proposed means of evangelizing Jews. The Presbyterian Department of Jewish Evangelization, under the leadership of Conning, and later Conrad Hoffman, introduced a number of innovations. Like the American Board of Missions to the Jews, it set out to evangelize among the second generation of Jewish immigrants. The generation that had come of age between the 1920s and 1940s had grown up in America and had been educated in the American school system. The mission developed new tactics to approach this younger group of people and relate to its aspirations and needs. It abandoned the storefront mission, which was in use until the 1920s among missions to the Jews and included weekly preaching meetings, and welfare work among newly arrived immigrants. It set out to establish "community center" mission houses that often served as the beginning of Jewish Christian congregations. In order to gain the hearts of this new generation, missions had to provide facilities and services directed at the needs of American youth. Among other things, the Department of Jewish Evangelization established three camps to serve as summer and recreation resorts for Jewish children and youth: Bethany in Roseland, New Jersey; Camp Grey near Chicago; and Hebron-by-the-Sea in Long Beach, California.[9]

The centers provided, in addition to weekly or twice-weekly prayer meetings, educational, cultural, intellectual, and recreational activities. They appealed to a young generation of Jews who were already familiar with the YMCA clubs, which were becoming increasingly less Christian and evangelical in nature, or Young Men's Hebrew Association (YMHA) clubs. Jewish congregations, particularly those affiliated with the Conservative and Reform movements in American Judaism, also began offering educational and recreational services, including summer camps for children and youth. Jewish Community Centers (JCCS) were soon to follow, offering their own variety of educational, cultural, and recreational activities. Missions did not usually establish large centers like those of the YMHA. Yet, although their centers were usually smaller, they still signaled to prospective converts that the missions fit in with the process of Americanization.

Missions considered their gospel message to be universal, transcending details of locality, ethnicity, personal ambition, and fashion. But even while holding to this ideal, missions in this second phase of the movement to evangelize the Jews showed a vital ability to adapt themselves to the changing demographic, sociological, and cultural realities in the Jewish community. This ability to adapt and develop new organizational modes and means to reach prospective Jewish converts was part of what kept the missionary movement going and allowed it to thrive.

The Presbyterian Department of Jewish Evangelization operated centers in Brooklyn and the Lower East Side of New York, Newark, St. Louis, Chester, Omaha, Baltimore, Philadelphia, San Francisco, Los Angeles, and Chicago. At its peak in 1932, there were almost forty missionaries working full-time on behalf of Jewish evangelization in the Presbyterian missionary endeavor.[10] Clearly, Jewish missions were a high priority of the Board of Home Missions of the Presbyterian Church. They were the second-largest item on its budget, the first being work among African Americans. This undoubtedly reflected the set of values and beliefs prevalent in some Presbyterian circles during the period. The ideology of the Department of Jewish Evangelization was clearly that of the conservatives. Yet much of the department's success in recruiting support for its activity came from what were perhaps the majority of Presbyterians at the time who did not share the messianic hopes of the fundamentalist segment of the denomination but were open to the latter's agenda of evangelizing the Jews. The department's rhetoric in trying to muster support within the denomination well reflected that reality. Conning established a journal of Jewish evangelism, which was published from the late 1920s until the mid-1930s, entitled *Our Jewish Neighbors*, like his book. The name reflected Conning's aim to promote interest in Jews and Jewish evangelism among Presbyterians. The journal, which had an overtly premillennialist overtone, was illustrated with Jewish symbols and views of the Holy Land. It reported developments in the Jewish world and in the Jewish settlement in Palestine; its articles reflected the theological basis of Jewish missions, the messianic hope, and the dispensationalist understanding of the role of Jews in history.

The directors of the Department of Jewish Evangelization, as well as the office staff, were non-Jews, yet the field missionaries were Jewish. Individuals such as Aaron Kligerman in Baltimore, David Bronstein in Chicago, and Daniel Finestone in Philadelphia came from the immigrant community and often served as father figures to prospective converts who were, as a rule, a generation younger than themselves. Such missionaries received training in theological seminaries and, at times, at the Moody Bible Institute in Chicago. They were natural candidates to become ministers of what would develop into Jewish congregations.

Women played a vital, yet often unrewarded, role in the Presbyterian missionary enterprise. The directors of the department, as well as all the heads of the mission's different centers, were men. Yet, although many women were not even officially mission employees, they fulfilled a major role in its evangelization efforts. Wives of missionaries usually worked at least part-time and often full-time (and more) as actual missionaries. This reality comes up time and again when one reads sources relating to the day-to-day operations of the missions. Women's involvement was perhaps even more noticeable during this period than during the previous one. Esther Bronstein, for example, officially was merely the wife of the director of the mission's center in Chicago, but in actuality, she worked with her husband in operating Peniel, a missionary branch and a Jewish congregation that provided a wide range of communal activities. A firm, determined, and outgoing person, Esther shared many of her husband's responsibilities.[11] She was not a minister and did not conduct services or preach like her husband, but she worked with the congregants, especially women and youth, for whom she represented the mission and what it stood for. She also performed other tasks, including fund-raising. Esther's role in the mission is illustrated in a photograph of the participants in a summer camp the mission organized on Lake Michigan during the summers of the late 1930s and 1940s.[12] She is standing alongside her husband among campers and staff, her predominance in the group undeniable. The role of women such as Esther Bronstein in the mission could be compared to that of politicians' or diplomats' wives at the time. They were not officially part of the staff and were not on the payroll, yet they were expected to dedicate much time and energy to their husbands' vocation. Bronstein, for example, identified herself completely with the missionary center she and her husband founded and its cause; she took pride in its accomplishments and credited herself for its achievements.[13]

In the course of his work, Conning encountered all sorts of people and life stories. One such person was George Benedict, a rabbi who became an openly confessed Christian. Benedict grew up in Sheffield, England, and received his rabbinical training at Jews' College in London. In the 1910s he moved to the United States, where he served in a number of rabbinical positions. Conning met Benedict while the latter was still serving as a rabbi and was seeking to confess openly of the Christian faith. Conning was positively impressed by the engaging and earnest rabbi, sensed that the latter's conversion could help promote Christianity among the Jews, and took it upon himself to help him.[14] Benedict resigned his rabbinical position, confessed his faith openly, and moved with his family to Philadelphia, where Conning helped him to publish and circulate his book *Christ Finds a Rabbi*.[15] The best thing for Benedict to do, they both concluded, was to become a minister. But Benedict, who was in his mid-forties at the time of his conversion, found it too difficult to complete the long and demanding course of studies in a Protestant seminary, which included, among other things, the study of Greek. Benedict decided then to become a missionary. Conning had no desire to hire the former rabbi, whom he now considered to be too free spirited and restless. Benedict decided to establish his own missionary enterprise. At this point the director of the Department of Jewish Evangelization decided to distance himself from his protégé. It was one thing to help a respectful rabbi become a confessing Christian; it was another altogether to tolerate the establishment of a new, potentially embarrassing missionary enterprise. Conning was not afraid of the competition Benedict could pose to his mission. Rather, he objected to a one-person mission established at the whim of an eccentric convert and was concerned about the reputation of such an enterprise. Missionary leaders such as Conning prided themselves on running large, organized, and well-supervised missionary enterprises. He and others were working on professionalizing the field and building a cadre of well-trained, carefully selected missionaries. Well aware of the sometimes problematic reputation of missions of the earlier period, he resented the small mom-and-pop missions that he considered to cause more harm to the missionary cause than good. Since Benedict was a former rabbi, Conning was particularly afraid of the reaction of the Jewish community; what was expected to be a great triumph—the conversion of a rabbi and his joining the Christian ministry—was threatening to turn into a defeat: Jews who might well seize on the embarrassing missionary career of the apostate rabbi. The Jewish reaction to Benedict's conversion was indeed less than appreciative.[16] In the end, Benedict did not prove to be much of an embarrassment to the Presbyterian cause. His missionary enterprise did not last very long, and he found a new occupation in the emerging interfaith activity of teaching interested Christians about Judaism.

Relating to eccentric converts was not the only concern of the department. Presbyterian missionaries, like many other missionaries who worked among Jews, showed special concern during the late 1930s and early 1940s for the plight of Jews in Nazi Germany. They were especially worried about the way "non-Aryan" Christians, Jews who had accepted the Christian (Protestant) faith, were treated by the Nazis. These people were regarded by the racist German regime as Jews and, as such, were treated as second-rate human beings subject to a series of abuses. Conrad Hoffmann, who replaced Conning as the director of the Department of Jewish Evangelization in 1937, was particularly active in trying to stir up Presbyterian public opinion to come to the aid of the harassed.[17] In 1939, he published a tract entitled *To Be a Non-Aryan in Germany*, in an effort to appeal for funds for the support of converted Jews in Germany.[18] Hoffman described the oppressive acts of the German government against Jews and the grave situation of the Jewish population there. He then moved to describe the particular hardships of "non-Aryan" Christians. Jews worldwide were making an enormous effort to help their brethren in distress, he claimed, but aiding Christians was not included in their efforts. Presbyterians, he contended, should contribute to the task of relieving the stress of persecuted Christians of Jewish origin in Germany. He urged that contributions be sent to his office.

Hoffman pursued his efforts and published another brochure, entitled *Emergency*. This second publication concentrated on describing some of the work carried out by the department on behalf of non-Aryan Christians persecuted in Germany. The department indeed put much effort into securing the evacuation of a small number of individuals and families from Germany to the United States. Such a mission was not altogether easy; immigration visas were scarce, and Christian refugees, Aryan or not, did not necessarily receive any priority over Jewish ones.[19] Each immigration visa was a struggle, and the Department of Jewish Evangelization exercised much effort on behalf of each of the Jewish Christian families it brought over from Germany and helped to settle in the United States.[20] During the mid- and late 1930s, the indefatigable Hoffman came out with a plan for the evacuation of the Jews from Nazi Germany. Realizing that most Western countries were unwilling to accept the Jews, he suggested building temporary camps to house the refugees until countries could gradually absorb them. As can be imagined, nothing came of this plan.[21]

That Conrad Hoffman, whose official task was to evangelize American Jews, decided to concentrate on rescuing Christians in Germany should not be surprising. His concern for the plight of converted Jews resulted directly from his understanding of his role as a propagator of Christianity among Jews. Other missionaries to the Jews in Scandinavia, Britain, and America were engaged in similar efforts to rescue converted Jews. Historically, missionaries have been advocates, in their own societies, of the people they were trying to Christianize and, particularly, of those who did accept the faith. This goes back to Dominicans protesting the maltreatment of Indians in Spanish-dominated America and Protestant missionaries working in Native American reservations in the nineteenth-century United States who protested the expulsion of the latter from their lands.[22] Missionaries felt responsible for the people they evangelized. In addition, they could not remain indifferent to persecutions inflicted on newly converted Jews by representatives of a Western Christian culture. Such a situation undermined their missionary rhetoric about the nature of Christianity and its ameliorating effect on human beings. The humanitarian efforts on behalf of converted Jews helped them to save face and strengthened their claim that the wrongdoings inflicted on Jews were not done by true Christians. In their ideology, true Christians repudiated the Nazis, cared for Jews, and were kind to them. It is a noteworthy fact that missions to the Jews in America were among the bodies most concerned with the fate of Jews in Nazi Germany and, later on, in Nazi-occupied Europe. They tried to alert the evangelical community and were among the first to grasp the full scope of the horrors.[23]

Meanwhile, the department continued its program of expansion. Conning's and Hoffman's policy of running it was intended to extend the scope of the department's work above and beyond the financial resources and personnel it could obtain. They did that, among other things, by turning the missionary outposts into semi-independent enterprises, transferring to them some of the responsibilities of the central office, and encouraging them to obtain large parts of their support from local Presbyterian sources.[24] Some branches, such as those in Chicago or Philadelphia, even organized their own boards of directors. Such centers during the late 1930s and 1940s began a process of moving from missionary posts to semi-independent congregations.[25] Whereas the motivation of the directors of the department was at least partially pragmatic, the consequences of their policy moved beyond such considerations. In actuality, the Presbyterian Church sanctioned the creation of indigenous Jewish churches, among the first such communities since the first centuries of Christianity. A long-standing debate in the history of missions in America had concentrated on whether to advocate Christian tenets of faith per se or to promote Anglo-Saxon cultural norms as well.[26] However, the establishment of Jewish Christian congregations cannot be explained merely as a triumph of those who advocated allowing ethnic and cultural expressions different from those of the prevailing culture. The historical and theological obstacles to establishing Jewish congregations were much larger than those faced by other ethnic groups, and creating such congregations should be viewed as a revolutionary act. Ethnic churches in America were usually formed on the basis of race or language or were brought over from the Old World as part of the religious-cultural heritage of a specific ethnic group. The term "Jewish," however, denoted another religious community and heritage altogether. For many, both Jews and Christians, such congregations seemed a bizarre hybrid. Moreover, traditionally Christians considered "Judaizing" as heretical, a dangerous deviation from Christian norms. The Presbyterian pioneering of such congregations was thus more than implementing a "Christ not culture" missionary policy and yielding to ethnic preferences. It touched on very sensitive and bitter nerves in the history of Jewish-Christian relations and attempted to write a new chapter in its complicated and ambiguous annals. It is ironic that it was conservative Christians who implemented such a daring innovation.

Not all Jews who were persuaded by the Christian message preferred to join Jewish congregations, even with assurances that such separate congregations were acceptable. Some were comfortable in regular churches. Indeed, most Jews who were converted through Presbyterian evangelization joined regular Presbyterian churches in which they felt welcome. The vigorous denominational effort at Christianizing Jews in those years obtained impressive results; by the early 1930s there were about two thousand Jewish converts who became members of Presbyterian churches.[27]

Yet some Jewish converts welcomed the opportunity to form congregations of their own and to create their own atmosphere.[28] Jewish converts often felt lonely in mainline Protestant churches, in which the mores and manners were completely different from those of eastern European Jews. Esther Bronstein recounted in her lively biography some of the differences in customs and manners between Jewish Christians and Anglo-Saxon Protestants and the feeling of estrangement the former felt in the latter's environment.[29] Yet it is doubtful whether Jewish Christians would have found the courage to organize as independent congregations without the encouragement and support of Protestant church authorities. Many converted Jews of that period felt that they needed to prove to the larger Christian community that they were genuine Christian believers, hence the need for some sort of formal backing for their separate organizations.[30]

The Jewish congregations between the 1930s and 1950s were dependent not only administratively and financially on the guidance and goodwill of the Presbyterian Church and Presbyterian benefactors but theologically and liturgically as well. These congregations did not aspire to be Christian synagogues or an amalgamation of synagogues and churches. Leaders of Jewish Christian congregations made some timid attempts to create a uniquely Jewish variant of evangelical liturgical practices.[31] Prayers and hymns in the Jewish Christian congregations were, for the most part, traditional Protestant hymns sung in English. Theologically, the Jewish converts in these centers were conservative evangelicals with a strong premillennialist outlook emphasizing (like many non-Jewish premillennialists) the special mission of the nation of Israel. These congregations often avoided the use of overt Christian symbols, such as the cross, sometimes substituting them for Jewish symbols such as the Magen David, the Star of David. They celebrated (at least partially) Jewish holidays such as Hanukkah and Passover and interpreted them in Christian terms.[32]

The Jewish Christian congregations did offer Jewish converts to Christianity a supportive environment, a Jewish milieu in which conversion to Christianity was acceptable and, at the same time, a Christian congregation in which being Jewish and acting Jewish was the norm.[33] Earlier attempts to build Jewish Christian congregations had been sporadic and short lived. Among other reasons, such previous attempts did not enjoy the active support of approving Protestants. Many converted Jews felt that the evangelical community would not tolerate separate Jewish churches and would treat them with suspicion.[34] The Presbyterian decision to establish and help to sustain Jewish congregations was the first major Protestant granting of legitimization of such separate Jewish Christian centers.

At the same time that the Presbyterian Church was building a large network of missionary work among the Jews and was encouraging the establishment of Jewish Christian congregations, liberal winds were blowing in the denomination's corridors, which brought about a decreasing interest of the church as a whole in evangelizing Jews. Between the 1920s and 1950s, the denomination became increasingly liberal; in fact, it became one of the most progressive American Protestant churches. The number of conservative premillennialists in its midst, and particularly within its leadership, dwindled. Presbyterians joined in goodwill and dialogue groups with Jews.[35] Dialogue and mission did not go hand in hand. They conveyed two very different understandings on the part of Christians of the Jews and the appropriate way to relate to that people and their religious heritage.[36] Jewish participants in the goodwill and dialogue groups expressed their resentment toward the evangelizing of Jews and presented it as an obstacle to a decent, respectful relationship between the two religious communities. Presbyterian participants in the dialogue, including the likes of John Foster Dulles, began relating to Judaism as a legitimate religion on equal footing with Christianity within the American polity.[37] For Presbyterian participants in the dialogue the missions became an embarrassment.[38] Something of an interest group developed among Presbyterian liberal theologians and activists against the continuation of the missionary enterprise among the Jews. Following World War II, the rationale that Conning employed during the 1920s and 1930s to convince the rank-and-file Presbyterians that they should evangelize their Jewish neighbors seemed weaker than ever. Demographic changes had taken place in the Jewish community that made the picture of Jewish social reality Conning had drawn a generation earlier irrelevant. In the years following the war, Jews moved rapidly into the middle classes and suburbia, increasingly becoming more accepted socially, just as Judaism became in the 1950s one of the three "public religions" in America.[39] In New York, a Presbyterian and a Jewish congregation shared the same house of worship, serving as both the Village Presbyterian Church and the Village Temple. In the atmosphere created by such an experiment there was, needless to say, no room for the missionary agenda.[40] Changes were taking place on the theological level as well. Leading Protestant thinkers such as Reinhold Niebuhr, who, although not a Presbyterian himself, had much influence on theologians and intellectuals in that denomination, advocated the idea that Jews were not in need of the Christian gospel and had a strong vital religious tradition of their own to sustain them.[41] The liberal demand for the abandonment of missionary work among Jews gained momentum. During the 1940s and 1950s, the budget and staff for Jewish missionary work declined steadily as the denomination as a whole became increasingly less committed to the cause.[42] The situation somewhat mirrored the atmosphere in mainline churches in general, which, during the postwar period, was marked by debate between "ecumenicals" and "evangelicals."[43] However, it went one step further: for many conservative evangelicals, it was particularly important to evangelize Jews, and for many liberals, following Niebuhr's model, it was particularly important not to evangelize them.

In 1949, the Presbyterian Department of Christian Approach to the Jews, as it had been called since 1937, underwent a second change of name. Its title could not hold through an age of dialogue, as it implied that the only accepted approach to the Jews was a mission. Its new title was the Department for City and Industrial Work, which was perhaps euphemistic but somewhat less objectionable to the dialogue group. It was no longer the thriving energetic department that Conning and Hoffman had led from 1920 until just after World War II. The new director or rather field secretary was Aaron J. Kligerman, a veteran missionary who had worked for the department since 1922 and had directed Emmanuel Center in Baltimore for more than two decades. Kligerman wrote a number of tracts that promoted evangelization work among the Jews. One such book was *Sharing Christ with Our Jewish Neighbors*, which advocated the idea Conning had tried so hard to promote, namely, that not only professional missionaries but dedicated Christians in general should take it upon themselves to evangelize Jews. Appropriately, Kligerman provided information on the Jews and guidelines on how to propagate Christianity among them. Another book, *The Gospel and the Jew*, reflected the situation of the mission during the period, its struggles for survival and its attempts to reason with the rank-and-file Presbyterians for its raison d'être. Kligerman forcefully called upon his readers in this work to support missionary work among Jews. Basing his argument on the dispensationalist premillennialist understanding of the Jews and their role in history, he again insisted that it was a Christian duty to share the Christian gospel with the Jews.

Such efforts at advocating the missionary agenda could not reverse the tide. The department was becoming weaker and smaller and concentrated mostly on protecting the existing Jewish congregations, including Kligerman's Emmanuel Center in Baltimore. Even the statements of policies and goals the Board of National Missions published annually reflected a more ambivalent and hesitant attitude toward the evangelization of the Jews, very different from the assured enthusiastic statements of the 1920s and 1930s.[44] This rather shrunken department was soon to die out altogether as the liberal forces advanced their agenda even further. By 1960, missions to the Jews as a denominational agenda were being phased out.

Ironically, the Department of Jewish Evangelization's policy of encouraging the independence of the missionary centers and congregations ensured the perpetuation of a number of Jewish Presbyterian congregations. Congregations of Jewish Christians in Chicago, Philadelphia, and Los Angeles were still operating in the late 1990s. They continue to serve as missionary centers, relics of times when the Presbyterians were aggressively engaged in evangelizing Jews. Activists in the few Jewish Presbyterian congregations, such as Herbs Link, who continued Daniel Finestone's work in Philadelphia, militated within the Presbyterian Church against the abandonment of the missionary agenda and the granting of recognition to the Jewish religion as a tradition capable of providing spiritual comfort to its adherents. Their voice did not carry much weight, however, as the progressive attitude gathered strength. In the 1960s and 1970s, the ecumenical atmosphere and the interfaith dialogue advanced even further. In the 1970s and 1980s the Presbyterian Church was among the more progressive churches in recognizing Judaism as a valid religion in its own right, capable of offering its adherents spiritual meaning and moral guidance.[45] By then, for the denomination that had been the most active in converting the Jews half a century earlier, missions to the Jews represented a forgotten history.

The rise and fall of the Presbyterian missionary work among the Jews is, in many ways, an amazing development. Within a generation, the denominational policy reversed, and the task of propagating the Christian gospel among the Jews was completely abandoned. This turn of events reflected the larger developments in the mainline churches, which defined themselves more and more in liberal terms. The initial American Protestant impetus for missionizing the Jews came from a prophetic reading of the Bible and an understanding of the Jews as historical Israel, God's first nation. Such voices, which were strong in the early decades of the century among Presbyterians, had died out almost completely by 1960. Other views advocating recognition and dialogue gained the upper hand. Ironically, it was in an interim period in the history of the church, when the liberal agenda was gaining ground but not completely dominant, that the missionary work among the Jews flourished. The premillennialist views were on the decline yet still alive and very influential in shaping the Presbyterian agenda. The eventual decline of the missionary agenda was inevitable considering the prevailing trends in the denomination.

13

The Chicago Hebrew Mission

While the Presbyterian Church underwent major changes in its attitude toward the evangelization of the Jews, other organizations did not alter their agenda. One group whose premillennialist outlook did not change was the Chicago Hebrew Mission. Its path, choices, and character during the period from 1920 through 1965 can be instructive in understanding the development of the movement to evangelize the Jews in America during that time.

From its inception, the Chicago Hebrew Mission held to a premillennialist conviction and made use of its messianic hope in its evangelization rhetoric. Yet the mission's board of governors in its early years had been composed of representatives of different churches, and it declared itself to be interdenominational. Following the fundamentalist-modernist debates of the 1910s and 1920s, however, the mission clearly cast its lot with the conservative wing of American Protestantism; its leaders advocated a more literal reading of the Bible. The mission established close contacts with the Moody Bible Institute, a major fundamentalist institution during the period, whose directors' and teachers' opinions and ideals on Scripture and Christian life were close to that of the mission. The mission worked together with the program for training Jewish evangelists at the Moody Bible Institute, serving as a training post for prospective missionaries. The good relationship with the MBI helped the mission maintain its reputation as a solid and respectable conservative institution.

The mission, like other evangelization agencies directing their efforts toward Jews, went through a process of professionalization, hiring graduates of the Moody Bible Institute and organizing a training program for prospective missionaries. The Chicago Hebrew Mission was noted, even by its Jewish adversaries, for maintaining irreproachable standards of integrity.[1] From its early days, the mission had already been in the habit of providing yearly budgetary announcements with detailed accounts of revenues and expenditures and publishing lists of donors and donations periodically.[2]

The Chicago Hebrew Mission during the period under discussion was also set on expansion. In addition to its main work in Chicago, it opened a number of branches in St. Louis, Milwaukee, Chattanooga, Seattle, Tampa, and New Orleans, among others. Some of the branches, as in St. Louis and New Orleans, operated as affiliate missions. They were autonomous and did not depend economically on the parent mission but followed the Chicago Hebrew Mission's ideology and evangelization techniques, used its publications, and carried its name. The spirit of expansion characterized the leadership of Charles P. Meeker, who became director of the mission in 1923, and his successor, Milton Lindberg. During Lindberg's tenure as the director of the mission in the 1940s and 1950s, the mission employed about twenty missionaries in a number of branches and itinerant posts in addition to a number of staff members in its headquarters in Chicago.[3]

In addition to opening new branches, the Chicago Hebrew Mission organized and initiated a system of itinerant evangelization that it called "cultivation": workers of the mission periodically visited cities and towns that did not have a permanent branch of the mission. To make such missionary endeavors work more efficiently the mission organized local "prayer groups." These were volunteer supporters in the various towns and cities that were "cultivated" and consisted of people committed to the cause of the mission, who prayed on its behalf and contributed money regularly. The itinerant missionaries would then coordinate their work with the local groups of volunteers. Such groups were established and "cultivation" was carried out in places such as Grand Rapids and Muskegon, Michigan; Akron, Ohio; Indianapolis, Indiana; and Kansas City, Missouri (where the mission eventually opened a branch), as well as in a number of cities in New England, New Jersey, and Iowa. Some of these towns had relatively small Jewish communities that did not, from the mission's point of view, justify the establishment of permanent local branches. But the Chicago Hebrew Mission could not afford to install full-time missionaries in these towns, and sending itinerant missionaries was the best it could do in its attempt to evangelize Jews residing in these places. It was also a means of promoting grassroots support. During the 1960s the mission abandoned its "cultivation" program, but prayer groups in some places continued to operate and serve as local support groups for the mission's activities well into the 1990s.

The Chicago Hebrew Mission was the largest mission to the Jews in America at the turn of the century. By the 1930s, although still dominant in the field of missions to the Jews and although it actually grew in size and activity, it was no longer the largest and played a secondary role in comparison with the larger, more dynamic missions that adapted themselves better to the changes in Jewish society in America: the American Board of Missions to the Jews and the Department of Jewish Evangelization of the Presbyterian Church in the U.S.A. The mission did not operate cultural community centers the way the Presbyterian Church or the American Board of Missions to the Jews did during that period. Neither did it encourage the establishment of Jewish congregations. It showed resourcefulness in enlarging the mission's geographical scope of activity, but its methods of approaching Jews remained conservative.

In Chicago, the mission located itself in central Jewish neighborhoods. It moved in the early 1950s from the older Jewish immigrant neighborhood southwest of the center of town, where it had been located since its establishment in the late 1880s, to Rogers Park, which, after World War II, became one of the central Jewish neighborhoods in the city. The mission relied in its work on approaching Jews through direct contacts. Its missionaries would visit Jews at home or work trying to interest the latter in reading the gospel and some of the mission's tracts.

Much of the fund-raising for the mission was done through the pages of its journal, the *Jewish Era*, and through its workers' speaking in churches on the mission and its cause. In later years, missionaries, particularly those working outside Chicago, were often expected to raise their own salaries. They received or solicited invitations from churches to speak, present the mission's cause, and call on the congregants to support it. The presentations were usually followed by collections that paid for the missionaries' salaries and expenses. This system of financing missionary work continued in Jewish evangelization well into the 1990s. It worked to sustain the missionaries and was often the only means through which missions such as the Chicago Hebrew Mission could maintain missionaries and at times expand their work to additional areas.

In some missions this system by which missionaries raised finances necessary for their maintenance and work occasionally helped to promote secession and factionalism. Field missionaries realized that they could cut their ties with the parent mission and still find the support necessary to carry out their work. In the case of the Chicago Hebrew Mission, the parting of the ways between the parent organization and some of its field missionaries was done on a friendly basis. The Midwest Messianic Fellowship in St. Louis and the International Messianic Fellowship of Chattanooga, Tennessee, parted from the mission in the 1930s and became independent organizations. These missions retained good relationships with their former parent mission, cooperating at times on various issues such as the publishing and distribution of tracts. The directors of the Chicago Hebrew Mission were often invited to visit and lecture at their former missions.

While the American Board of Missions to the Jews had a distinctly Jewish character (its directors and missionaries were almost always Jewish), the Chicago Hebrew Mission took a different course. In its early decades, it hired Jewish missionaries and even promoted them to positions of responsibility within its midst.[4] One of its noted missionaries at the turn of the century was, for example, Bernhard Angel, an eastern European Jew who worked among the Jewish immigrants in Chicago. But that policy was later reversed. Milton Lindberg, one of the mission's leaders during the period, expressed the mission's opinion when he stated that evangelization among the Jews was better served by non-Jewish evangelists.[5] Jews propagating the Christian gospel among their brethren provoked instant animosity and thus rejection of the Christian message, he contended. "It is the opinion of many . . . that the Gentile Christian has the best initial approach to the unconverted Jew, since he has not 'changed his religion for money,' as Jewish believers are accused of doing. . . . Jews have no prejudice against Gentiles as Christians, but against Jews who have become Christians there is strong antagonism which makes it more difficult to establish friendly contact."[6]

Lindberg had a point, as Jews often did react with anger, at least on a first encounter, toward those of their brethren who became missionaries. Non-Jews often were treated with more tolerance and respect when approaching Jews because Christian gentiles were expected to propagate their own faith. The mission, however, was working against the tide, since almost all missions to the Jews during the period were operating with Jewish evangelists. Jewish missionaries, although inspiring anger and bitterness at times, also provided for the newly converted an example of Jews who had embraced Christianity—indeed proof that such an option was possible. They often served successfully as father or mother figures to a younger generation of potential converts. Lindberg, accordingly, acknowledged that Jewish converts could participate in the second stage of the conversion process, offering example and reassurance to the newly converted.

In its early decades, the CHM was noted for its female director. But after Tryphena Rounds's retirement as director of the mission, women no longer held positions as directors in the mission or any of its branches. Yet women continued to hold central responsibilities, serving as field missionaries, carrying out administrative tasks, and editing the mission's journal. Women also sat on the mission's board of trustees. In 1937, when the Chicago Hebrew Mission celebrated its fiftieth anniversary, it proudly published the photographs of its trustees; out of nineteen members, three were women.[7] The situation, however, changed during Lindberg's tenure as director. By the 1950s, women no longer sat on the mission's board of trustees, and none joined the board until 1992. The mission, of course, employed women as missionaries; as a matter of fact, women made up the majority of missionaries during the period.[8] The pattern was in line with the position of women in missions to the Jews during that period: they served as evangelists and on the missions' staff in a vital manner but were not, as a rule, directors of missions or members of the board of trustees.

Although the CHM affirmed its conservative character and aligned itself with nonliberal Christians, who were often as conservative on social and economic issues as on theological and cultural ones, the salaries and even the lodging arrangements in the mission headquarters were run on an egalitarian and communal basis. All employees lived together in one building, and the mission even kept a communal kitchen and dining room. Needless to say, salaries were extremely low, as the mission actually provided its workers with most of their needs. The CHM was not necessarily innovative in that respect. This was often the way foreign missions were run, and at times, some home missions as well. Such a structure was organized in order to save money and enable the mission to carry out as many programs and keep as large a staff as possible within its budgetary limits. The mission directors and workers, being conservative American Christians, were unaware that the way the mission ran was in practice communal, one might even say kibbutzlike or communistic.

One feature the Chicago Hebrew Mission did share with other missions to the Jews of the period was the authoritarian, and at times imposing, nature of its directors. Like several of his contemporary missionary patriarchs, Lindberg, who became the mission's director in 1938, ran the mission with an iron fist. Some of the older, retired members of the mission remembered Lindberg (and his wife, Beth) directing all details of their work as well as their kibbutzlike life. In some ways his rule was felt even more strongly than that of other authoritarian directors of missions during the period, since in other missions employees did not necessarily have to live under the same roof with a pedantic, imposing director. In that particular mission Lindberg would even inspect the amount of hot water the missionaries were using for their weekly baths.[9]

In 1948, after more than two decades of evangelizing Jews, Lindberg wrote a guidebook for missionaries. The book, *Witnessing to Jews: A Handbook of Practical Aids*, enjoyed considerable popularity. It was in print for more than two decades and was printed throughout the years in six different editions, an indication that Lindberg's methods were alive and well during the period. The book is reminiscent, in its organization and agenda, of other such missionary publications. The director of the Chicago Hebrew Mission began his tract by making a case for the propagation of the Christian gospel among the Jews, which was "of supreme importance."[10] Basing his argument on the dispensationalist messianic worldview, he explained: "Only the sowing of the Gospel seed in their hearts can give them the basis of knowledge for their confession [of the Christian faith] during the time of Jacob's trouble. We can only sow that seed in their hearts before the rapture of the Church. Since the rapture is imminent, the evangelization of Israel is of immediate urgency."[11] The end of this era, Lindberg believed, was approaching, and the eschatological events were soon to begin. The Jews, in order to fulfill their role during the apocalypse, needed to be familiar with the gospel, so they could recognize the truth of the Christian message when the messianic events took place and be ready to accept Jesus as their Messiah during that time.

Lindberg offered his readers basic knowledge on Judaism and Jews, which, he thought, was a precondition for successful evangelism; he then went further to give potential evangelists firsthand advice on how to approach Jews. They should, he advised his readers, treat Jews with compassion as a prerequisite to persuading them of the truth of the Christian gospel. The experienced missionary cautioned his readers not to use certain terms and expressions when talking with Jews and recommended which terms to use instead. "The expression 'You Jews' is offensive to some Jews. It is better to use 'the Jewish People,' or to refer to Jews as 'Our Jewish friends,'" he recommended.[12] Lindberg also shared his experience concerning how to convince the Jews of the truth of the Trinity and of the Christian messianic hope. For the mission's director these two components of faith were inseparable.

Lindberg also referred in his book to possible Jewish objections to Christianity that propagators of the faith were likely to confront. One of the major issues was that Jews identified Christians with their persecutors and blamed the Christian faith for the abuses inflicted on them throughout their history as a minority group in Christian countries. Lindberg, like most missionaries, thought it essential for missionaries to disassociate themselves from the wrongdoings and make a point that true born-again Christians treated Jews with nothing but goodwill and compassion.[13] He ends his guide to future missionaries with such practical advice as when to visit Jews and how to engage them in conversation.

Lindberg also published a series of books on biblical prophecies, Christian eschatology, and the role of the Jewish people in the advancement of the messianic age. The most popular among them was *The Jew and Modern Israel in the Light of Prophecy*. First published in 1930, it was later revised and edited to bring it up to date with the developments in the Land of Israel. Lindberg was enthusiastic about the events there and interpreted them as a prelude to the messianic age. The settlement of hundreds of thousands of Jews in Palestine, the building of new villages and towns, the rejuvenation of the Hebrew language, and, later on, the birth of the state of Israel in 1948 were all "signs of the time" that indicated that this era was ending and the Messiah was to arrive very soon. It gave a stronger impetus to the missionary zeal and a sense of purpose in propagating Christianity among the Jews. Lindberg and his fellow missionaries believed that they were evangelizing not merely an ordinary group of people, a good aim in itself, but a unique nation that had a special task in history. The mission's purpose was to see to it that the nation of Israel really fulfilled that task by providing it with the knowledge of the Christian gospel that would make its impact in the messianic age. Almost all missions to the Jews in America during this period held to a premillennialist conviction that played a central part in their evangelization rhetoric, but in the Chicago Hebrew Mission, where Blackstone's heritage was alive and well, this ideology was particularly strong.

An ardent premillennialist and pro-Zionist organization, the CHM supported the state of Israel in its struggles against the Arabs and viewed the Jewish settlement of the Land of Israel as biblically sanctioned, something with which most Arabs could not agree. It was therefore somewhat surprising that the mission hired an Arab evangelist to spread the gospel among the Jews. Shukri Haik was born in Hammas, Syria, in 1899, to a family of Arab evangelical Christians. At age thirteen his family immigrated to America and settled in New Jersey, and Shukri attended the Northern Baptist Seminary. He served subsequently as a pastor in a number of congregations and then in World War II, as a chaplain in the United States Army. A premillennialist who believed in God's special plans for the Jewish people, Haik was invited by Milton Lindberg to join the Chicago Hebrew Mission and become its representative in Milwaukee. Haik had no problem advocating the idea that the return of the Jews to Palestine was a prerequisite before the return of Christ and the beginning of the millennial kingdom. During his many years of work in Milwaukee, Haik, the Arab Christian, was known for his annual Seders, demonstrations that he performed of the yearly Passover-night Jewish celebrations. From Haik's point of view his work among the Jews was an expression of devotion, goodwill, and appreciation of them. At times, his work included helping individual Jews and performing acts of kindness such as visiting sick people. Haik's positive position toward Zionism and the state of Israel and his decision to dedicate long years of his life to spreading the Christian gospel among the Jews were quite extraordinary for an Arab Christian. Even Arabs who were influenced by evangelical Christianity did not always favor the state of Israel, at least not openly, nor did they wish to engage in evangelizing Jews. Occasionally Haik had problems explaining his positive view of Zionism and Israel to Arab relatives.[14]

The CHM's interest in Zionism and the development of the Jewish settlement in the Land of Israel influenced its missionary agenda. Although it did not extend its work during the period to Jewish communities outside the United States, the mission decided to carry out missionary work in Palestine. There the representatives of the mission were Jews who made their home there or chose to live in the country for a number of years. The first such missionary, Hayman Jacobs, settled in Palestine in the early 1920s. Jacobs received attention in the missionary community following a tract he wrote, *Nationality and Religion*, which addressed an issue that has constantly preoccupied the missionary community. Jacobs expressed his opinion that Jews who have accepted Jesus as their Savior have joined the body of true believers in Christ and should not establish a church of their own. This was the opinion of the Chicago Hebrew Mission's people, who advocated the idea that Jews should join regular evangelical churches and not form their own congregations. Jacobs's opinion was published by the mission's organ and republished when such a debate erupted again a few decades later.[15]

In the 1950s and early 1960s the Chicago Hebrew Mission carried out a unique and rather daring evangelization enterprise in Israel. Its representative in the country, Jacob Blum, operated a radio program, intended to missionize Jews. Radio broadcasting in Israel was not open to free competition. There was only one official, government-run broadcasting station and an additional military station. Blum prepared the programs in his home in Jerusalem and then sent them to Monte Carlo, from where they were broadcast to Israel. In his program, which included music, he gave a post office box number in Jerusalem where interested listeners could send inquiries. Once the contact was established, Blum could then initiate further correspondence and personal evangelism.[16] The Voice of Hope, as the program was called, operated until the 1960s.

In 1953, the mission officially changed its name to the American Messianic Fellowship. The change of name was representative of the changes the mission underwent and the character it acquired. Long before the change of name, it had operated outside the Chicago area and saw itself as a national organization. Although it was headquartered in Chicago, its previous name had become inadequate and misleading. The new name also reflected the mission's commitment to the premillennialist messianic conviction and its conservative outlook on Christianity. In addition, the term "mission" was removed and replaced by the name "fellowship," which sounded friendlier and less offensive to Jews.

The Chicago Hebrew Mission remained from its inception the epitome of conservative evangelical respectability, and no scandal of any sort, including quarrels and secessions, ever tainted its good reputation.[17] It was, however, the more daring, innovative, and, at times, controversial missions such as the American Board of Missions to the Jews (and later on Jews for Jesus) that attracted more attention and made more of an impact on the field of Jewish evangelism. The more conventional, conservative, and reserved missions were often left in the shade.

14

American Missionary Work in Israel

The establishment of the state of Israel in 1948 made a strong impression on American evangelicals. It enhanced their messianic hopes and inspired them to devote more energy and personnel to evangelize Jews in the newly formed state. The American missionary experience in Israel in those years was in many ways unique and opened a new chapter in the history of the Jewish-Christian encounter. Contrary to all expectations, Christians were evangelizing in the independent Jewish state. The situation that developed was thus marked by paradoxes that often resulted from the gap between the missions' initial ideals and expectations and their actual modes of activity in Israel in its first two decades. The missionaries encountered unparalleled situations and found unprecedented means to carry out their agendas.

American missionary endeavors in the Holy Land, motivated by a premillennialist messianic view of Jews and their role in history, began as early as the 1820s, when the first American missionaries arrived in what was then called Palestine.[1] A renewed interest in converting the Jews and in carrying missionary work to the Holy Land took place in the late nineteenth century with the spread of dispensationalism. Missionary groups such as the Christian and Missionary Alliance and the Hope of Israel that were influenced by dispensationalist premillennialist beliefs sent missionaries to work among the Jews in Palestine.[2]

The First World War and the Balfour Declaration made a great impression on American premillennialists, whose missionary work in the Holy Land intensified.[3] In addition to the renewed interest in the Jewish return to Zion, the years 1918–48 were ones of prosperity and security for the Christian missionary community in what was then Palestine. The British who governed the country saw it as their duty to protect Christian interests, including the free operation of missions.[4] A number of American Protestant groups made their early beginnings in the country during these favorable years of British rule. These included the Southern Baptists, the Church of God, the Church of the Nazarene, and missionary agencies such as the American Board of Missions to the Jews. Groups that were already represented in the country, such as the Christian and Missionary Alliance, enlarged the scope of their activity.

This is not to suggest that missionaries did not face difficulties in propagating the Christian gospel to the Jewish population of British Palestine.[5] The prevailing ideology among Jewish immigrants in the 1920s to 1940s was Zionist, and to the vast majority Zionism seemed a fulfilling, preferable alternative to a religious worldview. They had no interest in missionaries whom many also saw as representative of the old hateful attitude of Christians toward Jews. Secular Zionists were, according to some accounts, even more hostile in their reactions to attempts to evangelize them than the more traditional Orthodox Jews.[6] Missions could not operate in Tel Aviv, the capital of secular Zionism, and centered their operation in cities with mixed populations such as Jerusalem, Haifa, Jaffa, and Tiberias. Many missions that had originally intended to evangelize Jews, such as the Christian and Missionary Alliance, placed increasing emphasis on evangelizing Arabs.

Circumstances changed considerably in 1948. A new wave of missionary enthusiasm and interest in Israel swept over premillennialist circles in America following the establishment of the state of Israel and its war with the Arabs in 1948–49. Many conservative Christians who adhered to a premillennialist faith had viewed the creation of an independent, internationally recognized Jewish state, and its somewhat surprising survival and victory over its Arab neighbors, as "signs of the time," an indication that history was unfolding according to plan and that the eschatological drama was soon to begin.[7]

The interest in and enthusiasm for Israel strongly enhanced the wish to evangelize the new nation. "Suddenly everybody seems to be 'called of God' to go to Jerusalem as a missionary!" wrote Joseph Cohn, the director of the American Board of Missions to the Jews, one of the larger missions to the Jews in America at the time.[8] George T. B. Davis, the director of the Million Testaments Campaigns, a mission headquartered in Philadelphia, wrote even more enthusiastically: "We desired to have further personal part in sowing the good seed throughout the length and breadth of that Land that has become one of the strategic mission fields of the world. Long centuries ago God chose that Land and that People to be His own, and we believe this is His appointment time to plant His Word there."[9] The American missionary position changed in the period following the establishment of Israel. Whereas before 1948 American missionary activity in Palestine was overshadowed by that of the British, who operated larger and more dominant missions, the situation now reversed. After World War II, Americans became the dominant force in Christian missions worldwide, directing more personnel and money than any other nation in the field.[10] By that time the evangelical messianic interest in Israel was much greater in America than Britain. The American missionary predominance in Israel manifested itself during the 1950s and 1960s in a number of ways. American missionaries became the leading figures in the missionary community; operated the larger, more aggressive, and more visible missions; and established, at times, a close relationship with the Israeli government.

The status of missions in Israel had changed considerably since the British period. The new state chose, to the surprise of many, to maintain the legal situation in religious matters as it existed during the British period, including the Christian right to carry on evangelization work in the country.[11] Missionaries, as well as Orthodox activists in Israel, expected the Jewish state to make different choices and ban attempts to evangelize Jews. Jews have traditionally viewed attempts to evangelize them as humiliating and hostile. But Israel's leaders thought differently. Christian opponents of Zionism had argued since the late nineteenth century that a Jewish state in Palestine would act against Christian interests and would harass Christian institutions.[12] The issue of protecting Christian rights and privileges arose often in the discussions that preceded the establishment of the state of Israel. From its inception, the Israeli government decided, therefore, to make a very strong point that it was protecting Christian rights and institutions, including not only freedom of worship but also property rights, tax exemptions, and the freedom to evangelize.[13] In doing so they sought, with some success, to reassure Christian churches that a Jewish state did not work against their old freedoms and privileges in the country.

The leaders of the new country did not wish to be blamed by foreign governments and churches or by the foreign press for restricting Christian liberties or allowing antimissionary activists to harass Christian representatives or deface their property. Allowing Christian missionaries to propagate the Christian gospel in Israel was, they believed, a small price to pay for establishing a record as a free, democratic, Christian-friendly country. In one extreme case in the early 1960s, when Orthodox Jewish resentment against the large and visible missionary activity in the country was growing, the police were sent to break up antimissionary demonstrations. Demonstrators were arrested and prosecuted.[14] One might conclude that while there was some antimissionary sentiment in Israel, the government chose to permit and even protect missionary activity.

From the point of view of the missions, however, there was one catch in the tolerant and protective government policy. The Israeli government took it upon itself to keep the status quo as far as missionary activity was concerned, which it interpreted to mean keeping the situation exactly as it existed before the establishment of the new state. Old, established missions could carry on their work freely, but new missions were not allowed officially to operate and could not be legally registered. Moreover, as far as the old missions were concerned, the number of missionaries given residence and work permits in the country was restricted to the number of missionaries employed prior to the birth of the state.

Many in the American evangelical community strove to evangelize in Israel and were not deterred by the administrative restrictions. American missions and independent evangelists who sought to work in the country found ways to overcome these bureaucratic obstacles. But administrative difficulties at times shaped the character of the mission's work. New missions discovered that they could operate in Israel, hiring and employing local residents or Jews who could come to the country and enjoy the privileges of new Jewish immigrants: automatic citizenship and, of course, right to reside and work. Missionaries could also come as tourists and carry out their evangelizing work in the country, stamping their passports to prolong their tourist status after three months and traveling back and forth, in and out of the country, in order to retain that status after nine months of residence.[15] The government did not wish to cause an international incident by refusing entry to respectable American citizens, let alone to expel Americans from the country. Missions had to contend with other bureaucratic problems as well. When the American Board of Missions to the Jews decided to buy an apartment in Haifa as a residence for its missionary there, it could not register the apartment in its own name, since it did not have legal standing in the country. It was therefore registered in the name of the mission's director, Daniel Fuchs.[16] Despite such administrative difficulties, a number of American missions, as well as many independent missionaries, began work in Israel in the 1950s, and some of the older missions in the country enlarged the scope of their activity considerably.

The socioeconomic and demographic situation became more favorable to the operation of missions after the birth of the state. Israel's sociological, cultural, and ideological infrastructure had changed dramatically since the 1920s, 1930s, and early 1940s. The population had grown rapidly, so that the country no longer consisted only of the Yishuv—the more ideological Jewish community of the British period—but was shaped by the mass immigration of the late 1940s and 1950s, which tripled the Jewish population of the country within a mere decade. Most immigrants were either Holocaust survivors from eastern Europe or immigrants from Middle Eastern or North African countries.[17] The percentage of the latter group within the population grew considerably and made up almost half the Jewish population by the early 1960s. Absorbing mass waves of immigrants, the country, during the late 1940s and early and mid-1950s, resorted to the rationing of food. In addition, there was a severe shortage of housing; new immigrants often resided in *maabarot*, or temporary lodgings, and shantytowns where people spent years without paved roads, electricity, running water, or heating. Immigration also brought to Israel mixed couples and some Jews who had already converted to Christianity in Europe or North America. Missionaries found that the new Israelis were more open to the presence of missionaries in their midst, although there was still resentment and anger.[18] It was against this background of an immigrant society that missions operated and left their mark.

Bureaucratic obstacles and the economic deprivation did not deter missionaries. Many American evangelicals were eager to work in Israel and propagate the gospel among its people. During the 1950s the directors of the American Board of

Missions to the Jews visited Israel or sometimes sent investigators to inspect the situation there. They concluded that missionary activity had grown so considerably that there was actually a surplus in missionary presence in the country. According to some calculations, Israel was the most evangelized country on earth.[19] Official sources reported a couple of hundred Christians engaging in missionary work in the country, which claimed a Jewish population of 630,000 at the beginning of the period and not much more than 2 million at its end.[20]

The presence of missionaries varied from one part of the country to another. Jerusalem during the 1950s was proportionately the most evangelized city on earth; dozens of enthusiastic American evangelical missionaries, among others, were evangelizing a population that grew in the Israeli part of the city during the period from 80,000 to 180,000. Missionary activity grew so considerably that in some areas of the country, such as Jerusalem, Jaffa, and Haifa, missions became part of the scenery. Charles Kalisky, who represented the American Board of Missions to the Jews in Jerusalem, wrote in a report he sent back to the board:

> The number of missionaries stationed in the country permanently and temporarily is relatively larger than in any other mission field in the world. As a result, the sum of money contributed for the work there is out of all proportion to the size of the country, which is somewhat smaller than the state of New Jersey. The fact remains that in the city of New York alone the number of Jews is three times the entire population of the State of Israel. Yet the number of missionaries working among the Jews in New York is no more, and possibly less, than the total number working in the city of Jerusalem alone.[21]

Kalisky also noted that many missionaries who were working in Israel never learned Hebrew properly, were unfamiliar with Israeli ways and manners, and had little or no knowledge of Judaism.[22] Joseph Cohn complained about what he considered to be the unprofessional attitude of many missionaries in Israel. "The basic difficulty is that these well meaning 'missionaries' . . . undertake to do whatever they wish, when they wish, and how they wish, all without supervision from anybody." Indeed, "the whole situation," claimed Cohn, the authoritarian director of a well-organized mission, "is a mess."[23] Cohn particularly objected to the fact that many missionaries were unaffiliated with established missions but rather came on their own initiative and operated on their own. Harold Sevener, who studied in Jerusalem in 1959–60 and later became the director of the American Board of Missions to the Jews, claimed that many missionaries during the period did not know Hebrew well and that some evangelical congregations met on Sundays, which alienated Jews from the services and what they represented. This, however, was more common for nonevangelical Protestant churches. Many American evangelical churches in Israel shifted during the 1950s to a Saturday

Sabbath service. One case in point was the Southern Baptist Convention, whose congregations in Israel moved their Sabbath on a pragmatic basis from Sunday to Saturday.

The American Board of Missions to the Jews, like many other missionary societies, was eager to evangelize in Israel. Not being represented in Israel in 1948, it could not officially register in the country and send missionaries there. It searched for Israeli residents who could carry on its work legally. It hired Haim Haimoff-Bar David, a Christian Jew, to represent the mission in Jerusalem. Born in Bulgaria, Haimoff had accepted the Christian evangelical faith as a student in Switzerland before World War II and was well respected by other Jewish Christians in the country, a fact that undoubtedly prompted the mission's decision to offer him the job. The financial arrangements and payments the American mission offered its local missionary were very generous.[24] The missions paid an American salary that was above the standards common among Israelis at the time. Haimoff, however, did not remain for long with the American Board; the reasons for the parting of ways were not disclosed.[25] The demand for missionaries was high, and he was soon hired by the American Association for Jewish Evangelism, a missionary organization headquartered in Chicago that was founded in the 1940s by missionaries who had broken away from the American Board. Since these two organizations were less than friendly with each other, the fact that Haimoff did not get along with the American Board did not count against him. Like the American Board, this organization, too, wanted to be represented in Israel and participate in evangelizing its people.

The American Board of Missions to the Jews also hired Jewish Christian residents of Israel in Haifa and Tel Aviv to carry out missionary work on its behalf in those cities. At one time its representative in Haifa, Peter Gutkind, was harassed by Jewish antagonists. That the mission's historian recorded the incident and highlighted it as the only time that such an event happened during the long years of the mission's operations in a number of Israeli towns suggests that missionaries did not have to fear for their lives or property and could live and work quite freely in Israel.[26] Actual physical attacks on missionaries or their property were rare. But emotional harassment did occur and included occasional incidents of unpleasant phone calls or letters. This was typical of the kind of harassment carried out in Israeli society during the 1950s and 1960s, particularly by members of the ultra Orthodox *haredi* community.[27] Such harassment was intended to express resentment and intimidate but almost never to inflict bodily injury. The situation was somewhat more difficult in Jerusalem, where antimissionary sentiments were the strongest.[28] On one occasion, two missionaries, a man and a woman, decided to attend an antimissionary meeting that took place in a synagogue in the *haredi* community of Mea Shearim. After revealing their identity, the two were subjected to abuse, both verbal and physical. But even in this case, they were not seriously injured, emerged in no need of medical treatment, and were soon at large to tell their story of near martyrdom. In actuality, cursing the missionaries, pushing them, and throwing their hats to the ground were the means for angry *haredi* people to express their resentment.[29]

Another missionary organization that carried out extensive work in Israel was Arthur Michelson's Hebrew Christian Witness to Israel. Like virtually all American evangelical missionaries to the Jews, Michelson was enthusiastic about the Zionist movement and its achievements. He was absolutely ecstatic about the birth of the state of Israel, viewing it, as did other American premillennialists, as a fulfillment of biblical prophecies.[30] The mass Jewish immigration to Israel opened up new avenues of missionary work for him. He established his Israeli center in Musrara, an old neighborhood in Jerusalem that between 1948 and 1967 was on the border between Israel and Jordan and was inhabited by poor immigrant families from North Africa. Michelson's mission, like others in Israel at the time, carried out relief work among the needy new immigrants and among youth and children as well. This aspect of missionary operation caused much resentment in Israeli society, particularly among the Orthodox.

As the government was unwilling to restrict missionary activity, some antimissionary activists realized that the missions were cashing in on neglect and deprivation in the poor neighborhoods of Israel. "It is the Israeli public who is responsible for the growth of the missions," wrote A. J. Brawer in *Hatsophe*, the Orthodox daily. Pointing to negligence in the face of poverty and deprivation, he contended that Jews should blame themselves and not the missionaries.[31] During the 1950s, antimissionary Jewish activists established social and educational organizations that aimed at working among children and youth in poor neighborhoods. One of the better known among them was Keren Yeladenu ("a Foundation for Our Children" in Hebrew), which opened youth clubs in neighborhoods such as Musrara. Another organization established and run by Orthodox Jews to combat missionary activity was Achiezer, which operated in Haifa and the vicinity. Like Keren Yeladenu, it concentrated its efforts on "the rescue of Jewish children from the mission." Its pamphlet lamented: "Openly in Jerusalem and the cities of Judea . . . thousands of Jewish children are led astray by the missionaries without anyone challenging or stopping them. Was it not enough that tens of thousands of our children were burned in Treblinka and Auschwitz that the missions have preferred stakes to burn the sons and daughters of the remnants of this nation?"[32] In the same vein, the chief rabbinate of Israel produced an antimissionary proclamation. "Terrible news, devastating the mind and the soul[,] arrives on the missionary menace . . . the Satan sent missionaries including converted Jews who betray their roots, and the smoke and ashes of the millions of saints, who burned in the ovens and suffocated in the gas chambers."[33] The rabbinate was an official government agency, yet its antimissionary declaration should not be surprising. The Israeli government did not speak with one voice when it came to the missions. The government policy on the whole protected the missionaries and the Christian right to propagate the gospel in Israel. Secular government agencies, such as the Foreign Office, the Ministry of the Interior, the Ministry of Commerce, and the police, insisted that missionaries be given complete freedom of operation and be protected.[34] But officials of the Ministry of Religious Affairs, such as Saul Colby, complied with the governmental policy half-heartedly, if not reluctantly.[35]

Since the missionary presence was legal and protected by law, Colby and the Department for Christian Affairs at the Ministry of Religious Affairs set out to minimize the possible effects of evangelism, especially on children. The department allocated funds to "rescue" Jewish children, often from deprived, one-parent families, whose fathers or mothers placed them in boarding schools sponsored by missionary societies. The department, aided by a number of volunteer societies, found alternative, Orthodox Jewish institutions for such children and took it upon itself (often indirectly) to pay the bill.[36] In some cases, the Israeli Ministry of Welfare took legal action to take custody of children who were placed by one or both of their parents in missionary boarding schools, making the case (which seems to have been often true) that the parents were dysfunctional.[37]

Colby's efforts did not stop the energetic missionary endeavors, in which many churches and groups took part. During the 1950s and 1960s the largest missionary enterprise in Israel was carried on by the Southern Baptists. The vigorous Baptist missionary work in Israel during those years points to the crucial role a charismatic leader can play in inspiring and directing a large and ambitious missionary enterprise. The Baptist representative in Israel was Robert Lindsey, whose personality shaped the character and priorities of the mission. Born in 1917 in Norman, Oklahoma, Lindsey came to Jerusalem as a missionary in 1937 and studied at the Hebrew University. He made a special point of learning modern, spoken Hebrew and becoming acquainted with the new Zionist-oriented Jewish culture of the day. During World War II, he went back to America and pursued his studies.[38] After the war ended, he returned with his wife to Israel to head the Baptist work in the country.

Lindsey proved to be a versatile person. Trained as a New Testament scholar, he felt dissatisfied with existing Hebrew translations of the New Testament. For decades, in approaching Hebrew-reading Jews, missionaries relied on Franz Delitzsch's late-nineteenth-century translation of the New Testament from Greek into biblical-like Hebrew. As a scholar of the New Testament, Lindsey found many inaccuracies in Delitzsch's work. In addition, he considered the translation to be archaic, stiff, and alien to the Israeli culture of the day, and he eventually initiated the translation of the New Testament into modern Israeli Hebrew. For Lindsey the task of translation was of the utmost importance. As he was supervising the large and expanding Baptist missionary work in Israel, the progress of the translation was somewhat slow. "Everyone in the mission is well aware of the importance of this project—begun ten years ago and still hobbling along. . . . They all wanted to let me go on with the work, and they all knew I could not do it and get involved in any of the active work of the convention," he wrote in a report to the Southern Baptist administration at home.[39]

In the course of translating the Gospels into modern Hebrew, Lindsey had come to believe that the synoptic Gospels were originally written in Hebrew and were only translated later into Greek. He concluded that the Gospel of Luke, which in his opinion contained fewer anti-Semitic remarks than the other two synoptic Gospels of Matthew and Mark, was the original. The Gospels of Matthew and Mark, he claimed, relied on Luke, in its original form, and on an additional source, "Q." This theory fit in nicely with the Baptist missionary agenda in Israel, since it enabled missionaries to present the New Testament as being devoid in essence of anti-Semitism.[40] It also served as a cornerstone for a new school of New Testament studies, which consisted of the very unlikely match of evangelical Christians and Orthodox Jews. The group, known later as the Jerusalem School of New Testament Studies, has been perhaps one of the most unexpected developments in the annals of the Jewish-Christian encounter in the modern age. It included Lindsey and some other evangelical scholars residing in Jerusalem, mostly members of the Baptist congregation, and a number of Orthodox Jewish Israeli scholars. Among them were professors at the Hebrew University of Jerusalem, notably David Flusser, a New Testament scholar, and Shmuel Safrai, a historian of Judaism during the Second Temple period. The Jewish scholars who joined with Lindsey in forming the school had a somewhat different agenda than the evangelical ones. They were interested in comparing the Gospels and the Jewish teaching of the period and made the claim that Jesus' message was not very different from that of Jewish sages of his time.[41] All members, for different reasons, were interested in emphasizing the Jewish origins of early Christianity. The Orthodox scholars did not conceive of Lindsey as a missionary endangering Jewish souls. They saw him as a scholar and a colleague who only incidentally held the title of missionary. They respected Lindsey's scholarship but, like many other members of the Israeli intelligentsia, did not take the missionary endeavor very seriously.

If the association between evangelical missionaries and Jewish Orthodox scholars was amazing, the encounter between the Southern Baptist missionaries and the Canaanites was almost in the realm of the unthinkable. The Canaanites (Cnanim, in Hebrew) were a small ideological-cultural group that originated in the late 1930s, mostly through the leadership of the Israeli poet Yonatan Ratosh.[42] The group was considered radical by most Israelis, for it stood outside the Zionist consensus of the day and advocated the building in the Land of Israel of a Hebrew nation and culture, divorced from traditional Judaism. Its proponents demanded, among other things, the separation of synagogue and state in Israel. Although the movement as such had only a very small following and no political power, it influenced Hebrew poetry and Israeli art insofar as it introduced pseudo-Canaanite motifs.[43] Some claimed that followers of the group had practiced what would later be known as neopagan rites. Although it is doubtful that such rites really took place, there were rumors that this was the case.[44] This did not deter Lindsey from establishing close connections with Canaanite ideologues and activists, including Yonatan Ratosh.[45] He hired Zvi Rin, brother of the Canaanite leader, to do translations into Hebrew of books published by the Baptist publishing house. He published articles in *Alef*, the ideological-cultural magazine the group had produced in the early 1950s, in which he advocated the idea of separation of church and state. The Canaanites, on their part, viewed the Baptists favorably: "They were the only Christian group whose language of prayer was Hebrew," wrote Rin. "I was also attracted to the Baptist outlook that religion was a personal faith, and not an inherited one. . . . Similarly, I was enchanted by their advocacy of complete separation of church and state."[46]

The Baptists who had prided themselves on their historical advocacy of separation between church and state took particular exception to the nonseparation of synagogue and state. The 1950s and 1960s were years of growth and expansion for the Baptists in Israel, yet Lindsey and others noticed the limitations the Israeli system was imposing on them. They could propagate the gospel freely, publish their materials, and build congregations, yet the system at large, they noted, was hardly working in their favor. Israeli children were receiving Jewish religious education as part of the official curriculum in public schools: religious affiliation in Israel was not a matter of choice; it was recorded at birth or upon immigration and was henceforth part of the official identity of all persons residing in the country. Rabbinical, church, and Sharaite (Muslim) courts had exclusive authority over their constituencies in matters of marriage, divorce, burials, and, at times, legacies and custody issues. The Baptists were therefore not competing in an open market of religion.[47]

When in the mid-1950s a group of secular Israelis, among them the brother of Yonatan Ratosh and Zvi Rin, Uzi Ornan, established a "League for the Prevention of Religious Coercion" (HaLiga LiMeniat Kfia Datit), Lindsey joined. He resigned his membership after a while, following both Christian and Jewish criticism.[48] Reacting to reports from its missionaries in Israel and other countries as well, the Southern Baptist Convention passed a resolution on May 1955 "believing in the complete separation of church and state. . . . We join with all who support the principle of religious freedom anywhere in the World, especially in Spain, Israel and Italy, and throughout Latin America."[49] Israel was obviously among the countries in which, the Baptists felt, the nonseparation between church and state was working against them. It is doubtful, however, if the Baptist leaders and activists were aware that their representative, in his efforts to seek separation of church and state, was joining with secular Israelis including the Canaanites.

Despite their desire for a separation of synagogue and state in Israel, the Baptist missionaries in the country did not ignore the Israeli bureaucratic system assigned to deal with Christian groups. Lindsey was in constant interaction with the Department for Christian Affairs at the Ministry of Religious Affairs. The Baptists had to obtain official residence permits for their missionaries (their quota was close to thirty persons) and to file and receive tax returns, as did all the other Christian denominations in the country. Like representatives of other churches, Lindsey did not wish to pay the high taxes Israelis were paying on imported cars, for example.[50] Moreover, at the same time that the Southern Baptists advocated the separation of church and state in Israel, they came to demand, on a pragmatic basis, that the state of Israel recognize them as an official religious community, which meant adjusting to the Israeli system of state-sanctioned religious communities with autonomy in religious and personal matters.[51]

Another group with which Lindsey established a relationship, curiously, was the American Council for Judaism. This American Jewish group was founded in the 1940s to oppose the establishment of a Jewish state in the Land of Israel and American Jewish support of this state. Members of the council advocated the idea that "nationality and religion are separate and distinct" and rejected "the concept that the State of Israel is the national homeland of the Jewish people."[52] Lindsey exchanged letters and views with Elmer Berger, the executive director of this small, elitist, and not very influential American Jewish group.[53] Lindsey's (and the Southern Baptists') expressed views favored the establishment of the state of Israel. As he stated in his letters to Berger, he saw Jewish religion and nationality as inseparable. Where he and the American Jewish anti-Zionist activist could find some common ground was in Lindsey's rejection of the prevailing notion among the Israeli elite that secular Zionist culture could replace religion.[54] For Lindsey, of course, the ideological and religious beliefs guiding Israel should have become the Christian evangelical ones.

In contrast to the majority of missions in the country at the time, Lindsey wished to propagate Christianity among members of the country's social, political, and cultural elite. Baptist centers were located in fashionable areas of Israeli cities, such as Rehavia in Jerusalem and Dizingof Street in Tel Aviv. The Baptists were particularly eager to convert young, educated Hebrew-speaking Israelis.[55] Lindsey, who was looking for means to reach that population, established Dugit, a Baptist Israeli publishing house, which, among other things, published translations into Hebrew of Roland Bainton's works on Martin Luther and the Reformation. The Baptist mission opened a series of bookshops in Israeli cities, including one in the heart of Tel Aviv, where it promoted evangelistic as well as scholarly

Christian literature and books intended for Christian tourists. Another Baptist enterprise aimed at evangelizing Israelis was the journal *Hayahad* ("Together" in Hebrew), published both in English and in Hebrew. Lindsey wrote extensively in *Hayahad* using an Israeli nom de plume, Reuven Lud. Other Baptist missionaries writing and publishing for *Hayahad* were Dwight Baker and Chandler Lanier.

In his articles, as well as in a number of books, Lindsey expressed his views on Israel's role in history.[56] Although Lindsey pointed out that he did not follow the dispensationalist messianic interpretation of Scriptures, his understanding of the Jewish people and its role in history was very similar to that of dispensationalist premillennialists. For him, the Jews were the chosen people, and he believed God's promises for the rejuvenation of Israel in its land to be still valid. In his vision, he expected the Jews to convert to Christianity and accept Jesus as their Savior before they could be fully rehabilitated.[57] His missionary agenda was thus, from his point of view, of special value. He, like many other missionaries to the Jews, saw his mission as transcending the mere spreading of Christianity to unchurched people. Evangelizing Jews was taking part in a historical, divinely inspired plan, the rejuvenation of God's chosen nation and land.[58] "The Jews . . . one day [will] be spoken of as having come into Christ's kingdom (Romans 11:26). . . . A certainty is that a relationship exists between Jewry and God's plan of world salvation. . . . The Jews are a remnant body in spiritual decline who nevertheless remind themselves and the world of God's beginning of redemptive history."[59]

Well acquainted with Israeli society of the 1950s and 1960s, Lindsey became even more convinced that the Jewish people could not redeem themselves on their own and were in urgent need of accepting Christianity as the force that would reform, heal, and secure their private and national well-being. Current Israeli society, he complained, was hedonistic and imitated materialistic Western styles of living.[60] The Baptist missionary did not care for the secular character and ideology of the Israeli elite. In the 1950s, when that elite was at the peak of its influence, he spoke about the failure of Zionism, as promoted by the older generation of leaders, to capture the hearts of the younger generation. Christianity should enter, he believed, into the existing spiritual and religious vacuum.[61]

During the 1950s and 1960s, the Baptists succeeded in establishing a series of congregations in Israel among both Hebrew- and Arabic-speaking people. Much of the Baptist energy during those years went into opening new branches, purchasing land and property, building schools and bookshops, and recruiting and maintaining a cadre of workers and volunteers. Among other enterprises, Lindsey and others purchased and built a "Baptist Village" near the Yarkon River not far from Tel Aviv, which served as a boarding school for Jews and Arabs, a convention center, and an agricultural farm. Real estate in Israel during the period was relatively inexpensive, which helped the Baptists to expand.[62] The

Board for International Missions of the Southern Baptist Convention financed much of the growing enterprise in Israel, but Lindsey mustered additional support such as that of Fédération des Églises Évangéliques Baptists de France and that of William Criswell, pastor of the First Baptist Church of Dallas. At times, Lindsey also became a patron to groups of Messianic Jews. Such groups of Jewish believers in Jesus, which did not have their own meeting places, would often meet in Baptist centers.

In line with the desire to approach young Israelis more efficiently and use terminology and language more familiar to them, Lindsey, together with others, compiled a dictionary of messianic terms.[63] The dictionary was intended to help missionaries in writing, preaching, and presenting the Christian evangelical cause in Hebrew. It chose attractive words for common Christian terms. One term that, together with others, was to create something of a revolution in the missionary vocabulary in Israel was *meshichi* ("messianic"). It came to replace the more familiar term *notzri* ("Christian"). Lindsey and other missionaries were only too aware of the instant resentment the term "Christian" raised among many Israelis. *Meshichi* meant Christian, but it had a completely different connotation and feeling to it than *notzri*. "Messianic" referred to the eschatological aspect of the Christian evangelical message the missions were trying to promote. It shifted the meaning of the term from an alien, hostile religion to a new, hopeful, biblically oriented, messianic religion. Other terms were also changed, invented, or adapted along the same lines. Although the new vocabulary did not help to bring about a large movement of converts during the 1950 and 1960s, it was instrumental in the 1970s and 1980s when circumstances changed and a much larger movement of conversion to Christianity occurred.

Lindsey's activity in Israel was, at times, amazing, considering the fact that he was accountable to the Southern Baptist Convention, which sponsored and financed his work in the country. Lindsey became attracted to the charismatic movement in Christianity that advocated personal manifestation of the divine in the believer's life, a more expressive and spontaneous religious service, and at times faith healing. Under his leadership, the Baptist House in Jerusalem, as well as other Baptist congregations in the country, turned charismatic. The Southern Baptist Convention had been in principle a noncharismatic denomination, and their missionary department was not in the habit of sponsoring charismatic congregations. It is doubtful whether such a change could have occurred without Lindsey's formidable and independent position both in the local Baptist community and vis-à-vis the church authorities in Richmond, Virginia.

Paradoxically, then, the Southern Baptists were sponsoring a missionary, who, on a number of issues, including biblical exegesis and prayer, deviated from usual Baptist practices. He certainly did not follow Baptist conventions in choosing the people and ideological groups he associated with or in defining his public image.

As a charismatic minister, Lindsey, among other things, practiced faith healing, including exorcism.[64] Some Jews, including those who had no interest in the Christian faith, approached him and asked him to heal them. Lindsey allowed himself freedom of expression and action rarely exercised among Baptist missionaries. Yet he was careful to update the Foreign Mission Board of the Baptist Missions headquarters in Richmond on the various plans and developments in the Baptist missionary enterprise in Israel.[65] Lindsey was to remain the senior Baptist missionary in Israel until 1987, at which time he retired in ill health and returned to Oklahoma.

In carrying out his mission Lindsey often demonstrated personal boldness. On one occasion he crossed the border to Jordan secretly and illegally to help an Arab youth—who was denied an education by his family—to cross the border (also illegally) back to Israel. In the course of this adventure he stepped on a mine, was injured, and consequently lost a leg. The Jordanians put him under hospital arrest, but the Israeli government interceded for his release and "repatriation" back to Israel. The incident curiously helped promote the Baptist minister's image in Israeli society. Israelis looked upon him as a sabra, or *hevreman*, one of their own. The Israeli secular press was beside itself praising Lindsey and what the journalists saw as his brave and self-sacrificing act.[66] His missionary intentions often overlooked thereafter, Lindsey became accepted in Israeli society and enjoyed the friendship and trust of the Israeli elite whose beliefs he criticized so vehemently. He was invited, for example, to serve on a special government committee that was intended to promote Christian pilgrimage to Israel. Similarly, he was selected to serve as a judge in the International Bible Contests initiated by David Ben-Gurion, then prime minister of Israel. Israeli journalists routinely interviewed him.[67]

Although there was much resentment (particularly among Orthodox Jews) toward missionary activity and there were, at times, attempts at harassing missionaries, many Israelis, particularly secular ones, were not overly bothered by the presence of missionaries, the scope and nature of whose activity they did not fully appreciate.[68] Their assumption was that very few Jews, if any, converted to Christianity on account of genuine religious persuasion. Jews typically held the notion that the attraction of Christianity to Jews had been mostly social and economic and that evangelization had little to do with it. It was assumed that those Jews who did convert were promised extensive economic support by missionaries.

The ambivalent, paradoxical relationship between the Israeli elite and Christian missionaries was also demonstrated by the career of William L. Hull. Strongly influenced by Aimee McPherson and the Foursquare Gospel Church, Hull started his Canadian Pentecostal missionary work in Israel in the 1930s.[69] Like Lindsey, he was interested in approaching the young Zionist society of his day. He established, with others such as LeRoy Kopp, the Zion Apostolic Mission, which was headquartered in Jerusalem. Like Lindsey, Hull openly showed sympathy and support for the Jewish struggle for free immigration and settlement and for independence from British rule.[70] He expressed his views in a journal he edited, *Pentecost in Jerusalem*, whose name was changed in 1948 to *Christian Voice in Israel*. The Pentecostal missionary also published a book on Israel and its role in history, *The Fall and Rise of Israel*. His understanding of the meaning of the birth of the state of Israel and the Jewish immigration to Israel were biblical-messianic in nature, in line with the dispensationalist premillennialist outlook.

Hull's missionary motivation was nourished by his dispensationalist understanding of the course of history. It was his duty, he believed, to save as many Jews as he could before the events of the End Times. Like other dispensationalist missionaries, Hull remarked, at times, on the stubbornness of Jews and the difficulty of convincing them of the truth of the Christian gospel.[71] Hull nonetheless expressed support for Israel's policy and for Jerusalem as Israel's capital under Israel's sovereignty. He remarked that the demand of the Roman Catholic Church for the internationalization of Jerusalem would have ended Protestant evangelical missionary activity, which, he noted, was protected under Israeli rule. A fundamentalist Protestant, Hull preferred to work under a Jewish government than a non-Protestant Christian one. Significantly, the Pentecostal minister dedicated his book to David Ben-Gurion, Israel's first prime minister, whose praise for the book was quoted on the dust jacket. From Ben-Gurion's words it is evident that he had no real knowledge of Hull's theology and assumed that Hull simply saw in the establishment of the state of Israel a fulfillment of biblical prophecy. Hull indeed saw in the creation of the new state a fulfillment of prophecy but understood it quite differently than Ben-Gurion. For him it was the first stage that was to lead to the establishment of the Kingdom of God on earth but certainly not the messianic kingdom itself.

Hull played a significant and revealing role in the case of Adolf Eichmann. In the early 1960s, the Israeli secret services kidnapped Eichmann, a Nazi officer who had coordinated much of the systematic murder of European Jews during World War II, and brought him to Israel, where he stood trial and was sentenced to death. Hull asked the Israeli authorities to allow him access to the mass murderer. Eichmann was reluctant to see a minister but eventually agreed to meet with Hull. Hull visited Eichmann in jail fourteen times and eventually was present at his execution. Throughout their meetings Hull tried to convince Eichmann of the truth of the gospel.[72] The Israeli authorities, in particular Arieh Nir, head of the Israeli prison system, fully cooperated with Hull. For his part, Nir hoped that Hull would serve as a reliable witness to the fair treatment and good living conditions the government offered Eichmann.

According to Hull's account, Eichmann was unrepentant until the last minutes of his life and held on to his Nazi understanding of history. With the rope around Eichmann's neck, Hull still tried to persuade him to accept Jesus as his Savior. Eichmann murmured: "Jesus."[73] Later on in interviews Hull claimed that if Eichmann had indeed accepted Jesus as his personal Savior, then he was saved, since Jesus' sacrifice on the cross atoned for whatever crimes the now converted criminal had committed.[74] The millions of Jews whom the Nazis had murdered during the Holocaust, on the other hand, died without accepting Jesus as their Savior and were doomed. Hull's opinions received wide notice in Israel and caused much shock and resentment. He lost favor with the Israeli establishment. Hull left Israel a short time afterward and returned to Canada. Some Israeli officials speculated that the negative Israeli reaction to Hull's evangelical under-standing of the fate of the Jews who perished in the Holocaust made him decide to leave.[75] But people who have worked with Hull in the Zion Apostolic Mission claim that personal family matters precipitated his return to his country.[76] Back in Canada, Hull continued to take an interest in the Jewish people, the prospect of their return to Zion, and their conversion to Christianity, and he remained a confirmed supporter of Israel. He continued to lead yearly tours of Canadian Pentecostals to Israel even when he was well into his eighties and even nineties.

Hull's career in Israel, like that of other missionaries, revealed the paradox inherent in the missionaries' attitude toward Israel and the Israeli reaction to it. Missionaries such as Hull supported Israel wholeheartedly. They sincerely ex-pressed goodwill and concern for the well-being of the young state and its inhabitants and took pride in its achievements. Their books on Israel read, at times, as if they were written by Zionist officials. Yet they were first and foremost motivated by their premillennialist messianic belief and biblical exegesis. As much as they were concerned for the well-being of the Jews, they at the same time considered them to be spiritually deprived, much in need of the ameliorating Christian gospel. Israeli leaders and officials, in turn, were, for the most part, unaware of the details of the Christian evangelical belief. Jewish leaders such as Ben-Gurion thought that Christians who supported Israel had an understanding of the Bible similar to their own. That the same belief that initiated support for Israel and warm feelings toward its people was the one that also inspired mission-ary efforts was something they often did not know or did not care to know.[77]

Another example of the paradoxical relationship that existed at times between the Israeli government and American missionaries was the warm reception of-fered by the Israeli leadership to visiting American evangelists who were engaged in propagating Christianity among the Jews. In 1959 Oral Roberts, a leading Pentecostal evangelist, visited Israel.[78] He met with David Ben-Gurion, and the two engaged in a cordial discussion on evangelism and biblical prophecy. It seems from the discussion that Ben-Gurion, who had lived in America for a while, had some general notion about American evangelists.[79] The two men found a common ground for a lively, amicable discussion of their interest in the

Hebrew Bible and their understanding that it served as the foundation on which the Israeli nation should build its life. Roberts was most pleased with Ben-Gurion and reported to his followers in America in very favorable terms on the country and its leader.[80]

Roberts was not the only Pentecostal who took an interest in Israel. In 1961, Pentecostals around the world decided to organize the Sixth World Conference of Pentecostal Churches in Jerusalem. William Hull was among the organizers of the conference, the location of which demonstrated the special relation of many Pentecostals to Israel. Jerusalem was then a city divided between Israel and Jordan. Israel declared Jerusalem to be its capital, but most countries did not recognize it as such and boycotted any international activity in Jerusalem. By choosing to conduct an international meeting in Jerusalem, the Pentecostals were thus making a political statement in favor of Israel's capital.

Eager to establish friendly contacts with Protestant churches, many of them American, the Israeli government made a special effort to welcome the conference.[81] Among other things, the Israeli Ministry of Religious Affairs published a special issue of *Christian News from Israel*—a publication of the ministry dedicated to promoting the Israeli cause among English-speaking Christian ministry and lay leadership—dedicated to the conference. The Israeli Government Company of Medals minted a special medal that was distributed to the delegates. And Prime Minister Ben-Gurion wrote a speech for the conference. His message to the conference serves as another example of the paradoxical relationship between the evangelical community and the Israeli leadership. The prime minister, needless to say, presented the state of Israel as a realization of biblical prophecies. The Israeli statesman and his aides thought that such a view would be embraced wholeheartedly by the Pentecostal delegates. They assumed that the latter's support of Israel was based on Christian evangelical recognition of the Jewish people as God's chosen people returning to their promised land. The difference between the secular Israeli view and the Pentecostal one (and the evangelical outlook in general) was that the Israelis were convinced that the country they had been building was the final stage in Jewish history. Christian evangelicals, on the other hand, had viewed Israel as merely a stage toward the realization of the messianic kingdom. They looked favorably upon Israel, but from their point of view it was a means to an end, a positive, welcomed development that prepared the ground for the arrival of the Lord; they refused to see in the Israeli state a fulfillment of the biblical prophecies, a restored Davidic kingdom.

In 1956, another amazing encounter took place between an American missionary who represented an organization of Jewish converts to Christianity in America and a senior Israeli official. Aaron Kligerman, a converted Jew and veteran missionary, came to Israel as a delegate on behalf of the Hebrew Christian Alliance of America accompanied by the group's secretary, Nate Schaiff, to express the alliance's concern about the condition of Jewish converts to Christianity in Israel. They sought ways to help the latter, particularly as far as their economic situation was concerned. Many converts, they asserted, were poor and in need of help. Hardship was not unusual in Israel, but matters were even more difficult for converts, so their fellow Jewish believers in Jesus in America believed. In their opinion, were the social and economic position of Jewish converts better, more would have professed their faith in the messiahship of Jesus. Kligerman and Schaiff met with the American ambassador in the American Embassy in Tel Aviv; the ambassador, according to the alliance's report, was supportive and offered the two delegates advice as to how to pursue their cause. Obviously, the American ambassador thought it only natural to offer help to representatives of missionary and converts' organizations.[82]

The ambassador arranged a meeting between the American visitors and the director general of the prime minister's office, Teddy Kollek. "Our interview with Mr. Teddy Kollek was a great encouragement for us. We thank God for the open door and the friendly sholem alechem (greetings) given us all along the way," wrote Kligerman in his published report. The Hebrew Christian delegates raised before Kollek the legal and social position of converted Jews in Israel. Kollek's reaction surprised the American Jewish Christian visitors. "Kollek informed us of the feeling of the ultra Orthodox who have brought about the anti-Christian attacks. . . . He continued to state that these men had come from ghettos, from behind the iron curtain, from . . . parts of Nazi-infested Europe and—having been hated, harassed, tortured, misunderstood, unloved . . . and persecuted by those who professed to be Christians . . . they had never known the culture of western civilization, had never had the teachings of tolerance or liberalism." Reminding the two representatives that "it took several generations to overcome prejudices in America," Kollek explained, "We are a new nation—please give us the same chance." According to Kligerman's report, Kollek approved of the idea of building Hebrew Christian congregations in Israel. Kligerman's enthusiastic report on his meeting with Kollek seems plausible. The energetic and open-minded lieutenant of Israel's prime minister would, in the mid-1960s, become the mayor of Jerusalem, where he put his liberal views into practice, offering help and protection to Christian churches and groups including a number of congregations of converted Jews that sprang up in the city during his tenure. He was perhaps particularly open to the Western idea of laissez-faire in the realm of religion and the idea that missionaries and converted Jews had the right to operate freely. He expressed, however, a view that was not much different from that of many in the secular Israeli elite. Kollek and his like did not identify with the beliefs or agenda of Christian missions and converts. They were nonetheless concerned about the character of Israeli society; they wanted Israel to be an open, pluralistic society and feared Jewish Orthodox intolerance. Missionaries and leaders of converts' organizations, for their part, remained convinced that if Israeli society was more tolerant they would have more of a chance to gain more converts.

As far as actual conversions were concerned, the missionary gains in Israel were very limited during the years 1948 to 1967 and were estimated at no more than a few hundred converts under the most liberal evaluations.[83] This should not be surprising. Missions in America were advocating a message that represented the values, norms, and beliefs of a large segment in society. This was not the case in Israel in its early years, where Christianity was a minority religion and evangelical Christianity had no standing or influence in the larger community. The missions represented a culture that existed only overseas and did not provide an avenue leading into Israeli society but rather outside it. Under the charismatic leadership of David Ben-Gurion, the early years of the new state, although years of severe economic shortage, were also years of national optimism and pride. Zionism served not merely as a political agenda during those years but as an all-encompassing ideology, providing a hopeful outlook on the course of Jewish history. Non-Zionist outlooks, such as those advocated by Communists or ultra Orthodox Jews, were regarded as completely marginal to the mainstream. Under such circumstances there was almost no chance that Israelis of the social elite would accept Christianity.

Much of the missionary efforts were directed, indeed, not toward the elite but toward the socially and economically deprived, the struggling new immigrants from eastern Europe, the Middle East, and North Africa. Many in this group suffered from something of a culture shock: they felt alienated from and did not share the values of the social elite. But among this segment of the population, too, the missionaries' gains were very limited. The Christian evangelical option did not seem a very attractive one in Israel in its early years. The younger generation of immigrants was busy absorbing itself into the predominant culture. Many were indeed looking for a new cultural framework and set of values, to replace that of their parents. They almost naturally sought it in the Israeli culture of the day, which was mostly secular. The mission's messages, if taken seriously, seemed alien and completely irrelevant to their lives and expectations.

As for the older generation of immigrants, they were even less open to changing their set of beliefs and religious affiliation. For many of them, immigrants from North Africa or the Middle East, the synagogue was the center of their social, communal, and spiritual lives. They had much to lose by converting to Christianity and very little to gain. Many of the new immigrants approached the missionaries seeking the services and relief the missions were offering but had no desire to commit themselves to accepting Jesus of Nazareth as their Savior. To many of them such evangelical terminology was completely incomprehensible and was far removed from their intellectual and spiritual framework. The only interest they showed in the missions was in the material help the latter offered at times. In one revealing photograph, the missionary Arthur Michelson showed his work among new immigrants from North Africa in Musrara, the border neighborhood in Jerusalem where his mission was located. Wishing to promote his work and impress potential supporters, Michelson titled the picture "Dr. Michelson . . . gives packages of food to some needy Jewish families and explains the Gospel to them." The missionary is indeed shown sitting and perhaps preaching, but his audience, as the picture shows, of older North African Jews, who are holding packages in their hands, are clearly not interested. Having received their packages, they seem eager to be on their way out.[84]

To realize how disadvantageous it was for Jews in Israel to accept Christianity during that period, one may turn to data provided by converts. A 1964 report presented by the secretary of the International Hebrew Christian Alliance, an organization of Jewish converts to evangelical Christianity headquartered in London, indicated that there were 160 adult Hebrew Christians or Messianic Jews, in Israel, that is, Jews who accepted Christianity in its Protestant evangelical form. But only twenty of them, he claimed, declared themselves openly to be Christians in a demographic census taken a year earlier by the Israeli government in which citizens were asked about (and had to disclose) their religious affiliation.[85] Since there was no separation between synagogue (or church) and state in Israel, Jews who accepted Christianity had to choose. They could reveal their decision to embrace Christianity, register as Christians, and be regarded by the authorities as Christians, or they could choose to keep that fact a secret and be registered as Jews. If they chose the latter, they had to live their lives under the jurisdiction of the rabbinate, including marrying as Jews and being buried as Jews. Obviously most chose that option rather than declare themselves openly as Christians. Many of these Jewish Christians were not really closeted; they were members of evangelical congregations and lived their lives within the evangelical subculture in Israel.

In some cases, however, Jews accepted the Christian evangelical faith but kept it secret, neither joining evangelical congregations nor interacting with fellow Christian believers. Such persons, often members of Orthodox communities, were afraid of arousing social resentment and lived something of a double life, revealing their belief only to a few people whom they could completely trust.[86] One does not know, of course, the exact number of such persons. Missionaries pointed at times to the existence of such people as an indication that the actual number of Jews who had accepted the Christian faith in Israel was larger than their recorded numbers.[87] They were well aware of the difficulties regarding the personal status of converted Jews in a country that did not separate church and state.

The only way missionaries could have turned their mission into a great numerical success was, in the words of the secretary of the International Hebrew Christian Alliance, "by turning into a travel agency."[88] Many Israelis in the 1950s and 1960s, immigrants from eastern Europe, the Balkans, or Middle Eastern or North African countries, felt that their lot might have been rosier if they immigrated to more affluent Western countries. Many approached the missions, inquiring if they would help them emigrate and settle in a Western country and expressing interest in converting to Christianity pending on a future emigration.[89] There was a prevailing assumption in Israeli society that missions were willing to bestow large material benefits on converts. In actuality, however, missions did not possess the economic resources many Israelis assumed they had. The missions' budgets, although generous by Israeli standards, certainly did not include any bonuses for the newly converted. Moreover, contrary to the Jewish stereotype, missionaries were, as a rule, interested in sincere converts and not in mere opportunists whose obvious motivation was economic benefits. In addition, helping Jews emigrate outside Israel was something evangelical missionaries would not do in principle, even if they could offer the material resources Israelis thought they possessed. They held a premillennialist view of history, according to which the immigration of Jews to Israel was understood as part of God's plan for the End Times, and they did not wish to support emigration out of the country.

Although the actual number of converts was relatively small, missionaries did not see their efforts as wasted. Living and evangelizing in Israel during the early years of the state seemed fulfilling and rewarding. As premillennialists, they felt that they had the obligation to make the Christian gospel known to Jews even if the latter did not accept it. They might, missionaries believed, accept it later on when the great events of the End Times began to unfold. They were "sowing the seed" for the future. Moreover, considering the legal and social obstacles and the ideological and cultural mood of the country, many saw reasons to be satisfied with relatively modest numbers of converts. Those Jews who did convert filled missionaries with an enormous sense of satisfaction as well as joy. They were, for the most part, young independent people in the prime of life looking forward to building families and careers. Their conversions were reported with pride and satisfaction. "It was a real joy to see such an intelligent fine looking young man, perhaps twenty five years of age, who had found the Lord Jesus Christ as his personal Savior," wrote George T. B. Davis, director of the Million Testaments Campaigns, on his encounter with a new convert in Israel of the early 1950s.[90] The few converts he met on his visit to Israel filled Davis with such joy that in his own eyes the missionary work in Israel was a great success.[91]

A number of factors created the unusual, often paradoxical reality in which American missionaries operated in Israel. Unexpectedly, a Jewish state allowed for Christian missionary activity (which was historically anathema for Jews) in its midst. This made for such incredible situations as when the prime minister and other top Israeli officials welcomed missionaries, trying to reassure them of Israel's friendly and protective policy. It resulted, at times, in missionaries seeking unlikely and even bizarre alliances and friendships. It also made for a strange relationship between missionaries and the Israeli government, which sought for political reasons to build a friendly relationship with missionaries, who represented large segments of Christianity.

The unusual character of the missionary endeavor in Israel was also enhanced by the fact that the missionaries did not treat Israel as just another country. Influenced by a dispensationalist premillennialist outlook, they believed they were evangelizing in a country where the great drama of the End Times was about to unfold and among a people who they believed were destined to play a crucial role in that drama. Their interests in the people and the country were much broader than trying to convince individual Jews of the truth of the Christian message. In their eyes they were witnesses to developments that had a global, cosmic significance. They had their own vested messianic interests in the country, which made them an interested party in the drama. Their aim was to try to influence the course of events, to educate the Jews as to how to better fulfill their historical role. The evangelical missionaries who came to Israel to influence the country, however, had to alter their activities to conform to the realities of the country. The evangelists, in the end, changed the country much less than they were changed by it.

15

The Converts' Community

The period from the 1920s to 1960s saw a rise in the number of Jewish converts to evangelical Christianity in America, significant changes in their demography, and the beginnings of a convert community. There are no accurate statistics on the number of Jewish converts to Christianity in America from the 1920s to the 1960s, and so in trying to reconstruct the picture one must rely on estimates gathered from contemporary observers and on partial data provided by various sources. All figures are undoubtedly no more than intelligent guesses at best, yet it seems that the number of converts grew during the period. The estimates for the earlier period were that about 150–200 Jews per year converted to Protestant Christianity in America from the 1880s to the 1910s. By the 1930s the rate had grown and might have reached as much as two or three times that number. Those estimates rely on denominational and missionary sources as to the numbers of Jewish converts who were members of Protestant churches in America. If such information is credible it might be that from 4,000 at the beginning of the century the number of converts had more than tripled by the early 1930s.[1] But no large-scale surveys were really taken to track all possible Jewish members of Protestant churches. Such a survey would not have revealed all Jewish converts, since not all of them declared themselves openly to be Jewish.[2]

A survey that the Presbyterian Department of Jewish Evangelization had conducted estimated the number of Jews in Presbyterian churches in the early 1930s at 2,000. If this is an indication of the larger picture, it does corroborate the missionary estimates of a growth in the number of Jewish conversions as of the 1920s. Like the growth in the missionary activity at large, the growth in the number of converts and the rise of a community of converts were relatively unheralded, not arousing much attention in either the Jewish or the Christian camps. Naturally, not all conversions were the result of the missionary activity directed specifically at Jews. There was also no differentiation in reports on the number of converts between members of evangelical and nonevangelical congregations.[3] Joining an Episcopalian church (not to mention Unitarian), for example, was remarkably different from joining a Baptist or a Bible church. The latter two indicated a different kind of conversion: being "born again" and accepting a premillennialist worldview.

Although the number of conversions was probably on the rise, conversion to

Christianity was a path that relatively few chose. The second generation of immigrants from eastern Europe were busy Americanizing. For almost all of them this meant leaving their parents' immigrant neighborhoods and abandoning the old eastern European immigrant's lifestyle in favor of a more Americanized, and usually secular, environment. A relatively large number of second-generation American Jews joined Conservative synagogues. A smaller, yet not insignificant, number joined Reform congregations. Many were content with no religious affiliation. Some adhered to secular ideologies such as socialism or communism, which explained the world in definitive terms, aimed at reforming society, and offered meaning to their lives. The 1930s were years of economic depression in America and saw the rise of the Fascist and Nazi regimes in Europe, as well as a growth of nativist hate groups in America. The numbers of young Jews embracing radical, left-wing ideologies escalated. Missionaries pointed out that many of the young people they approached had adhered to or at least explored secular ideologies, often socialism.[4] But such ideologies did not always seem the answer for those who sought a belief system that offered spiritual meaning and communal support rather than an ideological political framework.

Meeting with a missionary, or someone else who advocated the new belief, was crucial to the conversion process.[5] This is evident in all autobiographical accounts of converted Jews of that period, virtually without exception.[6] For young Jews who were looking for a new community and a system of meaning in their lives, the missionaries were at times agents of this new world, as well as serving as father or mother figures. The missionaries, as a rule, belonged to the converts' parents' generation; they usually had been born in eastern Europe and had come to America themselves as young men and women. It is significant, in this light, that missions continued to hire eastern European–born immigrants as missionaries long after it was evident that the missions' prospective converts had been born and raised in America. The American Board of Missions to the Jews, for example, took special pride in recruiting and training refugees from eastern Europe in the 1930s and 1940s, including Holocaust survivors.[7]

Prospective converts appreciated the attention and warmth the missionaries bestowed upon them. Naturally, the ones who tended most to build a parent-child relationship with missionaries were those who had been deprived of a father or mother or both. Toby Cantor, a teenager from Brooklyn, who had been orphaned and raised by his grandmother, wrote a letter in June 1929 to a Mr. E. Greenbaum, who operated a mission and a summer camp in New Jersey on behalf of the Presbyterian Church where the teenager spent a summer. Appreciating the treatment he received, he wrote: "You and Mrs. Greenbaum were two of the finest people I [have] ever known."[8] The warm fatherly attention that the missionary bestowed upon the young Toby alarmed his relatives, as well as other Jews in the community.[9] The parent-child aspect of relationships between missionaries and converts is further evidenced in the way they relate to each other in their writings. Converts wrote in laudatory terms of the missionaries who brought them to faith, and saw them as their mentors. Similarly, missionaries described converts they made in a manner reminiscent of uncles and aunts raving about the achievements of their favorite nephews and nieces or professors proud of successful doctoral students they have supervised who have done well in their careers.[10]

Converts in their autobiographical accounts often either mention the loss of parents in their childhood or describe a father who had been abusive, or weak and aloof.[11] Shlomo Sherman, who grew up in New York in the 1940s, describes an abusive and aloof father who later on left home altogether.[12] Hilda Koser operated a summer camp mission for Jewish children in Coney Island in the 1920s to 1950s. In her autobiography, she, too, describes an abusive, negligent, and absent father. The missionary she encountered served as a compensating father figure. She herself served as a mother figure to young prospective converts. Unmarried, and with no children of her own, she looked upon the teenagers she helped to convert as her children. She took pride in their progress in life and visited with them on her vacations.[13] Some doubt the usefulness of converts' biographical accounts as a historical source. Such accounts are frequently formulated and built into the expected patterns of such literary genres.[14] The narrators tend, for example, to portray their moral transformation following their conversion experience in radical terms. Moreover, students of this genre of literature caution that autobiographies do not always reflect the realities of the writers' lives but rather their feelings, beliefs, and perceptions when they sat down to write their memoirs.[15] Nonetheless, much of the information provided by Jewish converts to Christianity does not fall into the expected patterns of converts' testimonies. Such information as the convert's personal background varies from one writer to another and is not subject to the genre's prefixed narrative. These accounts are written innocently and give evidence—often unconsciously—of the social setting and personal moods and choices of the converts before, during, and after the process of conversion. One can definitely believe Sherman or Koser when they write that their fathers were negligent and abusive.

Such an observation does not dismiss in any way the claim of converts to have had a genuine experience of conversion, in which they had accepted Jesus as their personal Savior, and the spiritual and moral transformation this experience marked in their lives. A personal quest for a sense of family and community seems to have played an important part, whether consciously or unconsciously, in a person's decision to convert. Social and economic benefits, by contrast, had little to do with conversions to evangelical forms of Christianity. There were some Jews who converted to Christianity in America during the period out of social consideration. Some tended to hide their origins, and their life stories were exposed by their children a generation later.[16] Such people, as a rule, did not join conservative evangelical forms of Christianity, which did not enjoy much prestige at the time and could not offer the social mobility of the kind such persons were seeking. There were also some Jews of the period, often children of the Jewish social elite, who joined very progressive forms of Christianity such as the Unitarians, as well as humanistic and universalistic forms of religious-philosophical expressions, a pattern that began in the late nineteenth century.[17] The impetus for joining such groups was very different from that of those who chose conservative evangelical forms of Christianity. Their conversions had nothing to do with missionaries, since these progressive movements did not engage in missionary work (nor did they advocate "conversion" in its evangelical form). The attraction of these groups to some Jews was undoubtedly very different from that of evangelical Christianity.

Missionaries represented the beliefs and worldview of the conservative evangelical wing of Christianity. They did not propagate the Christian gospel among children of the Jewish elite but rather among the second generation of the masses of immigrant Jews, who had, at times, different agendas and aspirations than their better-settled elite brethren. Whatever the merits of converting to evangelical Christianity, they did not include a rise in social prestige and economic benefits. One should take into consideration that in the Jewish milieu from which they came, declaring their acceptance of Jesus as their Savior actually meant loss of face. To their Jewish friends, family, and neighbors, converts in this period often seemed strange, eccentrics who had chosen a path completely different from that of the overwhelming majority of American Jews of their generation. Jews viewed conversions to evangelical Christianity during the period more as an act of folly than treachery and continued to so view it, even after the movement to convert Jews to Christianity grew much larger in decades to come.

As for the non-Jewish community, many conservative evangelicals endorsed the evangelization of Jews in principle but did not necessarily go out of their way to welcome the newly converted and ease their path into their new community. Although evangelical Christians were favorably predisposed toward Jews on account of their premillennialist worldview, they were not devoid of prejudices against them.[18] Converts at times found themselves viewed in stereotypical terms.[19] The Jewish converts' entrance to evangelical society could be a painful one, as Esther Bronstein's memoirs colorfully portray.[20] Entering the conservative Protestant environment involved much more than simply proclaiming one's faith in the Messiah. Christianity was practiced by real people with long-established customs, tastes, manners, and ways of doing things. In addition, there were often sets of rules, of "do!" and "don't do," with which converts were not always very familiar. Some Jewish converts found their new faith comforting but often felt estranged and unsure of themselves when confronting the cultural particularities of the non-Jews and sensed that they were being judged by the latter. The Hebrew Christian congregations were one new option that could ease the feeling of intimidation that some Jewish converts felt when joining a culture that was basically welcoming but strange.

The Christian evangelical community was not necessarily hostile toward Jews. There are a number of indicators that show that the evangelical environment was, on the whole, willing to accept Jews. One is the number of Jews who served as pastors in evangelical churches. By 1930, according to one source, there were three hundred Jewish converts who were ministers of evangelical Protestant congregations.[21] This number is quite high when compared with the normal ratio of people serving as ministers. Obviously Jewish converts were, by comparison, particularly attracted to the ministry. This should not be surprising. From the converts' point of view, their conversion had been a major transformation, entailing a deep commitment. This often led to theological and pastoral studies motivated by intellectual curiosity concerning the essence of Christianity and to a wish to serve their new faith and help promote its cause. Study in theological seminaries and obtaining pastoral positions also served as a confirmation of their faith, an indication of their sincerity and seriousness. For the evangelical community, the appointment of Jewish pastors was an unmistakable act of trust. Ministers have always been leaders of their congregations and pillars in their communities. Pastoral positions in evangelical churches in America, one must recall, were rarely assigned by a church headquarters. Congregations usually selected their own ministers, or at least approved a candidate suggested by the church's headquarters. Obviously, a convert's Jewish background did not stand in the way of obtaining a pastoral position. Remarkably, some converted Jews, first- or second-generation immigrants who had grown up in the distinctive Jewish culture of the large East Coast cities, became pastors of evangelical congregations in the Midwest, the South, or the Northwest. It was not unheard of for evangelical congregations to have pastors with distinctly Jewish names. At times, Jewish converts even obtained positions of influence and prestige in the evangelical community, such as in institutions of higher education. Charles L. Feinberg, for example, who worked for some years as a missionary for the American Board of Missions to the Jews, became a professor, and later on dean, at Talbot Theological Seminary, a division of the Bible Institute of Los Angeles in La Mirada, California.

Appointments as missionaries were also a sign of acceptance and trust. By 1930, according to one source, a few hundred Jews were working as missionaries (in addition to many others working in Jewish evangelism).[22] In this regard, the convert's enthusiasm played a part, as many obviously wanted to share their new faith, either with their brethren or with people of other ethnic backgrounds. The signs of acceptance included, of course, the support for missions among the Jews, which remained a high priority on the evangelical agenda during the period.

There is no accurate information on the exact socioeconomic profile of the converts. A brochure published in the early 1970s by the American Board of Missions to the Jews, however, provides some insight as to the composition of the group of Jews that accepted Christianity during the 1930s to 1950s. This publication, which presents the stories of forty converts to Christianity, is not, of course, an unambiguous demographic source for the analysis of Jewish converts to Christianity during the period. The mission produced it as evangelizing material intended to convey the message that Jews should adopt Christianity. Thus the publication only presented persons who agreed to expose themselves and their life stories and only those who the mission felt would make a good impression.[23] Yet the mission also wanted to convey the message that conversion was for everyone. It did not try to impress potential readers that its followers were the rich and famous. Rather, it sought to advertise people of all walks of life: young, middle-aged, and older men and women, people of all professions as well as housewives and retired people. The picture the brochure reveals seems to reflect the American Jewish professional and economic realities of the time. Most of the older people presented in the brochure, those in their fifties, sixties, and seventies, were second-generation American Jews. Some in that generation had made it into the professions, but most had not. One of the group was a hairdresser, one a retired postal employee, another a meat cutter. There were a number of businessmen. One was a physician and one an aeronautical engineer; three were ministers. Most of the women, including some of the younger ones, were homemakers; some of the younger were administrative assistants; one was a retired businesswoman and one a physician.

The socioeconomic picture the brochure offers correlates, more or less, with that offered by other sources that offer anecdotal (but not statistical) data. David and Esther Bronstein, for example, described the congregation they had built and led in Chicago in the late 1930s to 1950s as composed of lower-middle-class people with only few members who had made it into the professions.[24] So does Shlomo Sherman, who recalls the congregation organized by the American Board of Missions to the Jews in its New York headquarters.[25]

The brochure unmistakenly conveys values and manners tuned to middle-class propriety and respectability. This is demonstrated, for example, in the choice of clothes and hairstyles of the persons presented.[26] The picture also correlates with that depicted by B. Z. Sobel, a Jewish sociologist who studied a Hebrew Christian congregation in New Jersey at about the time the brochure was produced. He describes a lower-middle-class American community and values.[27]

An important element in the new converts' lives was, of course, the issue of marriage. As there were no surveys taken during the period, one must again rely on scattered evidence given by contemporaries. It seems that the number of Jewish men who converted was higher than that of Jewish women, although the percentage of women within the ranks of the converts was on the rise. Converting and moving away from the Jewish community demanded a great deal of independence; it usually represented a rebellion against one's parents, their community, and the values and way of life they advocated. Women in the 1920s to 1950s were not yet fully "liberated" and were therefore less daring in stepping out of the conventions and routines of their generation. In addition, Jewish women of that generation were brought up to be marriage-oriented: to marry young, to seek a good match with a "nice Jewish boy," and raise a family. They were less inclined than men to make their own choices, study for a profession, build a career; certainly, they were less likely to choose a new religion and community.

With few Jewish Christian women available to marry, most converts found non-Jewish wives during that period. This is clear from abundant biographical data including obituaries of Jewish Christian activists and leaders, as well as the observations of members of the convert's community during the era.[28] Years later, some claimed that they might have preferred to marry Jewish women but that they had felt that the evangelical community expected them to marry non-Jewish spouses. The legitimacy of Jewish self-expression was only beginning to gain ground in the evangelical community, and some converts felt there was no justification, as far as the community around them was concerned, to marry a Jewish spouse, even if they felt more at home with such a spouse.[29] "There were a few Hebrew Christian girls . . . and if we were impudent or imprudent enough to cast an eye upon one of these maidens, flesh of out flesh, we were considered in danger of apostacy [sic]," wrote Elias Newman, many years later.[30] Such feelings might, of course, have reflected the insecurity many converts felt in their new society more than the actual demands of that society. There were converts during the period, after all, who were married to Jewish converts like themselves and nonetheless gained the trust and respect of the evangelical community. Examples abound and include some of the best-known missionaries of the period. The children of Jewish converts grew up, however, within the evangelical community and often in mixed marriages. They were fully integrated into the Christian evangelical community, with little or no indication of their Jewish background. One can occasionally trace the course of their lives in obituaries of the Jewish parent, in which one sees a complete divorce from any Jewish identity.[31]

During this middle period in the history of Christian missions to the Jews in America, organizations that offered converted Jews an opportunity to express their ethnic character and unique concerns were the Hebrew Christian Alliance of America and the Hebrew Christian congregations. The Jewish Christian subculture that developed in the 1970s to 1990s was only making its first hesitant steps. Most converts who were affiliated with non-Jewish congregations did not give much expression to their Jewishness and did not participate in the Hebrew Christian organizations. The Hebrew Christian Alliance attracted converts who were activists of the missionary movement, especially those in pastoral and missionary positions. They were by definition the more interested and committed among the converts. The alliance acted as a representative body for the converts within the larger evangelical community, advocating the cause of missions, which the alliance people saw as representing their own interest as converted Jews dedicated to the cause of spreading the Christian gospel among their brethren.

This was evident in its statement of purposes, which promises "to furnish a corporate witness to the Jews of the saving power of the Gospel of Jesus Christ" and "to be a testimony to the Christian Church in the program of Jewish Evangelization." That the activists of the alliance saw as one of their primary aims the promotion of the cause of Jewish evangelization was not surprising. Keeping Jewish evangelization high on the list of evangelical priorities indicated respect for the Jews and their role in history, as well as for individual converted Jews. It validated their status within the evangelical community. A lack of interest on the part of the evangelical community in propagating Christianity among the Jews would have been an insult to them and the path they had chosen. In addition, many of the alliance people were missionaries.

The statement of purposes also vowed "to publish suitable literature interpreting Christianity to the Jewish People"; "to assist as far as possible every agency engaged in the work of Evangelizing the Jews"; "to help educate Hebrew Christians for the Jewish Mission field"; "to carry on conferences on Jewish Evangelization seeking to establish a better understanding of the Jewish Problem and endeavoring to interpret the gospel of Christ to the Jewish People"; and "to aid through the International Hebrew Christian Alliance in a world witness to the Jews concerning the Messiahship of Jesus Christ."[32] The statement is instructive. In addition to advocating the cause of Jewish missions in the evangelical Christian community, the alliance hoped to be an instrument in the actual work of evangelism, which included helping to improve the quality of evangelism and setting higher standards for its work. This was in line with the general trend in the movement to evangelize the Jews in America during the period: the evolution toward a more professional, respectable, and effective mission. As previously noted, the alliance indeed helped establish and finance a program to educate missionaries to the Jews at the Moody Bible Institute. For a few years, it maintained a full-time position of an evangelist to the Jews, thus becoming a missionary agency itself. The position was eventually abolished owing to lack of funds. Only one clause in the list of purposes addressed an issue other than missions; it related to the alliance's role of providing communal support for new converts, helping them to adjust and find their niche in society. The struggle of the converts following their conversion was known to the activists of the alliance only too well.

Careful to avoid slander and defamation and keep a good public record, the alliance published its financial accounts and acknowledged every check it received.[33] Its budget consisted of hundreds of small donations from both Jews and non-Jews ranging from one dollar to a few hundred each. The position of the Hebrew Christian Alliance within the evangelical community was a complicated one and reflected in some ways the position of converted Jews in general within the evangelical milieu. On the one hand, many evangelical Christians offered the alliance warm support, demonstrated by donations from individuals as well as by invitations from congregations that hosted the yearly alliance conventions. The alliance was basically an accepted evangelical organization. But acceptance came at a price. The organization felt a need to prove its loyalty to evangelical values and to act in accordance with the norms and expectations of mainline conservative American evangelicalism of the period. Although there were, for example, some Jewish converts who, during that time, had joined Pentecostal churches, the organization gave expression only to non-Pentecostal Jewish Christians, who had accepted Jesus as their personal Savior and joined the more acceptable forms of evangelicalism. In giving expression to their Jewishness, the alliance activists went only so far as they thought the evangelical community at large would approve. Their organization during the period was a far cry from what it would become in the 1970s, when its members showed a much greater amount of independence.

The activists of the alliance were supporters of the Zionist cause. This was due both to Jewish national feelings and to their convictions as adherents of the dispensationalist premillennialist messianic hope that saw Zionism and the Jewish resettlement of the Land of Israel as necessary steps in the advancement of history and the beginning of the fulfillment of prophecies.[34] The converts' national sentiments thus received legitimation by the larger evangelical camp. The favorable attitude of the alliance toward Zionism was evident in its publication, which often included reports on the developments in the Zionist movement and described Palestine in favorable terms.[35]

During the 1920s and 1930s, the leaders of the Hebrew Christian Alliance approached the Zionist Organization of America asking to join as a group. "We are contending for a vital principle, the official recognition of Hebrew Christians as an integral part of the Jewish nation," wrote the editor of the *Hebrew Christian Alliance Quarterly* in explaining the request to be accepted into the Zionist organization.[36] In his appeals to the Zionist leadership, the alliance representative, John Zacker, declared that "the Hebrew Christian Alliance . . . has placed itself on record as favoring earnest efforts for the realization of Palestine as a Jewish homeland."[37] He demanded full rights for converted Jews in the Zionist organization and presented them as a division within Judaism. "Any Jew, be he Orthodox, Conservative, Reform, Messianic, Rationalist . . . should without shadow of doubt, be cordially received into your organization."[38] Zacker further claimed that the Hebrew Christian Alliance served as a representative of the Zionist cause in the Christian community. He also contended that the manner in which the Zionists treated Jewish Christians was a matter of concern for many Christians and would influence their attitude toward that movement.[39]

The leaders of the Zionist organization, such as Louis Lipsky, replied cordially. It was evident, however, that they were reluctant to grant the Hebrew Christian Alliance formal recognition, which, they were afraid, would be interpreted as granting legitimization to conversion of Jews and as such would cause resentment in the Jewish community.[40] Some activists of the alliance immigrated to Palestine after World War I, during the British mandate. One such activist was S. B. Rohold, who directed, under the auspices of the Canadian Presbyterian Church, a Jewish Christian congregation in Toronto and was a founder and leader of the Hebrew Christian Alliance in its early years. He immigrated to Palestine in 1920 and worked for eleven years as a missionary in Haifa, where he opened a Bible school.[41]

There was a certain amount of irony in the fact that an organization of Jewish Christians was operating on the conservative side of the American religious map, as did the fledgling congregations of Hebrew Christians, and that it was the conservatives and not the liberals who encouraged and supported the early beginnings of Jewish Christian expressions in America. Paradoxically, the conservatives were more apt to nourish such enterprises, their premillennialist faith and their understanding of the Jews and their place in history justifying their accepting attitude. In their turn, the converts' community as a whole was a product of the evangelical missionary endeavor, which was conservative and premillennialist in nature, and it was only natural for converts to find their place within that setting. Yet it was remarkable that an organization of converted Jews could operate within the framework of conservative Christianity and give expression to Jewish converts' concerns and national aspirations. Of course, these aspirations correlated with the messianic convictions of many conservative evangelicals and their understanding of the Jews and their role in history. Members of the alliance were careful to conform to what they perceived to be the evangelical norms and conventions. While converts to Protestantism in America were building their own network, meanwhile, the Protestant community was deliberating its attitude toward the evangelization of the Jews.

16

The Missionary Impulse

The Presbyterian Church was not the only church for which the period of the 1920s to the 1950s was a transitional one as far as the idea of evangelizing the Jews was concerned. The idea that the Jews should be missionized was alive among mainline Protestant churches in the period from 1920 to 1965, and such churches, as well as Protestant interdenominational bodies, invested much effort in missionizing the Jews. Yet it was during that period that many Protestants began to doubt the legitimacy of missions aimed specifically at Jews.

Ironically, the same period that saw, for the first time in Christian history, American Protestant theologians and leaders raise doubts over the legitimacy of missionizing the Jews also saw Protestants working toward professionalizing, systematizing, and coordinating missionary work among the Jews. As noted earlier, this took place on many fronts and levels ranging from the screening and training of missionaries, to studying the realities of the Jewish community and becoming acquainted with Jewish religious life, to producing more attractive and reliable translations of the Gospels as well as other publications. The representative bodies of American Protestantism saw it as their task to help raise the standards of Jewish missions. One means was the organization of special coordinating bodies on both the national and international level as well as conferences designated specifically to discuss issues relating to missions to the Jews. These conferences as well as the bodies, which were established specifically to coordinate the work of Jewish missions, were affiliated with the Federal Council of Churches of Christ in America, the International Missionary Council, and, after 1948, the World Council of Churches.

A series of international conferences on missions took place in the early decades of the twentieth century.[1] The first major international conference was convened in Edinburgh in 1910; it established a continuation committee that in 1921 was reorganized as the International Missionary Council. This new organization in its turn established the International Committee on the Christian Approach to the Jews. In 1927, the committee organized two international conferences in Europe, one in Budapest and a second one in Warsaw. A number of American Protestant missionaries, such as John S. Conning of the Presbyterian Church, participated as representatives in the conferences. The British and European Protestant missions to the Jews were still very strong during that period, and the Americans were in the minority. Most of the delegates represented German, Scandinavian, or British missions operating in various parts of Europe as well as in Asian and African missionary stations. The issues discussed in the conferences reveal some of the priorities of the missionary movement in America and abroad during the period.[2]

Some of the presentations dealt with the nature of Jewish-Christian relations and stated the Christian duty to evangelize Jews.[3] They denounced the treatment of the Jewish people throughout the centuries and urged Christians to oppose injustice against Jews, as such negative attitudes were stumbling blocks that stood in the way of effectively evangelizing them. Participants shared their experiences and offered one another advice as to how to improve the task of evangelizing the Jews. Speakers presented relevant data on the Jewish people, and the conferences also issued reports in which the participating missionaries offered their analysis of the realities of the field and the agenda they wanted to promote.

The Budapest report spoke about the need to recruit missionaries trained specifically for the field of Jewish evangelism.[4] Similarly, the report demanded that the missionary literature prepared for distribution among Jews should be reexamined and updated.[5] The Warsaw conference addressed similar concerns and also advocated the training of special workers for the field who had adequate knowledge of Hebrew and Yiddish as well as good knowledge of Christian theology.[6] The conference gave evidence of the ambivalent attitude of missionaries toward the people they were trying to convert. At the same time that the conference expressed its rejection of discrimination against the Jews, it also voiced negative opinions of the same people. A year before the conference the organizers distributed a questionnaire among the prospective participants. The conference then discussed the responses. Among other issues, participants listed what, in their opinions, were the obstacles that prevented more Jews from accepting Christianity. Some of the remarks were certainly valid, including such observations as "His treatment by non-Jews does not dispose him favorably to seek their society."[7] But the claim that "the higher moral standard of Christianity acts as a deterrent to many Jews" was one that most Jews would surely have contested and found offensive. Participants also made the claim that the Jews "have their own peculiar faults of character: selfishness, love of money and material prosperity, habits of lying, doubtful commercial dealing, lack of the sense of sin."[8] This assessment should be viewed as particularly extreme and cannot be taken as the standard missionary opinion of Jews. One can find in missionary tracts stereotypical imagery of Jews, often expressed with good intentions and without realizing that Jews might be hurt by such remarks. As part of the trend to professionalize the field, veterans in the field cautioned future evangelists not to use such potentially insulting language when approaching Jews. They had to state meticulously what such language included and explain that Jews did not appreciate stereotypes of themselves such as shrewd businessmen, for example.

The American missionaries found the European conferences unsatisfactory for their needs. They took place across the ocean, and very few American representatives could participate. And while these conferences related to issues that concerned missionaries to the Jews all around the globe, they did not concentrate their efforts on the realities of the American scene.

In 1931, at the demand of North American missionaries, the International Missionary Council organized a national conference in Atlantic City to discuss issues relating to the field of Jewish evangelism.[9] John R. Mott (1865–1955), director of the international department of the YMCA and chairman of the IMC, presided over the conference. Mott was an advocate of Christian unity and used his position in the IMC to promote his ecumenical vision.[10] His work, which helped bring about the establishment of the World Council of Churches in 1948, won him the Nobel Prize for peace a year later. The fact that Mott, one of the most outstanding leaders in Protestant ecumenical efforts in America, presided over the conference points to the importance of the gathering and the high priority American Protestants gave to evangelizing the Jews during the period. Mott and his like certainly considered evangelizing the Jews a legitimate and praiseworthy cause. Ironically, the ecumenical movement, which started around missionary conferences and organizations and which was at least partially stirred by the missionary demand that Christianity should unite in order to present itself more effectively to non-Christian societies, worked toward creating a more liberal, tolerant, and accepting atmosphere, which, in its turn, worked in the long run against a militant missionary approach. This would prove to be particularly evident in the realm of missions to the Jews.

Although the conference in 1931 and its agenda were meant to promote missionary work, the conference discussed at length the question of what the relationship of Christians and Jews should be. From a conservative missionary point of view, some of the presentations at the conference aroused discomfort, as they indirectly questioned the legitimacy of missionizing the Jews. Conservative advocates of missionary work among the Jews such as Joseph Cohn turned against the conference; in their view it did not endorse their missionary agenda without qualification, since it was willing to discuss other means and ways for Christians to relate to Jews.[11] It seems, however, that the indignation expressed by missionary advocates was an overreaction. In actuality, many of the presentations related to missionary work and attempted to systematize and professionalize the field.[12] Speakers emphasized the need for missionary literature of higher quality, more cooperation between the different missionary bodies, and well-trained missionaries as well as a more professional approach to prospective converts.[13]

One of the more important presentations in the conference, at least from a historian's point of view, was that of Charles Fahs, curator of the missionary research library at Union Theological Seminary. Fahs presented a report on the Jewish population in America and on the realities of the realm of missions to the Jews at that time. He did not necessarily provide any meaningful analysis, insights, or advice, but his detailed report serves as a reliable source for the scope and location of missionary work during the period.[14] According to Fahs's list, there were dozens of missions to the Jews in America, operating virtually in every Jewish community of a few thousand people or more (and at times in smaller communities, too). New York alone could claim more than thirty missionary stations. The evangelization of the Jews undoubtedly enjoyed a high priority in the missionary agenda of evangelical Protestant America during the period. Although by 1931 a number of major missionary organizations such as the American Board of Missions to the Jews, the Chicago Hebrew Mission, and the Department of Jewish Evangelization of the Presbyterian Church in the U.S.A. towered over the landscape of missions in their size and predominance and in the implementation of new ideas and methods, the report revealed that there were also many other small missionary enterprises working to evangelize Jews. Such missions were often snubbed by the larger, more established, and more professional missions as mom-and-pop missions, as they were small in size and scope and often operated by two full-time missionaries. Many of these missions continued to operate in accordance with the older paradigm of a storefront mission, without sufficient funds to change into the community center type of mission, a process that the larger missions advocated during the 1920s to 1950s. The report also revealed that the movement to evangelize the Jews in America was associated with mainstream conservative Protestantism and did not relate at that stage to the fledgling Pentecostal movement. Pentecostalism advocated a more immediate relationship with the divine, a more spontaneous worship, and a presence of the Holy Spirit in the believer's life, manifested by "speaking in tongues."[15] In the early decades of the century it was not part of the mainstream of conservative evangelical Christianity and was something of "the poor relation." The movement to evangelize the Jews in America made an ardent attempt to build itself a good reputation as solid and respectable, which meant the disassociation of itself from Pentecostal churches. The movement to evangelize the Jews in America would continue for decades to be non-Pentecostal in nature.

The International Missionary Council continued to promote the cause of Jewish evangelism through its Committee on the Christian Approach to the Jews. The committee was headquartered in New York and headed by an American, yet it was officially an international body representing missions to the Jews all around the globe. There were indeed a number of British, Canadian, and European missions that supported the activities of the committee.[16] Missions to the

Jews in Germany, some of which had been active for almost two centuries, were closed down during the mid- and late 1930s, but Scandinavian, Swiss, and Dutch missions participated in the work of the committee. The American missions that were affiliated with that body were mostly churches associated with the Federal Council of Churches of Christ in America, such as the American Baptists, the Reformed Church in America, and the Presbyterian Church in the U.S.A. The Presbyterians in particular valued the work of the organization and contributed a particularly large sum of money, much larger than any other church. This might have been because the director of the committee was Conrad Hoffman, who was also the director of the Department of Jewish Evangelization of the Presbyterian Church during much of the period. Most missions to the Jews in America at that time were not associated with the committee. This included some of the small missions as well as some major missions such as the Chicago Hebrew Mission, the American Board of Missions to the Jews, and the American Association for Jewish Evangelism. Perhaps some of the smaller missions did not care to join an international organization. The merits of its services were too abstract and remote. But there were other, deeper reasons for the refusal of many missions, including the larger ones, to join. As committed fundamentalists, they looked with suspicion at organizations representing mainline and liberal Protestantism even when such organizations advocated the cause of missions to the Jews. Fundamentalists had long resented the Federal Council of Churches, and when the World Council of Churches was established in 1948, they found little use for that organization as well. They kept their distance from ecumenical bodies, particularly those with international affiliations, viewing them with suspicion as too liberal and inclusive. Most missions to the Jews relied on fundamentalist supporters, and they would not join an ecumenical institution, not even one directed by Conrad Hoffman, who directed a mission that held views similar to their own concerning the Scriptures, biblical prophecy, and the destiny of Israel.

One should not, of course, overlook personal and institutional rivalries. Cohn, the director of the American Board of Missions to the Jews, did not join forces with ecumenically oriented missionaries on ideological grounds, but he had other motives as well. He considered his own mission to be the dominant all-encompassing one and worked to professionalize, systematize, and update its work. As has been noted, the American Board of Missions to the Jews organized its own conferences, which were oriented toward the more conservative elements in the Protestant camp, and Cohn disliked Conrad Hoffman precisely because the latter was the head of a rival mission.

In sum, the Committee on the Christian Approach to the Jews was an organization representing only a fraction of the missionary activity in America. It reflected the years 1920s to 1950s, which were an interim period in the history of missions to the Jews in America in which mainline Protestant churches sponsored missionary activity among the Jews, hiring Jewish converts to carry out work that was very similar in ideology and content to that carried out by more conservative organizations. Yet the conservatives did not trust the missionary enterprises of the mainline churches and often refused to cooperate with them because the latter's general theological trends were incompatible with the basic theological assumptions on which their missionary efforts were built. They were also aware that among mainline churches and their ecumenical network there were liberals voicing their opinions against the evangelization of the Jews and opting for a different means of relating to that people. Perhaps the conservatives could sense something that the mainline church's people could not: that since the mainline churches lacked the zeal and commitment deriving from a biblical prophetic worldview, in which the evangelization of the Jews had a very special meaning as part of God's plans for human salvation, they might very soon be convinced by the liberals to abandon the mission work among the Jews altogether, a scheme that eventually happened.

In addition to the International Missionary Council another Protestant body, the Home Mission Council, took it upon itself to help coordinate and promote missionary work among the Jews in America. In May 1932 it launched a department for the promotion of missionary work among the Jews that worked in cooperation with the Committee on the Christian Approach to the Jews of the IMC. John Conning, who headed the Department of Jewish Evangelization of the Presbyterian Church, was director of that department as well. But the Home Mission Council's involvement with evangelizing Jews came to a crisis in the 1940s, when opposition to continuing work among the Jews increased and the cooperation with the Committee on the Christian Approach to the Jews came to a halt.[17]

In some mainline denominations the missionary impulse was beginning to fade away in the 1950s, but not in all. It was a transitional period in which major Protestant churches often continued their missionary activity. Similarly, national and international interdenominational bodies, such as the World Council of Churches, continued to view missionary work among the Jews as legitimate and, at times, to operate agencies that were aimed at coordinating and improving evangelization work among the Jews. The World Council of Churches was established in 1948; for many this was the realization of a dream for Christian unity after decades of work toward building such an organization. In its early days the WCC was composed primarily of mainline and national Protestant churches. Later on Greek Orthodox, Eastern Orthodox, and third-world churches joined in. Conservative evangelicals, who saw the WCC as a liberal compromising institution, did not join. The WCC position on Jews in its early period paralleled that of mainline Protestantism in America, which both missionized the Jews and attempted to open a dialogue with them at the same time. In its first meeting in

Amsterdam the council issued a statement that related to the murder of 110,000 Dutch Jews by the Nazis. Yet it continued to view the evangelization of the Jews as a legitimate task that deserved a place on its own agenda.[18] It was, however, the last years of such systematic efforts among mainline churches and agencies, and one could (as many evangelical antagonists did) feel that in the air. As noted earlier, in some denominations, such as the Presbyterian Church, commitment and enthusiasm for the cause declined steadily throughout the 1940s and 1950s. In the 1960s, that organization's official standing on the evangelization of the Jews as well as on the Christian approach to the Jews in general would change to emphasize dialogue and recognition.[19]

Not only the International Missionary Council but, at times, other church bodies also established "consultations," or coordinating bodies, on the Christian approach to the Jews. A number of Lutheran churches in America organized such committees to coordinate Lutheran efforts at evangelizing Jews. In August 1959, a "theological consultation" arranged by the Department for the Christian Approach to the Jewish People of the National Lutheran Council was held at Lake Geneva, Wisconsin: "The program was related to the areas of inquiry proposed by the International Missionary Council's studies on the Christian Approach to the Jews. It was hoped that the report of this Consultation could be our American Lutheran contribution to that larger international study."[20] Participants included professors from Lutheran seminaries as well as missionaries and church officials. The agenda of this gathering was that of inquiry into the theological standing of the participants and the church at large, concerning the Jewish people and the prospect of their evangelization. The consultation issued a declaration that favored the idea of evangelizing the Jews.[21] This declaration suggested that missionary work among the Jews was a Christian duty, particularly if one adopted an appreciative attitude toward the Jewish people and the Jewish religion as a forerunner of Christianity. It expressed the conviction that evangelization efforts were a manifestation of goodwill and appreciation; to refrain from evangelizing the Jews was equivalent to indifference and negligence. The gathering, like many of its kind, was made up of people directly involved in the realm of missions to the Jews, and it would have been unlikely that they would have expressed a different opinion. As was the case in other denominations, the community of missionaries acted as an interest group in favor of continuing the missionary endeavor.

It would only be in the 1960s and 1970s that the Lutheran position would change and an atmosphere of interfaith dialogue would reach its peak and a new appreciation for Judaism and the Jewish people would become normative for mainline Protestants, who would completely abandon the missionary enterprise. The decline in missionary zeal and the rise of doubts over the legitimacy of Christian evangelization of Jews had to do with broader, long-range trends within the mainline churches. New attitudes toward other non-Protestant religions in general and Judaism in particular were making their impact on the agenda of major Protestant churches, such as the Presbyterians, American Baptists, Congregationalists, and Methodists.[22] A movement of interfaith cooperation and dialogue was making its way. The very first instances of interfaith dialogue could already be found in the late nineteenth century, particularly in conjunction with the World Parliament of Religions, which took place in Chicago in 1893. In the World Parliament of Religions liberal Protestants met with representatives of Reform and Conservative Judaism and Muslim, Bahai, Hindu, Buddhist, and other religious groups, as well as non-Protestant Christians.[23] An early proponent of the new liberal attitude was John Haynes Holmes of the Community Church in New York.[24] Holmes, who advocated a progressive social and political outlook, was a close friend of Stephen S. Wise, an independent Reform rabbi and a leader of American Judaism. As early as the late 1920s the prestigious Protestant minister was relating to Judaism as a religion that deserved respect as a religious tradition able to offer its adherents spiritual and moral content.

The attempts at dialogue took an organized form with the establishment in 1924 of the Committee on Good Will, which included liberal Protestants, Catholics, and Jews. The initiative for the creation of the Committee on Good Will might have been more social than theological and partly had to do with the rise of hate groups and bigotry in American public life during the early 1920s, a reality that alarmed Roman Catholics, Jews, and at times Protestants as well.[25] In 1928, an additional step was taken by the creation of the National Council of Christians and Jews. The establishment of this council marked an important development in Christian-Jewish relations in America and eventually had a strong influence on the attitudes of a number of Protestant churches toward the evangelization of the Jews and their eventual decision to abandon it. Protestant participants came from mainline churches associated with the Federal Council of Churches of Christ in America, in which churches that defined themselves as conservative did not take a part. Jewish participants in the Committee on Good Will and later on the National Council of Christians and Jews raised the issue of missions. From their point of view Christian attempts at evangelizing Jews were a stumbling block to a relationship of trust and goodwill. They could not accept the idea that Christians could sincerely express friendship and respect toward the Jews while at the same time seeking to convert them. Protestant participants in such gatherings began distancing themselves from the efforts to evangelize Jews.[26] Missionaries such as Conrad Hoffman reacted with alarm to such notions, which they saw as a betrayal of essential Christian imperatives and as a danger to their missionary cause.

A major proponent of the idea that Christians should not evangelize Jews was Reinhold Niebuhr, one of America's leading Protestant theologians between the

1930s and 1960s. Niebuhr, who was a professor at Union Theological Seminary in New York and advocated a neo-Orthodox theology, militated against the opinion that Christian propagation of the Christian gospel should include Jews. Niebuhr's attitude, which he expressed as early as 1926, signified a revolution in Christian Protestant thinking toward Jews and Judaism. His advocacy of nonmissionizing did not result from indifference or hostility toward Jews. It posed a liberal alternative to the conservative evangelical attitude toward Jews. Like the evangelicals, Niebuhr, too, supported Zionism, but on a political and historical basis rather than any premillennialist messianic hope. In the early 1940s he helped found the Christian Council for Palestine, which mustered Christian support for the establishment of a Jewish state in what was then British Palestine.[27] He did not view the Jews as destined to play a role in any eschatological era. Instead, he pioneered an approach that accepted the legitimacy of a separate Jewish existence outside the church and the idea that Jews, holding a valid religious tradition of their own, did not have to convert. Niebuhr was a rare voice among leading Protestant thinkers between the 1930s and 1950s; thereafter, however, his position became more accepted and was adopted and developed with great vigor by liberal Protestant theologians such as Roy A. Eckardt, Paul M. Van Buren, and Franklin Littell.[28]

The Liberal Protestant position shifted further when the ecumenical movement was greatly encouraged by the impact of Vatican II, the Roman Catholic ecumenical council that convened in the Vatican in the early 1960s. The council enhanced a new spirit of dialogue between the different Christian churches and between Christianity and other religions. It attempted to put to rest some of the old hostilities and bitterness and promoted an atmosphere of toleration and recognition.[29] During the mid- and late 1960s and 1970s a number of mainline church bodies adopted declarations and decisions in relation to the Jewish people and Judaism and their role in history.[30] Among other things, such declarations cleared the Jews of the historical accusation of the deicide. Mainline churches debated the issue of missions, and a number of those that had been engaged in evangelizing Jews during the 1950s decided categorically to stop missionizing them.[31] Their decisions were influenced by an increasingly prevailing attitude toward Jews and Judaism that recognized the right of the Jewish people to coexist alongside Christianity. They were also influenced by the strong Jewish objection to the missionary activity Jews voiced in the midst of the evolving dialogue. At this point, mainline Protestant churches also lacked the kind of conviction that could counterbalance the impact of dialogue and would sustain the desire to evangelize the Jews, namely, a premillennialist messianic belief that viewed the Jews as chosen to play a special role in God's plans for humanity. By the late 1960s the liberal Lutheran churches (now part of the Evangelical Lutheran Church), as well as other liberal Protestant churches associated with the National Council of Churches, abandoned their involvement in missionary activity among Jews. Evangelizing the Jews remained the declared agenda of more conservative Lutheran churches, such as the Missouri Synod, which not only continued its missionary efforts among the Jews but even intensified them. That particular denomination was strongly influenced by the fundamentalist conservative evangelical segment of American Christianity including the dispensationalist belief, which certainly shaped its evangelization efforts among the Jews.[32]

In sum, the years from the 1920s to the early 1960s should be viewed as a transitional period with the major denominations struggling over self-definition and over defining their theological views on many issues including their relation to the Jews. By the 1960s the liberal impetus triumphed over the agenda of many of the churches, the missionary impetus in those churches declined, and it would be up to conservative churches to promote missionary work among the Jews. While the Protestants deliberated the role of missions among themselves, the Jews had their opinion on the matter.

17

A Less Heated Reaction

The period 1920–65 was a relatively relaxed one as far as the relationship between the missionary movement and the Jewish community was concerned. Jewish leaders and activists did not regard attempts at evangelizing Jews favorably, but missions did not occupy the same place in the agenda of the Jewish community as in the last decades of the nineteenth century and the beginning of the twentieth, when Jewish reaction was heated and intense, or in the later period of the 1970s and 1980s when the Jewish community again gave the issue more notice.

Whereas during earlier decades Jewish journals such as the *American Israelite*, the *American Hebrew*, and *Menorah* periodically published articles expressing their disdain for missions to the Jews, the topic did not receive much attention in Jewish journals between the 1920s and the 1960s. The kind of former-convert literature that appeared in the earlier period, such as Samuel Freuder's *My Return to Judaism*, which vehemently attacked the missionary community and described it as fraudulent, did not repeat itself either. During the period, no specifically antimissionary Jewish organizations arose, and no Jewish activists dedicated themselves to fighting missionaries, as was the case in the earlier period and would become the case again in the 1970s to the 1990s. It was also a remarkable fact that the jealousies and rivalries in the missionary community during the period, which at times brought about the creation of new missionary organizations, were not used by mission antagonists in the Jewish community to defame and degrade missionaries and discredit the movement to evangelize the Jews. Jewish activists and the Jewish public were not really interested in such accounts.

The reasons for this relatively calm relationship to the missionaries' activity had to do with the character and agenda of the Jewish community and the image Jews held of missions during the period. Unlike in the earlier period, the Jewish community did not consider the missionary activity to be much of a threat. Following the Scopes trial the public and social image of conservative evangelical Christianity was not very high. In liberal eyes, it represented a declining anachronistic form of Christianity. The period between 1920 and 1965 saw the beginning of Christian-Jewish dialogue. Jewish leaders and activists who engaged in the dialogue met with liberal Christians, who seemed to represent the majority of Christianity. Neither liberal Christians nor Jews took fundamentalist Christianity very seriously. The Jewish leadership during the era looked upon missionaries as representing a marginal group of people who were irrelevant to major social and cultural trends. As such, they did not consider the latter to pose a danger either to Jewish survival or to the position of Jews within the American community.

During the 1920s to 1950s, the Jewish leadership considered other groups and movements to pose a much more immediate threat to Jewish life and status in the American polity than missionaries. These years were marked by the rise of nativist Anglo-Saxon or Christian exclusivist groups that American Jewry considered to be of real danger, whereas, the missions, they believed, were not. In comparison with outright anti-Semitism, the missionary movement, which previously seemed a serious threat to Jewish standing in American society, did not seem a threat any more. The 1920s to 1930s saw the establishment of a number of both national and local Jewish organizations aimed at combating harassment, defamation, and discrimination against Jews.[1] This included, on the national level, the Anti-Defamation League of B'nai B'rith and, on the local level, Relations Committees established in virtually all Jewish communities of a population of a few thousand Jews or more (and, at times, in smaller communities as well). Such organizations took it upon themselves to relate to all activities and occurrences that they considered harmful or intrusive; they collected material, exchanged information, expressed concern, and, at times, protested what they considered to be discrimination against or defamation of Jews. Dealing with missionaries fell under the rubric of these organizations.

An examination of the correspondence and material collected by Relations Committees, such as in Cincinnati, reveals that during the 1930s to 1960s missionaries were not of great concern to those organizations.[2] Among thousands and thousands of documents testifying to the worries of Jewish organizations during this period over the security, dignity, and civil equality of Jews in America, only very rarely is there a reference to missionary activity. Rather, these communities were busy over the rise of anti-Semitism in America during the 1920s to 1940s. They feared such anti-Jewish publications as Henry Ford's *Dearborn Independent*, or *The Protocols of the Elders of Zion*, which Ford also circulated in America, or Father Charles Caughlin's hateful radio program. They were similarly concerned over the work of nativist and Christian anti-Semitic groups, such as Charles Winrod's Defenders of the Christian Faith.[3] Groups advocating bigotry, such as the John Birch Society, continued to concern American Jewish organizations during the 1950s and 1960s as well. During those years the issue of missions to the Jews was a minor, secondary one.

Although anti-Semitism did not disappear after World War II, the situation for American Jews definitely improved. Following the war and during the 1950s, there was an institutional growth in American Judaism and an increase in synagogue building and membership. The status of Judaism improved, and it became to some extent one of the three accepted public religions in America.[4] Jewish social and economic opportunities also improved considerably. Jewish life in the American polity during the postwar years seemed more secure than ever. In such an atmosphere, Christian missions seemed completely irrelevant to the Jewish community in America.

In the early 1950s a leading historian of American Jewry, Anita Libman Lebeson, interviewed Archie Mackinney, the superintendent of the American Messianic Fellowship in Chicago. Unfamiliar with the premillennialist belief system, she was deeply impressed by what she considered his philo-Semitic and pro-Zionist stand. In her opinion, such a favorable attitude completely outweighed whatever missionary activity in which Mackinney was engaged. She did not consider such evangelization activities to be a threat. "They are missionaries. They are also . . . philo-semites who are moved to speak and act in behalf of Jewish restoration to a Jewish state. The Rev. Mackinney . . . has recently returned from Israel firmly convinced that the Jews and the State of Israel are part of the Divine Plan."[5] Such a favorable assessment of missionaries on the part of a committed Jew had not been heard since Zionist leaders at the turn of the century spoke to William Blackstone, the ardent missionary and Christian Zionist. But whereas Blackstone's Jewish friends did not care to know about his missionary activity, Libman Lebeson did know about Mackinney's and yet remained impressed at what she conceived to be his pro-Jewish attitude, though not everyone shared her opinion.

A number of other Jews wrote about missionaries between the 1920s and 1960s, and their opinions were not always so favorable. In the mid-1930s, David Eichhorn, a Reform rabbi, wrote a dissertation for the Hebrew Union College on the history of missions to the Jews in America. Eichhorn adopted a particularly harsh and resentful attitude toward the missionary endeavor, much in line with traditional Jewish views of proselytizers of Jews. His narrative takes at face value some of the worst accusations against individual missionaries and evangelization enterprises.[6] Eichhorn's work brings to mind, and indeed resembles, such nineteenth-century antimissionary tracts as those of Isaac M. Wise, from whose work Eichhorn quotes extensively. Another study of missions was not a Ph.D. dissertation but an essay. In an attempt to acquaint the Jews with the scope of missionary activity in 1948, *Jewish Social Studies* published an article by Max Eisen on missions to the Jews.[7] Although the essay appeared in an academic journal, it clearly reflected Jewish communal interests and concerns. The article was informative, consisting of lists and data on the missionary activity, but did not concern itself with the motivation and theological basis of the missionary work or attempt to understand the missionaries on their own ground. It had an antimissionary bias and described missionary work in resentful terms, albeit not as harsh as Eichhorn's, and indicated that the old resentful attitude on the part of Jews had not disappeared.

Another Ph.D. dissertation, by Robert Blumstock, who wrote his thesis at the University of Oregon toward the end of the period under discussion, reflected a different attitude. A sociologist not committed to Jewish leadership or community activity, Blumstock concentrated his work on the current activity of the American Board of Missions to the Jews. Unlike Eichhorn, he did not set out to defame missionaries but to study them. Consequently he shows a much better grasp of the group and its missionary drive and motivation and treats the mission in a more relaxed, detached, and scholarly manner.[8]

Writing dissertations on missionaries was not accidental. The period was marked by a small-scale Jewish attempt to study the missionary phenomenon. Mirroring the trend in the missionary community, the attempt was to systematize and professionalize the Jewish reaction to the missionary presence. This trend both reflected and enhanced the less heated and more relaxed attitude toward missionaries. In 1928, the Bureau of Jewish Social Research in New York carried out a survey of missionary activity among the Jews.[9] It composed a questionnaire that it sent to Jewish agencies in different localities such as the Federation of Jewish Welfare Organizations in Los Angeles. It asked the agencies to collect data in line with the guidelines of the questionnaire. The initiators of the survey were interested in information on the scope of the missionary network, the number of missions and missionaries, their location, and the number of converts they claimed to have made but did not inquire into the theology or motivation of the missionaries. Jewish community agencies such as that in Los Angeles did not have much difficulty in answering the survey's questionnaire. Missions were cooperative, and missionaries were quite open on their work and agenda.[10] A survey similar to that in America was carried out a few year later in Palestine, by the Department of Social Services of the Jewish Agency.

An illustration of the new, more systematic, and at the same time more relaxed attitude is provided by the Jewish community in Minnesota. In 1944, Erwin Oreck, a Jewish leader in Duluth, Minnesota, wrote to a number of Jewish organizations inquiring about Hyman Appelman, a Jewish convert and a missionary who was conducting evangelization campaigns there. He received answers from three Jewish organizations revealing an impressive and systematic fact-finding mechanism on the part of Jewish organizations regarding activities of groups and individuals, including Christian fundamentalists, suspected of hatred or malintention toward Jews. The interest Jewish groups took in evangelists such as Appelman was less on account of evangelization than possible anti-Semitism. Appelman's work in Minneapolis was conducted in cooperation with William Riley, whom Jews regarded as a hostile anti-Semite. Nissen Gross, director of the Fact-finding Department of the Anti-Defamation League of B'nai B'rith, Chicago, wrote to Oreck in Minnesota: "Schneider felt that Appleman [*sic*] was not a friend of the Jews because he is a fundamentalist . . . along the same lines as Rev. Riley. . . . However, Elias Newman, also a Hebrew Christian but very friendly and cooperative with us . . . claims that Appleman is a fine Christian but appears to be very gullible to the sinister influences of the Riley gang. Nevertheless we do not think Appleman should be put in the same class with Riley or other fundamentalists who are antagonistic toward the Jews, because of his desire to get converts to Christianity."[11] Gross's letter reveals a new, less hostile attitude toward missionaries. Elias Newman, a missionary, is described as "a friend" and "cooperative," a person with whom the Anti-Defamation League has a working relationship. Gross cites Newman's opinion, which he valued. He furthermore expresses his opinion that missionary work among the Jews does not qualify a person to be ranked as someone who is antagonistic toward the Jews.

Another letter came from Dorothy Nathan of the Community Service Unite, American Jewish Committee, New York City. "[Appelman] is a sincere and reputable person, not in any sense a racketeer." Such an evaluation of a missionary's character could hardly have been expected a generation earlier. She goes on to say that "[he] belongs with the very conservative Protestants . . . makes an emotional rather than an intellectual appeal. . . . He is pretty stiff-necked and there is nothing much to do about him." A third letter came from Rabbi Aaron Opher of the Synagogue Council of America in New York City. "Mr. Appelman," he writes, "endeavored to convert the Jews to Christianity. There was not anti-Semitic or subversive reference in any of his talks."[12] Obviously, Appelman did not bother Rabbi Opher and other Jewish activists as an evangelist; they would have been much more concerned had he been making anti-Semitic remarks.

Thus, there is a correlation between developments in the missionary community and the Jewish reaction. The years of the 1920s to the early 1960s were characterized by a missionary movement eager to gain respectability and careful not to antagonize the Jewish community and make a bad name for itself. The same years witnessed a more relaxed attitude in the Jewish community toward the Christian attempts at evangelizing Jews. Jews did not find the missionary efforts as objectionable as in the earlier period, and they were busy worrying about other complications in their relationship with the non-Jewish world. For both parties, those were years of growth and professionalization. Just as the missionaries who studied the Jewish community came to differentiate among different groups of Jews, so did the representatives of the Jewish community become conscious that there were different types of missionaries and that not all should automatically be regarded as enemies. In some cases Jews and missionaries even cooperated in what they saw as a mutual interest: fighting anti-Jewish bigotry. Although both sides were not fully aware of the matter, there was an unacknowledged dialogue and exchange between the missionary and the Jewish communities, which influenced both the missionary behavior and rhetoric and the Jewish reaction to Christian evangelists.

The period 1920–65 stands out as an intermediate era in the history of missions to the Jews in America. The movement moved away from the storefront missions of the earlier period that had been directed at the mass of immigrants arriving from eastern Europe and had been run by individuals with neither a systematic Christian education nor training for their posts. Missions grew in numbers, became more professional, and attracted increasing numbers of converts, but they had not yet stirred the mass movement of Jewish converts to Christianity witnessed from the late 1960s onward. Changes in the character of the missionary movement reflected the demographic developments in American Jewry. The missions during this middle period were targeting an intermediate generation of American Jews, with strong ties to eastern European traditions but eager to become fully American.

Similarly, new developments took place among the converts. The period saw the early beginnings of a converts' community and a subculture of Jews who, within evangelical Christianity, became advocates of the dispensationalist approach to the Jews and an interest group for the cause of Jewish evangelization. A number of Hebrew Christian congregations sprang up in major American cities, and an association of converted Jews took an active part in trying to shape the movement to evangelize the Jews in America. But the Hebrew Christian Alliance of America and the Jewish Christian congregations were still far from the more vigorous and independent Messianic Jewish movement that came about later. The emergence of a separate, albeit conformist, movement of converts reflected in its turn developments in the evangelical community that, within boundaries, allowed for moderate expression of ethnic distinctiveness.

In this second phase the missionary community learned much from the experiences and mistakes of the earlier period. Missionary leaders insisted on acquiring a more professional attitude toward evangelizing the Jews, along with a new set of norms for the supervision of missions and for the recruitment and training of missionaries. Consequently, the kind of scandals that erupted within the evangelical Protestant community over the conduct of missionaries did not repeat themselves. Similarly, the Jewish community ceased its aggressive attacks on the personal integrity of individual missionaries. Even though Joseph Cohn and Arthur Michelson stood out as controversial persons during that period, they retained their position as leaders of major missions and, despite challenges, enjoyed ample support among evangelicals that enabled them to carry on and even enlarge the work of their missions considerably.

In evaluating the period and its significance for the history of missions to the Jews in America, it is most important to note that the movement demonstrated great adaptability and resourcefulness. It showed a willingness to adjust to changes in the Jewish community and the new demands they brought with them. Its means of evangelization developed as the generation it was evangelizing changed. That adaptability secured the continuity of the movement and its growing success.

Missions to the Jews during the period were conservative evangelical institutions. It should be noted, therefore, that the years from the 1920s to the 1960s were not ones of decline but rather a period of growth for these enterprises in size, experience, organization, and sophistication. Contrary to the way many Americans viewed the matter, conservative evangelicalism did not consider itself defeated following the Scopes trial in 1925. The decades between the trial and the evangelical resurgence of the late 1960s and early 1970s were in actuality years of quiet growth for the movement. It had established or fortified a network of institutions: Bible schools, journals, radio stations, independent churches, and, of course, missionary organizations. In the 1970s many were surprised to discover that conservative evangelical Christianity was actually a large, vibrant, and growing segment of American religion. Similarly, many in the Jewish community were caught by surprise when they discovered in the early 1970s the existence of a large and dynamic movement of missions to the Jews.

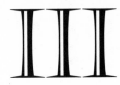

The Coming of Age, 1965–2000

18

The Changing Times

The late 1960s to early 1970s were marked by major changes in American society and culture, which strongly affected both the Jewish and evangelical communities. The new cultural trends influenced the realm of missions to the Jews and reshaped its character. Central among the developments that worked to change the missionary movement was the coming of age of the Jewish baby boomers, a generation with its own cultural characteristics and a new vision of American society and values, as well as stronger interest than its parents' generation in spiritual and religious matters.

The baby boomers, the generation born in the years following World War II, challenged much of their parents' generation's norms. Abandoning older, patriotic notions, many of them were unwilling to make personal sacrifices for the sake of American political goals and opposed the war in Vietnam. Opposition to the war served as a focal point for expressing their new values and agenda. Creating their own new young people's subculture, the counterculture, they adopted new exterior appearances, such as styles of dress and haircuts, and new music, as well as implementing more profound changes, such as more permissive norms of sexual expression and a mistrust of government and authority in general. Many among the younger generation embarked on spiritual journeys in an attempt to find more depth to life than they had found in the American culture of their parents' generation. Many sought spiritual meaning and a sense of community with little regard for their parents' religious affiliations, breaking many of the old ethnic barriers that had helped to reinforce a sense of inherited religious-ethnic loyalties.[1] The period saw a dramatic rise in new religious movements as well as an unexpected resurgence of evangelical Christianity, along with a continued or growing appeal of other veteran conservative religious groups, such as the Adventists and Jehovah's Witnesses.[2] Mainline, liberal middle-class denominations, which grew considerably in the post–World War II era, lost much of their appeal among the baby boomers and began to decline.[3] There was a strong awareness during the period that a profound cultural revolution was taking place, transforming accepted norms, values, and modes of living. In *Mr. Sammler's Planet*, Saul Bellow gave a literary expression to the sense of alienation and misplacement of old liberals confronting the new cultural realities. But among the members of the counterculture themselves, there were feelings of bewilderment and uprootedness, fueling the quest for new meanings, structures, and communities.[4]

The new cultural trends strongly influenced the Jewish baby boomers, even more so than any other ethnic segment in the American population. Young Jewish men and women were represented in new religious movements in particularly large numbers. In certain new religious groups, the percentage of Jews was five times greater than their percentage in the general American population.[5] In American forms of Buddhism, their representation has been even larger.[6] For Jews, the times were more promising than ever before. The new era brought with it a loosening of the old ethnic boundaries that characterized life in American cities until the 1960s. White baby boomers, for the most part, did not settle in ethnic neighborhoods, and their social milieu was more mixed and varied than that of their parents. The younger generation of Jews who came of age in the late 1960s and 1970s were already, for the most part, third-generation Americans. Whereas their grandparents were, as a rule, still part of the immigrant community and their parents had just reached the middle classes and suburbia, the Jewish baby boomers had usually been born and raised in comfortable middle-class homes. Making their way into America's middle class was not something they had had to make sacrifices to achieve. Unlike their parents, they did not strive to make it into America's mainstream. They were already there. Barriers and restrictions that affected their parents—quotas in colleges and universities, restricted residential areas, or nonadmittance to clubs or fraternities—were lifted during the 1960s. Whereas an earlier generation of Jews attending colleges clung together, joined the same fraternities, and courted exclusively Jewish mates, this was no longer the case for many among the younger generation.[7] They could be accepted to the colleges of their choice and could befriend and date (and marry) non-Jews, and they no longer congregated exclusively with fellow Jews. Jewish fraternities were dying out during the period, and the old Jewish ban on intermarriage, which held firm until the 1950s, was losing its hold during the 1960s and 1970s, with intermarriage rates growing steadily. By the late 1980s, intermarriages would become the norm rather than the exception. The Jewish taboo on crossing the lines and joining other alien religious groups had also weakened during the period, with many young Jews exploring and at times joining American forms of Asian religions, new religious movements, or evangelical forms of Christianity.[8]

How did the missionary movement react to the new era, the social and cultural changes that it brought about, and the vast new opportunities for evangelization that were embodied in this new generation? At the beginning of the era, the missionary community, for the most part, did not yet see the opportunities that the new era opened to its message, and its members were just as confused and resentful toward the new cultural trends as conservative Americans in general were. The missionary movement was associated with the conservative evangelical camp in American Christianity—mostly with what was then the mainstream, non-Pentecostal segment of evangelicalism. The missions had worked for decades to build a solid, respectable reputation as a means to secure their position in evangelical eyes. They identified themselves with and promoted evangelical middle-class propriety. They had, for the most part, a very difficult time relating to the counterculture and rejected it vehemently. The transition from one era to the next in the realm of Jewish evangelism was therefore not an easy and smooth passage, and the bulk of missionaries during the period had to be dragged into the new era in Jewish evangelism kicking and screaming. Nonetheless, within about a decade, the entire field of Jewish evangelism had transformed itself and acquired a completely new character.

The perpetrators of the change were two avant-garde movements within the missionary community that responded to the spirit of the age and took different courses than had been practiced by the missions. Jews for Jesus and Messianic Judaism paved the missionary way into new modes and methods of evangelizing the Jews, introducing a new character and a new spirit, one that took full notice of the social and cultural developments of the era. Their spectacular growth over the field reflected their better grasp of the changing realities of Jewish and evangelical life in America and thus their use of more effective techniques for both evangelizing Jews and gaining the support of the evangelical community.

Their story tells much about the history of missions during the period, since the other missions mostly reacted and responded to their innovative spirit. Other missions first rejected and struggled against the new groups, their ideas and character, but later embraced them, either enthusiastically or reluctantly. The relationship between the new missionary and messianic groups and their predecessors (and at times, sponsors) in the missionary camp resembled the relationship between the members of the counterculture and their parents' generation. It embodied rebellion on the part of the younger generation, severe criticism of their predecessors' ways and norms, and a wish to do things their own, new way.

On the old guard's side, the initial reaction was that of shock, alarm, and fear—perhaps not unlike that of the American establishment toward the young people's rebellious counterculture or of secure middle-class parents discovering that their children had joined that culture. There was definitely a generational struggle, one generation introducing new methods and styles and claiming its place in the center of the movement, the older generation clinging to its ways and means, rejecting and resenting the changes and its perpetrators. By the late 1970s to early 1980s, something of a rapprochement prevailed in the missionary scene. The older, veteran missionaries came to terms with the new trends and embraced them, at times wholeheartedly.

The core of the new approach, which by the 1980s would become prevalent in the entire missionary movement, was a reinforced emphasis on Jewish ethnicity and on support for the state of Israel. The period brought about a movement of searching for roots and a rise in ethnic pride at the same time that ethnic barriers were crumbling down.[9] The more avant-garde Jews for Jesus and the movement of Messianic Judaism and later on the entire missionary movement promoted, as never before, the notion that Jews were not betraying their heritage by accepting Jesus as their Savior but rather becoming better Jews and embarking on a journey of reclaiming their Jewish roots. The missions also emphasized their hopes and support for Israel. Missions reacted favorably toward Zionism from the beginning of that movement, but during the new era, in the late 1960s through the 1970s and 1980s, they proclaimed their attachment to Israel as never before. The emphasis on Jewish roots and the attachment to Israel have become the heart of the mission's rhetoric and their appeal in approaching both potential converts and donors.

A watershed event that helped to reinforce this attitude and played a role in initiating the ideology and rhetoric of the new missionary era was the Six-Day War. The war in June 1967 between Israel and its Arab neighbors had a profound impact on the image of Israel and Jews in America, with a particularly strong effect on both the Jewish and evangelical communities. For evangelicals, Israel's conquest of many of the major biblical sites of the country, including the historic parts of Jerusalem, seemed like the beginning of the events of the End Times. In their understanding, it indicated that the state of Israel had a role and purpose in God's plans for humanity and that the war was part of a larger plan that would lead to the messianic kingdom. Books by evangelical activists and thinkers in the years following the Six-Day War paid much attention to the role of the Jewish people and the state of Israel in history. Hal Lindsey's *The Late Great Planet Earth* was an evangelical premillennialist best-seller of the 1970s and sold more than twenty million copies. The book made elaborate references to the developments in the Middle East and presented Israel and the events that took place in that country as crucial to the premillennialist understanding of the course of history. Similarly, Billy Graham, the most prestigious evangelist of the period, produced a film on Israel in the early 1970s, *His Land*, which portrayed the country and the people in favorable and glorious terms. Following the Six-Day War, evangelical involvement with Jews and Israel intensified. Dozens of pro-Israel evangelical groups organized in the United States, and evangelicals have been counted among Israel's most loyal supporters in America.[10]

Evangelical leaders, among them major evangelists such as Billy Graham and Jerry Falwell, expressed their good feelings toward Israel, visited the country, and befriended its leaders. Evangelical opinions of Jews have improved dramatically since the 1960s, as a survey taken by the Jewish Anti-Defamation League pointed out.[11]

Missions benefited from the intensified evangelical interest in the Jews and the prospect of their eventual conversion to Christianity. In evangelical premillennialist eyes, they were working for a divine purpose, propagating the Christian gospel among God's chosen people. The evangelical community was willing to support such an enterprise generously. During the era, missions have turned (in addition to evangelization agencies) into centers for promoting interest in the Jews and their heritage, providing information on Israel, and organizing tours to that country. Missions to the Jews became part of the pro-Israel lobby in America, supporting Israeli policy more enthusiastically than left-wing or liberal Jews—not to mention liberal Christians, whose attitudes toward Israel grew increasingly critical throughout the 1960s to 1980s.[12]

For missions to the Jews, the era was particularly challenging and eventually unprecedentedly rewarding. Jews for Jesus and Messianic Judaism served as the avant-garde of this new era in missionary history. They wrote new chapters in the long and rich history of missions to the Jews in America, which, from the point of view of the missions, were more exciting and promising than ever.

19

Jews for Jesus and the Evangelization of a New Generation

In the early 1970s, Americans noticed a striking group of people: young men and women standing in crowded city areas, wearing T-shirts with the motto "Jews for Jesus" and distributing leaflets calling upon Jews to embrace Jesus as their Savior. These people made such a strong impression and attracted so much attention that, in the eyes of many, Jews for Jesus became associated with all attempts to evangelize Jews in America, as well as one of the better-known groups that were part of the "Jesus movement," the name given to the resurgence of evangelical Christianity among the younger generation during the 1960s and 1970s.[1] Directing its attention to members of the new counterculture and adapting to the young people's style and manners, Jews for Jesus differed sharply from evangelizing organizations of the earlier period. Whereas the older generation of missionaries strictly adhered to midcentury norms of conservative Protestant propriety, the new organization believed that its more daring approach would prove more effective with the younger generation and would eventually gain evangelical approval. During its early period, Jews for Jesus encountered much opposition from the old guard of missionaries and struggled for recognition and acknowledgment of the merits of its new style and methods. The challenges faced by the group in those years exemplifies larger developments in the evangelical community, which had gradually become more open to the spirit of the age—though not without inner struggles and conflicts.

Jews for Jesus was the informal name of a branch of an older mission to Jews in America—the American Board of Missions to the Jews; it later broke away from its parent organization and became independent, officially calling itself "Hineni Ministries."[2] Although Jews for Jesus acquired its own distinct character and introduced new evangelization techniques, the impetus to carry out its missionary work, its basic theological perceptions, and the essence of its message were not new. With all its resourcefulness and innovations in approaching prospective converts, the new missionary enterprise should be viewed in light of a long history of evangelizing the Jews in America, a history that began in the nineteenth century and has been largely motivated by a premillennialist messianic understanding of the role of the Jews in God's plans for humanity.[3]

At the time Jews for Jesus was formed, its parent organization, the American Board of Missions to the Jews, was large and well established. As noted earlier, the mission had been founded in 1894 by Leopold Cohn, who began his successful career as a missionary by operating a storefront mission in a heavily populated Jewish neighborhood in Brooklyn. The founder of Jews for Jesus, Moishe Rosen, looked upon Cohn as a hero and inspiration for his own work in founding a new missionary group. He also adopted Cohn's premillennialist messianic belief that emphasized the important role of Israel in the coming messianic age as well as a conservative outlook on biblical exegesis similar to that of the conservative segment of American Protestantism from which the mission received its support.

In its second phase, from the 1920s through the 1950s, the American Board of Missions to the Jews, under the leadership of Leopold's son, Joseph Cohn, proved itself to be an avant-garde group that noticed and responded to the changing character of the Jewish community and the culture in general. The dynamic mission developed innovative methods for reaching a new generation of prospective converts. After Cohn's death in 1953, the mission moved from a charismatic leadership to a bureaucratic one, and its character stiffened. The largest and most successful mission to the Jews, the American Board had been the target of endless accusations both from Jews and from rivals within the missionary community.[4] Its leaders felt they had to retain the trust of conservative Protestants, on whose support the mission relied for its survival. Thus, they worked hard on building its image as a solid, respectable institution, in line with conservative middle-class propriety. The last thing one could expect in the 1960s was for the mission to associate itself with a "beatnik" or a "hippie" movement or to acquire an image of a "freaky" group. Yet one of its more dynamic workers, Moishe Rosen, did just that.

Rosen is physically an enormous person, with an energetic, outgoing personality—the type of man whom one would neither ignore nor forget. Self-assured, decisive, and authoritarian, he made a natural leader and father figure for young men and women. Born in 1931 to a lower-middle-class family in Kansas City, he grew up in Denver, Colorado.[5] He was raised in a typical Jewish home of its day, observing the Jewish holidays and favoring liberal Democratic politics. During high school he worked in his father's junk business and enrolled in Colorado College, where he earned a certificate in business administration a year after his graduation from high school. Rosen's experience as a businessman served him later in running his missionary enterprise. Although inclined toward business, Rosen was also a "radical" involved in civil rights causes. Such an attitude was quite common among young Jews in the 1940s and 1950s, many of whom saw their well-being within American society as linked with progressive politics. Rosen was particularly influenced by Saul Alinsky (1909–72), a social activist in Chicago in the 1930s to 1960s, who advocated high-profile—and at times confrontational—tactics on the part of the underprivileged in their struggle to bring the establishment to act favorably on their behalf. Although Rosen later abandoned his political activity and became a conservative in his social outlook, he implemented some of Alinsky's ideas and emphasized confrontational tactics and high visibility in his missionary campaigns.[6]

At the age of eighteen, Rosen married Ceil Starr, who was the first to take an interest in the Christian faith. In 1953 they both converted and joined a Baptist congregation. Eager to learn about his new faith, Rosen enrolled as a student at Northeastern Bible School and also began his apprenticeship as a missionary with the American Board of Missions to the Jews. Upon his graduation in 1957, the American Board sent him to work in Los Angeles. Rosen's career there was successful, and during that period his relationship with the board's director for missionary work, Daniel Fuchs, was excellent, based on mutual fondness and appreciation. Rosen acquired a strong position within the mission, and in 1967 he was invited to the New York headquarters to direct a training school for entering missionaries. Rosen, more than others in the mission, began to notice that a new Jewish generation had come about and that the interests, opinions, and lifestyles of many of the young Jews differed from those whom the missions had previously approached.[7] He felt that the American Board needed new modes of evangelism to reach these young people. Admittedly Rosen himself held unfavorable views of the "counterculture," but like some other evangelists of the period he set out to approach this idealistic (albeit, in his opinion, misguided) generation and bring them to accept the Christian message.[8] He asked the mission to allow him to open a center for young seekers of the counterculture generation.

In 1970, Rosen was sent to San Francisco to operate a branch of the mission intended to approach the new generation there, in the capital of the counterculture. The city's residents were noted for their tolerance toward different groups, and it was a Mecca for tens of thousands of young men and women from all over the United States and elsewhere. A dramatic change in the political, social, cultural, and religious atmosphere in America was taking place. A new style of personal appearance, music, cuisine, and manners came into being, along with political protests, especially against the war in Vietnam and the draft and over civil rights issues, as well as a new or renewed interest in religion.[9] Young Jews were strongly influenced by the changing values and norms. At the same time that Rosen began his operations in San Francisco, thousands of young Jews were looking for new spiritual and communal identity. Many were attracted to Americanized versions of Eastern religions. There were followers of Meher Baba and the Reverend Sun Myung Moon, the "Hare Krishnas," practitioners of Zen and Transcendental Meditation, Sufis, and, of course, the "Jesus People." Others were drawn to renewed forms of Jewish life.[10]

The San Francisco mission was a branch of the American Board of Missions to the Jews, but it was in many ways independent and acquired its own characteristics, including its own striking name, Jews for Jesus. From its inception, it showed more flexibility as well as creativity and imagination in pursuing its evangelism. It used evangelization techniques completely different from those of other missions to the Jews. Rosen advocated more visibility on the part of the missionaries even if that meant provoking anger in the Jewish community. Jews, he contended, were confrontational people, and the means to arouse their curiosity and convince them of the truth of the Christian message had to match their nature. One could not approach Jews the same way one would approach Asians or middle-class Anglo-Saxons. In teaching prospective evangelists how to approach Jews, Rosen explained that a missionary need not adopt a specific formula in attempting to evangelize. Missionaries should use different techniques to approach different people, he contended.[11]

Jews for Jesus' new style, creativity, and resourcefulness were apparent in the new kinds of tracts it produced, which did not rely on elaborate quotes from the Bible and textual interpretation. It assumed that most young Jews were not very familiar with their religious heritage and thus quotations from Scripture would be of limited interest. Its leaflets were short, witty, handwritten, illustrated, and signed by the specific members of the group who wrote them. They also provided addresses and telephone numbers to establish contact. Producing these leaflets provided the young missionaries with a sense of personal creativity and fulfillment.

A leaflet signed by Steffi Geiser titled "Everything you always wanted to know about Jesus but were afraid to ask your Rabbi" was organized in question-and-answer form:

Q: Isn't Jesus really only for the Gentiles?
A: Nope. The Messiah was promised to the Jews and came as a Jew, through a Jewish woman, to the Jewish people.

This is a good illustration of the approach of Jews for Jesus. The leaflet's message was the same as had been propagated by evangelical missions since their inception, but here it was presented in a lively style with immediate appeal to the younger generation. "Jesus made me Kosher" reads Moishe Rosen's tract, emphasizing in its one-page format that "believing in Jesus is indeed the Jewish thing." Drawing on the younger generation's ignorance of but attraction to things Jewish, he stated, "Jesus is what makes some of us want to be more Jewish." Jews for Jesus and the missionary movement, generally, made use of Jewish ethnic identification, with frequent references to Jewish food, expressions, humor, and symbols. The new missionary branch also established its own musical band, the "Liberated Wailing Wall," which attracted a great deal of attention. Much of its music was original, composed around evangelical messianic and biblical themes and based on the new pop-rock style of the counterculture. The name of the band drew on Jewish national sentiments and was designed to demonstrate the mission's loyalty to the Jewish people. It also gave expression to the significance of the Six-Day War and its aftermath to both evangelical Christians and Jews.

Although Rosen's style, methods, and organizational structure certainly differed from the regular branches of the American Board of Missions to the Jews, his basic perceptions and ideology followed those of the parent organization. Rosen had served for many years in the ranks of the American Board and had no quarrel with its goals and doctrine; he only differed in the means he thought should be used to obtain the organization's goals. He believed that no one could enter the Kingdom of God unless born again; only those who accepted Jesus as their personal Savior were "saved" and promised eternal life. Others were doomed.[12] This core belief enhanced the group's zeal. Jews for Jesus also inherited the older organization's premillennialist outlook, which emphasized the central role of Israel in the messianic age. Basing its rhetoric on this worldview, Jews for Jesus could point to its faith's favorable attitude toward Jews. The group's view of the Bible and its exegesis were equally conservative. Rosen's group, like the American Board, did not join the charismatic movement, which had gained popularity among conservative Protestants at the time and emphasized a direct manifestation of the Holy Spirit in the believers' lives, divine healing, and a more enthusiastic form of service. Jews for Jesus was, however, more open to the charismatic style than its parent organization. It was, from the start, less formal in its manners and incorporated music and drama in its work.

Jews for Jesus was not the only evangelical group to accommodate its style of evangelism to the tastes of the counterculture. There were other evangelists who chose to concentrate their efforts on bringing the Christian gospel to the young generation and attempted to approach it using its own language.[13] Among the new evangelistic groups of the period were Tony and Sue Alamo's Christian Foundation, which was located at Saugus, north of Los Angeles; Chuck Smith's Calvary Chapel in Costa Mesa; and Duane Pederson's Hollywood Free Paper. Like Jews for Jesus, those groups all started in California, and all adopted the hair and dress style of the younger generation that they attempted to evangelize, promoted new forms of Christian music based on current pop and country trends, and often accompanied their prayer meetings with guitars or drums. Such groups also produced short, attractive, and witty leaflets that resembled those of Jews for Jesus; their methods of street evangelism were also very much alike.[14] There were undoubtedly mutual influences between the groups, all of which should be viewed as avant-garde missionaries, carrying the evangelical message by new means into a new social and cultural environment. Jews for Jesus differed from the other groups in that it directed its efforts toward a specific segment of the counterculture and had to confront the special sensitivities of

Jews, such as initial objections to Christianity, suspicions toward Christian missionaries, and feelings of guilt that often strongly affected Jews who considered converting to Christianity. The organization's newspaper advertisements, leaflets, and brochures show good marketing skills in confronting these issues.[15]

The missionary rhetoric emphasized the idea that Jews were not betraying their people, their history, or their parents by accepting Jesus as their Savior. Even Jews who had little or no knowledge of Judaism, Rosen contended, had been taught that Jews were supposed to reject Christianity.[16] An essential task of the mission, therefore, was to counter such an attitude. The Christian faith, the young evangelists assured prospective converts, was not a denial of their Jewishness but rather its true fulfillment. Jews should view the Christian faith as their own and not as an alien belief. The mission's name was intended to convey exactly that message.

Missions to the Jews had promoted the concept that accepting Christianity did not represent a denial of a convert's Jewishness since the nineteenth century but had met with much less success. Jewish taboos against joining Christianity were strong, and Jews were raised to look upon Christianity as an alien religion, but the new generation had grown up in a more open atmosphere, one in which Jewish customs such as spitting and exclaiming *shakets teshaktseno* ("thou shalt despise it") while passing near a church were long gone. Jews for Jesus repeated the evangelical claim that atrocities carried out by Christians against Jews in medieval and modern Europe had been perpetrated by Roman Catholics and Orthodox Christians who had not been "born again" in Christ and were not "real Christians" at all.[17] This claim seemed more credible to third-generation American Jews. They had grown up in suburbia; the basically friendly people whom they had encountered in schools or at work were not persecutors of Jews. They certainly could not associate the Jewish men and women of Jews for Jesus with pogroms and discrimination. The taboo on intermarriage, which had held until the early 1960s, was also beginning to loosen as a growing percentage of young American Jews married people of other religions without the other party converting.

Just at the time when Jews for Jesus was starting its work, a new movement within evangelical Christianity, Messianic Judaism, was beginning to make its way among the younger generation of Jewish converts to Christianity. Until the 1970s almost all Jewish converts joined regular evangelical "gentile" churches as a matter of course. Very few affiliated with Hebrew Christian congregations. There was a greater interest among the new converts of the 1970s in expressing ethnic pride and in establishing Jewish Christian congregations where they could relate to Jewish symbols and rites. The missionary claim that one could believe in Jesus yet continue a Jewish life found ready ears and led to the development of a large and assertive movement of Jewish evangelicals who wished to give expression to both their Christian faith and Jewish roots. Many of them established congregations independent of any church. In this, they were not unlike other evangelical groups of the era such as evangelical Native Americans who amalgamated rites taken from their traditional religions with evangelical theology and morality.

Ironically, Jews for Jesus—which for many became synonymous with Messianic Judaism—distanced itself initially from the Jewish Christian congregations and did not join ranks with the new movement.[18] Rosen was a missionary bringing Jews to accept Christianity rather than an activist in a converts movement. Upon his conversion, he himself joined a Baptist church and found it natural to direct converts to evangelical churches; and he insisted that his workers join denominational churches. Activists of the emerging Messianic Jewish movement were not altogether happy with Rosen's stance, but they felt that inadvertently he was rendering their movement a great service.[19] The visibility and aggressiveness of the missionary organization gave publicity to the Jewish Christian option and helped bring the fledgling Messianic Jewish movement into public awareness.[20]

Rosen's reserved attitude toward the rising movement of Messianic Judaism and the forming of Jewish Christian congregations reflected a common trend among missions to the Jews in the early 1970s. The American Board of Missions to the Jews, for example, pursued the same policy.[21] The missions held the opinion that such congregations were incompatible with evangelical norms. Things changed when Rosen and others realized that the attitudes of the evangelical community had shifted. The same trends that worked in favor of Jews for Jesus also worked to turn Messianic Judaism into an acceptable movement in evangelical eyes. The 1970s were marked by a rise in ethnic pride, the search for "roots," and an emphasis on ethnic cultural attributes. Another development that helped make the Jewish congregations that promoted Jewish rites and symbols more welcome and appreciated was the Six-Day War. The image of Jews in the evangelical community improved considerably during the late 1960s and 1970s, as indicated by a comparison of two surveys taken in the mid-1960s and early 1980s that examined the attitude of evangelical Christians toward Jews.[22] In such an atmosphere there was more room for converted Jews to present themselves proudly as Jews and openly relate to their ethnic and cultural heritage. Most Jewish converts to Christianity felt comfortable in joining regular evangelical churches, yet many decided to establish congregations in which they retained some Jewish traditional features such as conducting the weekly service on Friday night or Saturday morning instead of Sunday and incorporating a number of traditional Jewish prayers into the service. A pragmatic and shrewd evangelist, Rosen realized the great potential of Jewish symbols as well as Jewish congregations for evangelization work.[23] During the late 1970s to 1980s Jews for Jesus established a number of such Jewish Christian congregations.

Jews for Jesus' positive attitude toward the ethnic aspects of Jewish life served it well as it worked to reassure prospective converts that accepting Jesus as a Savior did not contradict their Jewishness. Missions to the Jews during the era began increasingly to emphasize their Jewish character. *Corned Beef, Knishes and Christ* and *You Bring the Bagels, I'll Bring the Gospel* were two titles of missionary tracts published during the 1970s and 1980s. As part of the renewed emphasis on Jewish ethnicity, Rosen shed his first name, Martin, and began to use his Jewish name, Moishe.[24]

Unlike the typical missionary branch with two or three hired employees, Rosen gathered around him a group of young people whom he had either converted during his early tenure in San Francisco or recruited a short time after their conversion. They were not employees in the usual sense of the word, although some of them received salaries from the American Board and many would become full-time employees of Jews for Jesus in due course. Nor could they have been defined as mere volunteers; they were a cadre of activists helping to form what they conceived to be a new movement, one with a special meaning and purpose in history. Not every convert could join the core group of activists whose spirit could be compared to that of an elite army unit. Members of the group had to demonstrate will, ability, and dedication. Evangelization campaigns on university campuses or in cities were planned and carried out like army operations, even using military terminology, such as "sortie." In its selective recruitment, the demands it put on its members, and its esprit de corps, the group might be compared to such elite and avant-garde missionary groups in the history of Christian evangelization as the sixteenth-century Jesuits. Rosen trained his people to withstand hardships and to be willing to face threats, abuse, persecutions, and even martyrdom.[25] The group seldom faced real dangers, but the possibility of such extreme situations helped shape its spirit. Although there were moments of personal tension, members of the group offered one another friendship and support. They celebrated holidays and birthdays together. Some shared apartments and houses. Most had a strong sense of fulfillment resulting from their belief that they were working for a great cause, from the special atmosphere of fellowship and camaraderie, and from the sense of creativity in expressing their talents in music, drama, writing, designing, and producing the group's publications and promotional material.[26] The old wish to evangelize the Jews had acquired a new enthusiastic spirit, and members of the group felt that they were participating in a historical mission that embodied eschatological implications and helped transcend the traditional boundaries between Judaism and Christianity.

As leader and teacher to the members, Rosen also directed the group in practical matters of administration, evangelizing, and fund-raising. Relating to Rosen as something of a father who both approved and reproached, the young activists were eager to prove themselves worthy of his trust and appreciation.

Rosen's standing among his followers, his understanding of his mission, and some aspects of his personality are revealed in *The Sayings of Chairman Moishe*, published by the mission. The sayings echo the biblical book of Proverbs and show a practical and witty person with the mind of a shrewd businessman: "Don't ask a man for a vow, if he has integrity that is enough, if he lacks integrity, no vow can bind him," he advised his followers.[27] "The church" he claimed, "isn't a country club for saints but a hospital for sinners."[28] "An idealist" he remarked, "is one who upon observing that a rose smells better than a cabbage concludes that it will make a better soup."[29] The title of the book also presents some humor that many people during the period understood, for it spoofs the Little Red Book of Chairman Mao Tse Tung, which was popular in the 1970s among leftists and would-be revolutionaries.

Jews in America during that period often looked upon the Jews for Jesus people as daring, even perverse men and women, who had broken an old, firm taboo by becoming Christian and had, in addition, joined a new "eccentric" hippie Jewish Christian group. Many of these seemingly radical young people who joined Jews for Jesus were, however, reserved and timid by nature. In high school or college they had not always joined other young people in rebellious activities; their work in Jews for Jesus gave them an opportunity to be engaged in an outgoing, daring activity and gave them access to the rebellious counter-culture youth whom they set out to evangelize. Contrary to the common Jewish image at the time, this was not a group composed of the mentally ill, high school dropouts, juvenile delinquents, or underachievers. Personal biographies of the group members reveal normal childhoods and adolescence.[30] Almost all had gone to college, and a high percentage went on to graduate school. A reading of their biographies reveals young people not rebellious by nature but in search of a new ideology and spiritual meaning in their lives. Many expressed disappointment with their parents, whose worldviews or intellectual guidance had proved unsatisfactory and who had no strong religious and spiritual commitment.[31] For many, joining a group such as Jews for Jesus meant moving to an environment that offered a sense of community and belonging as well as a sense of purpose and fulfillment.[32] It also offered them a constructive means of rebellion. They chose a path that appeared at first glance to be completely different from that of their parents, and their choice had often alarmed their families, seeming bizarre, even "sick." And yet it was not dangerous or destructive to their physical or emotional well-being. It placed them in a conservative environment, which banned the use of alcohol, tobacco, and recreational drugs. Their new evangelical guidelines also insisted on sexual abstinence until marriage and stable committed relationships centered on the family. In the guise of rebellion, Jews for Jesus actually promoted the conservative middle-class values of the parents' generation. As biographical accounts reveal, parents, after recovering from the first shock, often came to accept their children's choice of a new belief.[33]

Missionaries of the American Board of Missions to the Jews were usually older than the young men and women they were trying to convert and served as parent figures. Jews for Jesus was dramatically different. The members of the group who were busy evangelizing were the same age as their prospective converts. The generation gap and mistrust of the young toward their parents' generation were such during the Vietnam War era that the best evangelizers were those who wore jeans, had long hair, and opposed the war in Vietnam. Instead of a father or mother figure, the missionary was a peer, offering an acceptable example in addition to guidance and support. "Glenn turned out to be a 'regular guy,'" reminisced one convert of the period. "Glenn played college sports, was active in the student government association . . . was the kind of person who was there to help."[34] Another convert remembered, "Walking in mid-town Manhattan . . . I couldn't help noticing a young man who was conspicuous. . . . He was wearing a campaign button on his shirt. Being a naturally inquisitive person, and also finding this young man attractive, I wanted to know what his button said."[35]

Women had previously been hired as missionaries by the American Board, and of course, wives assisted their husbands in running the missions. But Jews for Jesus was more egalitarian and allowed for a greater role for women. Women served in a manner similar to that of men, including going out on "sorties" and being engaged in street-corner evangelism. Rosen recruited and trained women in his group's early days in even greater numbers than men.[36] This did not reflect any commitment to feminism. Jews for Jesus held to a conservative evangelical worldview; yet it was catering to a new generation in which women had equal access to education and increased expectations. In earlier years, Jewish women had converted to Christianity much less often than men, since they felt less free to break taboos and cross the community's boundaries into an alien faith. This now changed dramatically as women of the new generation took their equal share among those seeking new religious affiliation.[37] Since the group wanted to approach women—who from the evangelical point of view were equally in need of conversion and of having their spiritual needs met—it needed women evangelists who could present the message and provide an example. One of the early activists of the group, Sue Perlman, became assistant to the director, responsible for public relations, and editor of publications. But men eventually held most of the executive posts, such as directors of the various branches.

Just when Jews for Jesus was beginning its activities in the Bay Area in the early 1970s, a center of Jewish renewal, the House of Love and Prayer, was also in operation. It was associated with Rabbi Shlomo Carlebach, a former emissary of the Hasidic Lubavitch movement, who dedicated himself to bringing young

Jewish men and women closer to the Jewish tradition. A comparison between Jews for Jesus and the House of Love and Prayer can highlight the character of the missionary group and what it offered its prospective converts. The similarity between the two groups was that both of them answered the quest of younger Jewish men and women for meaning and community in their lives. Both groups offered a religious lifestyle that was very different than that which their adherents were used to in their parents' homes. The two groups presented their teachings as the true fulfillment of the religion of Israel. Both groups were messianic in their historical and national understanding and predicted a glorified future for the Jewish people when the Messiah arrives. They received enormous encouragement in their outlook from the Six-Day War and its outcome. A striking difference between the two groups lay in their advocacy of two irreconcilable interpretations of the Jewish religion: the one claiming the acceptance of Jesus as the Messiah and the teaching of Christianity in its evangelical form to be the valid manifestation of Jewish fulfillment, the other looking upon Jewish postbiblical tradition, as it evolved in the Jewish Diaspora, and particularly upon eastern European Hasidism, as the legitimate and preferred mode of Jewish practice and thought.[38]

But the two groups also had a very different relation toward the counterculture. Jews for Jesus adopted the new ways only as far as dress, haircuts, and music were concerned. It was less formal in style than the old, established missions initially were. It did not accept, however, other, more profound attributes of the era such as the new sexual morals of the day. Jews for Jesus was not a counterculture group. It catered to young Jews who were exposed to that culture but advocated a different way for these young people to live their lives. Conversion to Christianity through the group's advocacy meant, among other things, joining a community and a way of life that were much more conservative. Members of the House of Love and Prayer, on the other hand, were more receptive to the new mores and norms of the counterculture. Theirs was in many ways an attempt to amalgamate Hasidic Judaism and the hippie culture of the day. Members of the House of Love and Prayer wore not only jeans but clothes and ornaments of all sorts, including imports from East Asia and the Middle East. Some smoked hashish and marijuana and at times experimented with LSD. Although the group promoted marriage and family life, it was more permissive in its attitude toward premarital sex. While observing the Jewish Law and exploring Jewish Hasidic spirituality, members were engaged in practices borrowed from other religions—but practices that usually lost their original religious significance—such as yoga, meditation, and vegetarianism and at times took interest in mystical teachings of other religions such as Sufism. Last but not least, the House of Love and Prayer did not insist that those associated with it work diligently and build careers.

Studying the Torah held a supreme place in their worldview. Jews for Jesus and its evangelical environment, on the other hand, strictly promoted the work ethic.

The comparison reveals unmistakably the conservative character of Jews for Jesus and its explicitly nonpermissive nature. This should not be surprising. Jews for Jesus was an agent of evangelical Protestantism acting to Christianize Jews and bring them into the evangelical community. Its participation in the counterculture was mostly superficial, as it could go only as far as the evangelical community at large would accommodate to that culture. Accepting Jesus as Savior through the ranks of Jews for Jesus meant joining the conservative community of evangelical America and turning one's back on the hippie culture. It was in many ways, as biographical accounts of members of the group reveal, an escape from that culture and its risks.[39]

What determined who joined which group? This depended to a great extent on personal inclinations. Some were attracted to a community that responded positively to the counterculture and blended it with the Jewish tradition. Others sought to get away from the counterculture and find a more structured way of life. Some shopped around until they found a group that suited their needs.[40] Some disillusioned Jewish converts to Christianity ended up at the House of Love and Prayer. Yet evangelism had a great deal to do with the choices people made. Scholars of conversion point out that people are often influenced in joining religious groups by encounters with promoters of the faith, who, through their personal interaction, bring prospective converts to accept the message they propagate.[41] Effective evangelism was thus crucial in order to gain more converts. Missions to the Jews were active in America from the early nineteenth century, but Jews for Jesus and the more dynamic and innovative evangelization campaigns of the 1970s proved more successful than ever before. For the first time in American Jewish history, propagation of the Christian gospel among Jews proved successful and captured the souls of tens of thousands of young Jews.[42]

The converts of the new era had grown up in a different environment than those of earlier periods. The newly converted were usually third-generation American Jews. They were not new immigrants trying to become Americans, or sons and daughters of immigrants trying to make it into the mainstream. They were all born into second-generation middle-class Jewish families.[43] They were already part of American culture. Yet they wanted to find a community that would provide them with a framework and would offer more coherence and meaning. It is worth noting that until the 1950s most Jewish converts to Christianity in America came from an Orthodox background. In the 1960s the pattern changed, with most converts coming from either secular and unaffiliated homes or from families who were members of Reform or Conservative synagogues.[44] The converts made by Jews for Jesus were, among other things, rebelling against their liberal background, rejecting what they perceived as a cold and uncommitted religious life that did not offer them a sense of community and coherence in their life. The previous generations confronted by the missions were not, on the whole, "seekers" in the religious sense of the word. The general trends for Jews in America from the 1880s to the 1950s were those of Americanization and increasing secularization. Most Jews found their secularized Jewish community to be satisfactory, and many found meaning in political and social activities.[45] But the trend changed in the 1960s, and not only among young Jews. Since the late 1960s it has been the more conservative religious groups, those that have offered coherent intellectual, cultural, and personal frameworks and have put demands on their members and advocated self-denial rather than freedom of behavior, that have made substantial gains in new membership. On the other hand, liberal religious groups have, on the whole, been on the decline. The evangelical community at large has made millions of new converts since the late 1960s. Tens of thousands of them were Jews.[46]

Being innovative and successful did not guarantee a favorable reaction from the New York–based parent headquarters. The attitude of the directors of the American Board of Missions to the Jews toward Rosen and his innovative initiatives in San Francisco shifted considerably during the first three years of Jews for Jesus' operations. The board initially backed Rosen in launching his unique mission in San Francisco and placed eleven of the core group of activists on its payroll. However, Rosen's independent direction of his branch—which was an autonomous suborganization with a unique character—did not always please the leaders of the parent organization. Nor were they enthusiastic about the high profile and confrontational tactics advocated by Rosen, who soon became a controversial figure within the larger mission.[47] He was undoubtedly the mission's most energetic and resourceful figure and saw himself (and was viewed by others) as a natural candidate to inherit Daniel Fuchs's place as head of the mission. This, too, worked against him and his group. In August 1973, the American Board of Missions to the Jews fired Rosen.

The San Francisco missionary group, however, had a life of its own that did not depend, except for financial support, on the American Board. Those in the group who were on the board's payroll resigned, standing unanimously behind Rosen. Their work and energetic spirit continued without interruption. Jews for Jesus formed an independent corporation under California law. By that time, the group had sufficient connections and reputation to ensure widespread evangelical support. Following its official separation from the American Board, Jews for Jesus prepared a doctrinal statement. It emphasized the organization's conservative evangelical nature, reaffirmed the group's belief in the Second Coming of Jesus, and stated that "Israel exists as a covenant people through whom God continues to accomplish His purposes."[48]

Although Rosen's dismissal was something of an insult to him and shocked the group, and although it was associated with a power struggle over leadership, it should be viewed as the final stage in a natural process. Jews for Jesus, officially the San Francisco branch of the American Board of Missions to the Jews, had been, since its inception, independent in character and leadership, and its separation from the parent mission was bound to take place.

Jews for Jesus' vitality and visibility aroused widespread attention. It became one of the better-known groups taking part in evangelical missionary efforts. Evangelical leaders mentioned it when referring to Jewish evangelism and to the "Jesus movement." Many praised the organization, but others rejected its confrontational tactics.[49] One evangelical observer labeled the organization's style "Blitz evangelism." In his opinion, Jews for Jesus was successful in spreading the Christian gospel among Jews but was inconsiderate of Jewish sensitivities.[50] It was not surprising that its quick growth and predominance aroused envy among other missionary groups. Many among the older generation of missionaries resented Jews for Jesus' methods, its confrontational tactics, and visibility. Some openly criticized the organization, and the association of missions to the Jews, the Fellowship of Christian Testimonies to the Jews, denied its application for membership.[51]

Jews also reacted strongly to Jews for Jesus. In the period following World War II, the Jewish community did not give much notice to missionaries. The 1950s and 1960s saw an improvement in the position of Judaism in America. It became one of the accepted three religions, and interfaith dialogue between liberal Protestants, Roman Catholics, and Jews gained momentum.[52] In the 1970s, with the rise of Jews for Jesus, Jewish leaders and activists were confronted with a visible and energetic missionary movement. They often chose to react to missionaries and converts within the larger framework of "cults," as part of the new and, in their eyes, bizarre religious groups that came about during those years. They had a hard time taking the new missionary movement seriously. For many, it was something of a curiosity. Hillel centers for Jewish students on campuses invited representatives of Jews for Jesus to present their case.[53] In a 1979 article in *Midstream*, "Jews for Jesus, Are They Real?" Rabbi Ronald Gittelsohn wrote: " 'Jews for Jesus' is only one of several aberrant religious or pseudo religious cults flourishing today on the American scene."[54]

In a manner similar to the general anticult literature of the period, Jewish writers often looked upon Jews for Jesus as deceptive and as intentionally lying about its true nature.[55] Jewish activists did not follow the developments in the evangelical and missionary community and considered deceitful the Jews for Jesus rhetoric about conversion to Christianity as fulfilling one's Jewish destiny. Rabbi Shamai Kanter claimed that Jews for Jesus deceptively "offers conversion in an aggressively ethnic garb."[56] Orthodox rabbi and anticult activist Dov Fisch wrote: "If Rosen and his 'Jews for Jesus' seem less than kosher, it is not surprising. His Hebrew Christian gambit is a fraud. One can no sooner be a Christian and a Jew simultaneously than he can be a Christian and a Moslem. The claim that a Jew need not give up his Jewishness in order to join Christianity is a carefully constructed ruse . . . aimed at the enormous pool of young American Jews who were raised in assimilated middle and upper class areas."[57] Jewish writer and Nobel Prize laureate Elie Wiesel wrote in a similar vein in an article entitled "The Missionary Menace," in which he described Jews for Jesus as "hypocrites" who "don't even have the courage to declare frankly that they have decided to repudiate their people and its memories."[58]

On rare occasions Jewish groups or individuals have turned to physical violence in relating to Jews for Jesus. Ironically, Rosen welcomed such incidents, as they offered an aura of martyrdom to him and the group. He started his autobiographical book on Jews for Jesus by describing an incident in which a Jewish woman had hit him in the face. The readers are left impressed by the author's courage and unyielding determination in propagating the Christian faith among his brethren under threat of injury and possible death.[59] Rosen also managed to make use of other manifestations of Jewish antagonism to promote his group's goals. At one time, the Jewish Defense League sued Jews for Jesus for using its acronym (JDL), symbol (clenched fist), and motto ("Never Again") in its pamphlets while giving them a Christian meaning. "It had cost us $500 in attorney's fees to defend ourselves," remarked Rosen, "but all the Jewish newspapers carried the court story. . . . There would have been no other way to get so much publicity on such a small amount of money."[60]

In the mid-1970s, Jewish activists founded "Jews for Jews" to counter Christian missionaries, its name unmistakably inspired by that of Jews for Jesus. Disbanding after a few years, it was replaced by a new organization, "Jews for Judaism." The organization has sponsored lectures in Jewish centers in university campuses, published antimissionary material, and organized demonstrations at missionary gatherings. Orthodox activists established a number of other antimissionary organizations, some of them with the broader task of combating all religious groups, including "cults" or new religious movements that attracted young Jews.[61]

Many of the evangelical leaders during the late 1960s and 1970s, such as Billy Graham, Oral Roberts, Pat Robertson, and Jerry Falwell, expressed their sympathy and support for the Jews and for the state of Israel, which, particularly after the Six-Day War, they believed to be preparing the way for the Second Coming of Christ and his thousand-year reign on earth. Evangelical leaders established friendly relationships with American Jewish leaders as well as with Israeli officials. In 1973, concerned over Key 73, an ambitious evangelical campaign that was planned for that year, Jewish leaders approached Billy Graham and conveyed

Jewish resentment of Christian evangelism and their sense of the harm such evangelism could do to the fragile equilibrium of the Jewish-Christian relationship.[62] Graham published a statement in which he expressed his commitment as an evangelist to "establish contacts with all men concerning personal faith in Jesus Christ." Yet he denounced proselytizing that used gimmicks, coercion, or intimidation and expressed his disapproval of evangelistic efforts singling out Jews as Jews.[63] Such a declaration from the patriarch of American evangelism basically denied the right of missions to the Jews to exist and was a slap in the face for Jews for Jesus. Rosen's group had to campaign among the evangelicals to secure its position, clarify its goals, and promote its cause.[64] Such efforts became an important part of the group's agenda. Jews for Jesus as well as other missionary organizations and the fledgling groups of Messianic Jews became vigorous interest groups within the evangelical network. They advocated the cause of missions to the Jews and served as watchdogs against those who would remove it from the evangelical agenda or give it a low priority. Members of the group have given talks, played music, and collected money in conservative evangelical churches all around the country. Graham's opposition did not stop the group's growth. Many in the evangelical camp were impressed by the organization's vigor and visibility and were willing to support it.

Jews for Jesus became a national missionary enterprise with branches throughout the United States and in other countries as well. It came to equal and even surpass the American Board in its financial resources and personnel, not to mention its visibility and fame. It soon opened branches overseas and began operating in countries that have large Jewish populations, such as Britain, France, South Africa, Argentina, and Israel.[65] By the late 1970s, Jews for Jesus' income grew to more than $4.5 million a year, and by the 1990s, to more than $15 million, placing it among the larger and better-financed missions in America.

Before World War II, British missions such as the London Society for Promoting Christianity amongst the Jews and the Mildmay Mission to the Jews dominated the missionary activity among Jews worldwide. Following World War II American missions became the predominant ones in the field.[66] American evangelicalism influenced European forms of pietism and evangelicalism. American terminology such as the need "to be born again" became acceptable in other parts of the world. Jews for Jesus brought its aggressive missionary tactics to the international scene and applied sophisticated methods borrowed from the realm of marketing that were not always common outside the United States.[67] In the international arena, Jews for Jesus became the best known and active of all Jewish missions to the Jews, often becoming synonymous with the entire phenomenon of missions to the Jews and the movement of Christian Jews in general. The organization was reluctant, for many years, to establish a branch in Israel; its leader felt that such a move would not agree with the mission's principles. Following in the footsteps of the American Board of Missions to the Jews, Rosen insisted on the mission presenting itself for what it was. Its evangelists dressed in T-shirts or sweatshirts emblazoned openly and proudly with "Jews for Jesus." By the late 1970s, the group and its agenda were well known in both Jewish and Christian circles, and evangelizing in Israel, where sensitivities ran high, became a problem. The group did not establish a permanent outpost there until the mid-1990s. On the other hand, Jews for Jesus was among the first organizations to evangelize Jews in the former Soviet Union, where it carried out a number of projects, including seminars for local activists.[68] It also extended its work to Russian-speaking immigrants in America and Germany.

Some of Jews for Jesus' evangelization tactics are currently unique among missions to the Jews. The organization continues to carry out "sorties," consisting mostly of street evangelism and campaigns on university campuses. Teams of evangelists arrive on campus, distributing leaflets, singing, and inviting students to establish contact. Such campaigns have given Jews for Jesus a great amount of exposure and publicity, boosting the support it receives from evangelical Christians. Over time, the group has turned into a missionary organization that evangelizes not only Jews but non-Jews as well. In fact, as time has progressed, many, if not most, of its converts have been non-Jews. The group's raison d'être has consistently been the propagation of Christianity among the Jews, and its Jewish Christian character has throughout the years become, if anything, stronger. But it has turned, in actuality, into more than a mission to the Jews. While many of its messages and publications continued to concentrate on Jews, it began to direct its attention to non-Jews as well. Unlike the Lubavitch Hasidic group, the Jews for Jesus people would not ask passersby if they were Jewish or not before offering them tracts. Such an attitude was perhaps appropriate for a Jewish ultra Orthodox group that limited its work to bringing nonpracticing Jews back into the fold. After all, traditionally Jews were not supposed to aim at converting members of other religions. But an evangelical organization could not adopt such a policy and had to relate to non-Jews as well.

By the late 1990s, the organization's agenda went one step further. Its campaigns on campuses were now designed for the general student population, and not for Jewish students alone. The leaflets its evangelists were distributing on campuses, such as the University of North Carolina at Chapel Hill, carried general Christian evangelical messages, with no special appeals to or mention of Jews. The pamphlets continued to be short and witty but of a general, generic evangelical genre. "Beware of Religious Fanatics . . . Handing Out Pamphlets!!" reads the provocative title of one of the new leaflets. "The religious fanatic who handed you this pamphlet wants you to know that there is a BIG (as in huge, large, and vast) difference between being 'religious,' and having a *relationship* with *God* (who loves us lots!)," it declares, following a well-paved evangelical path. In line with the changing times, it provides, in addition to the writer's name and the organization's address, an e-mail address, a Web site, and the request not to litter.

The new nature of the campus campaigns has given the group a new aura. It signified the prominent position Jews for Jesus had acquired in the Christian evangelical world, as well as the favorable status of Jewish converts in general. They have been regarded as legitimate evangelists to the general public just as their Jewish Christian ideology and communities have become accepted features of evangelical culture. Such a reality is also reflected in the Passover demonstrations that Jews for Jesus staff members and field evangelists have been conducting in recent years in churches all around the United States. The demonstrations have become an important part of the campaign to muster support for the mission and promote favorable public opinion in the conservative Christian camp toward the evangelization of Jews. The Passover celebrations have similarly given expression to the growing interest in Jews and their heritage in the evangelical camp, as well as the growing consensus among evangelical scholars that the roots and early beginnings of Christianity are in the Judaism of the Second Temple period. Evangelicals have begun viewing Passover as a biblical holiday, which was celebrated by Jesus and his disciples, and have, in recent years, shown growing interest in celebrating it.

Jews for Jesus' high visibility and at times provocative modes of evangelism have not been limited to street evangelism. In the 1980s and 1990s, Jews for Jesus has run ads in major American dailies and weeklies, such as *Time* magazine. "Why Can't Christmas Be a Jewish Holiday?" reads one of the ads. "Isn't Christmas the birthday of the greatest Jew who ever lived?" it goes on. "Of course. Y'shua (that's the Jewish way to say Jesus) was born in a Jewish place—Bethlehem—to a Jewish mother—Miriam—according to the Jewish prophets for a Jewish purpose, 'the salvation of the world.'" The ad, placed on a whole page, features a young Jewish woman who fits into the popular image of how Jews look, with Star of David jewelry and a big, friendly smile. The ad includes the headquarters address and an invitation to order the book *Jesus for Jews*, a compilation of autobiographical accounts of Jewish converts to Christianity who are associated with Jews for Jesus.

Another mode of evangelism used by Jews for Jesus is a short monthly magazine the mission sends to prospective converts and donors. In *Issues: A Messianic Jewish Perspective*, the Messianic Jewish style that Jews for Jesus has adopted reaches its peak. The magazine features a regular section, "In the Little Shtetel of Vaysechvoos," in which it features Shalom Alechem–style short stories with an underlying evangelical morality. By the late 1990s, Jews for Jesus' adoption of the Messianic Jewish symbols and language was extensive. It named its yearly summer camp "Gilgal," and its advertisement for the camps read: "Messianic Jewish summer camps for children ages 8 to 18." It is only at the end of the page that one discovers that the camp is run by Jews for Jesus. Similarly, the catalog of goods that Jews for Jesus offers for mail order is called *Messianic Resources*. It features on its cover artistically designed Shabbat candle stickers, complete with a picture of a woman reciting the traditional blessing over the candles, her hands covering her eyes. In the background it advertises a traditional *talit* (prayer shawl), a Shabbat silver wine cup, and underneath it a book with the title *Y'shua*.[69] The catalog, produced by Purple Pomegranate Productions (a division of Jews for Jesus), offers a large variety of traditional Jewish artifacts that no mission to the Jews would have even contemplated promoting in an earlier generation. Among them: kiddush cups (for blessing the wine), Passover Seder plates, matzo plates, Sabbath candles, Hanukkah menorahs, dreidels, shofars (rams' horns), and mezuzahs (for the doors). People viewing the Judaica parts of the catalog might easily mistake them for pages in a catalog of an Orthodox or a Conservative Jewish group.[70] Other parts of the catalog would, however, have set the record straight. The books, tapes, and videos section reveals the mission's theology very clearly. Among other things, it features a number of publications and productions on the Second Coming of Jesus.[71]

Although the group's messianic theology has not changed since its inception, its organizational patterns have changed considerably throughout the years. From a group of a few dozen very young and enthusiastic men and women who evangelized in the Bay Area, it grew to be the largest mission to the Jews and an international organization with branches all over the Jewish world. Its techniques of recruitment and training have changed dramatically. In its early years, it was the group's leader, Moishe Rosen, who interviewed the prospective members and trained them. The organization has, since then, gone through a process of institutionalization and bureaucratization. Candidates are screened by a committee, and prospective evangelists go to a special training school the group established in New York. In its size and stature, Jews for Jesus became in the 1980s and 1990s what the American Board of Missions to the Jews had been in the 1930s and 1940s, when it was the largest and most influential mission—towering above all others in the field. Like the American Board, Jews for Jesus made it its business to evangelize all over the nation and the globe, attracting much attention and controversy. The organization claimed its central place in the larger movement and became a well-respected member of the new organization of missions to the Jews: the Lausanne Consultation on Jewish Evangelism. In a manner also reminiscent of the American Board, Jews for Jesus has produced leaders for the movement to evangelize the Jews at large. Two members of the early group of activists, Sam Nadler and Mitchell Glaser, for example, have become directors of the Chosen People Ministries (as the American Board of Missions to the Jews came to be called). Another early activist, David Stern, became a major Messianic Jewish theologian.

In the mid-1990s, the group's founder and leader, Moishe Rosen, decided to step down, and the board of governors chose a new director: David Brickner. Brickner was relatively young when he was elected to replace Rosen. He was not a founder of the mission but joined its leadership when the organization was well established. The source of authority in the organization seems to have begun shifting, in Max Weber's terms, from charismatic to bureaucratic.

Jews for Jesus has come a long way since its establishment in 1970. In its beginning, it was an avant-garde group that set out to approach the generation of the counterculture, accommodating itself to the new trends. Although the group encountered resistance on the part of the older generation of missionaries, which rejected both its style and methods, many in the evangelical community were willing to lend the new mission their support. Jews for Jesus should be viewed as a revitalized form of the old evangelical quest to evangelize the Jews. Its novelty and uniqueness were not in its message, which missionaries had been preaching to American Jews for several generations, but in the fact that its leader was the first to realize that there was a new generation of American Jews with new interests and values and that he was willing to use new forms to approach them. Rosen's achievement was not in creating a new missionary agenda but rather in using new strategies and means that made the mission more effective in achiev-ing its goals. In doing so he and his group gave a new lease on life to the movement to evangelize the Jews in America and helped maintain the efforts to evangelize the Jews as a top priority on the American evangelical missionary agenda.

The rise of Jews for Jesus demonstrated vitality on the part of the evangelical camp in adapting evangelization techniques and style of worship to meet cultural changes. It manifests a surprising amount of openness on the part of conservative evangelical Protestantism in America in relating to new cultural trends during this period. Concentrating on the ultimate goal of converting young people and bringing them into the fold of evangelical Christianity and its basic tenets of faith and worldview, avant-garde evangelical groups such as Jews for Jesus were willing to compromise and adopt the style of the counterculture without really abandon-ing their conservative nature. The same can be said for the growing use of Jewish symbols and rites by Jews for Jesus and the movement of Messianic Judaism. In an attempt to evangelize more effectively, Jews for Jesus promoted symbols and rites that came from what had been traditionally viewed as a different religious community, yet its goal remained to Christianize Jews and persuade them to join the evangelical community and share its values. In the final analysis, Jews for Jesus should be viewed as an avant-garde arm of the movement to evangelize the Jews and of evangelical Christianity in one of its more adaptable, expansive modes. It has proved to be more successful than ever.

20

The Rise of Messianic Judaism

In the late 1960s and early 1970s, both Jews and Christians in America were surprised to see the rise of a large and vigorous movement of Jewish converts to Christianity; this offshoot has since developed into the major arm of the movement to evangelize the Jews. These new, more confident, and assertive Jewish converts to Christianity have defined themselves as Messianic Jews.

The roots of the ideology and practices of the new movement can be traced to the nineteenth-century pietist and evangelical missions to the Jews in central Europe, Britain, and America. Such missions were motivated by a premillennialist messianic view that considered the Jews to be the chosen people, heir to the covenant between God and Israel. Pietist and evangelical missions refrained from using overt Christian symbols such as the cross. Instead they promoted Jewish symbols, such as the Star of David or the menorah, and advocated the position that accepting the Christian faith did not stand in contradiction to retaining Jewish identity.[1] The first attempts at establishing congregations of Jewish converts to Christianity were carried out by missions. Between the 1850s and the 1870s, there were a number of attempts in America at creating Hebrew Christian brotherhoods. These organizations were designed to serve both as centers for carrying out missionary work among Jews and as congregations in which Jews who had converted to Christianity could feel at home. Jewish converts established their own organization in Britain as early as 1860 and in America in 1915.[2] Most members of these Hebrew Christian organizations were active missionaries or ministers in various Protestant churches, and their willingness to create separate Jewish Christian congregations was limited. Yet some missions made sporadic attempts at establishing such communities.[3]

In the late nineteenth century Joseph Rabinowitz, a Zionist activist who converted to Christianity, directed a congregation of Jewish Christians in Kishinev, Russia, on behalf of the London-based Mildmay Mission to the Jews.[4] In the early 1890s, the Hope of Israel mission established a congregation of Jewish converts to Christianity on the Lower East Side of New York. This was an outstanding experiment because the mission's directors, Arno Gaebelein and Ernest Stroeter, advocated for a number of years the idea that Jews who had accepted Christianity had the right to observe the Jewish Law.[5]

Most of the early attempts at building Jewish congregations were short lived.

Gaebelein, for example, gave up on the idea of separate Jewish Christian congregations and disbanded his group. Rabinowitz's congregation in Kishinev, to cite another example, closed down following his death. The evangelical community as a whole did not see a particular merit in encouraging the establishment of Jewish Christian communities. For Christians, "Judaizing" had traditionally been considered heresy, and many still expressed alarm at "Judaizing tendencies" and had a difficult time relating to the new Jewish congregations as legitimate churches. The converts, for their part, were often afraid of arousing suspicion and joined non-Jewish churches willingly.[6] Even those converts who did wish to congregate with other fellow Jews were reluctant to do so because they did not feel that their Protestant environment approved of separate communities of Jewish Christians. In the 1930s a new development came about: Presbyterian missionaries initiated the establishment of a number of Hebrew Christian congregations under their auspices. The director of the Department of Jewish Evangelization of the Presbyterian Church in the U.S.A., John S. Conning, considered it more economical to create independent Jewish congregations that served as centers of evangelization and raised funds on their own. The leaders of the Presbyterian Jewish communities themselves believed that many converts would feel more at home in communities of their own, where being Jewish and acting Jewish was normative. Some of those congregations made timid attempts at creating a unique Jewish Christian liturgy, but for the most part, they followed the Protestant Presbyterian hymnology. They owed their existence to church missionary initiative and had no desire to overstep what they felt the Christian Protestant community was willing to tolerate.[7]

The self-perception of being simultaneously Christian and Jewish could be found in the writings of a number of Jews who had converted to evangelical Christianity prior to the rise of the Messianic Jewish movement. This included, for example, Joseph Cohn, the director of the American Board of Missions to the Jews during the 1920s to 1950s, who manifested in his autobiography a strong sense of Jewish identity and pride vis-à-vis the evangelical community whose approval and support he strove to receive.[8] The question that preoccupied the community of converts was what this double or mixed identity meant and how to express it.[9] The novelty of the Messianic Jewish movement that came about in the 1970s and its Jewish Christian ideology was that a set of notions and aspirations that had previously been expressed only sporadically, partially, and hesitantly found a stronger and more assertive voice and became a more acceptable option for Jewish converts to Christianity. It also gained respect and support in the larger evangelical community, though not without a struggle.

In the first phase of the movement, during the early and mid-1970s, Jewish converts to Christianity established a number of congregations on their own initiative. Unlike the previous communities of Jewish Christians, the new congregations of Messianic Jews were largely independent of the control of missionary societies or Christian denominations. This does not mean that the Messianic Jewish movement did not seek the acceptance of the larger evangelical community. Nor were all Messianic Jewish congregations established by converts' initiatives or always independent of missionary control. Most congregations of Messianic Jews that came about during the late 1970s, 1980s, and 1990s were, in fact, established on the initiative, or at least the assistance, of missionary societies that had come to appreciate the relative success of such communities in promoting conversions of Jews to Christianity. Yet the fact that the early congregations were independent of missionary or denominational control shaped much of the self-perception of the movement as well as its image in the evangelical camp. In its own eyes, it has been an independent movement that made its own choices and decisions and as such was much more assertive and outgoing in its Jewishness than previous expressions of Jewish Christian life.[10]

In a manner reminiscent of other new religious movements, Messianic Jews have made a claim to the antiquity of their movement. According to that notion, Jews who had embraced Christianity were the original Christians, making Messianic Judaism the authentic ur-form of Christianity. In the *Jewish New Testament*, David Stern, a leader in the Messianic Jewish movement in America and Israel, changed the traditional translation of Paul's Epistle to the Hebrews into "A Letter to the Messianic Jews." Messianic Jews have also viewed Jewish converts to Protestant Christianity throughout the centuries as their predecessors.[11] At the same time, Messianic Jews see their movement as innovative and daring, as carving a completely new path for Jewish converts to Christianity and for the relationship between the two traditionally alien religious communities.[12] The notion of having created a movement and a formula that have managed to transcend the historical differences between the two religions and unite them has served as a major inspiration and offered an enormous sense of purpose for the movement and its esprit de corps.

The term "Messianic Judaism" points, however, to the history of the modern movement. The term came into public use in America in the early 1970s, although it was not entirely new, having been used in internal debates in the community of converts as early as the beginning of the century. At that time, it referred to a very small minority of converts who wanted to retain elements of the Jewish tradition and law.[13] When the term was revived in Israel in the 1940s and 1950s, its meaning changed, and it came to designate all Jews who had accepted Christianity in its evangelical form. Missionaries such as the Southern Baptist Robert Lindsey noted that for Israeli Jews the term "Christians" (*nozrim* in Hebrew) meant, almost automatically, an alien, hostile religion. Because such a term made it nearly impossible to convince Jews that Christianity was "their" religion, the missionaries sought a more neutral term that did not arouse strong negative feelings. They chose the term *Meshichyim* ("Messianic") to overcome the suspicion and antagonism that the term *nozrim* was provoking.[14] The term *Meshichyim* also emphasized messianism as a major component of the Christian evangelical belief that the missions propagated. It held an aura of a new, innovative religion rather than an old, unfavorable one. The term was used to refer to those Jews who accepted Jesus as their personal Savior and did not apply, for example, to Jews accepting Roman Catholicism, who in Israel called themselves Hebrew Catholics. The term "Messianic Judaism" was adopted in America in the early 1970s by those converts to evangelical Christianity who advocated a more assertive attitude on the part of converts toward their Jewish roots and heritage.[15]

Messianic Judaism, although it advocated the idea of an independent movement of Jewish converts, remained the offspring of the missionary movement, and the ties would never be broken. The rise of Messianic Judaism was, in many ways, a logical outcome of the ideology and rhetoric of the movement to evangelize the Jews as well as its early sponsorship of various forms of Hebrew Christian expressions. The missions have promoted the message that Jews who had embraced Christianity were not betraying their heritage or even their faith but were actually fulfilling their true Jewish selves by becoming Christians. The missions also promoted the dispensationalist idea that the Church equals the body of the true Christian believers and that Christians were defined by their acceptance of Jesus as their personal Savior and not by their affiliations with specific denominations and particular liturgies or modes of prayer. Missions had been using Jewish symbols in their buildings and literature and called their centers by Hebrew names such as Emanuel or Beth Sar Shalom. Similarly, the missions' publications featured Jewish religious symbols and practices such as the lighting of a menorah. Although missionaries to the Jews were alarmed when they first confronted the more assertive and independent movement of Messianic Judaism, it was they who were responsible for its conception and indirectly for its birth. The ideology, rhetoric, and symbols they had promoted for generations provided the background for the rise of a new movement that missionaries at first rejected as going too far but later accepted and even embraced.

In some ways, the relationship of the more established missions to the new movement is reminiscent of the relationship of parents to their rebellious teenagers. The latter often consider their parents to be inconsistent and compromising on their own teachings. They have, on the other hand, a perception of themselves as being idealistic and noncompromising on their beliefs. The new movement embodied a generation gap that involved a move from one stage in the history of evangelism of Jews in America to another. Messianic Judaism signified a new chapter in the life of the movement to evangelize the Jews, one in which congregations of converts would become the major vehicle of evangelism.

The establishment of the first Messianic Jewish congregations demonstrates the link between the missionary movement and Messianic Judaism. Beth Messiah in Cincinnati holds the honor of being the first congregation of the new movement. Its founder and first leader, Martin Chernoff, began as a missionary on behalf of the Chicago-headquartered American Association for Jewish Evangelism. What later developed into an independent Messianic Jewish congregation started as a missionary center.[16] A veteran of World War II and a convert, Martin Chernoff settled in Cincinnati with his family in the late 1950s after working previously as a missionary in Atlanta. Martin's wife, Johannah, who assisted her husband in his work as a missionary, built a warm relationship with the Jewish community of Cincinnati, became active in a number of Jewish organizations including B'nai B'rith and the Jewish Hospital Auxiliary, and wrote a column for the local Jewish newspaper. Her Jewish peers in such groups perhaps found it easier to accept her because she was not born a Jew, and they did not conceive of her as such. They obviously appreciated her contribution to their work.[17] The Jewish response to Johannah's activity in Jewish organizations was typical of Jewish reaction in general to missionaries during the 1950s and 1960s. Jews, as a rule, did not take the missionaries very seriously and did not look upon them as a threat.[18] The Jewish women who accepted Johannah Chernoff into their organizations saw her as a fellow volunteer and friend. They did not conceive of her as a person who could capture Jewish souls. But the Chernoffs' ministry was growing.

In the late 1960s and early 1970s, a relatively large number of Jewish students from the University of Cincinnati responded to Chernoff's evangelism and declared their belief in Jesus as the Messiah. Never before had a mission to the Jews succeeded in converting such a large and dynamic group of young people on an American campus. This group held, therefore, a great promise for the community of Jewish converts to Christianity and for the movement to evangelize the Jews and produced in later years a number of the leaders of the Messianic Jewish movement in America. The Cincinnati congregation chose to become independent. It acquired a distinct character that went far beyond what the sponsoring mission had bargained for. It was assertively Jewish, and in contrast to the American Association for Jewish Evangelism (and other major missions to the Jews during the period) the community became charismatic, incorporating enthusiastic modes of prayer, such as extensive use of music, the raising and clapping of hands, and dancing during the service. The new community struggled throughout the 1970s and 1980s to find a path that would give expression to its Christian beliefs, its charismatic style, and its renewed emphasis on its Jewish roots. The move toward the incorporation of Jewish elements was gradual, as would be the case in other Messianic Jewish congregations, and was not without inner debates and struggles.

Another early and even more central congregation within the larger movement of Messianic Judaism has been Beth Yeshua in Philadelphia. The story of Beth Yeshua resembles that of Beth Messiah, as the new group also broke away from a missionary center to create a new community. Its history offers a window into the reasons young Jews during the late 1960s and early 1970s were attracted to evangelical Christianity. The group that served as the nucleus for Beth Yeshua was known originally as Fink's Zoo. In the late 1960s, Joe Finkelstein, a chemist and a Jewish convert to Christianity, gathered at his home in Philadelphia a group of Jewish teenagers who were looking for an alternative to their parents' middle-class environment, as well as a haven from the more dangerous aspects of the counterculture. In the guise of a rebellious act—choosing a new and historically alien religious community—the converts actually joined a conservative lifestyle that promoted middle-class values and offered a sense of security.[19] Finkelstein brought the new converts to the Presbyterian-sponsored Hebrew Christian center in downtown Philadelphia, where they joined in for a number of years. But the young converts did not take well to the older Jewish Presbyterian congregation. They viewed the downtown community, which had been established in the 1930s by the Department of Jewish Evangelization of the Presbyterian Church in the U.S.A., as too stiff and "square," lacking in both spiritual expression and Jewish atmosphere.[20] They decided to establish their own congregation. Since Finkelstein wished to pursue his work as a chemist, the new group approached Martin Chernoff and asked him to become its leader.

Like Beth Messiah, Beth Yeshua also chose to become charismatic, incorporating such features as the raising of hands and the performing of songs and dances as part of the members' expression of faith. Also like the congregation in Cincinnati, it struggled throughout the 1970s and 1980s to give expression to its identity as simultaneously a Christian, a Jewish, and a charismatic community. The most fundamental dilemma was how many of the traditional Jewish artifacts and symbols to incorporate. The congregation eventually chose to conduct its weekly prayer meetings on Friday nights, asked its male members and guests to wear yarmulkes during prayers, and decided to light Shabbat candles before the service and even to install an ark with a Torah scroll in the prayer hall. These changes did not come about at once, and not without deliberations and struggles within the community.

Beth Yeshua is composed of middle-class, well-to-do professionals. The socioeconomic fabric of the community, which is above the average for Messianic congregations, has helped the community take independent stands and develop its own agenda. It is able to do well on its own without the support of missionary societies or denominational bodies and therefore does not have to abide by the latter's tastes and expectations. This does not mean that the congregation wishes to exclude itself from the larger evangelical and charismatic community—on the contrary, but it does allow the congregation a large amount of freedom in pursuing the incorporation of elements from the Jewish tradition.

Beth Yeshua's affiliation with the charismatic movement is manifested in its style of worship and in its relationship with the larger charismatic community. In the 1990s, the congregation adopted a charismatic practice known as the "Toronto Blessing" or "Being Slain in the Spirit," a devotional scene attributed to the Holy Spirit in which members fall on the floor, helped by other congregants, who hold them and see to it that they stay safe. Members of the community traveled to Toronto to study the new practice and have kept in touch with other charismatic congregations around the world. On traveling to Israel, for example, they visit and pray at charismatic Messianic congregations rather than at noncharismatic ones.

Loyalty to the Christian evangelical theology and agenda is manifested in its insistence that all people need to accept Jesus as their Savior in order to ensure their salvation, become better human beings, and join the body of Christ, the community of true believers. Like all Messianic congregations, Beth Yeshua is strongly committed to the evangelization of Jews and has established its own evangelism agency. But even without an adjunct missionary organization, the Messianic congregation serves as a natural and vibrant center of evangelism. Messianic congregations promote the Christian message by simply being there. Members invite friends to attend services, and curious observers and seekers also come by. Almost all sermons are evangelistic in nature, promote the Christian evangelical creed, and strive to inspire the nonconverted in the audience to convert. They emphasize the necessity of accepting Jesus as a Savior, the need of Jews to be born again in Christ just like any other group of people, and the view that Jews become better Jews when they accept Jesus as their Savior. Messianic leaders consider their achievements in evangelism to surpass those of specially designated missions to the Jews when comparing the personnel and resources spent. They therefore consider their enterprises to be much more beneficial for the propagation of the Christian gospel among the Jews and criticize missionary societies that insist on carrying on missionary work divorced from congregations of Messianic Jews.[21]

Situated in a middle-class Jewish neighborhood in Philadelphia, Beth Yeshua is one of the larger Messianic congregations, with a few hundred adults participating in its activities. A few of the congregation's members have played an active role in the Messianic Jewish movement. Martin Chernoff and David Chernoff, father and son who served consecutively as the pastors or Messianic rabbis of the congregation, also served as successive presidents of the Messianic Jewish Alliance of America. Joel Chernoff, also a son of Martin Chernoff, has led "Lamb," one of the better-known Messianic Jewish musical bands, and has also served for a number of years as the president of the Messianic Jewish Alliance. Joe Finkelstein also served as a president of that organization. Another member of the congregation, Dr. Robert Winer, a neurologist, an author, and a historian of Messianic Judaism, has served as the head of the alliance's public relations committee. The congregation established a day school, Chalutzim ("Pioneers" in Hebrew), where children of members can study from kindergarten to high school. The school's name, which carries a strong Zionist connotation, is indicative of Messianic Judaism's strong support of Israel. Messianic congregations incorporate Israeli songs into their hymnals, organize tours to Israel, and take a deep interest in the fate of that country. Their understanding of Zionism and the state of Israel resembles that of premillennialist evangelicals.[22]

For Messianic Jews, their relation to Israel serves to reaffirm their Jewish identity at the same time that it carries the theological perceptions and political agenda of the evangelical camp.[23] The day school points to another development—Messianic Judaism has become something more than being both Jewish and Christian. Throughout the 1970s and 1980s, it built its own subculture, complete with national organizations, a youth movement, prayer books and hymnals, and a series of publications and periodicals including Messianic Jewish theological, apologetic, and evangelistic treatises. One series of yearly Messianic conferences takes place each summer at Messiah College in Pennsylvania with many of the members of Beth Yeshua taking part in the events. Sponsored by the Messianic Jewish Alliance of America and other Messianic organizations, the gathering offers a window into the Messianic movement's varied activities and groups, which includes bands of singers and dancers and youth activities as well as the participation of missionary organizations such as Ariel Ministries and Jews for Jesus.[24]

Chalutzim, the school Beth Yeshua had built, represents this particular Messianic Jewish subculture. Members of the congregation did not wish to send their children to public schools, where they confronted "impending strikes, lack of quality academic opportunities . . . and the teaching of secular humanism, situational ethics, and decadent sexual mores."[25] At the same time, the congregations' members felt that neither Christian evangelical nor Jewish day schools would do, for neither fully represented the congregations' values and needs. Similarly, Messianic Jewish hymnologies are not merely Christian evangelical ones. Many Messianic hymns do resemble contemporary evangelical ones, and the music is unmistakably the rock-influenced "New Christian music" of the 1960s to 1980s, yet they remain in a category of their own. Most hymns have been written and composed by Messianic Jews, offering an opportunity for Messianic Jewish songwriters and musicians to express literary and musical talents. Many of the hymns relate to Israel's role in history, convey a messianic hope, and refer to Jesus as the Savior of Israel. In addition, small changes differentiate them from the general genre of contemporary evangelical hymns, such as in the use of the name Yeshua instead of Jesus.[26] Messianic hymnals, such as that of Beth Yeshua, also include a large number of Israeli songs.

Another social, cultural, and spiritual institution that offers an illustration of the special subculture of Messianic Jews is the Messianic Bar Mitzvah. The Bar Mitzvah serves as a major social and communal institution in American Jewish life.[27] It is therefore understandable that Messianic Jews have decided to incorporate it as one of their rituals and celebrations. Giving up Bar Mitzvahs would have meant giving up a major Jewish rite of passage, whereas embracing it has served as a statement that Messianic Jews do practice Jewish culture. Yet the Messianic Bar Mitzvahs are different. They follow the standard Jewish Bar Mitzvah as far as the social institution is concerned—a major celebration to which family members gather from all around the country and to which friends and colleagues are invited as well as members of the congregations in which the Bar Mitzvahs are celebrated. But the religious ceremony takes a twist. It does not follow traditional Jewish rites such as the chanting, according to old melodies, of a full *parasha*: a portion from the Pentateuch, the Five Books of Moses, followed by a portion from the Prophets. Instead, there is a reading from the New Testament, and the *drasha*, the sermon, is turned into a public declaration that comes to reaffirm and promote the Messianic Jewish creed.[28] By the age of thirteen, Messianic Jewish children are expected to accept Jesus as their Savior and become fully acquainted with the Messianic Jewish theology. The Bar Mitzvah serves therefore as a communal forum for such a child to declare his or her faith, affirm the Messianic Jewish agenda of being Jewish and Christian at the same time, and, like all Bar Mitzvah children, receive the community's attention and approval. It demonstrates, together with the day school, the summer camps, and other Messianic youth activity, the community's determination to raise a second generation of Messianic Jews and to transfer the community's faith and character to its children.

Most remarkably, Messianic Judaism has created its own vocabulary, strongly influenced by the evangelical rhetoric of conversion yet somewhat different. Messianic Jews avoid using terms that might scare potential converts away or that do not go hand in hand with both the theological perceptions of Messianic Judaism and its unique sensitivities. The use of the terms "mission" and "missionaries," which had been quite legitimate in the previous generation, became something of a taboo. Similarly, the term "proselytizing" was rejected because Messianic Jews do not see themselves as moving from one religion to another.[29] In their eyes, they were, and have remained, Jewish. So new terms have been employed instead. Rather than "evangelizing," Messianic Jews speak about "sharing" and "witnessing" and talk about "coming to the faith" or "coming to know Jesus" or, preferably, "coming to know Yeshua" (the term "Christ" being equally

passé). They speak about "believers" to designate born-agains, and they differentiate between "gentile believers" and "Jewish believers," the first being non-Jewish
evangelical Christians and the second, Jews who have accepted the Christian
evangelical faith. This language was adopted by the entire missionary community.[30] The vocabulary takes some getting used to and so helps shape a communal
spirit among the converted. Converts learn this special language along their
spiritual and communal journey towards conversion. The adoption of this language signifies the acceptance of Messianic theological perceptions and communal norms and plays an important part in the conversion process.[31]

Converting to Christianity means accepting evangelical morality and turning
one's back on some of the freedoms of the general culture.[32] In principle, members of Messianic congregations do not smoke, refrain from drinking hard liquor
(although some Messianic Jews occasionally drink wine), and view sexual relations as reserved for marriage. Messianic Jews share the values of the general
culture in the realm of finances, money, and professional goals. Most of them,
like conservative evangelicals in general, subscribe to conservative social and
political views.[33]

The rise of congregations such as Beth Yeshua, with their unique character
and language, had much to do with the atmosphere that developed in America in
the late 1960s and early 1970s. The Six-Day War had strongly affected both the
Jewish self-perception and the manner in which evangelical Christians viewed
the Jews. It profoundly affected Jewish converts to evangelical Christianity. It
worked to raise their status as individuals and as a group within the larger
evangelical milieu. It also worked to boost their self-esteem, their interest in their
roots, and their desire to remain part of the Jewish people. A number of Jewish
converts published articles and books to convey their impressions of the Six-Day
War and its impact. Their writings conveyed a sense of pride in Israel and in their
Jewish heritage.[34] Impressed by the positive attitude that developed in evangelical
circles toward Jews and Israel, converts felt that they had more room within the
larger evangelical community to give expression to their unique heritage and
their feelings of attachment to the Jewish people.

Another cultural development helped reinforce such an attitude. The same
years that saw a profound shift in the self-image of the Jews and their status in
American society also saw dramatic changes in the way Americans related to
ethnic heritage in general and to their roots in particular. Whereas previously the
trend for American Jews was to eradicate tribal features, the trend in those years
reversed.[35] Not only Jews, but African Americans, Native Americans, and others
were taking a renewed pride in their roots, emphasizing their unique ethnic
attributes.[36] In such an atmosphere, the prospect of Jews joining Anglo-Saxon,
"gentile" Christian congregations and disappearing into the general non-Jewish
milieu seemed less attractive than before. Most of those who came of age during

the 1960s and 1970s were third-generation American Jews. Americanizing and joining the heart of American culture was not something they strove for, since it had already been accomplished by their parents. Influenced by the cultural trends around them, they often took greater interest than their parents in their heritage. Their encounters with the evangelical community only helped to reinforce such notions, since evangelicals were also taking a renewed interest in Jews and their culture. The 1970s witnessed something of an awakened interest in Jewish culture, history, and spirituality among young American Jews. This expressed itself, among other things, in the creation of programs of Jewish studies in dozens, and later hundreds, of American universities and colleges, in the growth in the numbers of Jewish adults studying Hebrew or Yiddish, and in the resurgence of popular eastern European Jewish musical bands (*kleizmers*), which began performing at Jewish weddings and community celebrations. There was also a renewed interest in Jewish Hasidic spirituality and a Jewish movement of Return to Tradition.[37] For Jews, as for others, the resurgence of ethnicity was not merely nostalgia but rather helped build their perceptions of their collective past and heritage into their current identities.[38] This was definitely the case with Messianic Jews.

This new emphasis in American culture on ethnicity, ethnic pride, and interest in one's roots and heritage, together with a renewed interest in and appreciation for Jews and Israel in the aftermath of the Six-Day War, stands in the background to the rise of the new movement of Messianic Judaism and its unique character and to its relative success in attracting young Jewish men and women. The cultural context also explains the movement's acceptance by the evangelical community and its transformation into the central arm of the movement to evangelize the Jews in America. The emphasis on Jewish ethnicity and pride would eventually shape the agenda and rhetoric of the entire missionary movement. By the late 1970s, most missions to the Jews embraced the Messianic Jewish ideology and rhetoric and began promoting Messianic Jewish congregations that were intended to serve as centers of evangelism. This was not a smooth process and was marked by some bitter struggles and a great amount of resistance on the part of the older missions toward the new movement that challenged their long-established methods. Yet the Messianic Jewish way eventually won.

The initial reaction of the older, more established missions of the Jews in America to the movement of Messianic Judaism could best be seen by the reaction of the Fellowship of Christian Testimonies to the Jews, the organization of missions to the Jews in America at the time. The FCTJ had just reorganized in 1972. Initially, the organization was based on a representation of the member missions in proportion to their size: each mission had a voting power in the organization according to the number of missionaries it employed.[39] This organizational structure created tensions and resentment, mainly between the large and powerful American Board of Missions to the Jews, which employed dozens of field missionaries, and the smaller missions that felt that they did not exercise much influence on the organization. The new organization was based on the equal standing of all member missions. Ironically, the organization that was reorganized to create a more democratic atmosphere found itself, during the mid-seventies, trying to keep at bay new forms of missionary approaches and groups. In 1975, about a year after its legal incorporation as an independent organization, Hineni Ministries, the official name of Jews for Jesus, asked to join the FCTJ. Most members voted against it, and its application was turned down. The FCTJ did not offer any official explanation, but it seems that the FCTJ's rather conservative members were suspicious of a new, controversial organization that had a new character and employed innovative techniques different from the ones previously practiced in the realm of missions to the Jews.[40] Oral tradition has it that another consideration was the charismatic and energetic personality of Jews for Jesus' director, Moishe Rosen; the members of the FCTJ feared that Rosen would take over and would run the organization.[41]

Even more antagonistic was the organization's reaction to Messianic Judaism. The members of the FCTJ treated the rise of the new movement with great alarm. In their eyes, it represented misguided forms of evangelism and extreme notions of Jewish pride and was compromising the status and achievements of the entire missionary movement. Unlike Jews for Jesus, no Messianic Jewish congregation or organization asked to join the FCTJ, but the members of the organization thought that they should, as a representative body of the missions to the Jews in America, express their negative opinion on that movement. Members of the FCTJ resented not only the more assertive liturgical innovations of the Messianic Jewish movement but also the fact that these Jewish Christians created a new movement of congregations outside the auspices of established missions or denominational bodies. The representatives of the missions were aware that it was their work and ideology that had brought about the new movement. They feared that this unintentional creation of theirs was going beyond the accepted theology and manners the evangelical community was willing to tolerate and was therefore threatening to become an embarrassment for them in the evangelical camp. Their own status and security were in danger. Their attitude could be compared to that of parents to rebellious radical youth who feel embarrassed by their children's opinions and activities and are afraid that they might compromise their own social status.

The FCTJ decided to appoint a committee of three members to compose a resolution on Messianic Judaism, which would then be adopted as the group's official position and statement on the matter. Its members were Harold Sevener, then deputy to the president of the American Board of Missions to the Jews; William Currie, director of the American Messianic Fellowship; and Marvin

Rosenthal, director of the Friends of Israel. All three men represented some of the largest, oldest, and most well respected missionary organizations in the country. All of them were at that point sternly against the new movement. Of the three, Rosenthal was to remain in opposition to the idea of separate Jewish congregations for decades to come; the other two missionary leaders would change their mind. In its annual meeting, the organization adopted a statement that the committee composed and that denounced Messianic Judaism. It read:

> Inasmuch as many within the modern movement of Messianic Judaism publicly declare themselves to be a fourth branch of Judaism, we of the Fellowship of Christian Testimonies to the Jews at our annual meeting held at America's Keswick, October 16–19, 1975 feel constrained to make the following statement:

> Whereas a segment of Messianic Judaism strives to be a denomination within Judaism alongside Orthodox, Conservative, and Reform Judaism, thus confusing Law and Grace, we of the FCTJ affirm that the New Testament teaches that the Christian faith is consistent with, but not a continuation of[,] biblical Judaism, and is distinct from rabbinical Judaism.

> Whereas a segment of Messianic Judaism claims to be a synagogue, and not a church, we of the FCTJ affirm that the New Testament clearly distinguishes between the synagogue and the church; therefore, Bible-believing Hebrew Christians should be aligned with the local church in fellowship with Gentile believers.

> Whereas a segment of Messianic Judaism encourages Gentile Christians to undergo a conversion to Judaism, we of the FCTJ affirm that this violates the tenor of the New Testament in general and the books of Galatians and Hebrews in particular, for it involves converting to a religion that clearly denies the Messiahship of Jesus.

> Whereas a segment of Messianic Judaism adopts the practices of rabbinic Judaism (instituted by Jewish leadership who rejected the Person and work of Jesus Christ), e.g. kosher laws, wearing skull caps and prayer shawls, et al., we of the FCTJ affirm that any practice of culture, Jewish or non-Jewish, must be brought into conformity with New Testament theology.

> Whereas a segment of Messianic Judaism isolates itself from the local church rebuilding the "middle wall or partition," thus establishing a pseudo-cultural pride, we of the FCTJ affirm the necessity of the Hebrew Christian expressing his culture and his spiritual gifts in the context of the local church, thus edifying the Body of Christ as a whole, and not an isolated pseudo-culture.

Whereas a segment of Messianic Judaism opposed the usage of terms such as "Jesus," "Christ," "Christian," "cross," et al, and insists on using the Hebrew terms *exclusively*, we of the FCTJ affirm that though we endorse tactfulness in witness, we reject a presentation of the Gospel which is a subtle attempt to veil and camouflage the Person and work of our Lord Jesus Christ.

Whereas segments of Messianic Judaism, by portraying themselves to be synagogues with rabbis for the purpose of attracting unsuspecting Jews, employ methods which are unethical, we of the FCTJ affirm that Jewish missions must be honest and biblical in their message and approach, and reject the concept that "*the end justifies the means.*"

Be it resolved, therefore, that we of the FCTJ stand apart from and in opposition to Messianic Judaism as it is evolving today."

The resolution indicates that what particularly alarmed some missionaries was the fact that among the first wave of Messianic Jews there were some who manifested a positive attitude toward the observance of the Jewish Law. The number of such people was small, and no fully observant congregations, according to Jewish Orthodox norms, came about, yet the phenomenon received much publicity—disproportional to its size and significance within the larger movement.[42] The language used by the FCTJ indicates that the members of the organization were not always fully acquainted with the atmosphere of the new Messianic congregations. Their statement expresses alarm that was often based more on the reputation of the new movement than on a careful examination of the facts. The document suggests that the entire movement or large parts of it were practicing Jewish rites or that non-Jews who wished to join Messianic congregations underwent the traditional process of conversion to Judaism under the supervision of rabbinical authorities. This was hardly the case. By the time the FCTJ issued its condemnation, hundreds of non-Jews had joined Messianic Jewish congregations, but very few underwent any process of conversion, and almost none underwent the process of a traditional rabbinically supervised Jewish conversion. Similarly, though Messianic Judaism strove for recognition by both Christians and Jews, it did not attempt to become a Jewish denomination alongside Orthodox or Conservative Judaism. Many Messianic Jews would have, in fact, agreed with the theological standing reflected in the resolution. They did not try to join the synagogue but rather attempted to become a new subdivision within evangelical Christianity with its own distinctive characteristics and set of congregations, but not beyond the accepted theological norms of the evangelical world. What the missionaries who gathered at the annual meeting of the FCTJ did not perceive accurately was the willingness of the evangelical community to accept such a subdivision. The independent tendency of the new converts' movement frightened the veteran missionaries, who were under the impression not only that the rise of Messianic Judaism would cause the evangelical community to treat the new movement with suspicion and hostility but that anger might be directed at them, too.[43]

The last clause of the FCTJ's statement reveals that the members of the older, established missionary organizations were also taken aback by the new methods employed by Messianic Jews and considered some of them to be unethical. They felt that persons engaged in propagating the Christian gospel should declare themselves openly as missionaries and that followers of Jesus should present themselves to be Christian and not "Messianic." Such a clause in the resolution reflected an awareness on the part of the representatives that Messianic Judaism was an evangelizing movement turning into a new arm of the movement to evangelize the Jews and as such they were concerned over its ethical missionary conduct. For an entire generation, the missionary movement had been attempting to set standards in this realm. In the early stages of the movement, in the late nineteenth century and early twentieth, Jews and Christians alike accused missions and missionaries of using unethical practices in propagating the Christian gospel among the Jews. From the 1920s to the 1960s, missions worked hard to make sure that they would not have to face such accusations that had harmed their reputation in earlier days. Many among them were therefore uncomfortable with methods that deviated so sharply from the standards they had set and that they believed had worked well for the movement and helped improve its reputation in the evangelical camp. Similarly, the old-guard missionaries thought that Jewish converts to Christianity calling themselves Jewish and not Christian were not presenting their true identity. They also disapproved of what they considered to be the use of other euphemistic terms and saw them as a deceit. Ironically, the missionary criticism of Messianic Judaism at this point, although motivated by different concern, resembled that of Jewish critics of the movement.[44] The missionaries were afraid that the new groups would be building themselves a bad reputation which would reflect poorly on the movement to evangelize the Jews as a whole.

This clause revealed a gap between the two groups—that of the old missionaries and the young Messianic Jews—that went further than different understandings of how Jews who have accepted Jesus as their Savior should express their faith. The gap was also between two generations within the movement to evangelize the Jews in America who differed over the ways and means of evangelism. Should evangelizing the Jews be carried out by professional evangelists operating on behalf of established missions and openly declaring themselves to be missionaries propagating the Christian belief? Or should it be carried out by Messianic Jews who advocated accepting "Yeshua Ha Mashiah" as part of the

Jewish faith and, as a rule, were neither professional missionaries nor full-time evangelists?

The older generation reacted with suspicion, alarm, and perhaps fear to the rise of a new generation that brought about new methods that seemed to the older generation to challenge their own. The missionary establishment was reacting against a new wave, resisting the changes, even without being fully aware of all their details and nuances. The new trend was, in actuality, much less radical than the missionaries thought it to be. It did not deviate in essence doctrinally from what the older movement stood for. It was, after all, a child of that movement. The doctrinal basis of the FCTJ was the traditional, almost standard evangelical-fundamentalist creed of the time, reminiscent of those adopted by many conservative Christian organizations in America. It included clauses that asserted the supreme authority of the Scriptures and reaffirmed an orthodox view of the Trinity and of the nature and role of Jesus Christ. As a body representing a premillennialist outlook, it also endorsed the belief in the Second Coming of Jesus. Now, in sharp reaction to Messianic Judaism, the FCTJ made an official addendum to its constitution regarding the doctrines it stood for. The new clause read: "The local church is the visible manifestation of the Body of Christ. It is a company of believers called out from among Jews and Gentiles, separated unto the Lord Jesus Christ and voluntarily associated for the ministry of the Word, the mutual edification of its members and observance of the ordinances. All believers are bound to join themselves unto local assemblies when and where they have the opportunity, for discipleship involves church membership."[45] The second part of the addendum in particular reflects suspicion toward separate Jewish congregations. The members of the FCTJ were of the opinion that Jewish converts should join "local assemblies" and were in need of "discipleship," and they did not think that converts could achieve that in their own communities. In an even sharper statement, the American Board of Missions to the Jews stated: "We cannot understand how one can confer a 'Messianic Synagogue' with the body of Christ. We decry any movement, no matter how well-intentioned, that would erect the 'Middle War of partition between us' which our Lord destroyed."[46] Although the FCTJ was suspicious and even hostile toward the Messianic Jewish movement, its members nonetheless invited Larry Rice, the general secretary of the Messianic Jewish Alliance, to present his objections to the FCTJ's negative standing on Messianic Judaism. This sign of openness in the midst of suspicion proved significant. Not long after the FCTJ condemnation, the missionary movement began coming to terms with Messianic Judaism and its methods, adjusting itself to the new changes and trying to make the most out of the new Messianic ideology and methods, in an attempt to advance the cause of evangelism among Jews. Missions that had promoted the FCTJ denouncement of Messianic Judaism and published it in their journals, such as the American Board of Missions to the Jews, changed their mind on that matter just a few years later and became, in the 1980s, sponsors of Messianic congregations.

The change in the missions' attitude had to do with the realization that they had not really read the situation correctly and that the evangelical community was much more open to the new movement, its style, and its methods than they had thought. Evangelicals did not necessarily share the attitudes, feelings, and fears of the veteran missionaries who convened at the FCTJ and condemned Messianic Judaism. There was a certain amount of uncertainty in evangelical circles during the early and mid-1970s concerning Messianic congregations. It was a new development, and many in the evangelical community were uninformed as to its exact nature and purpose. Major evangelical publications such as *Christianity Today*, *Missiology*, or the *Moody Monthly* published articles to inform their readers and let spokespersons of Messianic Judaism present their case. As such accommodations indicate, there was no immediate rejection or censorship of the movement. The evangelical community was willing to give the new trend a hearing and was willing to be persuaded.

By 1974, the topic had become particularly relevant, and the evangelical journal *Christianity Today* wanted to present the subject. To that end, it published an article that told the story of a Jewish family of converts, "More Jewish Than Ever—We've Found the Messiah." This article was preceded by a more theological essay by Louis Goldberg titled "The Messianic Jew." A professor at the Moody Bible Institute and the director of its department of Jewish evangelization, Goldberg presented himself as a Messianic Jew, a daring act considering the antagonism of the missionary community that historically had cosponsored the department at Moody. Messianic Jews, he claimed, were Jewish believers in Jesus as the Messiah who were part of the Church—the body of the true believers. As such, the professor of Jewish evangelism argued, they were "princes of God," persons who came to know God. But as Goldberg saw it, Jews who accepted Jesus were not merely Christians who happened to be of Jewish origin. As Jews, they had a special role in serving as witnesses to their brethren. So the call to the evangelical community to accept Messianic Jews as a legitimate group was based on the idea that they should serve effectively as evangelists to other Jews. Nonconverted Jews, regular Christians, and Jewish believers in Jesus each had different roles in history, the Moody professor asserted. The place for Jewish believers in Jesus, he concluded, was with all Christians in the local assemblies, but they still had the right to take interest in their brethren and be attached to them. His definition of Messianic Judaism was a very moderate one. He did not endorse the establishment of separate Messianic congregations and did not even mention the option to observe Jewish rites by Jewish converts to Christianity.

Goldberg's position calls for an explanation. As director of the program for training missionaries to the Jews at the Moody Bible Institute, he worked closely with missions. His name appeared on the list of boards of governors or referees for a number of missions, such as the American Messianic Fellowship and the American Board of Missions to the Jews, yet he adopted a different view than that of the established community of missionaries at the time. Active in the Hebrew Christian Alliance of America from the 1940s to 1960s, Goldberg served, in a way, as a link between the older and younger generations of Jewish Christians.[47] He himself did not join a Messianic Jewish congregation but remained a member of a regular "gentile" Baptist church. However, his response to the rise of a young and enthusiastic generation of Jewish Christians who wished to remain connected with their Jewish roots was a positive one. In a similar vein, Goldberg did not find fault with Jews for Jesus, either, and developed a cordial relationship with the new missionary organization and its leader, Moishe Rosen, who invited the professor to sit on the organization's Board of Governors. Goldberg spent three decades of his life training future missionaries and carried out campaigns of evangelism with his students, but he was not an employed missionary, was not committed to a particular mission, and did not see a vested interest in defending the existing missionary establishment or in perpetuating the missionary status quo.

As the director of the program at Moody, Goldberg had to retain cordial relationships with the directors of all missions and be as open as he could to different trends in the field. This, in many ways, reflected the institution in which he was working. The Moody Bible Institute in general tried to remain in the respectable center of conservative evangelical Christianity and avoid taking sides in conflicts or schisms resulting from partisan or sectarian viewpoints. The program for Jewish evangelism, and Goldberg as its director, were in a similar position within the community of missionaries and converts. Following the controversy over Messianic Judaism, Goldberg managed to keep a polite relationship with all parties involved, even with the most vocal opponents of Messianic Judaism. Marvin Rosenthal, the director of the Friends of Israel, on learning from Goldberg himself of the latter's sympathetic views of Messianic Judaism, expressed explicit alarm, yet he remained cordial.[48] In taking such an attitude, Goldberg was more daring than he realized. He supported the new missionary expressions before they became established as the prevailing modes in the field of Jewish evangelism and before it became absolutely clear that such attitudes were acceptable to the evangelical community. His opinions proved not to have hurt his standing as a professor at Moody, and the new trends in Jewish evangelization did not decrease interest in the program he directed. Many among the new generation of Messianic Jews became interested in the very kind of education the program offered. Similarly, the new, dynamic organization Jews for Jesus built a working relationship with the department at Moody—among other things, students in the program did fieldwork at Jews for Jesus. The program at Moody served as a vehicle through which Messianic Jewish activists became members of the missionary or Messianic Jewish leadership. Since the 1980s, graduates of the program pursued careers not only as missionaries but also as leaders and pastors of Messianic congregations and institutions. None of the Messianic Jews who studied at the Moody Bible Institute were "traditionalists," wore *kipot* (yarmulkes), or kept the Jewish dietary laws. The Jewish program, however, did celebrate Jewish holidays such as Rosh Hashanah, the Jewish New Year, and Goldberg, and at times others in the program, explicitly refrained from eating pork.

Another open defender of Messianic Judaism was James Hutchens, who wrote a doctoral dissertation at Fuller Theological Seminary, "A Case for Messianic Judaism." Hutchens, who converted to Judaism while holding his belief in the messiahship of Jesus, advocated Messianic Judaism as a means for Jews to accept the Christian faith while retaining the cultural components of their Jewish heritage. He believed that it would help overcome Jewish opposition to conversion. Beyond "the core faith," the cultural dress was variable, he contended, and open for choice.[49] That such a dissertation could be written and approved in a conservative evangelical theological seminary was proof that evangelicalism as a whole was much more open and inclusive than the old-guard missionaries had presumed. Fuller Theological Seminary might have been more inclusive and open to cultural variations than other conservative evangelical schools,[50] but other evangelical institutions of higher learning, such as Trinity Evangelical Divinity School, the Moody Bible Institute, and Dallas Theological Seminary, also opened their doors to Messianic Jews. Being admitted to such schools signaled acceptance by the heart of the conservative evangelical community. Hutchens pursued his course of presenting the movement to the general evangelical community. In an article he published in *Missiology* in 1977, he offered a "progress report" on Messianic Judaism. Writing for a general mission's journal, Hutchens presented the movement as varied and complex and reflected on its problems and limitations no less than on its growth and successes.

Non-Jewish evangelical observers did not take the missionary point of view, either. The *Moody Monthly*, the bulletin of the Moody Bible Institute, published, as early as 1972, "A Breakthrough for Messianic Judaism," an article that presented the movement in very positive terms and noted its potential for converting large numbers of Jews. "The ministry of sharing Jesus with Jewish people is a much more rewarding enterprise than it was a decade or so ago," the journal noted.[51] *Christianity Today* published a series of articles starting in 1971 on Messianic Judaism in an approving, even enthusiastic tone.[52] *Christianity Today* continued to publish favorable articles on Messianic Judaism, demonstrating the interest in and support for the movement by the mainstream of American evangelicalism. The positive response of members of the evangelical camp toward Messianic Judaism is best illustrated by a book published in the early 1980s by an evangelical scholar. Davis Rausch, a professor at Ashland Theological Seminary, traveled throughout the fledgling congregations of the late 1970s and early 1980s and wrote with much sympathy for the movement. He was particularly appreciative toward those individuals choosing to incorporate Jewish observance with Christian evangelical beliefs.[53] Rausch set out to defend Messianic Judaism in the pages of the more liberal *Christian Century*. "The fact that Judaism and Christianity are not incompatible has, it seems, been a well-guarded secret," he approvingly quoted a Messianic leader as saying.[54]

Whereas evangelical Christians were open to accepting Messianic Judaism, liberal Protestants were one group of Christians that did not look favorably upon the new movement. The years in which Messianic Judaism made its debut were also the heyday of the Jewish-Christian dialogue. The Second Vatican Council (1962–65) had brought about an atmosphere of interfaith reconciliation and dialogue. Protestant denominations such as the Episcopalians, Presbyterians, and Methodists had come out with declarations absolving the Jews from the deicide charge and asserting the legitimacy and validity of the existence of Judaism alongside Christianity.[55] Liberal Protestant theologians such as Krister Stendahl, James Parkes, Franklin Littel, and Paul van Buren dedicated theological tracts to promoting the new attitude. Representatives of liberal churches met with Jewish leaders and thinkers in interfaith meetings. In sharp contrast to conservative Christianity, liberal Protestantism had moved to recognize the merits of rabbinical Judaism as a rich religious tradition, one that could offer moral guidelines and spiritual comfort to its adherents. Liberal Christians have, since the 1970s, taken interest in the Jewish religious heritage, and the study of Judaism has become an integral part of the curriculum in almost all liberal Christian institutions.[56] Most significant, liberal Christian denominations closed down their missions to the Jews. From the liberal point of view, there was no need for Jews to turn to Christianity, certainly not to conservative evangelicalism, a form of Christianity many liberals cared little for in any event.[57] Neither the Jewish nor the Christian aspects of Messianic Jews appealed to them. They were interested in speaking with "real" Jews and in learning from authentic rabbinical Judaism, a "brother religion," not in Messianic Judaism, which they did not consider to be a valid form of the religion they were now looking at in a new light. Ironically, liberal Christians shared the prevailing Jewish view, which refused to see Messianic Judaism as a legitimate expression of Judaism. The Messianic Jewish creed sounded too much like that of evangelical Christianity to be Jewish. Liberal Christians also became aware of how resentful Jews were of missionary activity in all forms, and as long as evangelizing of Jews went on, they themselves—as liberal and accepting as they were—were perceived by Jews as members of a proselytizing religion. In 1977, the Board of Governors of the Long Island Council of Churches noted "with alarm": "Certain groups are engaging in subterfuge and dishonesty in representing the claims of their faith groups. There is a confusion which results in mixing religious symbols in ways which distort their essential meaning. The Board also deplores the pressures which result when any faith group calls into question the right to continued existence of another faith group."[58] This unfavorable attitude on the part of Christian theologians and activists toward their movement, its claim to be authentically Jewish, and its methods of evangelism did not really bother Messianic Jews. Most of them took very little notice of liberal Christianity, which they viewed as an unsatisfactory form of the Christian religion. For Messianic Jews, as for conservative evangelicals in general, the definition of Christians were persons "born again in Christ," an experience that liberals have refused to deem essential. Messianic Jews were therefore not taken aback by liberal Christians, whose support and approval they never sought in the first place.

Unimpressed by attacks and criticism and encouraged by growing evangelical acceptance and support, Messianic Judaism developed throughout the 1970s and 1980s into a large movement. By the late 1990s, there were more than two hundred congregations with a noticeable presence on the American evangelical scene. Whereas previously membership was almost insignificant in comparison with the larger Jewish population, the size of the current movement is larger than that of Reconstructionist Judaism. From both a Jewish and a Christian point of view, it signified the coming of age of the convert's movement and of the movement to evangelize the Jews.

The movement is, however, far from united or uniform and has, in fact, many subdivisions and groups, colors and shades. A major division between Messianic congregations is between charismatics and noncharismatics. Most of the early congregations chose to become charismatic, but many of the ones established by the mostly noncharismatic missionary societies are not. This reflects the developments within the larger evangelical community.

The relative success of the movement to evangelize the Jews in America during the 1970s and 1980s should be viewed to a large extent as part of the evangelical resurgence and its appeal to millions of young Americans during those years. Within the framework of evangelicalism, the charismatics were particularly successful. Their advocacy of a direct personal encounter with the divine and their more joyful and expressive services appealed to many young people, including Jewish converts. Charismatic Messianic Jews and noncharismatic Messianic Jews have formed different union organizations; yet despite differences, arguments, and rivalry, the mutual campaign for recognition by the evangelical community as genuine Christians and by Jews as authentic Jews and the basic sense of identity as Messianic Jews often transcended the divisions.[59]

Another major difference between Messianic congregations is over the relation of Jews who have accepted Christianity toward Jewish tradition and rites. On the one end of the spectrum stood those who have adopted the name "Messianic Jews" but have followed in the footsteps of Hebrew Christianity, the older, milder form of Jewish Christian congregations. The latter were very hesitant to observe Jewish rites and customs and have adopted a liturgy close to that of non-Jewish "Anglo-Saxon" congregations. On the other end of the spectrum stand "traditionalists," who advocate preservation of Jewish rites, such as the wearing of yarmulkes during prayer and at times even on a daily basis, as does the Messianic ideologue and writer David Stern. Some have introduced into Messianic services rites such as the wearing of *talitot*, traditional Jewish prayer shawls, by the leaders of the community; reading from the Torah as part of the service; chanting of prayers according to traditional Jewish melodies; and holding the major weekly services on Friday nights or Saturday mornings. None, however, have made the claim that there is a requirement to observe such rites as a prerequisite toward salvation.[60] Messianic Jews have, without exception, shared the evangelical dictum that the road to eternal life was in the acceptance of Jesus as a personal Savior and that no obedience to the Law was necessary in order to obtain that goal. Those insisting on the need to observe elements of the Law as a prerequisite for salvation had gravitated toward another movement, B'nai Noah ("the Sons of Noah"), composed of evangelical Christians who had adopted some modes of Jewish observance.[61] But, as a rule, such groups neither presented themselves as part of the Messianic Jewish movement nor were accepted by it. Messianic Judaism in general adheres to evangelical Christian doctrines without qualification. Salvation depends on the acceptance of Jesus Christ as a personal Savior, and on nothing else. Remarkably, for many Messianic Jews, it was exactly this adherence to the basic Christian evangelical faith that allowed them to adopt and promote Jewish rites and customs. They were Christians in good standing and could retain whatever cultural attributes and rites they chose. There was no reason, as far as the genuine Christian belief was concerned, to follow in the customs, habits, and regulations of mainstream Anglo-Saxon churches, and Jewish manners and cultural heritage were just as good.[62] Jewish converts to Christianity were not the only ones during the period to build communities that amalgamated ethnic heritages, including religious rites borrowed from preconversion ethnic religions and evangelical Christianity. A striking example of such a mixture was evangelical Native Americans who incorporated symbols, artifacts, music, dances, dress, rites, and customs taken from traditional North American religions into their evangelical congregations.

It was perhaps not a coincidence that when the Promise Keepers launched their rally in Washington, D.C., in 1997, two groups of born-again Christians who participated in the rally were particularly visible. Messianic Jews came to the gathering dressed with *talitot* and holding *shofarot* (rams' horns), and Native Americans dressed in their traditional attire. Both groups signified the inclusiveness of the rally, which emphasized the unity of all conservative evangelicals by allowing for cultural diversity, at the same time that a common faith and set of values were declared. It also signified the acceptance of these two traditions in their evangelical form by the larger community of born-agains. Native Americans and Jews were not alone. There were other religious groups during that era that amalgamated rites taken from religious traditions that only a few years earlier were considered irreconcilably alien. The most striking example was Pentecostal Roman Catholicism, which first appeared on the scene in 1964 and was accepted in the post–Vatican II atmosphere by the Roman Catholic Church hierarchy and laity. Another hybrid that would have been previously unthinkable was evangelical Greek Orthodoxy, which came about in the 1970s.[63]

Messianic Judaism was not different from other new religious movements of the period that, while making a claim to the antiquity of their practices, allowed themselves a remarkable freedom of choice and selection, including the amalgamation of traditions that were considered by previous generations to be alien and hostile to each other. The crossing of historical boundaries and old animosities offered members of Messianic Judaism a sense of mission—they were working to "make things right" and bring together the truth and beauty of both religions: the faith in Yeshua with the belief in the special role of Israel in history and the traditional symbols of Judaism. This sense of mission and the particular atmosphere it created account for the relative success of Messianic Judaism as an effective arm of the movement to evangelize the Jews in America. In previous generations, the missionary claim that Jews could be true to their Jewishness while adopting the Christian faith did not hold much water with potential Jewish converts. In Jewish and Christian minds alike, Jews were Jews, and Christians were Christians. But for the generation that came of age in the 1960s and 1970s, things were different. They felt that they could make their own choices and did not have to abide by old boundaries and taboos that they believed they could transcend. Judaism and Christianity could go hand in hand. Its conservative character in matters of personal morality notwithstanding, Messianic Judaism is a product of the age and the generation that allowed itself unprecedented freedoms of choice and self-fulfillment. The new movement has turned conversion to Christianity into an exciting option, as one was not joining the traditional "old" Christianity but rather a young, enthusiastic version that worked around the traditional definition of Christianity as an alien religious community.

Since the late 1970s, the tensions between the established missions and the Messianic movement have eased considerably. In June 1976, merely a year after the statements of condemnation that the FCTJ and the American Board of Missions to the Jews issued, both missionary and Messianic leaders met together in Chicago to reconcile their differences. The initiative for the conference came, not surprisingly, from leaders of evangelical missionary institutions such as Arthur

Glasser, the dean of Fuller Theological Seminary School of World Missions, and Herbert Kane, the president of the American Society of Missiology. Its resolution read: "We recognize that different methods may be used to communicate the message of Jesus the Messiah to the Jewish people. We accept the validity of the various congregations' structures and modes of worship for Jesus believers."[64] The varied modes of evangelism, however, soon changed in the direction of the Messianic Jewish paradigm. A few congregations of Jewish converts, serving as centers of evangelism among Jews, existed before the rise of Messianic Judaism. But the new movement of Messianic Jews was to become, throughout the 1970s, 1980s, and 1990s, the predominant missionary vehicle of the era, forcing many of the older missions to adapt their ideology and methods to the new trends. Missions have come to recognize the merits of Messianic congregations as centers of evangelism and began founding such congregations themselves. Missionary societies such as the Chosen People Ministries, Jews for Jesus, and Ariel Ministries and denominational missionary bodies such as the Assemblies of God, the Christian and Missionary Alliance, and lately (and famously) the Southern Baptist Convention have decided to establish and support congregations of Messianic Jews.[65] In the eyes of such missionary groups, these congregations proved to be effective in evangelizing Jews, as they demonstrated both the spiritual and communal merits of the Christian evangelical faith and were particularly compelling for those Jews who wished to retain their Jewish identity and continued to identify with Jewish causes. The missionary system had been based, until the 1960s, on evangelization societies employing professional missionaries whose sole vocation was propagating Christianity among the Jews. Since the 1970s, Messianic congregations have replaced much of the older paradigm, serving as centers of evangelism. They presented a new relationship between evangelists and prospective converts based on interaction between peers of similar ages and backgrounds.[66] Messianic Jews in all walks of life have served as undeclared and nonprofessional evangelists, by just being who they were: arousing curiosity, answering questions, offering literature, and inviting friends and acquaintances to attend services.

The American Board of Missions to the Jews became a major initiator in that field, sponsoring the establishment of dozens of new congregations. This became the major missionary agenda of the mission and the means through which it has attempted to carry out its goal of propagating Christianity among the Jews.[67] Ironically, the mission that denounced Messianic congregations became, in a relatively short period of time, its promoter and defender in the evangelical community.[68] The first congregation the mission opened was the Olive Tree congregation in a northwestern suburb of Chicago.[69] This congregation, like many of the early ones, emerged out of an older missionary outpost. Adus was a Presbyterian missionary center (not to be confused with Peniel, another Presbyterian center in Chicago that had become a Hebrew Christian congregation decades before). By the 1950s, Presbyterian commitment to evangelizing Jews decreased considerably, and by the 1960s, it ceased altogether. To overcome a budgeting crisis and to avoid closing the center, the Presbyterians first turned Adus into a joint project with the American Board of Missions to the Jews and later transferred it altogether into the hands of the American Board. In 1976, the board decided to turn the missionary center into a Messianic Jewish congregation. From the perspective of the board, it had proved to be a spectacular success: bringing a substantial number of Jews and non-Jews to hear the Christian gospel and a relatively large percentage of them to accept it.[70] Its first years as a Messianic congregation were so successful that the Olive Tree produced another congregation, the Vineyard, in a western suburb. This left the Olive Tree a not very large community. About thirty to forty people meet each week, with a membership of no more than sixty to seventy people. Some of the members also belong to non-Jewish churches. The small size of the assembly gives, at times, a feeling that one is encountering a fledgling congregation struggling for survival, although it has been there since 1976. Having been established by the American Board of Missions to the Jews, the Olive Tree is noncharismatic and takes a nontraditionalist outlook on expressing its Jewishness.[71] The Olive Tree's noncharismatic character explains in part its small constituency. Many Jewish converts to evangelical Christianity in the northern suburbs of Chicago have preferred to join charismatic non-Jewish congregations, such as the Vineyard Fellowship in Evanston.[72]

In a manner typical of many Messianic communities, the Olive Tree shares a building with a Korean congregation. The Jewish group meets on Saturdays and the Korean one on Sundays. This is not just a mere coincidence. The Olive Tree congregation would not have shared territory with a Muslim or a Buddhist group. The Korean congregation is similar in faith and character, and the sharing of space signifies the affinity. It also demonstrates mutual recognition and acceptance of ethnically oriented congregations by the larger evangelical community. The name of the congregation is suggestive in that it demonstrates a premillennialist understanding of the Jews and their role in history yet it is an English and not a Hebrew name, like the names of more traditionalist congregations. The service in the Olive Tree is not traditional, and no chanting of the Torah in its customary Jewish form is done. Similarly, the members do not wear yarmulkes or *talitot* during service, and the assembly hall does not contain an ark.[73]

Although the American Board has embraced the idea of Messianic congregations and turned them into its means of evangelism, the congregations it established were not the independent, more traditionalist and charismatic congregations that formed the emerging Messianic Jewish movement of the early 1970s. By sponsoring congregations, the board influenced their character, and as a result they have been milder, more reminiscent of the Hebrew Christian congregations of the 1930s to 1960s. In describing the first congregation in northern Chicago, its first pastor, John Bell, spoke about "planting Jewish oriented Church[s]." Another missionary of the American Board wrote: "If we can share the Gospel with a Jewish accent, we can have a local congregation with a Jewish flavor that is reaching out to Jews and Gentiles."[74] The missionary sponsorship of congregations affected Messianic Judaism, which has blended more and more with the missionary organizations, turning in essence into one movement. Perhaps not surprisingly, the American Board of Missions to the Jews decided in the 1980s to change its name, removing the term "missions" and adopting a more neutral name. It chose "the Chosen People Ministries," which was reminiscent of the name of the magazine the mission had published since its very early days. It signified the mission's premillennialist understanding of the Jewish people and its role in history. It also demonstrated a wish not to be identified with "missions" but rather to adopt the Messianic Jewish rhetoric and vocabulary.

Jews for Jesus, which unlike the American Board of Missions to the Jews has continued extensive campaigns of field evangelism, has also established a number of congregations. One of them, Tiferet Israel, is located in the Sunset area of San Francisco. Like its parent organization, the congregation has been noncharismatic, yet it carries some charismatic features, such as rising and clapping hands and the playing of musical instruments. Although it meets in a building of a local Presbyterian church, it is much more traditionalist than the Olive Tree congregation. During the service, which takes place on Friday evening, members of the congregation read a portion of the Torah in a traditional eastern European Jewish chant, accompanied by the recitation of blessings that accompany the traditional Jewish weekly Torah reading. The person chanting from the Torah wears a *talit*. The blessings over the Torah reading have been altered in part, so as to fit the members' Christological understanding.[75] Following the service, the congregation meets for an *oneg shabat*, an hour of socializing and refreshments, which include home-baked challah and Jewish delicacies. The congregation is small, no more than a few dozen members, but it operates a religious school that teaches, among other things, Hebrew. As is the case with practically all Messianic congregations, a large percentage of the congregants are non-Jews who join either because they are married to Jews or because they find the Messianic communities acceptable and even preferable evangelical assemblies.[76]

Many, if not most, Messianic congregations have found a middle road between the more traditionalist and the more moderate Hebrew Christian approach. Many retain some traditional rites, the most popular of which is the yearly celebration of Passover and a reading of a Messianic Haggadah. An examination of Messianic Jewish Haggadoth reveals that they are different from the conventional Jewish ones.[77] One of the more popular ones, by Eric Peter Lipson, *Passover Haggadah: a Messianic Celebration*, is distributed by Jews for Jesus, attesting to the Messianic Jewish spirit the mission had decided to promote. The Haggadah is almost entirely in English and assumes no prior knowledge of Jewish customs or previous participation in a Passover celebration. It maintains major features of the traditional one, such as the Four Questions, the four cups of wine, and an additional fifth, for Eliah the Prophet. Lipson's version, however, cuts out passages of the traditional Haggadah, most notably those of the midrash, rabbinical exegesis of and elaboration on the exodus story. Instead, the text offers numerous quotations from the New Testament, such as from John 20:19 on Jesus' appearance before his disciples after his resurrection from the dead.[78] The Haggadah also includes prayers relating to Jesus and his role as a Savior. It includes the following prayer: "Blessed art Thou, O Lord our God, king of the Universe, who had sent Thy son, Thine only son, Y'shua the Messiah, to be the light of the world and our Paschal Lamb, that through him we might live. Amen."[79]

J. Ron Tavalin's *Kol Hesed Messianic Haggadah* incorporates more Hebrew than many other Messianic Haggadoth. "The Messianic Believer's Haggadah," Talvin explains in the preface, "differs from the traditional Haggadah in that we who maintain the Messiahship of Yeshua (Jesus) see an even greater blessing and redemption than that one contained in the book of Exodus. Even as the Israelites were redeemed from Slavery to Pharaoh, so all peoples, Jew and non-Jew, through the New Covenant of the Messiah, are redeemed from bondage to sin and death." Like Lipson, Tavalin assumes no prior knowledge on the part of his readers of the customs and terminology of the Seder, the Passover night, and offers both a glossary of terms and ample explanations throughout the text. Like the *Passover Haggadah*, *Kol Hesed* eliminated the midrash passages and instead relates to Jesus and his role as the Redeemer. The first blessing reads: "Blessed are you, O Lord our God, King of the Universe, who has sanctified us through faith in Yeshua Ha Mashiakh and commanded us to remove the leaven."

Messianic Jews evidently wish to celebrate and retain many of the traditional features of the Passover Seder, the most widely celebrated Jewish holiday, yet they also give expression to their Christian evangelical faith. Celebrating the Passover night had become, during the 1970s and 1980s, fashionable in the evangelical camp. Evangelical churches have begun conducting Seder demonstrations, usually under the leadership of Messianic Jewish guests. This had become a common means for missions such as Jews for Jesus to approach the evangelical community, advertise their agenda, and apply for funds. Evangelical scholarship in the last generation had paid attention to the Jewish roots of Christianity, a reality that works to enhance the interest in Jewish holidays that go back to Jesus' era and that had been mentioned in both the Hebrew Bible and the New Testament.[80] Similarly, the Passover Seder is a prime time to invite potential converts to Messianic Seders, either at private homes or in congregational or missionary settings.[81] The unique manner in which Messianic congregations choose to celebrate the Passover points to the dialectical approach of that movement that cherishes and promotes attributes of the Jewish heritage, while remaining within the boundaries of evangelical theological correctness and public approval.

In addition to the divisions between charismatics and noncharismatics and varying levels of observation of Jewish rites and customs, congregations differ as to the percentage of Jews versus non-Jews they have as members. According to a survey conducted by Michael Schiffman, "most Messianic congregations . . . have percentages of Jewish membership between twenty-five and fifty percent." "This," Schiffman declares somewhat apologetically, "illustrates that Messianic congregations are not putting up a 'middle wall of partition' between Jewish and non-Jewish people."[82] The percentage of intermarried couples within the congregations surpasses the average for the general Jewish population.[83] Ironically, Messianic congregations serve not only as centers of evangelism for Jews and non-Jews but also as assemblies where non-Jews receive education in and are oriented toward knowledge and celebration of Jewish holidays and customs. Although such communities are Christian, the non-Jewish members nonetheless resemble non-Jews joining conventional synagogues. In both cases, non-Jews show interest in elements of the Jewish tradition and join in as members in houses of worship that define themselves as Jewish.[84] Such a phenomenon could not have taken place before the late 1960s and the new attitude that had come about toward Jews and Israel. Ironically, a movement that came to propagate Christianity among the Jews had built communities in which non-Jews join in as members of congregations that amalgamate Jewish customs with the Christian faith and celebrate Jewish holidays.[85]

Communal affinity also varies from one Messianic congregation to another. Members of Beth Yeshua tend to live in the same area. Some have even moved in order to be part of the community, in proximity to one another. In other congregations such as the Olive Tree, this is not the case: members come to services once a week but are scattered geographically and live in various neighborhoods in northern and western suburbs of Chicago. They do not necessarily interact with one another during the week. Their social milieu includes non-Jewish evangelicals and not only Messianic Jews. There are differences between congregations regarding the socioeconomic profile of the community. The gap in this respect between Beth Yeshua in Philadelphia and Beth Messiah in Cincinnati or the Olive Tree in Chicago is too striking not to be noticed.[86] No comprehensive survey on the socioeconomic nature of Messianic congregations has so far been conducted, and so assessing this aspect of Messianic life is based merely on observation.[87] Yet it seems that Beth Yeshua is an exception, and most congregations do not possess such a high socioeconomic profile; most of their members tend to be in the lower middle class. Whereas the congregations are not short on people holding college and, at times, graduate degrees, there are very few, if any, academicians in the humanities and social sciences or people in the arts whose work would be accepted outside Messianic and evangelical circles. In sharp contrast to the demographics of American synagogues, the Messianic communities consist mostly of persons of the baby boom and baby buster generations and Generation X—those who have come of age in the 1960s and later. It lacks older generations.

Having built a unique subculture within the larger evangelical camp, Messianic Jewish thinkers have produced a series of theological and apologetic tracts that have come to define and defend the movement's path. In accordance with the relatively pluralistic nature of Messianic Judaism, their work has not been unified or uniform and has given voice to a large spectrum of opinions. Among the better-known theologians are John Fischer, Arnold G. Fruchtenbaum, Daniel Juster, and David Stern. All were initially associated with missions to the Jews or with denominational bodies and made a theological and communal journey—moving from a "Hebrew Christian" identity and membership in non-Jewish congregations into a Messianic Jewish one.

Arnold Fruchtenbaum, who converted as a teenager in Brooklyn, began his career as a missionary for the American Board of Missions to the Jews before establishing his own missionary enterprise, Ariel Ministries. In the 1970s, Fruchtenbaum defined himself as a Hebrew Christian and was skeptical about the more assertive forms of Messianic Judaism.[88] In *Hebrew Christianity: Its Theology, History and Philosophy*, Fruchtenbaum presented his views on Jewish converts to Christianity, their faith, community, and their relation to the Jewish people. He defended Hebrew Christians and presented them as solid Christian believers in good standing: "Do Hebrew Christians behave differently from Gentile Christians? Regarding the basic doctrines of the Christian faith, the answer is no. Among fundamental believers, certain teachings are held in common, such as the substitutionary atonement of Christ for our sins. On some minor issues, such as baptism, there are differences of opinion. These differences however are . . . between believers in general; Jewish and Gentile Christians will be found on both sides." On this issue, Hebrew Christians and Messianic Jews of all colors and shapes would have agreed with him. But the assertive elements of Messianic Judaism might not have shared his views on where Jewish converts look for a community. Having emphasized the idea that Jewish converts were an unalienable part of the Christian community, Fruchtenbaum categorically declared that "the Hebrew Christian should be a member of the local church along with Gentile believers."[89] Like others in the missionary camp, he modified his views a number of years later, and Ariel Ministries has been instrumental in the establishment of a number of Messianic congregations. In 1985, Fruchtenbaum defended the right of Jewish believers in Jesus to establish congregations and observe Jewish rites if they so wished, as long as they looked upon it as an option and did not consider it a requirement toward salvation.[90] A graduate of Dallas Theological Seminary and a veteran missionary of the American Board of Missions to the Jews, Fruchtenbaum has been a committed adherent to the dispensationalist premillennialist messianic hope and constructed his arguments accordingly. Not surprisingly, he emphasized the missionary role of all Jewish Christian congregations.

Next to Fruchtenbaum's *Hebrew Christianity*, David Stern's *Messianic Jewish Manifesto* is one of the better-known Messianic theological tracts.[91] In it, the author, an American businessman from California who immigrated to Israel and became a leader in a traditionalist Messianic congregation, presents a comprehensive defense of Messianic Judaism, its ideas and goals. "By providing a Jewish environment for Messianic faith, Messianic Judaism is useful in evangelizing Jews," argues Stern. He goes on: "It is useful in focusing the Church's attention on the Jewish people."[92] The last argument relates also to evangelism. Messianic Jews have been active in trying to keep the evangelization of the Jews a high priority in the evangelical camp.

Another major Messianic theological work is Daniel Juster's *Jewish Roots: A Foundation of Biblical Theology For Messianic Judaism*. Juster has been one of the earliest and better-known leaders of Messianic congregations. A graduate of the Presbyterian McCormick Theological Seminary in Hyde Park, Chicago, Juster pastored, in the early and mid-1970s, Adat Hatikvah, a Presbyterian-sponsored Hebrew Christian congregation in Chicago that had later joined ranks with the emerging Messianic Jewish movement. In the late 1970s, Juster moved to Rockville, Maryland, where he has led Beth Messiah, one of the largest and most influential Messianic congregations, comparable in its centrality and influence within the larger movement to Beth Yeshua in Philadelphia. Like the latter, it chose a more traditionalist path but not necessarily an outright charismatic one. Juster's definition of Messianic Judaism is, however, broad and inclusive: "It is a movement among Jewish and non-Jewish followers of Jesus of Nazareth who believe that it is proper and desirable for Jewish followers of Jesus to recognize and identify with their Jewishness." Juster's definition acknowledges that Messianic Judaism is a movement in which non-Jews take part. "The central question" in Juster's view, is "whether there is a biblical basis for Messianic Judaism." The author examines numerous passages in the New Testament, such as Galatians 3:28, "There is neither Jews nor Greek, for you are all one in Christ Jesus," which is potentially (and often in actuality) used to negate the idea of separate Jewish Christian congregations. He refutes such a notion: "Both may be called to different styles of life and witness to different fields of service, yet they are spiritually one in the Messiah."[93] Like other apologists of the movement, Juster emphasizes that congregations fostered by Messianic Jews serve as primary means of facilitating the goals of Jewish outreach and evangelism.[94]

Another Messianic Jewish thinker and writer is John Fischer, who began his career as a missionary with the American Messianic Fellowship in Chicago. There he tried to implement Messianic Jewish practices. He went on to become a pastor of a Messianic Jewish congregation in Florida and director of Menorah Ministries and compiled a Messianic Jewish siddur (prayer book), which became popular in the Messianic movement.[95] Like Messianic Haggadoth, the siddur selectively picks elements of the traditional Jewish prayer book. It makes up for passages it left out with prayers that give expression to faith in Jesus Christ and his role as the Redeemer. Fischer attempted to establish a Jewish Christian yeshiva, a theological seminary for Messianic Jews, which was designed for the specific needs of Messianic Jewish ministers.[96] Fischer's *The Olive Tree Connection: Sharing Messiah with Israel* can be described as a Messianic Jewish call to non-Jews to give a high priority to and support evangelism of Jews. The book reflects the new attitudes toward Jews and Israel brought about by the Six-Day War and the relative success of the new missionary era.[97]

Whereas the different theologians vary in their vision of Messianic Jewish life and practices, they all agree on some major points, among them the centrality of evangelism to Jewish Christian congregations and the fact that such communities do not separate Jews from the church but rather allow them, on an optional basis, their own space and a connection to their roots and ethnicity. The writers also emphasize the high priority Messianic Jews should give to evangelism and the duty of non-Jews to support them in their efforts.

At the start of the new century, Messianic Judaism is a growing movement. It has passed its stage of infancy but has retained its youthful vigor and enthusiasm. It is characterized by a large degree of optimism, resulting from its relative success and growth, and a strong sense of mission. This relates not only to the successful proclamation of the Christian gospel to the "chosen people" but also to a notion Messianic Jews have of taking part in a groundbreaking historical experiment—amalgamating the Christian faith with Jewish heritage, thus mending old wounds. They have come up with just the right formula to set things right. "The Messianic Jewish community will be the vehicle for healing the worst schism in the history of the world, the split between the Christians and the Jews," declared David Stern enthusiastically.[98]

Messianic Judaism has been the logical outcome of the rhetoric and activity of the missionary movement and its dispensationalist theology. It was, however, the spirit of the age that brought about the move from the more moderate and hesitant forms of Hebrew Christianity to the large, proud, and assertive movement of Messianic Judaism. The post-1967 image of Jews and Israel in evangelical eyes; the rise in the interest in and the emphasis on roots, heritage, and ethnic pride; and the self-proclaimed liberties and prerogatives of a new generation that not only felt more at ease in crossing religious and communal boundaries but also saw no difficulty in picking, choosing, and bringing together rites and customs from different traditions—all worked to push the Hebrew Christian movement a step forward.

Messianic Judaism changed the missionary scene, turning the Jewish Christian congregations into the centers of evangelism par excellence. Together with the innovative and energetic Jews for Jesus, the Messianic Jewish movement gave a new burst of enthusiasm to the missionary goal and helped keep the evangelization of Jews high on the evangelical priority list. It gave the movement to evangelize the Jews a more dynamic and more promising image than it had a generation earlier. Although the younger and more enthusiastic movement challenged the old guard of missionaries and its assumptions about the relationship between Judaism and Christianity, it quickly became an accepted segment of the evangelical scene in America, one of the more noticed new groups that came about in the 1970s and added color, life, and bodies to the larger movement.

21

The Missionaries Become Real

The rise of Messianic Judaism and Jews for Jesus, the aggressive missionary activity, and the unprecedented growth in the number of Jewish converts to Christianity in America brought about a strong Jewish reaction. The Jewish community's reaction to the missionary presence and to the movement of converted Jews was not always unified or consistent. One can detect, however, some common denominators that demonstrate the Jewish understanding of the legitimate boundaries of Judaism as a religion and as a community, the perceptions Jews have had of their position in the American community, and the prospects of their survival as a unique group.

Jews encountered missionaries in America long before the 1970s. The Jewish reactions to Christian missionaries began with the establishment of missions to the Jews in America as early as the 1810s. Throughout the nineteenth century and until World War I, Jewish leaders and activists reacted with great alarm to attempts to evangelize their brethren. The Christian evangelization efforts stood in the center of the interaction between the Jewish community and the non-Jewish Christian majority and ranked high on the Jewish communal agenda.[1] The Jewish reaction changed dramatically in the decades following World War I. The missions that worried the Jewish community endlessly in the nineteenth century became almost a nonissue. Worries over other, new, hostile manifestations on the part of the non-Jewish society took their place. The 1920s and 1930s saw the rise of Christian and nativist anti-Semitic groups in America. Jewish national organizations that became active during the period, such as the Anti-Defamation League or the local Jewish federations, through their committees for public relations, began collecting data on and protesting against the activities of hate groups and anti-Semitic propaganda. One can go over the documents collected by public relations committees in the 1920s to 1960s, view thousands and thousands of documents, and not find even one reference to missionaries. The 1950s and 1960s saw an improvement in the position of Judaism and Jews in America. Judaism became one of the accepted three religions in the American public arena, and interfaith dialogue gained momentum.[2] In the 1960s and 1970s, the Catholic Church, as well as mainline Protestant churches, underwent something of a revolution in their relation to Judaism and Jews. Liberal Catholic and Protestant theologians and leaders expressed a new appreciative understanding of Jews and their role in history, granting legitimacy to the separate existence of Judaism and the nation of Israel outside the Church. Such views were reinforced in a number of declarations, and these churches abandoned their missionary work among the Jews.[3]

Evangelical, fundamentalist, or charismatic groups within Christianity, on the other hand, held to their missionary agenda. Adhering to a premillennialist messianic conviction, many in this segment of Christianity developed a theological view of the Jews as the chosen people, destined to play a dominant role in the events of the End Times.[4] The dramatic occurrences in the life of the Jewish people in the twentieth century, particularly the establishment of the state of Israel in 1948 and the Six-Day War in 1967, reinforced the messianic expectations and the belief that the Jews were indeed a people worthy of the hopes invested in them.[5] Such views strengthened the missionary impetus. Conservative evangelical Christians did not join in the atmosphere of interfaith dialogue and recognition and were unimpressed by liberal teachings. They believed that their interest in the Jews should manifest itself by sharing the Christian gospel with that people.[6]

On their part, Jews often shared, during the 1960s and the 1970s, the prevailing liberal image of conservative evangelicals as anachronistic and marginal to the cultural and intellectual trends of the day.[7] They had a hard time taking the evangelical missionary attempts seriously. That evangelicals could successfully evangelize thousands of young Jews was something many Jews could not comprehend. The same attitude marked the Jewish reaction toward Jewish converts to Christianity. As a rule, Jews looked upon converts to evangelical Christianity as a small group of marginal, eccentric people, whose abandonment of the faith had no real significance for the future of American Jewry.[8] In the early 1970s, many in the Jewish community looked upon groups such as Jews for Jesus as no more than a curiosity. Holding such an outlook, some Hillel campus centers invited representatives of Jews for Jesus to present their case.[9] They ceased inviting them when they became more aware of the nature of the group and the scope of its activity.[10]

Significantly, Jewish activists and writers often related to missionaries and converts within the larger framework of "cults," as part of what they conceived to be the attraction of young Jews to new "bizarre" religious groups. Jews were influenced in that regard by their impressions of the messages and symbols of the new wave of missionary activity. In the 1970s, Jews for Jesus and Messianic Judaism increasingly promoted the idea that Jews could embrace Christianity and remain loyal Jews; they used Jewish symbols, Jewish names, and Israeli music and emphasized their support for Israel. Jews did not take seriously the Messianic Jewish claim that one could embrace Christianity and remain Jewish. Many Jews found the new character of the missionary movement to be strange and confusing. They saw the claims to be both Jewish and Christian either as fraudulent or as an indication that the missionaries and Messianic Jews were just another "crazy cult." "Beth Yeshua," wrote Michael Mach on a Messianic Jewish congregation in Philadelphia, "is part of . . . an Orwellian world of Jewish-Christian confusion where things are never as they ought to be, and rarely as they seem."[11] This attitude is manifested in numerous books and articles dealing with missionaries in which there was often little attempt to differentiate between conversions to Christianity and joining such new religious groups as the Unification Church.[12] Rabbi Ronald Gittelsohn, in a 1979 article in *Midstream*, entitled "Jews for Jesus: Are They Real?," gave expression to what was a common Jewish perception: "Jews for Jesus is only one of several aberrant religious or pseudo-religious cults flourishing today on the American scene."[13] He offered a Marxist-Freudian explanation to the attraction of young Jews to these religious groups: "What a blessed and wonderful relief to throw all this heart-breaking, back-breaking, brain-breaking worry onto a gentle Messiah who will solve everything! Jesus or Krishna, or Sun Myung Moon—represents to them the kind, loving daddy they knew, or for whom they desperately yearned as children, the daddy who would answer all their doubts, assuage all their hurts."[14] Much of the Jewish reaction to the extensive missionary activity followed the pattern of the anticult movement, which prevailed in America in the 1970s and 1980s and looked upon new religious movements as a harmful, illegitimate phenomenon. Scholars who studied the reaction to new religious movements have pointed to common themes that appear in anticult literature. Harvey Cox has pointed to four such recurrent themes: the belief that the new religious movements are socially or politically subversive; that sexual and behavioral deviancy occurs within the groups; that the groups are deceptive and intentionally lie to outsiders about their true activities; and that new religious movements brainwash their members.[15] These themes indeed appear in varied frequency in the Jewish literature on missionaries and messianic Jews.[16] One motif that is particularly visible in Jewish writings on missionaries is deception.

One writer who made the claim was Elie Wiesel, the famous Holocaust survivor and Nobel Prize laureate, who took great exception to the Christian missionary activity and related to it several times in his writings.[17] In an article entitled "The Missionary Menace," he declared Jews for Jesus to be "hypocrites" who "don't even have the courage to declare frankly that they have decided to repudiate their people and its memories."[18] In *Keeping Posted*, a publication of the Union of American Hebrew Congregations, Annette Daum repeated that accusation. The missionaries, she claimed, were evangelizing minors, distorting Jewish symbols, using deceptive language, and making false claims. "Missionaries are taught to avoid Christian terminology and are trained in the use of deceptive language which masks the missionary intent," she complained.[19] In a 1984 article in *Moment*, Rabbi Shamai Kanter claimed that Jews for Jesus deceptively "offer conversion in an aggressively ethnic garb."[20] Dov Fisch, an Orthodox rabbi and an anticult activist, writes: "If Rosen and his 'Jews for Jesus' seem less than kosher, it is not surprising. His Hebrew Christian gambit is a fraud. One can no sooner be a Christian and a Jew simultaneously than he can a Christian and a Moslem. The claim that a Jew need not give up his Jewishness in order to join Christianity is a carefully constructed ruse . . . aimed at the enormous pool of young American Jews who were raised in assimilated, middle and upper class areas."[21]

A number of Jewish organizations issued statements on missionaries and "cults." The General Assembly of the Union of American Hebrew Congregations adopted a resolution in November 1977 on "missionaries and deprogramming." Their statement reflected a common Jewish understanding of missionaries as deceptive and as being part of the larger phenomenon of "cults." It reads:

> While the right to proselytize in our society is protected by constitutional guarantees of religious liberty, we are concerned, nonetheless, by the current intensification of missionary activity directed towards Jews in many parts of this country. Those guarantees neither legitimize nor justify tactics which some missionary groups and cults use when directing their efforts towards Jews: coercion, misrepresentation of the meaning of religious symbols, abuse of religious rites and practices. This deception and manipulation often violates the civil rights of those members who are its victims.[22]

The resolution reflected, among other things, the Jewish opinion on what the standing of "cults" (and missionaries) should be on the legal level. Unlike much of the general anticult literature of the 1970s that often suggested taking legal measures to combat new religious movements, (i.e., banning them), Jewish organizations and literature explicitly argued against taking such steps. Religious freedom was a value Jews felt they should protect. Their commitment to the open, pluralistic nature of American society and their belief that their standing in the American polity depended on its democratic nature took precedent. Instead, Jewish activists suggested that combating missionaries and stopping desertion from the faith should be done through inner reform: strengthening the Jews' commitment to their tradition, strengthening Jewish education, and reemphasizing the spiritual dimensions of Jewish religious life. In fact, Jewish anticult literature did not direct its criticism so much against missionaries and new religious movements as against Jews. It criticized Jewish parents for failing to raise their children in committed Jewish homes, the Jewish community for its inadequacy in making Judaism attractive to the younger generation, and Jewish education for failing to transfer Judaism to the next generation. Many of the writers also criticized Jewish congregations for their lack of spirituality, warmth, and a sense of community. Gary Eisenberg, author of *Smashing the Idols: A Jewish*

Inquiry into the Cult Phenomenon, writes: "Our synagogues must become conducive to spiritual growth. Rabbis must work to strengthen the bonds unifying their congregations, and must be true teachers, not the politicians they have become in so many synagogues today. . . . The spiritual heart yearns for something beyond the intellect . . . a yearning for transcendent experiences. Jews must be able to find substance in the synagogue or they will turn to religious, psychological, social, psychic, or political cults."[23] Lita Linzer Schwartz, in a 1978 article entitled "Cults and the Vulnerability of Jewish Youth," makes the claim that contemporary Jewish youth "tend to be secularized rather than religiously observant, poorly educated in their faith," and "subject to emotional difficulties."[24]

For some Orthodox anticult activists such as Dov Fisch, relating to Christian missionaries and new religious movements provided an opportunity to criticize non-Orthodox Jews. Fisch writes: "Most Jewish students do not have any background in traditional Judaism. Denied a Yeshiva education by 'enlightened' parents, or subject to a Talmud Torah/Bar Mitzvah Factory which never really taught Talmud or Torah—these young Jews cannot begin to cope with attacks against traditional Judaism. Not only have they no avenue on which to travel in search of answers, they also have no desire, no reason to look for answers in defense of Jewish tradition."[25] Orthodox antimissionary activists such as Fisch felt at ease in pointing to the lack of appropriate Jewish education among liberal Jews. They felt that their community was more immune to the dangers of being seduced by alien religions. They also believed that Orthodox Judaism was better equipped to offer an alternative to young Jews who were seeking spiritual meaning and a sense of community in their lives.

The Orthodox community came out with initiatives to counter the missionary work and offer alternative Jewish options to Jewish youth seeking spiritual meaning in their lives. Orthodox Jewish evangelists such as the Lubavitch Hasidic movement found themselves, at times, competing with evangelical missionaries over Jewish souls.[26] Orthodox activists established a number of anticult and antimissionary organizations, such as Emes, headed by Rabbi Yaakov Spivak and headquartered in Monsey, New York. Among other things, Spivak purposely encountered missionaries propagating Christianity in New York in order to argue with them.[27] Another organization, Beth Shifra, concentrated its efforts on Jewish immigrants from Russia in Brighton Beach, Brooklyn. "In Brighton Beach, Brooklyn, the first home for a majority of Russian Jewish arrivals to our shores, numerous missions and cults ply their evil trade with unlimited funds, legions of 'volunteers' and a high success rate," reads Beth Shifra's leaflet. "Through selfless dedication and round-the-clock efforts, Beth Shifra has managed to stem the tide. Classes, trips, Shabbatons, Holiday parties, a free nursery and a host of other social, religious . . . services help the Russians . . . live as happy and vibrant Jews," it continued. "But all this takes massive amounts of money." The leaflet concluded with an appeal for funds.[28] In the mid-1970s, Jewish activists founded Jews for Jews, its name unmistakably inspired by that of Jews for Jesus. Disbanding after a few years, it was replaced by a new organization, Jews for Judaism. The organization has sponsored lectures in Jewish centers on university campuses, published antimissionary material, and organized demonstrations at missionary or messianic Jewish gatherings.

One of the larger Orthodox Jewish organizations to take issue with missions has been Yad L'Achim ("A Hand for Our Brethren"). Its antimissionary, anticult department is, however, only one segment of its larger agenda—promoting Jewish observant life.[29] Another organization that existed for a number of years was the Anti Missionary Institute (AMI), which in the late 1970s and early 1980s became a notable organization in the field. The antimissionary groups were, as a rule, small in size, budgets, and scope of activities. They were no match for the much larger, better-funded, and more experienced missionary organizations. Most of the antimissionary enterprises, such as AMI or Jews for Jews, disbanded after a number of years. Their small size and short-lived histories were indications of their standing on the list of priorities of the American Jewish community. American Jews gave large sums of money to such causes as the arts, higher education, or the state of Israel, but they did not show the same generosity toward combating missionaries. Most Jews did not take the missions (or their fighters in the Jewish camp) very seriously. Unlike the Anti-Defamation League, such organizations did not become household names in the Jewish community, and most Jews did not even know they existed.

Most antimissionary activists were "cult busters" who related to missionaries as part of a larger phenomenon. One exception to the rule was Shmuel Golding, who concentrated his efforts exclusively on Christian evangelization. A convert to Judaism from evangelical Christianity, Golding, who immigrated to Israel, has called his small center the Jerusalem Institute of Biblical Polemics.[30] Unlike other polemicists and authors of "know what to answer" tracts, Golding has related in his brochures mainly to passages in the New Testament, in an attempt to discredit the evangelical beliefs in general and the missionary rhetoric in particular. Among other things, Golding has claimed the New Testament to be the root of anti-Semitism.[31] In a leaflet entitled "Jews Beware!" Golding blames the New Testament teachings for anti-Semitism, bursts of brutality against Jews, the fires of the Inquisition, the blood libels, and the Holocaust. To substantiate his claims, he attaches verses from the New Testament to each accusation. In one of his leaflets, he promises a ten-thousand-dollar reward to "any 'Jew for Jesus' who can find in the Hebrew Bible any prophets who have said 'He shall be called a Nazarene' as is recorded in the New Testament (Matthew 27:9, 10)" or "a virgin, shall bear a child, as is recorded in the New Testament (Matthew 1:23)," and other such New Testament verses.[32]

Golding has published a number of guides to Jews who have encountered missionaries. Unlike other guides of this kind, Golding's *Guide to the Misled* is intended for Jews who have accepted the Christian faith and attempts to persuade them, basing its polemics on the New Testament. "Let us assume that you are a believer in Jesus. . . . Let's see if you observe everything that is written in the New Testament."[33] The antimissionary crusader also published a *Counselor's Guide*, intended to provide suggestions and advice to antimissionary counselors.

Golding's roots in evangelical Christianity and his extensive use of the New Testament aroused enormous anger among missionaries and Messianic Jews. Ironically, most of his audience came from these groups. Few missionaries bothered to react to guides and pamphlets written by Jews coming from the Orthodox tradition, who relied in their polemics on alternative Jewish interpretations of biblical passages. But Golding was different. Making use of the New Testament in order to challenge the validity of Christianity touched upon sensitive evangelical nerves. A number of missionary and Messianic Jewish activists turned out against Golding, who became something of a red flag to angry bulls.[34]

Only rarely have Jews turned to violence against missionaries. Such behavior was almost always the initiative of individuals or small groups and did not represent official Jewish policy on behalf of local communities or national organizations. This does not mean that there were no instances of intimidation against missionaries. Such sporadic acts of hostility were directed against the new congregations of Messianic Jews. In February 1980, two young men who, according to some sources, were members of the Jewish Defense League entered a Messianic Jewish congregation, Ahavat Zion ("Love of Zion") in Encino, Los Angeles. What occurred next became a matter of opinion.[35] No one disputes the fact that a Torah scroll was missing following that unsolicited visit. The young men were convinced that they had liberated the scroll, since its use by a Christian congregation was desecration, whereas for members of the congregation as well as the police, it was a theft.

According to newspaper reports, the Messianic Jewish congregation in Philadelphia, Beth Yeshua, encountered Jewish opposition when it tried to build its center in a Jewish neighborhood.[36] An additional source of embarrassment for the congregation was an ad placed in one of the local newspapers, by an unknown antagonist, with the phone numbers of Messianic Ministries, an offshoot organization of the Messianic congregation.[37] In addition, an unidentified Orthodox group called for an *oneg shabat*, an after-service social gathering on Friday night, not far from the messianic group's prayer house as a protest against the activities of the Messianic congregation. The description of the missionaries in the leaflet announcing the *Oneg* echoes common Jewish perceptions of Christian evangelists and Messianic Jews. The appeal to the *Oneg* reads: "Jewish residents of Overbrook Park: There is a cult in your midst. Like the Moonies and the Krishnas . . . they are the Messianic Jewish Movement."[38]

The sporadic, unorganized, and unsystematic nature of attempts to intimidate missionaries and members of Messianic congregations is demonstrated by the activities of the Jewish Defense League in this realm. According to some sources, members of this organization occasionally engaged in acts of hostility against Messianic congregations.[39] But this evidently differed from one location to another. In the mid-1970s, the local branch of the Jewish Defense League in Philadelphia established a cordial relationship with the Messianic congregation Beth Yeshua. Members of the congregation participated in the activities of the branch and donated money. Their identities as Messianic Jews were known to the executive director of the Jewish Defense League, who responded in friendly terms. Her letter to members of Beth Yeshua opened: "Dear fellow Jews, Messianic Jews, and Believers."[40] Three years later, with a change in leadership in the local JDL branch, the amicable relationship ceased. The JDL in Philadelphia added Messianic Jews to the list of groups it opposed.[41] These incidents of hostility on the part of members of the Jewish community did not achieve their goal. If anything, they served to strengthen a sense of camaraderie among members of the Messianic Jewish community.

On one rare occasion, the JDL sued Jews for Jesus for what it saw as an infringement on its common-law trademark. Moishe Rosen, the leader of Jews for Jesus, described the incident: "The tract is entitled *Never Again*, which is the Jewish Defense League's slogan, and refers to the Nazi Holocaust. In our tract, however, JDL stands for Jesus Delivers Life. . . . The judge found that we could not use the clenched fist symbol in a Jewish star, the initials JDL, or the slogan 'Never Again' unless we clearly identified the pamphlet as coming from Jews For Jesus. But . . . under the judge's ruling we could continue to hand out the broadside . . . since it met the legal requirements." Rosen concludes: "It had cost us $500 in attorney's fees to defend ourselves, but all the Jewish newspapers carried the court story, and quoted a substantial amount from our tract. There would have been no other way to get so much publicity on such a small amount of money."[42] Jewish organizations learned their lesson and did not sue missions again. Ironically, incidents involving open Jewish hostility were more or less welcomed by missionaries, who, at times, highlighted such occurrences beyond all proportion. As was noted earlier, Moishe Rosen starts his book on Jews for Jesus by describing an incident in which a Jewish woman in San Francisco hit him in the face.[43] The readers are left impressed by the author's determination and courage in propagating the Christian faith among his brethren in the face of severe persecution and possible martyrdom. Missionary organizations have even related to nonviolent Jewish antimissionary efforts as a menace and a serious obstacle to their operations and have used them in their appeal for funds. Harold Sevener, the president of the Chosen People Ministries, one of the larger missions to the Jews in America, wrote:

> The most serious problem facing us today [is] the well-organized anti-missionary efforts of the Jewish community. Their tactics range from one to one friendships with Jewish believers to using the legal system to harass missionaries. They seek to cause a rift between evangelical churches and mission agencies such as ours. They hold seminars to train people how to counteract the "missionary message." And they have considerable effect. . . . We are sowing the seed faithfully by the Spirit of God, and through our missionary workers, the seed is being watered and cultivated. Yet the enemy is always present, ready to snatch the seed of faith. Never before in the history of Jewish missions has there been such an organized assault by the Jewish community on missionaries and Jewish evangelism.[44]

Jewish antimissionary activists would have probably considered Sevener's description a compliment. But the president of the Chosen People Ministries was paying Jewish antimissionary activities compliments they did not deserve. The Jewish response to Christian missionaries was not as comprehensive, well organized, unified, or energetic as Sevener described it. The missionary leader was not, however, so much interested in patting his Jewish antagonists on their back as in promoting his own organization. He and the other missionaries, he implied, were doing a wonderfully heroic job in the face of enormous opposition and deserved appreciation and support. He ended his article with an appeal. "We need your prayers and your support to win the battle."

Just as Jews tended to relate to missions as cults, Sevener's description of the Jewish antimissionary activity strongly resembled Jewish (and non-Jewish) images of "cult activity." "By the code of the anti-missionaries," the president of the Chosen People Ministries asserted, "the end justifies the means. Half-truths, deliberate distortions, heavy emotional appeals, guilt, even physical abuse are all justified if, in the end, a Jewish person renounces Messiah." "Where is the believer's greatest fear and weakness: acceptance, parents, children? The antimissionary will exploit them all for 'the good of the cause,'" he concluded.[45] Ironically, Sevener's harsh accusations sound like some of the Jewish complaints in reverse. They point to the often one-sided manner in which both Jewish and evangelical activists viewed each other. What for representatives of one religious community was a legitimate propagation of their faith was an unscrupulous assault for the others; and what for one group was a justified defense of its ranks was, for the group engaged in evangelizing, a vicious denial of its right to make converts.

In contrast to Sevener's claims, much of the Jewish antimissionary activity that did take place was directed inward—to the Jewish community. Jewish activists, thinkers, and organizations thought that they should prepare Jewish youth for a possible encounter with Christian missionaries. They wanted to provide young Jews with interpretations of theological claims and biblical exegesis. In the 1970s and 1980s a number of Jewish activists published "know what to answer" books and pamphlets. These tracts did not speak in one voice; each book represented a different Jewish point of view and a different denominational affiliation. *What to Say When the Missionary Comes to Your Door* was one such brochure, prepared by Rabbi Lawrence M. Silverman of Beth Jacob, a Reform congregation in Plymouth, Massachusetts. Written from a liberal Jewish point of view, the booklet demonstrated the Reform opinion of the Messianic idea. It included statements such as "The messianic age will come to pass in this world! Whatever else it may be, in our view, the Messianic Age will at least be a this-worldly happening" or, "We do not believe that personal salvation and eternal life should be overriding concerns in one's life." Many conservative and most Orthodox Jews would probably not have agreed with Silverman's views.

Another "know what to answer" instructional article was published in *Kol Yavneh*, a publication of the Orthodox National Religious Jewish Students' Association. Produced by an Orthodox activist, Gad Malamed, it differed sharply from the Reform booklet. The author did not dispute the existence of the afterlife or of the world to come. He shared those tenets of faith, which are held by many Orthodox Jews, with the missionaries. He differed, however, from the missionaries in interpreting the content of the world to come and how to reach it. The Orthodox polemicist challenged the Christians' claim that Jesus was the Messiah proclaimed in the Bible.[46] The author examined biblical verses that were often quoted by Christian missionaries to prove their position and claimed that they were mistranslated. For example, the verse in Isaiah that has often been quoted to prove that the birth of Jesus through a virgin was already prophesied in the Old Testament ("Behold, the virgin has conceived and will bear a son") was based on translating the Hebrew word *alma* as a virgin, whereas it actually meant a young woman.[47]

None have gone to as much trouble in attempting to repudiate Christian missionary rhetoric as Gerald Sigal, who responded in detail to the missionary exegetical claims. Sigal's lengthy book, *The Jew and the Christian Missionary: A Jewish Response to Missionary Christianity*, takes issue with the Christian missionary interpretations of biblical passages that have been employed to prove the truth of the Christian faith and used by missionaries as part of the rhetoric of evangelization.

Sigal's book and other such "know what to answer" publications were based on a naive view of the process of conversion. They viewed the interaction between missionaries and potential converts as a theological academic exegetical discourse. Their assumption was that if only the converts had the right answers at the right moment they would have remained in the Jewish camp. This outlook overlooked some of the most important aspects of the conversion process and of religious affiliation in general, which had only partially to do with theological arguments, official creeds, or biblical verses.[48]

This is not to say that missionaries did not relate to the theological aspects of evangelical Christianity and to biblical exegesis. They did. They promoted such views as the New Testament being the second part of the Bible and that events and personalities in the Old Testament or Hebrew Bible pointed to persons and occurrences in the New Testament. But many of the Jews who became attracted to Christianity did not join their new faith on a theoretical, theological basis. Their new evangelical environment offered them a sense of community and a network of fellowship and support. Promoting a conservative evangelical world-view, their new environment also put demands on them and imposed clear boundaries and guidelines. By preferring evangelical Christianity, the newly converted were signaling that they had found in their new religious community a more nurturing environment than in liberal Jewish congregations or in secular, unaffiliated Jewish life. The writers of these books found it easier to believe that the adoption of the Christian faith resulted from a lack of biblical-exegetical knowledge; all would have been well if only converts to Christianity were provided in time with the right answers. They were right to assume that many of the young Jews attracted to Christianity had a poor knowledge of their Jewish heritage and faith. They were mistaken, however, in their assumption that "know what to answer" tracts could have made a significant difference when such Jews encountered missionaries propagating the Christian faith. Some did read the "know what to answer" tracts scrupulously. Louis Goldberg, the director of the program for Jewish evangelization at the Moody Bible Institute, wrote a booklet, which was published by Jews for Jesus, to combat Sigal's claims. Ironically, it was the missionaries who, more than anyone else, read books such as Sigal's and responded to them.[49]

Influenced by public criticism and the need to "do something" to counter the missionary threat, the Conservative and Reform movements developed educational programs for their youth in an attempt to immunize them against the missionary appeal. The United Synagogue of America's Department of Youth Activities circulated a guidebook for conducting such a program: *The Missionary at the Door—Our Uniqueness*. Developed and edited by Rabbi Benjamin Segal, it is composed of a series of essays discussing such issues as "Why Aren't We Christians?" and "Was Jesus the Messiah? Let's Examine the Facts"; in the latter essay, its author, Pinchas Stoper, argued that biblical descriptions of the Messiah do not relate to Jesus. The book includes a "Discussion Leader's Guide" for workshops of the conservative youth movement. The guide illustrates some of the problems Jews faced in trying to counter present-day missionaries. The evangelists of Jews for Jesus as well as Messianic Jewish groups claimed pride in their ethnic Jewish identity and made extensive use of Jewish symbols and language. It had become increasingly more difficult for defenders of Judaism to discredit the missionary claim that Jews could retain their Jewishness while accepting Jesus as Messiah. The discussion guide thus insisted that Judaism was a religion and not merely an ethnic grouping and that being a "Jewish-Christian made no more sense than a capitalist-communist." Another essay was entitled "Put the Problem in Perspective." Although its authors saw missionaries and conversions to Christianity as a danger for the Jewish community, they downplayed the scope of those conversions.

The Orthodox National Conference of Synagogue Youth produced a somewhat different type of guide. Editor Aryeh Kaplan intended the guide, *The Real Messiah?: A Jewish Response to Missionaries*, less for Jews who might become convinced of the truth of the Christian gospel than for guides who could talk to such youth and present the Jewish side of the picture to them. The editor assumed that people growing up in the Orthodox milieu were basically immune to the Christian message, and he believed that Orthodox Jews had a mission and duty to provide answers to those Jews who were not fortunate enough to have received a thorough Jewish education. "We must strive, with loving concern, to restore erring individuals to their faith and community," he wrote.[50] The booklet, like other publications of its kind, included chapters explaining Jewish traditional positions, such as "Why Aren't We Christians?" and "The Real Messiah."

Responding to growing concerns in the Jewish community, some Jewish federations decided to take action. "It is only recently that our communal agencies have begun to develop effective techniques to respond to . . . proselytizing activities," wrote Burt Siegel in *Jewish Exponent*, the Organ of the Jewish Federation of Metropolitan Philadelphia. "The Jewish Community Relations Council serves as a clearing house for information regarding missionary groups, we continue to monitor their activities and publicize throughout the Jewish community the name and nature of the programs of the dozen or so local missionary groups. . . . The Jewish Family Service now has a full time counseling service specifically resulting from cult and missionary activities. JFS runs parent support groups, youth support groups and families who get caught up in cult or missionary problems," he informed.[51] Other Jewish federations also took action. The Jewish Federation–Council of Greater Los Angeles established a special task force on missionary efforts. Its brochure, "The Missionary at Our Door," offered guidelines on how to relate to missionaries, including "Do not be taken in by the 'Jewish Christian' ploy"; "Do not debate, dialogue or argue with missionaries," and "Do not lose your cool." The Jewish Federation was offering help to families of those who joined Christian groups. Like much of the Jewish reaction, the task force called upon Jews to show more awareness: "Since much of the missionary appeal is to those on the fringes, we urge all Jews . . . to be sensitive to those around them who might be helped. . . . By helping each other, we help ourselves and strengthen the whole of Judaism."

The largest attempt on the local level to combat missionaries was that of the New York Jewish community. The Jewish Community Relations Council of New York established the Task Force on Missionaries and Cults. The largest Jewish community in the country, New York Jewry could support a special organization or subdivision dedicated to the activity of missions and new religious movements among Jews. Directed by Philip Abramowitz, who held a Ph.D. in special education, the task force concentrated much of its efforts on collecting data on new religious movements and missions. "Our files," the report of activities declared, "house information on nearly eighteen hundred cult and missionary groups."[52] The task force also provided counseling services, complete with a twenty-four-hour-a-day hotline, which reflected the scope of the anxiety and state of crisis in which families of converts found themselves.

The task force's policy reflected much of the Jewish feeling toward missionaries. In response to ads posted by Jews for Jesus in major newspapers in which it asked, "Why can't Christmas be a Jewish holiday? Isn't Christmas the birthday of the greatest Jew who ever lived?" the task force sent letters in which it stated, "The Task Force respects the right of others to uphold and pursue their faith. However, the tactics of Jews For Jesus seem to us to violate the commitment to ethics and honesty. . . . Their right to advocate beliefs should not preclude their legal and moral responsibility to inform the public of their true intentions."[53] Like other anticult movements of the period, the task force circulated the testimony of a former Messianic Jew who described his double odyssey to and from the belief in Jesus.[54]

Jewish community leaders tried, at times, to approach the Christian community and to alert it to what they considered to be the unfairness of the missionary activity and its destructive nature.[55] The same years that saw the rise of Jews for Jesus and Messianic Judaism were also witness to the heyday of the Jewish-Christian dialogue, a movement of rapprochement between the religious communities whose participants were liberal Jews, liberal Protestants, and Roman Catholics. Jews voiced their objections to the Christian evangelism of Jews. Liberal Christians did indeed become convinced that evangelizing the Jews was inappropriate. Some liberal Protestant thinkers, such as Franklin Littel and Robert Handy, denounced the ongoing Christian evangelism of Jews.[56] But their voice did not carry much weight among conservative Christians, who sponsored the missionary efforts.[57]

In the 1970s, Jewish activists made attempts to enter into a dialogue with evangelical Christians. This was done on a smaller scale and in a more reserved manner than between liberal Christians and Jews. Many in the Jewish community looked suspiciously at the conservative segment of Christianity. Evangelicals, for their part, remained committed to evangelism and would not modify their theological standing. Ironically, during those years, conservative evangelicals became ardent supporters of the state of Israel. Many evangelical leaders, such as Billy Graham, Oral Roberts, Pat Robertson, and Jerry Falwell, expressed sympathy for the Jews and support for Israel. Influenced by their premillennialist messianic hope, many evangelicals saw the Six-Day War in 1967 as a sign that Israel was established for a purpose and was about to fulfill a crucial role in preparing the way for the Second Coming of Jesus and his thousand-year reign on earth.[58]

Israeli leaders and officials welcomed evangelical support warmly, responding with friendliness to evangelical leaders, activists, and organizations.[59] They were often unaware of the fact that the same groups that were supporting Israel were the ones to sponsor missionary activity among Jews, both in America and in Israel. Pat Robertson, for example, whose evangelization network, the 700 Club, broadcasts to Israel, is also the recipient of the Jabotinsky Order Medal. Many Israelis did not take the missionary activity very seriously. They shared the view that conversions were few in number and involved marginal persons. It was a small price to pay in exchange for a good relationship with Christians who backed Israel so ardently. Some Jewish American activists, notably Nathan Perlmutter of the Anti-Defamation League and Marc H. Tannenbaum of the American Jewish Committee, welcomed and promoted the evangelical interest. Support for Israel, they asserted, took precedence over other considerations.

Establishing cordial relationships with evangelical leaders, Jewish activists tried to use their newly acquired connections to influence their evangelical friends to give up on missionizing the Jews. One such event took place in 1973 in connection with Key 73, an ambitious evangelical campaign that was planned for that year, with the goal of spreading the Christian gospel to the entire generation. As was noted earlier, Jewish leaders voiced resentment over the idea that Jews were included in the evangelization plans.[60] They were not necessarily concerned about the possibility of a mass Jewish desertion of the faith so much as the implications concerning Christian attitudes toward Jews and the nature of religious life in America. Perlmutter and others approached Billy Graham and conveyed to him the Jewish views on Christian evangelism in general and their specific concern over the Key 73 evangelical campaign in which Graham took no part and with which he was not directly connected. Following his meeting with the Jewish leaders, Graham published a statement in which he expressed his commitment as an evangelist to spread the Christian message to all human beings.Yet he denounced proselytizing "that used gimmicks, coercion, or intimidation"—a clear reflection of the Jewish image of the missionary tactics. Graham also expressed his disapproval of evangelistic efforts that singled out Jews as Jews.[61] Pleased with Graham's attitude, the Anti-Defamation League awarded the evangelist its Torch of Freedom Award, and the American Jewish Committee, sometime later, its National Inter-religious Award. Missions to the Jews, however, were less pleased. Missionaries approached Graham and presented their case, and the evangelist did not repeat his declaration. Graham's denunciation notwithstanding, evangelical support for missionary work among the Jews did not weaken.

Jewish activists did not, however, give up on the attempt to convince conservative evangelicals that evangelizing Jews was wrong. One such Jewish activist has been Rabbi Yechiel Eckstein. An ordained Orthodox rabbi, Eckstein, a former national codirector of the Inter-religious Affairs of the Anti-Defamation League of B'nai B'rith, founded in the mid-1980s an organization with the aims of bringing Jews and evangelical Christians together. The Holy Land Fellowship of Christians and Jews has encouraged conservative Christians to support Jewish causes and has concentrated much of its efforts on projects on which both communities can agree, such as support for Israel or for Russian Jewish immigration to Israel. Eckstein excluded from the activity of his organization persons directly involved with missions to the Jews, thus attempting to promote an atmosphere among evangelicals that would discourage the evangelization of Jews and to direct the evangelical interest in the Jewish people to more constructive (from a Jewish point of view) channels. In a book he wrote to familiarize evangelical Christians with Jews and Judaism, Eckstein dedicated a chapter to the Jewish attitudes toward Christian missions to the Jews and toward Messianic Judaism. Demonstrating a good knowledge of evangelical theology, he asked evangelicals "to leave the conversion of the Jews to God, who may or may not bring it about when the time of the Gentiles arrives."[62]

Viewing the various Jewish reactions to the missionary activity might, at first glance, give the incorrect impression that the missionary threat ranked high in Jewish intellectual discourse. Considering the scope of the movement to evangelize the Jews in America during the period and the escalating numbers of Jewish conversions to evangelical Christianity, not to mention the distress it brought to thousands of families, it is surprising how little attention the Jewish community was willing to give to the missionaries. The issue was discussed on local and national community levels by the official voices of American Jewry. Jewish intellectuals, academicians, writers, and journalists, on the other hand, hardly addressed the issue. One can search the pages of major Jewish publications such as *Moment* or *Commentary* during the 1970s and 1980s and find almost no mention of missionaries or of the growing movement of Messianic Jews.[63] Other issues, such as developments in the state of Israel, the fate of Russian Jewry, American political, social, and cultural issues, the women's movement, and the Jewish-black relationship enjoyed a higher priority. Most evaluations of the actual numbers of conversions were reassuringly minimal. American Jewry as a whole did not consider the Christian missionary activity a threat to Jewish survival in America or to the well-being of the Jewish community. The missionaries did not seem to affect the sense of security that Jews had gained in American society and were not conceived of as a threat to the Jewish standing in the American polity.

Jewish scholarship of missionaries and converts followed the pattern of underrating the scope and importance of the missionary movement. Academic or semiacademic studies during the period strengthened such an outlook. In 1978, David Eichhorn, a Reform rabbi, published a historical survey of Christian missions to the Jews in America.[64] Throughout this work, Eichhorn degraded and mocked both missionaries and converts. His treatment of the resurgence of the missionary movement in the 1970s was no different, and he described it as a failure.[65] Another study was that of the sociologist B. Z. Sobel. Beginning his research while working for the Anti-Defamation League, Sobel studied a congregation of Jewish converts to Christianity. His conclusion was that converted Jews were sad, marginal people, who were defeated on all fronts of life. The studies thus confirmed what Jewish leaders and activists wished to believe.[66]

The 1970s and 1980s were years of optimism for American Jews. Charles Silberman gave expression to the spirit of the age in his best-selling book *A Certain People: American Jews and Their Lives Today*, which related, with unprecedented confidence and pride, to the realities of American Jewish life and to the place and status of the Jews in American society and culture. In a more academic tone, sociologists Calvin Goldscheider and Alan Zuckerman marveled at the minirevival that had taken place in American Judaism since the late 1960s. Choosing to see elements of renewal and growth, they wrote: "Since the Mid 1960s there has been an enormous growth in Jewish activities, and new forms of Jewish identity, and new sources of Jewish cohesion have emerged. These have been particularly concentrated among teenagers, college students, and young adults. The impressive growth of Habad houses, Jewish consciousness among students, kosher facilities, Jewish studies, and Israel-Zionism-Soviet Jewry activities, among others, have been revolutionary forces in American Jewish life."[67] Silberman, Goldscheider, and Zuckerman, like other writers during the 1970s and 1980s who dedicated their books to evaluating the position of American Jewry, did not even mention missionaries, whom they obviously did not consider to be playing any role in shaping the future of American Jews.

Toward the late 1980s, Leonard Fein and Arthur Herzberg began voicing their concern over the course of American Jewry and its ability to survive into the twenty-first century.[68] But their opinions were not necessarily the prevailing ones. Matters changed in the 1990s, following the publication of the findings of the 1990 National Jewish Demographic Survey. Many read in the survey alarming data pointing to the dwindling of the Jewish ranks, a result of negative demographic trends—decline in reproduction, intermarriage, and desertion of the faith.[69] The survey's estimates of the number of Jews who had joined non-Jewish religions confirmed the most pessimistic estimates. Concern over the future of American Jewry as a distinct and vital religious and ethnic community became the norm. That was perhaps one of the reasons for a change of attitude in the way the Jewish community began approaching the subject of Jewish conversions to Christianity.

As the data emerging from the survey became more and more known and discussed among Jews, Jewish publications began reporting on missionary activity and the community of converts in a new manner. Articles on Messianic Jews in *Moment* and the *Jerusalem Report* appearing in 1994–95, for example, treated the converts to Christianity respectfully and presented their case in a surprisingly impartial tone—a long shot from the articles of the 1970s and 1980s that related to that movement in a condescending manner or attributed to it conspiratorial motives.[70] The writers described the converts, many of them actively evangelizing among their brethren, in realistic terms as perfectly normal people, whose faith offered them meaning, community, and a sense of purpose. By the mid-1990s, it became clear to many in the Jewish community that the aggressive missionary movement of the 1970s and 1980s had created large and vital groups of converts, that their numbers were far above what most Jewish activists had previously estimated, and that such groups were not necessarily composed of the down and out. It further brought into realization the fact that the missionary activity and the growing Messianic Jewish communities were posing a challenge to the continuity of Jewish life in America in its traditional sense. The missionaries had become real.

There were elements of irony in the Jewish response to Christian missionaries during this period. The resurgence and intensification of the missionary activity came about during a time of unprecedented social and economic well-being for American Jews. Old restrictions and prejudices disappeared, and Jews became accepted members of America's professional class. Being part of a liberal milieu, Jews (like many non-Jews) had a hard time taking conservative evangelists seriously and could not grasp the scope of the latter's success in capturing the hearts of young Jews. The Jewish intellectual elite usually ignored the phenomenon, and academic studies reassured the community that no serious harm was done to its ranks. There was, therefore, an element of coming of age when, in the 1990s, Jews began relating to missionaries and converts in more realistic terms, giving up on the "anticult" attitudes that characterized their responses for two decades.

Ironically, too, Jews were firmly committed to the pluralistic nature of American society, and organizations that did relate to the missionary challenge could, in essence, do very little to combat it. Most of the activity concentrated on collecting data and offering counseling to families. Another realm of activity attempted to strengthen Jewish spiritual life and education. In the final analysis, the energetic missionary endeavor had exposed the vulnerability of Jewish continuity in a free, open culture in which religious affiliation had become increasingly a matter of choice and not inherited obligation and in which the social boundaries between Jews and Christians crumbled and no longer worked to reinforce religious identity. Jews' responses along the years moved from denial to a partial recognition of the new realities.

22

The New Face of the Missionary Movement

The rise of Jews for Jesus and Messianic Judaism has strongly affected the missionary movement and reshaped much of its character. Jews for Jesus and the Messianic Jewish congregations replaced the American Board of Missions to the Jews as the avant-garde of the era and introduced new methods of evangelism. They became so predominant and captured so much attention that the existence of other missionary organizations often went unnoticed. But the older missions, such as the American Board of Missions to the Jews, did not die out. On the contrary, they continued carrying out their work with great vigor. The older missions were now reacting to innovations brought about by the new, more dynamic groups. Yet they remained on the scene and altered their character in line with the spirit of the age, which was determined mostly by the new Messianic Jewish congregations. Missions did not change their basic theological creeds or evangelistic messages, but the language they were now using and the means they employed to propagate the faith changed and shifted in the direction of Messianic Judaism.

Influenced by the new trend, missions have adopted a new vocabulary that has come to describe evangelism, conversion, and converts in a manner devoid of their historical meaning and connotations. In this new language, converts are not depicted as persons becoming Christians and moving from one religious community to another but as persons who have become "believers" or "Jewish believers," "were saved," and have found the true meaning of their identities as Jews. For many, such terminology was not euphemism. They internalized the language, which became part of their new selves. But some also adopted it for its utilitarian value, as a more effective tool of evangelism. Like the Baptist missions in Israel in the 1940s and 1950s, missions in America in the 1970s and 1980s discovered that the use of a more neutral language untainted by the long and bitter history of Christian-Jewish relations has helped them approach Jews more successfully.[1]

The terms "mission" and "missionaries" were voluntary casualties of the new era and disappeared from the missionary scene. During the 1970s and 1980s, the term "missions" became more and more discredited by postcolonial intellectual trends that viewed missionaries as no more than an arm of the colonial nations, coming to strip indigenous populations of their cultural heritage and political power.[2] But in no other missionary field did the terms "missions" and "missionaries" so completely disappear. The new missionary terminology wished, first and foremost, to overcome the instant reluctance of Jews to listen to missionaries and to take their message seriously. The adoption of new terminology to describe their work to potential converts became a matter of survival. If they wished to succeed and preach their messages effectively, they had to adapt and accept the Messianic terminology. Missions changed their names, mottoes, and symbols, in accordance with the new language. Ironically, Jews for Jesus, the innovative new organization that became identified with the spirit of the age, was one organization that continued to insist on its missionaries presenting themselves openly, publicly, and proudly for what they were. Although they avoided mentioning the terms "mission" or "missionaries," the evangelists wore T-shirts, sweatshirts, or sport jackets with the organization's name.

Giving up on their old principles and becoming more pragmatic, missionaries concentrated on their goal, and their tactics changed dramatically. In the previous era, the missionary movement was tuned on middle-class propriety and made every effort to persuade the conservative Protestant community that its methods of operation and evangelization were beyond reproach. Missionary leaders took pride in being able to account for every penny they received, for every hour of a missionary's activities, and for truth and accuracy in presenting themselves to potential converts.[3] Now missions were willing to disguise or conceal their missionary intentions and to use language that did not overtly present their goal of Christianizing the Jews.

The new missionary tactics were adopted with dramatic effect in Israel. The missions operating in Israel during the 1950s and 1960s had already sought ways to beat the system in their struggle to expand the missionary operations in the country, but they changed their mode of operation in the 1970s and 1980s. The older system imposed by the Israeli government that was based on a quota of the number of missionaries permitted to reside in the country did not disappear completely, but it relaxed considerably. Missionaries could settle in the country more easily, and the number of new evangelical groups operating in the country grew.[4] The question facing the missions became not so much how to bring more missionaries into the country but how to approach and interact successfully with young Israelis. In previous decades missions had concentrated their efforts on the poor, immigrant neighborhoods in Israeli cities. Now, their focus changed. Their aim in the 1970s and 1980s became the heart of Israeli culture and society: young men and women who had grown up in the country, served in the army, and received high school and college education.

Whereas the Israeli scene of the 1950s and 1960s left little room for missions to make converts in the heart of the Israeli society, the 1970s and 1980s brought about new opportunities. Israeli society changed dramatically during this period as it moved away from the pioneer spirit of the pre-state period and the early years of independence and became a Western-oriented consumer society. Following the Yom Kippur War of October 1973, the Israeli elite lost much of its self-confidence, and its faith in Zionism as an all-encompassing ideology, providing hope, meaning, and a sense of purpose, weakened considerably. With the fading away of a central secular national faith and the moral and spiritual vacuum it left, there was plenty of room for alternative faiths to make their way in the Israeli religious market.[5]

In the years following the Yom Kippur War, thousands of young Israelis joined new religious movements that had not been represented in the country just a few years earlier, including EST, the Church of Scientology, the Hare Krishnas, and the Unification Church. Thousands became "returnees to tradition" and joined Orthodox forms of Judaism. Many others accepted the Christian faith. As was the case in America, Messianic congregations became the leaders in the field. Israel had originally been the cradle of what might be called the "new missionary language," a language in which words such as "missionary," "evangelization," and "conversion" from one religion to another (*hamarat dat* in Hebrew) ceased to exist.[6] Reinforced by the invention of equivalent terminology in America, it now became the prevailing vocabulary in whatever language missionaries to the Jews were using.

Impressed by the mystique of the kibbutz as the epitome of the Israeli Zionist elite, missions paid special attention to "the Children of the Dream," as Bruno Bettleheim called those who grew up in kibbutzim. As early as the 1960s, the kibbutzim opened their doors to volunteers from all around the world, offering them room and board, Hebrew school courses, and tours in the country in exchange for their working as unskilled laborers in the various kibbutz agricultural enterprises. Tens of thousands have, throughout the 1960s, 1970s, and 1980s, taken part in this program. Many of them befriended young kibbutzniks, and hundreds of them married kibbutz members and remained in the kibbutzim on a permanent basis. For the youth of the kibbutzim, volunteers from Western countries were representatives of foreign cultures, acquainting them with the fashions of the outside world in music, dancing, clothing, sexual norms, and, at times, also with drugs. Missions realized the potential for evangelism embodied in the encounter between the volunteers and the kibbutz youth and decided to send missionaries to the kibbutzim.

Such missionaries did not present themselves as what they were, nor did they evangelize openly. Such frankness would have ended the attempts at evangelism before they even started. Instead, evangelists came as regular volunteers. They befriended young kibbutzniks, invited people to join them in celebrating holidays, answered questions about their faith, and offered literature. If the encounter proved fruitful and kibbutzniks were interested and eventually accepted Jesus as their Savior, the evangelists would acquaint the newly converted with congregations in Israeli cities or send them to Bible schools or Christian colleges in America or Britain. Some information about missionaries in kibbutzim has been revealed in missionary brochures.[7] But missions tried to remain discreet. By the late 1980s, after a series of conversions among its youth, the kibbutz movement decided to put an end to the volunteer program.

The extensive and varied work carried out by missionary groups and individuals notwithstanding, Messianic congregations have served in Israel as a major arm of the missionary movement. The community of Messianic Jews in Israel grew considerably during the 1970s and 1980s. From no more than three hundred people in the mid-1960s, it grew to about three thousand in the mid-1980s and then to about six thousand in the mid-1990s. Some of the growth came from immigration, as hundreds of Jewish converts to Christianity from America settled in Israel in the years following the Six-Day War in 1967. Many more came in the 1980s and 1990s from the former Soviet Union and Ethiopia, but many new converts were Israelis who had been raised in the country. By the 1980s, the demography of the Messianic congregations was a far cry from the realities of the earlier years of the state. It became evident that the evangelical zeal missionaries had invested for decades had come to fruition, and the missionary movement had been making converts in almost all segments of Israeli society. Much of the stigma surrounding conversion to Christianity has faded away as Israeli society became more inclusive and tolerant throughout the 1970s and 1980s and as new religious movements have become part of the Israeli cultural scene.[8]

The terminology adopted by the missionary community in Israel has helped ease the stigma and guilt surrounding conversion. Those accepting Jesus as their Savior have called themselves "maaminim" (believers), not "converts," and have spoken about "lehagea laEmuna" or "kshenaaseti mamin" (when I become a believer) and not about their "conversion." They were "Yehudim" (Jews) and not "Notzrim" (Christians), even after their conversions. Moreover, for most Israelis, the image of Christianity, particularly in its Western Protestant, English-speaking or Scandinavian form, has changed dramatically. It has moved from a hostile faith that wished to suppress, if not annihilate, Judaism and Jews to the religion of friendly visitors, volunteers, colleagues, and friends. Israelis' self-confidence has been shattered since the Yom Kippur War of 1973, but at the same time, their self-image has moved away from that of a persecuted minority. For many secular Israelis, Messianic Jews were just a friendly new religious movement, and they did not see Jewish Christian communities as a threat to Jewish survival. In the 1990s, Messianic Jews marched under their own banner in the yearly Jerusalem Marches, a reality that could not have taken place earlier.[9] A public opinion poll solicited by Messianic Jewish activists in the late 1980s discovered that most Israelis were willing to accept Messianic Jews.[10]

Was the conversion pattern in Israel different from that in America? Unlike in America, Israelis accepting Christianity were converting to a minority religious group, one that advocated a different faith and set of values than the major cultural trends of the country. In choosing Christianity, they have not necessarily rejected their Israeli identity but rather found a protective niche in that society. Some of the autobiographical accounts of Israeli converts point to a rejection of their parents' worldviews and values and a strong sense of spiritual and communal voids prior to their conversion.[11] They have also signaled that they have found Israeli secular culture and values unsatisfactory and even unacceptable.[12] In this, ironically, they have shared similar outlooks with many Orthodox Jews, who, like them, had rejected Israel's open and permissive culture. This accounts, among other things, for the bitter animosity of Orthodox propagators of the faith toward Christian missionary activity and Messianic congregations, since both groups compete over the same pool of potential converts. Similarly, Messianic Jews have held a less than favorable attitude toward Orthodox Judaism, as they, too, have felt that the many converts made by the other group should have joined their camp.[13] Even though Messianic Jews reject Israeli cultural values, their relationship with Israeli society has, paradoxically, improved in the past few decades, and they have come to feel much more at home in it. One factor that allowed for the growth of Messianic Judaism and its relative successful appeal to young Israelis has been the growing legitimization of the movement at the same time that it was offering an alternative to Israeli secular permissive culture. As in America, it became more adapted to the general culture while offering a sense of security against some of its more permissive elements.[14] Similarly, it has provided a sense of community within a society that, as a whole, has lost much of its sense of unity, coherence, and purpose. Consequently, the Messianic Jewish option has become attractive to many members of Israeli society. Jews (and their non-Jewish spouses) who had converted to Christianity in the former Soviet Union or in Ethiopia (and other countries) but not necessarily to evangelical Christianity joined Messianic Congregations in Israel. Such a choice has helped them reconcile their loyalty to their Christian faith with the culture of their new country. The Messianic congregations have also served to ease the tensions of building their lives in a new country.

The Messianic Jewish community in Israel is far from being united. There are a number of organizations, national meetings, conferences, publications, and summer camps to give the movement some coherence and sense of unity.[15] But the movement as a whole is remarkably diverse and, within the boundaries of evangelical Christianity, pluralistic. Congregations operate in a number of languages, including Hebrew, English, Russian, and Amharic. As in America, there are charismatic and noncharismatic Messianic congregations, and there are differences regarding the amount of Jewish traditional rites the congregations incorporate. In addition, as Menahem Benhayim, an Israeli Messianic Jewish leader and writer, has pointed out, congregations have different characteristics depending on the different traditions they have inherited from their former or present missionary sponsors, such as Reform, Plymouth Brethren, Anglican, Lutheran, Baptist, and the Christian and Missionary Alliance.[16] Messianic congregations often depend on missionary support; many of them are located on the property of churches, and foreign missionaries take part in the life of many communities. Benhayim summarizes the atmosphere as the following: "Most Israeli congregations and fellowships reflect the Evangelical Christian streams from Calvinist to Charismatic, which have influenced their leaders and members. We sometimes hear gentile Christian visitors from abroad making significant comments during visits to Israel, 'Oh, we feel so much at home here; the service and atmosphere was just like ours!' "[17] He concludes by expressing a wish for more independent and authentic Israeli content to Messianic Jewish life in that country.

Messianic Judaism has demonstrated a great amount of energy and vitality in the Israeli scene and has transformed itself in the past decades from a small marginal group to a large and dynamic movement. This was due in no small part to changes in Israeli society and culture, as well as to waves of immigrations that brought about many Jewish converts to Christianity. But some of the growth was due to the fact that Messianic congregations were effective in conveying to prospective converts a strong sense of community and a safe haven with an alternative set of morals to that of the general culture. As perhaps the fastest-growing religious movement in the country, Messianic Judaism serves effectively as the most vital arm of the movement to evangelize the Jews in Israel.

The relationship between the missions and Israeli society has been marked by ironies. This feature of missionary work reached a peak in the late 1970s, 1980s, and 1990s. Evangelical interest in Israel during that era was at its height, and conservative evangelicals, influenced by a premillennialist messianic understanding of history, became ardent supporters of Israel in the American political arena. The Likud government that came to power in 1977 had developed a particularly friendly relationship with evangelical leaders and organizations. Similarly, a number of Jewish Orthodox activists and organizations such as the Temple Mount Faithful have developed cordial relationships with evangelical supporters. A paradoxical situation developed. Members of the same camp in American society that sponsored missionary activity among the Jews were also Israel's supporters and on excellent terms with its right-wing government. Even more ironic, right-wing and Orthodox Jews encouraged the friendship of groups and individuals that have lent their support to missionary organizations or carried out such work themselves. In the 1980s, for example, the Likud government honored Pat Robertson by presenting him with the Jabotinsky Order Medal. Robertson's 700 Club has operated a special radio station, "Kol Hatikva," or "The

Voice of Peace," broadcasting evangelical messages to Israel from Lebanon and Cyprus. This did not deter right-wing Orthodox Israeli activists from appearing on Robertson's television program in an attempt to muster support for their activities.

Support for Israel has been the other side of the missionary coin, arising from the same theological perceptions that have motivated the evangelization of Jews. The missions themselves became part of the evangelical network of support for Israel and have operated as centers of production and distribution of material on Israel, promoting the country in accordance with their Christian Zionist views.[18] This has come about in a variety of means and media uses, ranging from radio broadcasts on Israel to the distribution of videotapes, brochures, and articles on that country in mission newspapers. The promotion of pro-Israeli views and evangelism were often interwoven, being featured side by side in the same magazines, the one serving as the reason for the other. The interest in Israel manifested itself in more than writing and broadcasting. A new feature of missionary life that came about in the 1970s was organizing tours to Israel for donors and supporters of the missionary cause. Missions, such as the Chosen People Ministries, Ariel Ministries, the American Messianic Fellowship, and Zola Levitt's Ministries, have periodically organized tour groups to Israel.[19] Most tours were similar to those organized by churches, Bible schools, and other nonmissionary evangelical organizations. Avoiding the use of the term "missions," such groups have often invited Israeli officials to give talks. Most Israeli government agencies could not tell the difference between one pro-Israeli evangelical group and another and could not determine whether evangelical organizations were engaged in missionary work or not, especially since there was little to differentiate between missions and other pro-Israel evangelical organizations. Some tours have occasionally engaged in evangelism, distributing material in homes or in public spaces, such as beaches or open-air music or dance festivals.

To what extent pro-Israel and missionary activities have been intertwined can be seen from the travail of the one organization operating in Israel that made a solemn decision not to evangelize. Since its establishment in 1980, the International Christian Embassy in Jerusalem has been one of the largest evangelical pro-Israel organizations. Headquartered in Jerusalem and mustering support among evangelicals all around the globe, the ICEJ has built a particularly warm relationship with the Israeli government. In order to ensure the trust and cooperation of the country's leadership, the organization decided to refrain from missionizing. This decision enabled the organization to gain the trust of the government, but it also turned many evangelical activists against it.[20] Evangelists in Israel lashed out at the ICEJ, accusing it of betraying one of its major duties.[21] Even if many of the other organizations operating in the country were not very overt in their missionary nature, and some were not particularly energetic in carrying out their goals, evangelizing was one of their purposes, and they were upset that evangelicals like themselves were willing to give up on it. In their view, no reason was good enough to justify such a move.

The paradoxical nature of the Israeli-missionary encounter could also be seen by the attempts to pass laws in Israel curtailing or banning missionary activity. Antimissionary sentiments ran high in Israel in the 1950s and 1960s, with many in the Orthodox community resenting the missions' presence. But the Labor government refused to yield to demands to ban missionary activity, a move that, it believed, would have harmed Israeli interests abroad.[22] Matters changed in 1977 with the Likud rise to power. Like Labor leaders before him, Menachem Begin relied heavily on the Orthodox parties taking part in his coalition government. The importance of such parties grew considerably after 1977, as they were often the ones to determine which of the two contenders, Likud or Labor, would lead the government. In negotiating with Begin, the Orthodox demanded that a stop be put to missionary activity.

In 1978, at the time that the Israeli-evangelical relationship was reaching the height of its friendliness, the Israeli Knesset passed an antimissionary law prohibiting the offering of money or economic benefits in exchange for conversion. The law was based on the old Jewish myth that missionaries were offering substantial material gains to converts and that financial rewards served as the major impetus for moving from Judaism to Christianity. The missionary community became anxious over the possible implications of the law for its work in the country, but it soon discovered that it had no reason to fear. The 1978 law proved to be a fiasco and had no bearing on Christian evangelism. For one thing, economic promises had rarely, if ever, been part of the evangelization message. But the Israeli government took no chances. Passing a law was one thing; implementing it was another. The attorney general had no intention of allowing the law to become anything more than a dead letter.[23] The minister of justice, Shmuel Tamir, stated publicly that the attorney general had given instructions "that no action, or even inquiry, be instituted by virtue of this law without the prior direct authorization of the Attorney General in person, or the State Attorney in person." There were thus no practical implications to the law. For a while, it pacified Orthodox demands, but it made no real impact on the missionary scene in the country. Missionary work went on as usual, and the Messianic Jewish community was growing.

In the 1990s, antimissionary sentiments were again running high, and a number of Orthodox and non-Orthodox members of Parliament came out with initiatives to outlaw missionary activity.[24] In 1996, an initial, first-round proposal passed the Knesset vote.[25] But then the complex and paradoxical nature of the relationship between the missionary community and Israeli society became unprecedentedly clear. Missionaries operating in Israel called upon their evangelical supporters in America to raise their voices against the impeding law. "We call upon the international Christian community to join us in our opposition to this law," read one of the appeals; "as Christian believers in the God of Israel and in Jesus the Messiah and Savior of the world, we have a special respect and appreciation for the Jewish people and the nation of Israel. We seek and pray for the welfare of all of God's people in the land. We view with grave concern the erosion of Israel's democratic freedom by this proposed law."[26] The Israeli Embassy and consulates in America as well as embassies and consulates in other countries with substantial evangelical populations were virtually flooded with letters of protest against the law. Evangelical opponents of the law circulated forms to protest the law through the Internet.[27] Many wrote directly to the prime minister in Jerusalem.[28] The standard letters emphasized that they were written by friends of Israel who wished the country well and were writing to warn the government against the consequences that the passing of such a law might bring with it. Such legislation, they claimed, would place Israel in the same category with third-world dictatorial regimes and would turn its current supporters against it. Prime Minister Benjamin Netanyahu, who at first offhandedly supported the bill, changed his mind and promised evangelical activists he would oppose it. Other non-Orthodox supporters of the bill, such as Nisim Zwili, a member of the Knesset from the Labor Party, also withdrew their support of the proposed law. As a means of backing out of the law yet saving face, the government's opposition to the proposed law came in exchange for a promise by Christian groups not to evangelize. This agreement, which allowed the government to present its abandonment of the law as a triumph, or at least not as a defeat, had its catch. The Christian groups that promised not to evangelize Jews were not engaged in such activity anyhow, and those who made it their goal to missionize Jews made no promises to stop their activity. "It is not quite clear how the Christian groups with whom the deal was made themselves construe the agreement. . . . The important thing is that Messianic Jews, along with foreign organizations whose ministry is to reach the Jewish people with the gospel, have made not such pact," wrote Kai Kjaer-Hansen in an editorial in *Mishkan*, a journal providing a forum to groups and individuals involved in evangelism in Israel.[29]

The rise and fall of the antimissionary laws was marked by a number of paradoxes. There was an ironic element in antimissionary law being promoted by the Orthodox segments of the Israeli population. Some Orthodox, namely, the settlers' circles, had come to rely on evangelical support, and some of them had established close ties with evangelical organizations.[30] Similarly, the rise and fall of the laws revealed as never before that evangelical political support for Israel and the special relationship that developed between Israel and evangelical Protestant leaders and organizations stood as a block against any action Israel might have taken against the missionary presence.

Even without the realization that the legislation would be politically costly on the international arena, it is doubtful whether the Israeli government would have put the law into effect. The government had no intention of risking the mess of being involved with prosecuting missionaries in 1978. The 1997 law was meant to have more "teeth" to it than its 1978 version, but was based on a misconception. Orthodox pressures notwithstanding, the government was not more willing in the late 1990s to implement an antimissionary law than before. In addition, trying to implement the law would have been almost impossible. As a rule, missionaries in Israel do not present themselves as such, and all missionary societies have chosen neutral names, mottoes, and declarations of purposes. If the Israeli government had gone so far as to implement the law, its agencies would have had to utilize information based on intelligence reports. It would also have had to deport evangelists. The cost to its international image, not to mention the loss of Christian evangelical support, would have been enormous.

In discussing the proposed law, missionaries had also pointed out that keeping professional missionaries at bay hardly would have worked to stop evangelism in Israel, as much of current evangelism was carried out through Messianic congregations. Moreover, many evangelists in the country were students or came on short excursions. Missionaries have reminisced about how they had beaten the system before and how there had, in the past, already been disguised modes of evangelism that did not declare themselves openly as such, such as in the kibbutzim. Moreover, current-day evangelism is carried out in part by such means as the Internet, where missions have home pages, or by e-mail exchange. Brochures and leaflets are sent by mail. Short of turning Israel into an Orwellian police state where free speech, tourism, the mail service, and even the electronic mail would be scrutinized and censored, attempts at implementing the law would be ineffective.

The inability of the Israeli government to censor or curtail missionary activity, even if it had decided to do so, points to the changing nature of evangelism during the current generation. If previously much of the missionary work among the Jews had been carried out by professional evangelists in storefront missionary stations or missionary centers, this had by and large ceased to be the case. The new missionary era has been marked by the predominance of converts' congregations serving as centers of evangelism, on the one hand, and the missionary headquarters carrying out other means of evangelism, through the Internet or by mail, on the other hand. Many of the evangelization efforts outside the Messianic congregations have been taking place in the office, utilizing computers as the major means of production. Missions create home pages, send leaflets, answer e-mail and telephone inquiries, and take orders for books, audiocassettes, videocassettes, and, at times, artifacts and T-shirts. The production of printed or recorded literature has become a major line of action for the missions. Appeals to donors and fund-raising visits to churches also keep the missionary agencies busy. All those activities no longer demand day-to-day interaction between the missionary staff and the Jewish population. Electronic communication has replaced a direct, person-to-person appeal to potential converts. Historically, evangelists in America had been quick to adopt new technologies as a means of conducting their work more effectively.[31] Missions to the Jews were no exception and have embraced the new communication devices of the late twentieth century wholeheartedly. Their offices began to look like those of sophisticated commercial companies that specialize in the promotion of goods or of political candidates. The growing emphasis on producing attractive books, leaflets, audio- and videocassettes, and home pages has allowed missionaries to give expression to their talents in fields such as writing, editing, and translating, as well as computer graphics, designing, and painting.

Missions have shut down centers that formerly attracted Jewish inquirers and have moved to commercial-industrial areas outside the centers of Jewish population. In previous generations missions and missionaries were part of the scenery in Jewish neighborhoods, and children growing up in such neighborhoods would encounter them regularly, but this reality came to an end. Although the effects of evangelism had reached their peak, the missionary centers themselves were gone. Historically located in New York, the American Board of Missions to the Jews moved its headquarters, which had also served in the past as a center of local evangelism and prayer meetings, to an industrial park in Charlotte, North Carolina. The mission chose a place where real estate was cheaper and salaries allowed for a higher standard of living than in the Big Apple. A similar move was taken in the 1980s by the American Messianic Fellowship. After being located in Jewish neighborhoods in Chicago for a hundred years, the mission moved to a commercial-industrial area in the southern part of the city. In the 1960s and 1970s, Jews were moving farther north, into safer neighborhoods, and Rogers Park, the area in which the mission had been located for decades, lost its Jewish character. Considering its options and realizing that the nature of missionary work had altered, the mission's leaders concluded that they did not need to reside among the people they were trying to approach. They could evangelize those people just as effectively from their offices.

Whereas in the United States missions moved more and more into the electronic age, giving up on older methods such as storefront bookshops and reading rooms, community centers, home visitations, and street evangelism, matters were different in Israel. For one thing, missionaries there could safely assume that most of the people they were approaching were Jews, and so older methods of evangelism were still effective. Moreover, street evangelism, home visitations, and the sending of unsolicited material by mail, or placing it in people's mailboxes, were often regarded by Americans as uncivil.[32] This was not a point missionaries felt they had to take into consideration in Israel. This had to do, in part, with the conventions of the country, its ways and manners, which were very different than in the United States. In addition, missions did not think that they had to take into consideration how their tactics affect their image. Their perception has been that large segments of Israeli society were antagonistic anyway and that propagating the gospel in the country demanded courage. Because public sentiment in Israel has often been less than favorable, missionaries have considered it a daring act to evangelize in that country, distribute material on the streets, and discuss Jesus with Israelis. Ironically, such a perception led to a great amount of boldness.[33] Missions and Messianic groups have evangelized in the streets, on beaches, at music and dance festivals, on public buses, and even on El-Al transatlantic flights.[34] Similarly, they did not refrain from placing missionary material in private mailboxes or conducting unsolicited home visitations. Those activities offered a spirit of adventure, which made the missionary work in the country more exciting and rewarding.

In recent years, not only Israel but also the Soviet Union has been a place where missionary enthusiasm ran high. The opening of the countries of the former Soviet Union gave American missions unexpected new territories where they could propagate the gospel among Jews. In this realm, too, missions to the Jews were not unlike the evangelical movement at large, which has paid much attention to the former Soviet bloc once the Communist regimes there crumbled. Many evangelical groups have been active in the former Soviet Union since the late 1980s, but missions to the Jews were a category of their own. In evangelical premillennialist eyes, Jews were not just people to evangelize like everybody else. Motivated by a premillennialist understanding of world history and armed with a Messianic rhetoric, the missions emphasized the role and destiny of the Jews. Missions to the Jews, again in line with the American picture as a whole, have, in relative terms, been more active there than others. The Soviet Jews proved to be a promising and fertile group for evangelism with immediate rewards. The use of Messianic vocabulary and the Jewish Christian option proved particularly attractive to many Soviet Jews. After seven decades of Communist rule, which destroyed all Jewish educational, cultural, and religious infrastructure, most Jews were completely devoid of Jewish knowledge and practices, and a high percentage of them had intermarried. They had no preconceived notions of what Judaism was supposed to look like and no concept of the content of traditional forms of Judaism. They did not have to be convinced that Messianic Judaism was Judaism. For many, it was the only Judaism they had ever encountered. Some Soviet Jews have also been influenced during the 1970s and 1980s by the Christian revival in Russia. The Messianic option, whether advocated by Messianic Jews or by missionary organizations, allowed them to connect with their Jewish identity while embracing Christianity.

Like Israel, the countries of the former Soviet Union became, since the late 1980s, something of a promised land: a place that called for a special mission and effort, that conveyed a sense of enthusiasm and triumph. Missions and Messianic Jewish organizations sent dozens of evangelists, organized tours, and established seminars to train local activists. Missions implemented the Messianic paradigm there as well. This manifested itself in the building of Messianic congregations as an effective means to attract potential Jewish converts. Jewish observers in the mid-1990s have remarked that the Messianic congregations in the former Soviet Union were larger, younger, and more active and enthusiastic than the few conventional Jewish synagogues in the former Soviet Union.[35]

Missions have also carried out extensive evangelization of Russian-speaking Jews outside the former Soviet Union. They have given special attention to this group in America and Israel, the major destination of Russian Jewish immigrants, where hundreds of thousands of immigrants arrived in the 1980s and 1990s, as well as other countries, such as Germany. The inclusion of Russian Jews as a major object of evangelism has strongly affected the character of the missions. Missions have hired Russian-speaking missionaries, and since the late 1980s, Russian literature, books, brochures, and audio- and videocassettes have become an unalienable part of the missions' line of production and can be found on every missionary shelf.

Geography was not the only element in the massive change that affected the movement to evangelize the Jews. The character of contemporary missionary activity has also been influenced by the changing role of women. The place of women in the missions has been influenced by developments in the general culture, and more specifically the evangelical community. The 1960s and 1970s saw a dramatic change in the role of women, their expectations, and the opportunities open to them. They joined the ranks of spiritual seekers and felt free to join or abandon religious communities as never before. Female evangelists have always played an important role in carrying out much of the missions' work, both in field evangelism and in office work, but the new era brought new challenges in that realm to evangelical institutions, which had to approach a new generation of women, more liberated and aspiring than ever before. Missions have continued to regard women as essential members of their staff, carrying out much of the work of evangelism as well as administration and the production of printed or recorded material. The more daring and pragmatic Jews for Jesus allowed women to rise to positions of branch directors or directors of publications. In other missions, positions of leadership remained exclusively in the hands of men. The same could be said about Messianic Jewish congregations, in which women have shared in the various chores and duties, including the teaching of Sunday school. Yet only men could become pastors and hold positions of leadership in the various Messianic Jewish organizations. In many communities, women could not even join in the official lay leadership and become elders of the congregation. The missionary environment has also remained one of the last areas in which women have been expected to quit working and stay at home when their children were young. This points to the nature of the cultural environment that sponsors the missions as well as to the motivation for and the price of conversion. In converting and joining in with the Messianic Jewish community, or with regular non-Messianic evangelical congregations, women make a conscious decision to adopt a more conservative and restrictive lifestyle. For some it is a trade in which they give up some of the liberties and opportunities that a more liberal environment would offer in exchange for a sense of community, spiritual fulfillment, and purpose. For others, it is part of the gains of conversion and a relief.[36] Some observers of the evangelical scene, however, have not seen women there as powerless and have pointed to conservative modes of women's liberation.[37] Some changes in the position of women have definitely taken place. After decades of boards of governors run only by men, for example, women began joining such boards in the 1980s. The electronic age has offered women in missions new avenues to give expression to their talents in writing, editing, graphics, and design. In the realm of giving opportunities to women, the missions have proved to be adaptable, but going only as far as the conservative evangelical norms allowed.[38] Although they kept men at the head of the hierarchy, they did allow women to participate and express their energies and gifts. In relative terms they fell quite a bit short of women's missionary roles in the nineteenth century, when missions were pioneers in allowing women opportunities they did not as a rule enjoy elsewhere.[39]

The contemporary missionary scene has been transformed in more ways than one. Did the changes affect donations to the missions? Did the economic basis of support that provides the means for missionary activity also change dramatically during the period? The answer to these questions is on the whole negative. The arrival of Jews for Jesus and the Messianic congregations challenged the older missions on many fronts but surprisingly did not cause any economic strain. The missionary scene, although not without its rivalries, competitiveness, struggles, and bitterness, proved to be anything but a zero-sum game. There has been room for many organizations. The evangelical community has evidently been willing to offer support to many groups, as donations to missionary enterprises have been a means to express interest in and goodwill toward the Jews and Israel. The era since the Six-Day War in 1967 has brought evangelical interest in the Jews and their role in the Messianic era to a peak. This was reflected in the realm of missions, which benefited enormously from the growing evangelical interest in the Jews.

Although not as well known as Jews for Jesus, additional new missions came about during the period, such as Ariel Ministries or Zola Levitt's Ministries. Both were established by former employees of the American Board of Missions to the Jews who had no theological argument with the board but wished to become independent and open their own missionary enterprises. They did not attract the same amount of attention that Jews for Jesus did and were perhaps not as innovative, but both of them have thrived.

As in the previous period, each mission has built its own network of support, carving its niche within the evangelical community. Organizations have traditionally differed as to the geographical area of their base of support and the constituency to which they had appealed, but during the current era this has become less prevalent. Groups that were previously restricted to certain geographical areas, such as Friends of Israel, went national. The American Messianic Fellowship, which had originally been a Chicago-based organization operating mostly in the Midwest, had, during the 1970s and 1980s, enlarged the geographical scope of its activities, building networks of support among evangelicals outside the United States, including in Mexico and Japan. Charismatics and noncharismatics might have differed as to which missions they chose to support, but this division was not absolute and did not always prevent charismatics from offering support to noncharismatic missions. Since many evangelicals see in missions a means of expressing their premillennialist hopes for a predominant role for the Jews in bringing about the Messianic era and expect the conversion of large numbers of Jews in the years preceding the arrival of the Messiah, it has not been unheard of for supporters of the missionary idea to give their money to missions even if the latter did not represent their views in all matters—for example, charismatics supporting an organization that is, in principle, noncharismatic. The 1960s to 1980s changed the position of charismatics within the evangelical camp, turning them into a much larger and more central and respectable force.[40] Many of the leading Messianic congregations have chosen to become charismatic, but most major missionary organizations, old and new, have remained noncharismatic. This goes back in many ways to the history of the movement to evangelize the Jews and its strong attempts to remain within the respectable mainstream. The larger, older missions, such as the Chosen People Ministries, the Association for Jewish Evangelism, the Friends of Israel, and the American Messianic Fellowship, have therefore been, almost by definition, noncharismatic. Jews for Jesus and Ariel Ministries, being (like many of the older missions) offshoots of the American Board of Missions to the Jews, have retained their noncharismatic character. The fact that most of the major missions have remained noncharismatic does not mean that Pentecostals and charismatics have not shown interest in evangelizing the Jews. Some Pentecostal and charismatic groups, such as the Assemblies of God, have increased their efforts and were expending more personnel and resources on that task. But the missionary movement as a whole remained mainly noncharismatic.

Convincing the evangelical churchgoers that they are supporting a worthy cause has remained a major part of the missions' work. The more effective missions are in this realm, the more successful they are in raising funds and enlarging the scope of their activities. Missionaries visit churches and give talks about the Jewish people and Israel and the importance of sharing the gospel with that nation. In line with the new Messianic trends, they have also joined in by organizing Passover Seders or demonstrating the use of Jewish religious artifacts such as the shofar. One missionary who tours churches dressed as an ancient Levite, demonstrating the blowing of a shofar, is Zola Levitt, whose mission also sells a large variety of music, cassettes, books, videotapes, and artifacts.[41] Levitt's experiment—opening a mission that emphasizes the premillennialist conviction of the centrality of the Jews to the realization of God's kingdom on earth and promotes Jewish biblical themes—has proved very successful. Within a few years, it turned into a medium-sized missionary enterprise, with a yearly seven-figure budget. The evangelical community took a special interest in the Jews and was favorably predisposed toward supporting their evangelism. There was clearly room for many evangelists and missionary enterprises to thrive.

As in earlier periods, missions found a means of coming together and discussing issues of interest to the movement at large. The Fellowship of Christian Testimonies to the Jews (FCTJ) collapsed a few years after its decision not to include Jews for Jesus and its attack on Messianic Judaism. The organization's policy of exclusion undermined its own goals, since it created a situation in which major and most dynamic parts of the missionary movement were not included. By the early 1980s, the FCTJ faded away, and a new forum for missionary activists to discuss issues and exchange views came about: the Lausanne Consultation on Jewish Evangelism. The creation and dynamics of the new forum shed light on the character of the movement to evangelize the Jews and the frequent inability of missions to overlook small differences, personal rivalries, and ego clashes in order to cooperate more effectively and build a united front or merely to get together to discuss issues of mutual interest. Starting in the early 1970s, the Lausanne Conference was an international evangelical event organized to enhance and promote evangelism worldwide. One of its "consultations" was dedicated to the evangelization of Jews. Activists of the movement to evangelize the Jews decided to maintain the consultation as a more permanent forum for missionaries to the Jews to meet. Having been originally created as part of the Lausanne Conference, a prestigious evangelical institution, the Lausanne Consultation on Jewish Evangelism had a more neutral and inclusive aura to it than the FCTJ and so enabled missions that had previously not cooperated with one another to get together. Among other things, the consultation allowed Jews for Jesus to take its place as a central group within the larger movement and its people to sit together with representatives of other missions. Similarly, Messianic congregations were allowed to join in as regular members. Rivalries and competitiveness notwithstanding, some amount of rapprochement and cooperation came about.[42]

The LCJE is divided into European and North American chapters but represents missionary and Messianic Jewish organizations in other parts of the world as well, such as Australia, South Africa, Latin America, Israel, and Japan. In the 1980s and 1990s, evangelical Christians in Latin America and Asian countries joined in the evangelization of Jews, both as supporters of existing groups in America, Europe, and Israel and through organizations of their own.[43]

At the turn of the century, the movement to evangelize the Jews is vibrant and busier than ever. Since the latter decades of the twentieth century, the movement as a whole has proved to be particularly dynamic. Much of the continued vitality and the relative success of the movement results from the growth of evangelical Christianity as a whole and the new openness of this branch of Christianity to the new modes of evangelism and congregational life, as well as from the increased evangelical interest in Jews and Israel. But the movement can also take credit for its own resourcefulness, for the creation of avant-garde groups within its ranks that advanced the movement by responding to the changing cultural trends and by adapting new modes of evangelism that the movement at large embraced and made its own.

Conclusion

Since the late nineteenth century, missions to the Jews have held an important place on the agenda of conservative American Protestants. The high priority this segment of American Christianity has given the attempts to evangelize the Jews has been the outcome of its theological understanding of the Jews and their role in history. The theology that motivated the movement to evangelize the Jews conceived of that people not as a rival religious community but as a remnant of an ancient people who carry a special mission and are predestined to help bring the drama of Christian salvation to its conclusion. The unique theology of the missions to the Jews created a missionary movement that has demonstrated a great amount of goodwill and appreciation for the Jews and their cultural heritage and, at the same time, a view that the Jewish religion could not provide its adherents with spiritual comfort, moral guidelines, and, most important of all, salvation. Only in Christianity could Jews, as individuals, find eternal life and, as a nation, the peace and security they sought, as well as the fulfillment of their destiny as the chosen people.

The theological perceptions that inspired the movement were extraordinary. In no other case has one religious community assigned a predominant role to another religious community in its vision of redemption or claimed that the other group held a special relationship with God. Similarly, in no other situation has one religious group invested so much hope in another group as the key brokers on the road to universal salvation. This unusual attitude in the history of the relationship between religious communities created the unique character of this special missionary movement. Although on a practical level the movement to evangelize the Jews shared some of the characteristics of other Protestant missions, its understanding of itself and its prospective converts were unique. Protestant missionaries in other missionary fields have also seen their work as a calling and found special merit in evangelizing various nations, but, as a rule, in no other field have missionaries found merit in the religion whose members they were trying to convert into Christians. Nor have missionaries to other groups made the claim that by adopting Christianity the people whom they were evangelizing were fulfilling their true selves as members of the religious communities with which they had been originally affiliated. None have used major symbols of other religions to attract members of the religious communities that they were evangelizing. And in no other field of evangelism did evangelists point to the sacred Scriptures of the religious community they were trying to Christianize as a source that both parties could relate to as authoritative.

From a dispensationalist Protestant point of view, the fact that the Jews were

God's chosen people, essential for the fulfillment of messianic hopes, and at the same time in urgent need of being evangelized embodied a special calling and a unique mission. This seemingly contradictory outlook accounts for this extraordinary missionary movement that aimed at evangelizing a nation it considered chosen.

A series of paradoxes have come to characterize this unusual missionary scene. The missionaries whose vocation and aim was to spread the Christian faith among Jews became ardent supporters of Jewish national causes. In order to advance the cause of the missionary movement and muster support in the Christian world, missionaries advocated the idea of the special destiny of Israel, emphasizing the merits and achievements of the Jews. While they worked to promote Christianity among Jews, the missionaries studied the Jews, learned the realities of Jewish life and customs, and educated the Christian evangelical community about Judaism and Jews. They laid the foundation and have been the driving force for the building of Christian congregations in which Jewish ethnicity, symbols, and rites are preserved and celebrated.

In relating to such an unusual missionary phenomenon, Jews have also shown contradictory inclinations. Although Jewish leaders have resented the missionary presence and have often viewed the attempts to evangelize their people as an intrusion and an insult, they have, at the same time, welcomed missionary friendliness when they felt it was advantageous for Jewish causes. Jewish popular response was similarly inconsistent. Resentment and, at times, hostility toward missionaries did not deter the masses from taking advantage of the services missions offered, nor did it stop young men and women from exploring the missionary message and the Christian option.

The socioeconomic and cultural background of prospective converts changed dramatically throughout the more than one hundred years of unflagging American Protestant missionary work among the Jews. From newly arrived, Yiddish-speaking immigrants, to second-generation American Jews who wished to become more integrated into American culture, to Jewish members of the counterculture—the various generations targeted for evangelism seem to differ sharply from one another. Yet, although the cultural backgrounds of prospective converts have shifted greatly during the years, the object of missionary attention has fundamentally remained the same: the young, the seekers, those in transition. Most converts in all the different generations were young people moving from one cultural framework, and at times geographical territory, to another. They were seekers of new spaces, communities, and meanings. The converts' inner deliberations before, during, and after conversion also remained similar. For converts of all generations, a major dilemma was how to reconcile their identities as Jews with the Christian faith. This was a major concern the missionaries had to address and on which much of the missionary rhetoric concentrated.

The converts' choices and the communities they strove to build have also been marked by paradoxes. In contrast to the aims and choices of Jewish converts to Christianity in previous centuries, many of the converts to evangelical Christianity in America in the late nineteenth century and throughout the twentieth century wished to retain their Jewish identity. In the latter decades of the twentieth century, this trend intensified, with many converts building their own congregations and taking pride and interest in their Jewish roots. Ironically, it was a conservative segment of Christianity, evangelical Protestantism, that allowed Jewish converts to Christianity more freedom of expression than other branches of the Christian faith had done.

Something of a symbiosis developed between the missionaries, the people they evangelized, the converts, and the Jewish activists reacting to the missionary presence. All responded to one another, altering their rhetoric and activities in accordance with developments among the other parties. Missions changed their methods and modes of operation in response to the demographic, socioeconomic, and cultural trends of the Jewish communities. The missions' rhetoric and working methods also took into account Jewish responses and concerns. Jewish reactions to missionary activity in turn reflected the changes that took place in the standing of the Jewish community within the American polity: the sense of vulnerability or security that the Jews felt. The changes in the methods of operation of missions also reflected the developments in the Protestant community that sponsored the missions: its cultural perceptions, the modes of behavior it accepted or rejected, and its set of priorities. Unwittingly, the different players in the missionary drama were dialoguing with one another. Jewish actions and arguments responded to the missionary presence and rhetoric, and the missionaries, in turn, altered their arguments and methods in accordance with Jewish ones. In building their life and community after conversion, the converts took notice of both Christian and Jewish attitudes and claims.

The movement to evangelize the Jews has demonstrated a great amount of adaptability, taking notice of developments in the Jewish and Protestant communities, and American culture in general, and changing its tactics and rhetoric accordingly. Although many missionaries found it difficult to change their modes of operation, others proved to be more attuned to the spirit of the age, implementing new ideas and styles. Yet, while the missionary scene has been characterized by periodic changes, it has also been marked by a great amount of continuity. The theological perception that motivated and guided the movement persisted throughout the decades with amazing consistency. Adhering to a biblical premillennialist understanding of the development of world history and the role of the Jews in the messianic age, missionaries carried out their work with a special sense of mission. In their own eyes, they were propagating Christianity among God's chosen people, the historical nation of Israel. This core belief affected all spheres of the missionary experience: symbols, rhetoric, appeals to potential converts and donors, the character of the community of converts and its agenda, as well as the movement's relationship with different segments of the Protestant community.

The persistence of the missionary zeal has been a direct result of the continued interest of conservative Protestants in the Jews as a people destined to play an important role in the messianic events of the End Times. Attempting in their early decades to include a large spectrum of Protestant supporters, the missions have become part and parcel of the conservative evangelical network in America. They have come to depend on the support of this segment of American Christianity, which they have received generously. Many among the conservatives, including some of the nation's most acclaimed evangelists, have shared the missions' theological perceptions of the uniqueness of the Jews and their role in the messianic age and have lent their support to the missionary cause wholeheartedly. From their inception in the late nineteenth century and into the twenty-first century, missions to the Jews have been high on the evangelical missionary agenda and have received more aid, in relative terms, than any other missionary field. The developments in the life of the Jewish people during the twentieth century, as viewed by conservative evangelicals, enhanced support for the movement to evangelize the Jews. The missions became the means through which the evangelical community could be actively involved in the life of the Jewish people and help direct its course.

The other realm in which evangelical Christians expressed their special understanding of the Jewish people was political support for Zionism and, later, the state of Israel. Missions and pro-Zionism became expressions of interest in and involvement with the Jews. The combination of the two worked to create much of the paradoxical nature of the interaction between missionaries and Jews. Evangelizing a nation that they understood to be chosen for a distinct purpose in the drama of the End Times, evangelists lent the Jewish national movement of restoration to Zion their enthusiastic support. Missions and those sponsoring them have sincerely seen themselves as friends and supporters of Jewish causes, while at the same time aggressively evangelizing the Jews. Thus, at least from a Jewish point of view, they have also been actively involved in the disintegration of the Jewish community as it was traditionally known.

The missionary efforts have come to fruition in the latter decades of the twentieth century and into the twenty-first as an unprecedentedly large movement of converts has come into being. The missionary rhetoric that spoke about Jews finding their fulfillment as Christians has found more ready ears as the definition of what being Jewish means has changed dramatically. In previous generations, Jews had a very clear notion of what being Jewish consisted of in contrast to being Christian. Jews formed a separate social and cultural group within the larger society and were very different from Christian Protestants. But the social and cultural separateness of Jews has been seriously eroded in the past few decades, and with it the sense of what it means to be Jewish. A number of nontraditional expressions of Jewish identity have come into being during the period. Many Jews came to believe that they could practice other religious forms, such as Buddhism, and retain a sense of Jewish identity. The social and cultural trends that have weakened the traditional Jewish sense of ethnic and religious identities have enlarged the number of converts to evangelical Christianity. The missions' success was nourished by the paradoxical nature of Jewish existence in the twentieth century, when a national Jewish movement arose alongside forces that worked to erode the traditional sense of Jewish cohesion and identity. The missions cashed in on this double development: on the one hand, the success of the Jewish national movement served to strengthen their basis of support among evangelical Christians, and, on the other hand, the erosion of the traditional Jewish sense of identity helped them gain more converts.

At the turn of the century, the movement to evangelize the Jews is as energetic as ever, and its sense of accomplishment and triumphalism is at its height. In their own eyes, the missions have gone from better to best, and the missionaries are more than optimistic about their future stature and growth. Yet the future of the movement, like its past, is clouded in paradoxes. There can be no movement to evangelize the Jews without Jews. At present, however, the Jewish existence has become precarious. The objects of the missionary zeal, the Jewish people, are facing an unprecedented demographic crisis, and the prognosis some analysts are offering is pessimistic. In a paradoxical manner, there could be an "oversuccess" of the missionary movement. If masses of Jews move away into other communities, there might not be a vital people called Jews. Moreover, the energetic evangelization of that nation has been motivated by the idea that Jews are a distinct people with a special role in history. Such notions have received great encouragement from events and developments in the life of the Jewish people. The rise and partial success of the Jewish national movement have, in that respect, been an endless blessing for the movement: promoting interest in the Jews and their historical role and consequently enhancing support for the missions. The Six-Day War, for example, offered evangelical Christians much enthusiasm and hope, but recent developments, including the Israelis' withdrawal from territories they conquered in 1967 and the internal crisis in Israeli society, have been less promising. Such "negative" developments could work to weaken interest in the Jews and the prospect of their conversion to Christianity. It might well be that the movement to evangelize the Jews will, within a few decades, face new crises and challenges that will alter its character considerably.

Yet, looking at the current scene and predicting the immediate, short-term future, it is more than likely that the missionary movement will thrive in the coming generation. The number of Messianic congregations will grow, and the movement's sense of accomplishment and triumph will persist. At the turn of the new century, the missionary movement is at the peak of its self-confidence, looking forward to a bright future.

Notes

INTRODUCTION

1. On the history of the relationship between the two religions, see Talmage, *Disputation and Dialogue;* Ruether, *Faith and Fratricide;* Cohen, *Friars and the Jews;* Toon, *Puritans, the Millennium, and the Future of Israel;* Feldman, *Dual Destinies.*

2. An example of the first kind of literature is Sevener, *Rabbi's Vision,* and of the second, Eichhorn, *Evangelizing the American Jew.* Both books are very informative.

3. William R. Hutchinson, *Errand to the World,* 2.

4. Sarna, "American Jewish Response to Nineteenth-Century Christian Missions," 35–51.

5. On the attempts to build missions to the Jews between the 1810s and the 1870s, see Eichhorn, *Evangelizing the American Jew,* 1–140.

6. On the Millerites and the Mormons and the Jews, see Malachy, *American Fundamentalism and Israel,* 19–56; Ricks, "Zionism and the Mormon Church"; Epperson, *Mormons and Jews.*

7. On dispensationalism, see Bass, *Background to Dispensationalism;* MacPherson, *Incredible Cover Up;* Sandeen, *Roots of Fundamentalism;* Weber, *Living in the Shadow of the Second Coming.*

8. For example, Brookes, *Maranatha;* Blackstone, *Jesus Is Coming.* More recent publications include Billy Graham, *World Aflame;* Lindsey, *Late Great Planet Earth.*

CHAPTER ONE

1. On the British movement to evangelize the Jews in the nineteenth century, see Tuchman, *Bible and Sword,* 175–207; Scult, *Millennial Expectations and Jewish Liberties.*

2. On such attempts, see Eichhorn, *Evangelizing the American Jew,* 6–140.

3. On the impact of nineteenth-century missions on American Jews, see Sarna, "American Jewish Response to Nineteenth-Century Christian Missions," 35–51.

4. On the British missionary enterprises directed at the evangelization of the Jews in the nineteenth century, see Gidney, *History of the London Society for Promoting Christianity amongst the Jews;* Tuchman, *Bible and Sword,* 175–207; Scult, *Millennial Expectations and Jewish Liberties,* 80–130.

5. Cf. Shipps, *Mormon Tradition;* Numbers and Butler, *The Disappointed.*

6. Cf. Malachy, *American Fundamentalism and Israel,* 19–56; Greenberg, *Holy Land in American Religious Thought,* 191–96.

7. On dispensationalism, see, for example, Bass, *Background to Dispensationalism;* Ehlert, *Bibliographic History of Dispensationalism;* Sandeen, *Roots of Fundamentalism;* Timothy P. Weber, *Living In the Shadow of the Second Coming.* On Darby's understanding of the nature of the church, see Geldbach, *Christlich Versammlung.*

8. On the details of the dispensationalist eschatological scheme, see, for example, Blackstone, *Jesus Is Coming.* For a contemporary version, see Lindsey, *Late Great Planet Earth.*

9. Cf. Marsden, *Fundamentalism and American Culture*.

10. For example, Gray, *Great Epochs of Sacred History*; Scofield, *Addresses on Prophecy*; Torrey, *Return of the Lord Jesus*; Riley, *Wanted—A World Leader!*.

11. Rausch, *Zionism within Early American Fundamentalism*; Merkley, *Politics of Christian Zionism*.

12. Ariel, "American Initiative for a Jewish State: William Blackstone and the Petition of 1891," 125–38; Merkley, *Politics of Christian Zionism*, 59–74.

13. Cf. Meyer, "Directory of Protestant Jewish Missionary Societies," 114–22.

14. Eichhorn, *Evangelizing the American Jew*, 141–76.

15. Cf. Hutchison, *Errand to the World*, 112.

16. Warnock, "To the Jew First"; Warnock acknowledges when describing an Episcopalian mission in New York that missions to the Jews were marked by a premillennialist theology that gave it its impetus. Warnock, "This Year They More Nearly Approached Us Than Ever," 35.

17. See, for example, such journals as *Our Hope*, the *Jewish Era*, the *Chosen People*, the *Glory of Israel*, *Immanuel's Witness*, and *Prayer and Work for Israel*.

18. For example, Blackstone, *Jesus Is Coming*, 208–9.

19. Torrey, "Blessed Hope," 22; Burrell, "Signs of the Times," 69.

20. Gaebelein, "Capture of Jerusalem," 146; Riley, "Last Times," 175.

21. See the statement adopted by the Philadelphia Prophetic Conference in Pettingill, Schafter, and Adams, *Light on Prophecy*, 12.

22. A second edition of *Jesus Is Coming* came out in 1886 and a third one in 1908. The book was translated into more than forty languages with a distribution of more than a million and a half copies.

23. For example, Blackstone, *Heart of the Jewish Problem*.

24. For example, Gaebelein, *Messiah and His People Israel*; Gaebelein, *Hath God Cast Away His People?*; Gaebelein, *Jewish Question*.

25. For example, West, "Prophecy and Israel"; Eerdman, "Structure and Book of Isaiah and Part II. 40–66"; Stroeter, "Second Coming of Christ in Relation to Israel."

26. For example, Leopold Cohn, "Editorial," 3–4; Kuldell, *Some Hindrances in Jewish Missions*, 8–9; Cohn, *I Have Fought a Good Fight*, 75; White, "Gospel to the Jews a Neglected Work," 56–59; Cooper, *Why Evangelize Israel in This Generation and How*.

27. For example, Cooper, *Why Evangelize Israel in This Generation and How*.

28. For example, Blackstone, *Jesus Is Coming*, 162.

29. See, for example, Rounds, "Pale of Settlement," 94–96.

30. Chalmers, "Blood Accusation," 57–59; Gaebelein, "Same Old Accusation," 556.

31. For example, Scofield, *Addresses on Prophecy*, 54; Levi, *Christianity*, esp. 85–109; cf. also Conway, "Protestant Missions to the Jews," 132.

32. Thompson, *Century of Jewish Missions*, 270.

33. *Twenty Second Annual Report of the Society for Promoting Christianity amongst the Jews*, 1; quoted by Warnock, "To the Jew First," 27.

34. Stroeter, "Second Coming of Christ in Relation to Israel," 138–39.

35. For example, Cohn, *What Is His Son's Name?*; Cohn, *Behold the Virgin Shall Conceive and Bear a Son*.

36. For example, Blackstone, *Millennium*; Rounds, "Liberal Judaism," 69–70.

37. Cf., for example, Gaebelein, *Half a Century*, 28; Blackstone, "Jerusalem," 70–71.

38. For example, Rounds, "Reformed Judaism—a Failure," 74–75; Gaebelein, "Aspects of Jewish Power in the United States," 103.

39. Gaebelein, *Conflict of the Ages*, 151.

40. Rischin, *Promised City*, 199.

41. See the mission journals, such as *Jewish Era, Immanuel's Witness*, and *Glory of Israel*.

42. For example, Cohn, *What Is His Son's Name?*

43. Ibid., 2–9.

44. "Notes from Our Mission," 24.

45. For example, Angel, "Day of Atonement," 225–28; Cohn, *Jewish Holidays and Their Significance*.

46. Gaebelein, *Half a Century*, 67–68.

47. Meyer, "German Jewish Missions from 1517 to 1800," 136–41; for British missions, in addition to works cited above in note 4 of this chapter, see Thompson, *Century of Jewish Missions*, 93–117.

48. Cf., for example, Tuchman, *Bible and Sword*, 175–207.

49. For example, Denman [Secretary of the London Society for Promoting Christianity amongst the Jews], "Second Coming of Our Lord and Its Relation to the Jews," 1–6.

50. For example, "Zionist Movement," 96; "The Zionist Movement," *Jewish Era* 27 (1918): 44.

51. For example, Gaebelein, *Hath God Cast Away His People?*, 28–29, 69; Seiss, "Who Are the 144,000?" 10; Cohn, "Questions and Answers," 15.

52. For example, Scofield, *Addresses on Prophecy*, 21.

53. On Gaebelein, see Rausch, *Arno C. Gaebelein*.

54. From "The Principles of the Hope of Israel Movement," in Gaebelein, *Messiah and His People Israel*, 65.

55. Gaebelein, *Half a Century*, 39–45.

56. On Rabinowitz, see Kjaer-Hansen, *Joseph Rabinowitz and the Messianic Movement*.

57. Rabinowitz, *Jesus of Nazareth, the King of the Jews!*.

58. Hutchison, *Errand to the World*, esp. 15–42, 62–90.

59. Gaebelein, *Half a Century*, 52.

60. Ibid., 39–45.

61. Brookes, "Work among the Jews," 15–16.

62. For the response of the Hope of Israel directors to such criticism, see Stroeter, "Misapprehension Corrected," 55–58.

63. Gaebelein, "Short Review of Our Mission," 68–71.

CHAPTER TWO

1. Meyer, "Directory of Protestant Jewish Missionary Societies," 114–22. Louis Meyer's report is conservative. Others evaluated the number of missions and missionaries as much higher.

2. Ibid.

3. On Jewish immigrants in New York during that period, see Rischin, *Promised City*; Goren, *New York Jews and the Quest for Community*.

4. Weber, *Living in the Shadow of the Second Coming*, 148.

5. Cf. Hutchison, *Errand to the World*, 100.

6. Angel, "Report of Work during 1891," 19.

7. For example, Gaebelein, *Half a Century*, 35.

8. Cohn, *I Have Fought a Good Fight*, 106–16; Weber, *Living in the Shadow of the Second Coming*, 148.

9. Gaebelein, "How the Hope of Israel Became Undenominational," 3–5.

10. Cf. Thompson, *Century of Missions*, 239. After Thompson published his book, the CHM inspired the establishment of a few more missions.

11. For example, Blackstone, "Letter," 75; Mauro, "Zionism."

12. On William Blackstone, his role in the development of the dispensationalist movement in America, and his interest in Jews and their role in history, see Ariel, *On Behalf of Israel*, 55–96; Ariel, "Neglected Chapter in the History of Christian Zionism in America," 68–85.

13. On Jane Addams, see Marty, *Modern American Religion*, vol. 1, *Irony of It All*, 82–84; Davis, *American Heroine*.

14. On the role of women in the fundamentalist movement, see Bendroth, *Fundamentalism and Gender*, 1–12.

15. Lindberg, *Witnessing to Jews*, 10.

16. Angel, "Mistakes," 4.

17. Ibid.

18. See Eichhorn, *Evangelizing the American Jew*, 172–76.

19. See, for example, Sevener, *Rabbi's Vision*, which treats Cohn as a saintly figure. In contrast, see Eichhorn, *Evangelizing the American Jew*, 172–76; Warnock, "To the Jew First," 221–305. Both Eichhorn and Warnock portray Cohn in very negative terms.

20. Cohn, *Modern Missionary to an Ancient People*, 16–17.

21. For a biography of Cohn, see Sevener, *Rabbi's Vision*, 7–27, which very much follows Cohn's autobiography (*Modern Missionary to an Ancient People*).

22. Bacon, *Strange Story of Dr. Cohn and Mr. Joszovics*.

23. Ibid.; Eichhorn, *Evangelizing the American Jew*, 172–176; Warnock, "To the Jew First," 221–305. Cf. also Angel, "Mistakes."

24. See some of Cohn's essays, for example, the tracts *Behold the Virgin* and *The Broken Matzo*, both published by the mission for distribution among Jews. See also *Chosen People Question Box*, which is a collection of Cohn's answers to theological inquiries published throughout the 1890s to 1910s in *Chosen People*.

25. Cohn, *I Have Fought A Good Fight*, 95–105.

26. Cohn, "Mr. Needleman," 7.

27. See, for example, *Chosen People* 5 (October 1899): 1.

28. Cohn, "Announcement," 7.

29. Cohn, *I Have Fought a Good Fight*, 68, 165.

30. Cohn, "Christian Duty to the Jews," 4–5; Cohn, "Reasons for the Immediate Evangelization of the Jews," 7.

31. Cohn, "Salutation," 4–5; cf. also Cohn, "Talks with Girls and Boys," 5–6.

32. Cohn, "Salutation," 5.

33. Sherburne, "Our Mission Hall," 5; Sherburne, "Our Schools," 5.

34. Cohn, *I Have Fought a Good Fight*, 40–44.

35. Ibid., 17–26.

36. Ibid., 25.

37. Pearlstein, "Physician's Report," 8.

38. This included tracts that dealt with such issues as the Trinity, the virgin birth of Christ, or the interpretation of Isaiah 53.

39. "Question Column," 7.

40. Cohn, "Salutation," 1.

41. Cohn, *Modern Missionary to an Ancient People*, 49–50.

42. "Williamsburg Mission to the Jews," 191–92.

43. Niklaus, Sawin, and Stoesz, *All For Jesus*, 71.

44. The Christian Alliance was organized as a local American organization to provide support for the International Missionary Alliance, which evangelized abroad. The two societies were virtually one in purpose and constituency. In 1897 they formally united as the Christian and Missionary Alliance. A. B. Simpson, who directed both organizations, was elected president and superintendent. On the early history of the Christian and Missionary Alliance, see Padington, *Twenty-five Wonderful Years, 1889–1914*; Niklaus, Sawin, and Stoetz, *All for Jesus*.

45. Quoted in Niklaus, Sawin, and Stoetz, *All for Jesus*, 73.

46. On Albert B. Simpson and the alliance's early theological principles, see *Four-Fold Gospel*; cf. also Thompson, *Life of A. B. Simpson*, 235–40; Pyles, "Missionary Eschatology of A. B. Simpson," 29–47.

47. For example, Simpson, *Gospel of the Kingdom*, 172.

48. Ibid., 173–75; Thompson, *Century of Jewish Missions*, 148–50. For an analysis of Simpson's views on the Jews and on the need to evangelize them, see Schmidgall, "American Holiness Churches."

49. Simpson, *Gospel of the Kingdom*, 185.

50. Ibid.

51. Tucker and Liefeld, *Daughters of the Church*, 291–92.

52. Cf. Ariel, "American Dispensationalists and Jerusalem, 1870–1918."

53. Smalley, *Alliance Mission in Palestine, Arab Lands, and Israel*, 19. I am indebted to the Reverend and Mrs. William and Swannie Currie for letting me know about the manuscript and allowing me to read it.

54. Cf. Vester, *Our Jerusalem*, 62–148.

55. Cf. Welter, "She Hath Done What She Could," 119.

56. Cf. Crombie, *For the Love of Zion*.

57. Schmidgall, "American Holiness Churches," 64.

58. On the alliance's work in America, see Evearitt, "Jewish-Christian Missions to Jews," 262–75.

59. Ibid.

60. See, for example, *Menorah* 35 (November 1903): 325.

CHAPTER THREE

1. On converts to other forms of Christianity during the period, see, for example, Appel, "Christian Science and the Jews," 100–121. The Jews who were attracted to Christian Science were mostly American-born, educated, middle-class women. The Christian Scientists did

not make an effort to evangelize among Jews, and the reasons for the attraction of the Jews to this church were very different than those that brought Jews to embrace evangelical Christianity.

2. Cf. the description, for example, in Rose Cohen's memoir, *Out of the Shadow*.

3. Ibid., 161.

4. See the testimony of John Hoffman in *American Hebrew* 44 (August 29, 1890): 62–63.

5. Cf., for example, Starr, "Story of the Life and Conversion of Jacob Starr," 156–57; Starr, "Report of J. R. Lewek," 31–32.

6. Rischin, *Promised City*, 199; Cohen, *Out of the Shadow*, 160–61, 244–45, 247–48, 254.

7. See a quotation from an article in the *New York Observer* of October 1891 in Douglas, *Herman Warszawiak*, 10–11. The reporter clearly states that it was men who came to hear the preaching.

8. This new sense of freedom and its influence on the minds and lives of new immigrants are manifested in the works of Abraham Cahan, a Jewish immigrant journalist and writer in turn-of-the-century New York. See Cahan, *Imported Bridegroom and Other Stories of the New York Ghetto*.

9. Meyer, "Protestant Missions to the Jews," 910–11.

10. Rischin, *Promised City*, 115–235; Cowan and Cowan, *Our Parents' Lives*, 249–86.

11. Cf. Rambo, *Understanding Religious Conversion*, 56–57.

12. For example, Starr, "Story of the Life and Conversion of Jacob Starr".

13. Steiner, *From Alien to Citizen*, 213–18.

14. Hellyer, *From the Rabbis to Christ*, 46.

15. Ibid., 217.

16. Cf. Freuder, *My Return to Judaism*, 89; Cohn, "Possibilities," 1. Cohn blamed the influence of Jewish society and sought ways to overcome that.

17. Rambo, "Psychology of Conversion," 160.

18. Steiner, *From Alien to Citizen*, 211.

19. Allison, "Religious Conversion," 23–38; Ullman, *Transformed Self*, 29–74; Rambo, *Understanding Religious Conversion*, 157.

20. Steiner, *From Alien to Citizen*.

21. Bernstein, *Ways of God*, 13–5.

22. Hellyer, *From the Rabbis to Christ*, 9.

23. Goldstein, *All the Doors Were Opened*.

24. Koser, *Come and Get It!*.

25. Bronstein, *Esther*.

26. Freuder, *My Return to Judaism*, 7–35.

27. For example, Hellyer, *From the Rabbis to Christ*; Goldstein, *All the Doors Were Opened*; Koser, *Come and Get It!*.

28. Stark and Bainbridge, "Networks of Faith," 1376–95; Rambo, *Understanding Religious Conversion*.

29. Lofland and Stark, "Becoming a World-Saver," 865–75; Lofland and Skonvod, "Conversion Motifs," 373–85; Rambo, *Understanding Religious Conversion*, 15.

30. Lofland and Stark, "Becoming a World-Saver."

31. Cohn, "Possibilities"; Cohn, "Daughters of Zion Class," 32.

32. Samuel Freuder in *My Return to Judaism* states that as a complaint.

33. "Jesus Saves," 77–78.

34. See accounts and testimonies of converts in the period. For example, see Steiner, *From Alien to Citizen*; Koser, *Come and Get It!*; Needleman, "My Conversion," 3–4; Newitz, "Story of My Conversion," 3–4.

35. Cf. Stromberg, "Impression Point," 56–74.

36. See Gaebelein, "Herman Warszawiak's Methods," 2–5.

37. Cf. Rambo, *Understanding Religious Conversion*, 160.

38. For example, Freuder, *My Return to Judaism*, 98–99.

39. Gaebelein, *Half a Century*, 29.

40. Angel, "Mistakes," 4.

41. Freuder, *My Return to Judaism*.

42. "Report of Dr. F. Charles," 33.

43. "First Annual Report," 7.

44. Cohn, "Possibilities," 1.

45. Reuben, "Conversion of Maurice Reuben," 16–17; Needleman, "My Conversion," 3–4.

46. Freuder, *My Return to Judaism*.

47. Ibid., 35–59.

48. Newman, "Looking Back Twenty-five Years," 24.

49. Ibid.

50. Joseph H. Cohn, for example, recalls such remarks in his book, *I Have Fought A Good Fight*, 35–37. On rejection, see Warnock, "This Year They More Nearly Approached Us Than Ever," 43.

51. On Dwight Moody and his attitude toward Jews, see Ariel, "An American Evangelist and the Jews," 41–49.

52. *Immanuel's Witness* 3 (1901): 101.

53. Steiner, *From Alien to Citizen*.

54. On the *Fundamentals*, see Sandeen, *Roots of Fundamentalism*, 188–207.

55. Cf. Rambo, *Understanding Religious Conversion*, 161.

56. Steiner, *From Alien to Citizen*, 261.

57. Sorin, *Jewish People in America*, vol. 3, *Time for Building*, 39.

58. One might point here again to the literary work of Abraham Cahan, who gave voice to the realities of the immigrant's community. See Cahan's descriptions of such personal situations in his *Imported Bridegroom and Other Stories of the New York Ghetto*. See also Cowan and Cowan, *Our Parents' Lives*, 144–55.

59. Cf. Todd M. Endelman, introduction to Endelman, *Jewish Apostasy in the Modern World*, 13; Kaplan, *Making of the Jewish Middle Class*, 82–83; Hyman, *Gender and Assimilation in Modern Jewish History*, 20. Hyman claims that women held more firmly than men to Jewish religious practices.

60. Cf. Fishman, *Breath of Life*, 28.

61. Cf., for example, Newitz, "Story of My Conversion," 3–4.

62. Cohn, "Gathering of Christian Jews," 3. On Gaebelein's attempts to build a congregation of converted Jews, see Ariel, *On Behalf of Israel*, 97–108.

63. Cf., for example, Evearitt, "Jewish Christian Missions to Jews."

64. See Ariel, "From Judaism to Christianity," 122–29.

65. For example, Metshnick, "Meshumod," 74–78; Cast, "Story of the Conversion of a Young Jewess," 71; Reuben, "Conversion of Maurice Reuben," 16–17; Goldstein, *All the Doors Were Opened*, 24–26.

66. For example, Freuder, *My Return to Judaism*, 53.

67. Angel, "Mistakes," 4.

68. Cf. Warnock "To the Jew First," 148–82.

69. See Winer, *The Calling*, 1–12.

70. For example, Rohold, *War and the Jews*; Newman, *Jewish Peril and the Hidden Hand*; Dushaw, *When Mr. Thompson Got to Heaven*; Reich, *Messianic Hope of Israel*; Cohn, *I Have Loved Jacob*.

71. Rausch, *Messianic Judaism*, 21–49; Winer, *The Calling*, 5–27.

72. *Minutes of the First Hebrew-Christian Conference of the United States*, 14–16.

73. This comes through in almost all articles and tracts written by converts to evangelical Christianity during the period; see, for example, articles written throughout the years in the *Hebrew Christian Alliance Quarterly*.

74. "Jewish Ordinances," 23–36.

75. Baron, "Messianic Judaism or Judaising Christianity."

76. Cf. Ariel, *On Behalf of Israel*, 103–8.

77. See, for example, resolutions offered on that matter by a number of Episcopalian bishops. *Journal of the General Convention of the Protestant Episcopal Church in the United States of America* (1907): 128–29, 136; (1910): 605–11.

78. Baron, "Messianic Judaism or Judaising Christianity"; Rausch, *Messianic Judaism*, 55, 58.

79. Cf. Hutchison, *Errand to the World*, 91–124.

80. Cf. Newman, "Looking Back Twenty-five Years."

81. See lists of donors in the pages of the *Hebrew Christian Alliance Quarterly*.

82. Cf. Rausch, *Messianic Judaism*, 21–49.

83. See Winer, *The Calling*, 77–81.

84. "We Have Not Lost Our Hope," back page.

85. A classical testimony of that sort was Freuder, *My Return to Judaism*.

86. I am thankful to Robert I. Winer, M.D., for bringing to my knowledge the works of Dushaw. James Warnock in his dissertation also relates to this rather forgotten writer and provides biographical background in Warnock, "To the Jew First," 177–82.

87. Dushaw, *When Mr. Thomson Got to Heaven*, 1.

88. Dushaw, *The Rivals*.

89. Dushaw, *Proselytes of the Ghetto*.

90. See, for example, in Dushaw's works such as *Proselytes of the Ghetto* or *The Rivals*.

91. Cf. Hagner, *Jewish Reclamation of Jesus*.

92. Dushaw, *Proselytes of the Ghetto*, 106.

93. Dushaw, *The Rivals*, 116.

94. Ibid.

95. Ibid., 111.

96. Cf. Winer, *The Calling*, 80, 118.

CHAPTER FOUR

1. Cohen, *Out of the Shadow*, 160.

2. For example, Gaebelein, *Half a Century*; Eichhorn, *Evangelizing the American Jews*, 168.

3. Cohen, *Out of the Shadow*, 161.

4. For example, Wise, *Defense of Judaism versus Proselytizing Christianity*; Wise, introduction to Freuder, *My Return to Judaism*.

5. Simon, "Conversion," 7.

6. Sarna, "American Jewish Response to Nineteenth-Century Christian Missions," 42.

7. For example, in *Defense of Judaism versus Proselytizing Christianity*.

8. Ibid., 8–9.

9. On Reform Judaism during the period, see Meyer, *Response to Modernity*, chaps. 6–7. On the Reform attitudes toward Christianity, see Berlin, *Defending the Faith*.

10. For example, Blackstone, *Heart of the Jewish Problem*, 16.

11. Handy, *Christian America*, 155–83.

12. Gaebelein, *Conflict of the Ages*, 147.

13. Cf. Cohn, *To Both Houses of Israel*.

14. Quoted by Gerhard Deutsch in his response to Hertz's accusation. Deutsch, "Has Reform Judaism Stimulated Apostasy?," 307.

15. Ibid.

16. For example, "Want to Drive Out Missionaries?," 399.

17. "Jews Warned against Missionaries," 182.

18. See, for example, the exchange of letters between F. de Sola Mendes, rabbi of Shearith Israel in New York, and W. R. Huntington, rector of Grace Episcopal Church in New York, following the decision of the New York diocese of the Episcopal Church to engage in missionary work among the Jews, in Sola Mendes, "Missionary Work in New York," 250–51. Huntington replied to Sola Mendes justifying the evangelization of the Jews. He argued that Jews were moving away from the religious beliefs of their parents, becoming agnostics, and there was a rise in Jewish crime in New York. He further made the claim in line with the spirit of Jewish evangelism during the period that by converting the Jews he did not mean to gentilize them and that he showed sympathy to Jewish suffering.

19. On conversions to Judaism, see, for example, Rosenbloom, *Conversion to Judaism*.

20. Simon, "Conversion," 7.

21. Felsenthal to Blackstone, October 16, 1891, in Blackstone's personal papers, at the archives of the Billy Graham Center, Wheaton, Ill.

22. See, for example, Blackstone's reply to Rabbi Bernhard Felsenthal of December 8, 1891, a copy in Blackstone's personal papers, at the archives of the Billy Graham Center.

23. This is an underlying assumption in a number of Jewish publications. For example, Eichhorn, *Evangelizing the American Jew*, and Freuder, *My Return to Judaism*.

24. Simon, "Conversion," 7.

25. See a letter-pamphlet written and circulated by Alexander S. Bacon, a Baptist lawyer from New York, dated July 12, 1918, and addressed "to the Moderator and Members of the Long Island Baptist Association." Copy in the American Jewish Archives, Cincinnati, Ohio.

26. For example, Freuder, *My Return to Judaism*; Eichhorn, *Evangelizing the American Jew*; see also Eisen, "Christian Missions to the Jews," 31–72.

27. Freuder, *My Return to Judaism*, 160–70; Eichhorn, *Evangelizing the American Jew*, 172–76; Eisen, "Christian Missions to the Jews," 35. Cohn's name does not appear in a book containing a list of the rabbis who functioned in Hungary, but this, of course, could be a consequence of his being ostracized by the rabbinical world from which he emerged. Schwartz, *Schem Hagdolim*.

28. For example, Freuder, *My Return to Judaism*; Eichhorn, *Evangelizing the American Jew*.

29. For example, Benedict, *Christ Finds a Rabbi*; Wertheimer, *From Rabbinism to Christ*.

30. After the conversion of Abraham Jaeger to Christianity, Isaac M. Wise, who had previously supported him and helped him obtain a position as a rabbi, turned against him and declared, "It is not true that Mr. Jaeger is or ever was a rabbi." *American Israelite*, July 12, 1872, 8.

31. *American Hebrew* 91 (September 27, 1912): 617.

32. "West Side Organization to Oppose Missionaries," 219; "Want to Drive Out Missionaries," 399.

33. Sarna, "American Jewish Response to Nineteenth-Century Christian Missions," 35–51; Sarna, "Impact of Nineteenth-Century Christian Missions on American Jews," 232–54.

34. See, for example, Dushkin, *Jewish Education in New York City*, 45, 53–54; Dushkin relates to educational organizations that were established as early as the 1830s and continued their work vigorously at the turn of the century.

35. On the Jewish motivation for initiatives to improve the conditions of the immigrant population, see Rockaway, *Words of the Uprooted*.

36. "West Side Organization to Oppose Missionaries."

37. "Jews Mob a Mission."

38. See, for example, "Jews Mob a Mission," 531; "Raiding the Missionaries," 617, describes a more premeditated attempt at disrupting a missionary service. See also "Working against Missions," 264, which describes picketing of a mission.

39. "Stealing Jewish Children," 705–6.

40. Eichhorn, *Evangelizing the American Jew*, 171, 182–83; Gurock, "Jewish Communal Divisiveness in Response to Christian Influences," 257.

41. See "Jewish Bill against Missionaries," 87. The article quotes non-Jewish resentment of the bill.

42. Ariel, "Neglected Chapter in the History of Christian Zionism in America," 68–85.

43. Eichhorn, *Evangelizing the American Jew*, 143; Michelson, *From Judaism and Law to Christ and Grace*, 82–83.

44. Paula Hyman adopts such an interpretation in *Gender and Assimilation in Modern Jewish History*.

45. Ellinger, "Editorial," 320–23.

46. A striking example was Isaac M. Wise's rhetoric against converted Jews. Eichhorn, who records some of Wise's remarks, follows, to a large degree, in his footsteps.

47. Jeffrey S. Gurock describes the short-lived Jewish Centers Association, established in 1906, as aimed mainly at combating the missionary efforts. "Jewish Communal Divisiveness in Response to Christian Influences," 257; Gurock portrays Orthodox Jewish activists as standing in the forefront of antimissionary activity.

48. See, for example, some of the illustrations in Rischin, *Promised City*.

49. Gurock, "Jacob A. Riis," 29–48.

50. On Riis and the Jews, see Fried, "Jacob Riis and the Jews," 5–24; Tuerk, "Jacob Riis and the Jews," 179–201.

51. Gurock, "Jacob A. Riis."

52. For example, Thompson, *Century of Jewish Missions*, 45; "Builders of Israel or Anti missionaries," 7–10; Hinz, "Some Discouragements in Jewish Mission Work," 183–84.

53. On the interaction between evangelists and prospective converts, see Rambo, *Understanding Religious Conversion*.

54. Berlin, *Defending the Faith*, 45–75.

55. Weiss, *Some Burning Questions*, 12–15. Felsenthal, *Why Do the Jews Not Accept Jesus*, 3–6.

56. "Open Letter to Bishop Greer," 881.

57. See Wilkinson, "Moral Defensibility of Some of the Methods Employed in Jewish Missions," 60–67.

CHAPTER FIVE

1. Gaebelein, "Herman Warszawiak's Methods," 2–5. Cohn, *I Have Fought a Good Fight*, 28–30.

2. Gaebelein, *Half a Century*, 29–30; Freuder, *My Return to Judaism*, 109–10; Eichhorn, *Evangelizing the American Jew*, 163–76.

3. For example, Wilkinson, "Moral Defensibility of Some of the Methods Employed in Jewish Missions," 60–67.

4. Ibid.

5. *Glory of Israel* 1 (1903): 134.

6. Douglas, *Herman Warszawiak*, 10.

7. On Warszawiak's saga, see Eichhorn, *Evangelizing the American Jew*, 167–72, and Cohn, *I Have Fought a Good Fight*, 40–44.

8. On Freshman's career as a missionary, see Eichhorn's rather unfavorable account, *Evangelizing the American Jew*, 163–65.

9. See Bacon's *Strange Story of Dr. Cohn and Mr. Joszovics*.

10. Angel, "Mistakes," 4.

11. In describing the financial management of the Federation of American Zionists prior to World War I, Melvin Urofsky, historian of American Zionism, writes:

Of all the Zionist functions, none had been so sloppily handled as finance. . . . Soon after Brandeis took over, he installed Robert D. Kesselman, a certified public accountant, in charge of finances. Kesselman had a most difficult time getting the old-line Zionist workers to accept the need for proper money handling and record keeping. They had always been rather casual about it, collecting when they could, keeping donations in their coat pockets or in paper bags, and turning it in whenever they happened to stroll by the office.

Urofsky, *American Zionism from Herzl to the Holocaust*, 157.

12. Ibid.

13. For example, Bernstein, *Some Jewish Witnesses for Christ*; Einspruch, *When Jews Face Christ*; Meyer, *Eminent Hebrew Christians of the Nineteenth Century*; *Good News* (Good News Society, Johannesburg), Special Rabbis' Edition.

14. *Good News*, Special Rabbis' Edition, 18; Cohn, *I Have Fought A Good Fight*, 20.

15. Tuchman, *Bible and Sword*; Scult, *Millennial Expectations and Jewish Liberties*; Eichhorn, *Evangelizing the American Jew*.

16. For example, "Sixth Annual Conference of the Chicago Hebrew Mission," 174.

17. For example, Tuchman, *Bible and Sword*; Eichhorn, *Evangelizing the American Jew*.

18. On revivalism and evangelism among people of Protestant descent, see William McLoughlin, *Revivalism, Awakenings, and Reform.*

19. Rambo, *Understanding Religious Conversion,* 14.

20. Ibid.; cf. also Viswanthan, *Outside the Fold.*

21. Neill, *History of Christianity in India,* 2:131–63.

22. Hutchison, *Errand to the World,* 99; Neill is more generous in his evaluation, *History of Christianity in India,* 362.

23. For example, Gaebelein, *Half a Century.*

24. For example, Dushaw, "Hebrew Christian Literature," 36.

25. For example, Einspruch, "Literature for the Christian Approach to the Jews," 97–102.

26. Ibid.

CHAPTER SIX

1. On the developments in American Protestantism during that period, see Marty, *Modern American Religion,* vol. 1, *Irony of It All.*

2. On the rise of liberal Protestantism, see Hutchison, *Modernist Impulse in American Protestantism.*

3. Marsden, *Fundamentalism and American Culture.*

4. Cf. Weber, *Living in the Shadow of the Second Coming.*

5. Ariel, *On Behalf of Israel.*

6. See, for example, Marty, *Modern American Religion,* vol. 2, *Noise of Conflict, 1919–1941.*

7. Hutchison, *Errand to the World,* 112.

8. See, for example, Cohn, *Will They Psychoanalyze God?.*

9. Cohn, *Tomorrow for the Jews.*

10. Newman, *Why I Became A Lutheran,* 6–8.

11. Peltz, *Christian Modernism and Reform Judaism,* 7.

CHAPTER SEVEN

1. Lindberg, *Witnessing to Jews,* 49.

2. Gartenhaus, *Winning Jews to Christ,* 124–33.

3. Hanson, *These Also I Must Bring,* 43.

4. Ibid., 72.

5. Among them, Kligerman, *Gospel and the Jew* and *Sharing Christ with Our Jewish Neighbors.*

CHAPTER EIGHT

1. Inadequate translations of the Bible were a common feature worldwide. In the first decades of the twentieth century, missionaries in a number of countries took it upon themselves to produce new, more accurate, and more reliable translations. See Smalley, *Translation as Mission,* esp. 39–59.

2. Much of the information about Einspruch is provided in an autobiographical account, *Man with the Book*.

3. This church no longer exists, as it incorporated into what is today the Evangelical Lutheran Church in America.

4. Einspruch, *Man with the Book*.

5. Einspruch, "Christ, Christians, and the Jews," 151–52.

6. Einspruch, "Literature for the Christian Approach to the Jews," 97–102.

7. Ibid.

8. Cf. Smalley, *Translation as Mission*, 16, 39–40.

9. Ibid., 83–104; on the options and choices Bible translators make, see ibid., 105–32.

10. For former New Testament produced in America, see *Das Neu Testament*. This was an edited version produced in conjunction with the Bible Society.

11. A translation of the article appears in Einspruch, *Raisins and Almonds*, 15–17.

12. On Krelenbaum and his translation of the New Testament into Yiddish, see Praeger, *Yiddish Culture in Britain*, 383–84.

13. The Million Testaments Campaign also eventually made peace with Einspruch and distributed his translation.

14. I am indebted to Barbara and Dr. Leonard Praeger of Haifa, Israel, who during the late 1970s and early 1980s interviewed Aaron Krelenbaum a number of times in London, for sharing their knowledge and impressions with me.

15. On the way Yiddish writers treated one another during the period, see Cynthia Ozick's short story "Envy or Yiddish in America," in Ozick, *Pagan Rabbi and Other Stories*, 39–100; Shulman, "Boulevard Isaac Bashevis Singer," 38–40.

CHAPTER NINE

1. On Moody's attitude toward the Jewish people, see Ariel, "American Evangelist and the Jews," 41–49.

2. For example, *Moody Bible Institute Bulletin* 6 (May 1920).

3. Newman, "Place of the Moody Bible Institute in Jewish Evangelization," 176–77.

4. Winer, *The Calling*, 25. The Moody Bible Institute archives do not bear witness to the Hebrew Christian Alliance support.

5. On Levy and his appointment, see Joel Levy to James Gray, published in the *Moody Bible Institute Monthly* 22 (March 1922): 854, and Elias Newman's obituary "Late Rev. Joel Levy," 1147.

6. On Solomon Birnbaum, see his file at the Moody Bible Institute archives, Chicago, file CB B619.

7. *Moody Bible Institute Bulletin* 6 (June 1927), 21.

8. Ibid.

9. Birnbaum, "Preaching to Jews at Atlantic City," 199.

10. Sevener, *Rabbi's Vision*, 114–15.

11. See a report of an unpleasant incident that took place in Chicago in the early 1930s, Peltz, *Christian Modernism and Reform Judaism*, 4.

12. On Max Reich, see obituaries "Home Going of Max Reich"; "Dr. Max I. Reich, Moody Bible Institute Teacher, Wrote Religious Books"; and "Dr. Max Isaac Reich."

13. See, for example, Reich, *Sweet Singer of Israel*, 155–74.

14. Reich, *Sketches of Messianic Prophecy in the Book of Isaiah*; Reich, *Messianic Hope of Israel*.

15. Reich, "Israel," 45.

16. For example, Gray, "God's Covenant with Abraham, or Why He Chose Israel," chap. 2 in *Textbook on Prophecy*, 18–26.

17. Chap. 5, "Israel Restored and Renewed," and chap. 22, "Jerusalem's Capture in Light of Prophecy," in Gray, *Textbook on Prophecy*, 41–47, 200–206.

18. *Moody Bible Institute Bulletin* 10 (April 1931): no pagination.

19. Cf. Getz, *MBI*, 182.

20. *Catalog of Moody Bible Institute*, 1948–49, 35–36.

21. See reminiscences of a Jewish student at the Moody Bible Institute in the early 1950s, Strober, "My Life as a Christian," 38.

22. On Nathan J. Stone, see Pfefer, "We Salute the Rev. Nathan J. Stone," 19–20.

CHAPTER TEN

1. Cohn dedicated large parts of his autobiography, *I Have Fought a Good Fight*, to describing his earliest experiences in his father's mission.

2. Cf. Warnock, "To the Jew First," 230.

3. On the change of leadership, see Sevener, *Rabbi's Vision*, 86–87.

4. For example, Cohn, *Behold the Virgin Shall Conceive and Bear a Son*; Cohn, *Jewish Holidays and Their Significance*.

5. Cohn, *Behold the Virgin Shall Conceive an Bear a Son*.

6. Heydt, *Chosen People Question Box II*, for example, 152–56.

7. Hutchison, *Errand to the World*, esp. 15–42, 62–90.

8. See, for example, Cohn, "Russian Envoy Comes to Israel," 1–2; the same article was published in Yiddish on pp. 3–4. See also a tract by Daniel Fuchs, *Is Sputnik Another Tower of Babel?*.

9. Cohn "Russian Envoy Comes to Israel," 1, 4 (the Yiddish version).

10. Sherman, *Escape from Jesus*.

11. On the conferences, see Sevener, *Rabbi's Vision*, 84.

12. Sandeen, *Roots of Fundamentalism*, 131–61.

13. *Chosen People* 23 (October 1917): 3–4.

14. Bradbury, *Light for the World's Darkness*.

15. Chafer, "Coming Destruction of Ecclesiastical and Political Babylon," 52–62.

16. Lindsey, "Church and the Jews," 201–7.

17. Ibid., 202.

18. Ibid., 207.

19. Eisen, "Christian Missions to the Jews," 31–72. Although published in a scholarly journal, Eisen's article, in which he takes great exception to the American Board, should be read as a Jewish community leader's reaction to the missions.

20. In the early 1960s there were twenty-seven women and twenty men working as active missionaries for the American Board. See *North American Protestant Foreign Mission Agencies*, 25.

21. On the American Board of Missions to the Jews' work overseas during that period, see Sevener, *Rabbi's Vision*, 96–97, 154–229.

22. See Kjaer-Hansen, *Joseph Rabinowitz and the Messianic Movement*, 63–65.

23. *Chosen People* 35 (May 1930): 9; Sevener, *Rabbi's Vision*, 157.

24. See Sevener, *Rabbi's Vision*, 184.

25. For example, the Baptist magazine *Watchman Examiner* presented Cohn's photograph on its front cover accompanied by a favorable article inside (p. 65), January 21, 1943.

26. See, for example, a letter written (but not sent) by the Department of Jewish Evangelization of the Presbyterian Church in the U.S.A. to the American Board of Missions to the Jews, March 23, 1923, in the archives of the Presbyterian Church in the U.S.A., Presbyterian Historical Society, Philadelphia, group 127, box 15, folder 9.

27. See Joseph H. Cohn file at the Moody Bible Institute archives, which holds a number of clippings from newspapers regarding such incidents. The names of the newspapers and dates are missing. For example, "Cohn vs. Riley" of August 1939 and "Joseph Cohn and Russian Communism."

28. On William B. Riley and his network of evangelism, see Trollinger, *God's Empire*.

29. See Ariel, *On Behalf of Israel*, 45, 47, 112.

30. Newman, *Fundamentalists' Resuscitation of the Antisemitic Protocol Forgery* (Minneapolis: Augsburg Publishing House, 1934).

31. Sevener, *Rabbi's Vision*, 288.

CHAPTER ELEVEN

1. For example, Eisen, "Christian Missions to the Jews."

2. See, for example, correspondence between the two missionary bodies, archives of the Presbyterian Church in the U.S.A, Presbyterian Historical Society, Philadelphia, group 127, box 15, folder 9.

3. On the accusations concerning Cohn's salary, marital life, and dictatorial character, see a pamphlet privately published by J. Palmer Muntz, a former member of the board of directors of the American Board of Missions to the Jews, in May 1944, and another circular letter of the same year (published by the American Association for Jewish Evangelism), *Why We Resign from the American Board of Missions to the Jews*. A copy of the letter is in the Joseph H. Cohn file in the archives of the Moody Bible Institute.

4. Muntz, *Why We Resign from the American Board of Missions to the Jews*.

5. On Abraham Machlin, see Gordon, "House of the Prince of Peace," 184–85; Gordon, "Machlins Will Celebrate Two Anniversaries." See also Machlin's recollections, A. B. Machlin, "Leaf from a Missionary's Diary," 130–47; from the point of view of the American Board, see Sevener, *Rabbi's Vision*, 131, 133, 231–41, 244–47, 249, 250–53.

6. See lists of members of the advisory council published in the different editions of *Salvation*, the mission's magazine. Among the names on the list were presidents of the Moody Bible Institute, William Culbertson and George Sweeting; president of Dallas Theological Seminary, John Walvoord; and William Criswell, pastor of First Baptist Church of Dallas.

7. Bradbury, *Israel's Restoration*.

8. Chafer, "Introduction to Eschatology," 148–62.

9. Ironside, "Fulfilled Prophecy Concerning the Jew," 163–80.

10. Bradbury, "New State of Israel," 37–54.

11. Appelman, "Suffering People," 27.

12. Ibid.

13. Muntz, "Jew in History and Destiny," 83–99.

14. Ibid., 98.

15. See lists of the executive board members and reports of the field missionaries in the pages of the mission's journal, *Salvation*.

16. William B. Riley to C. W. O'Neill, of Kansas City, Mo., December 9, 1937, copy in the Jewish Community Relations Council of Minnesota Papers deposited in the Minnesota Historical Society, Minneapolis, P445, box 45. I am thankful to Dr. James Warnock for enlightening me as to the existence of this material and for sending me copies of it.

17. Brooks, *Lies Have Wings*.

18. Riley to O'Neill, December 9, 1937.

19. "In connection with the coming of the Lord there will be, as Gaebelein teaches, a remnant of Jews saved . . . and that remnant will become the great evangelizing agency during the millennium—in which time many will be saved." In ibid.

20. See, for example, in the pages of *Jewish Hope*, the journal the mission published during the 1940s. See also Michelson, *Jewish Passover and the Lord's Supper*.

21. See photographs in Michelson, *Out of Darkness into Light, From Judaism and Law to Christ and Grace*, and *Jewish Passover and the Lord's Supper*.

22. For example, Michelson, *Jewish Passover and the Lord's Supper*, frontispiece; Michelson, *Out of Darkness into Light*, 2, 7, 9.

23. Cf. Pruter, *Jewish Christians in the United States*, 98.

24. A copy in the files of the Jewish Community Relations Committee of Cincinnati, Ohio, microfilm no. 527, American Jewish Archives.

25. See, for example, Eisen, "Christian Missions to the Jews," 39.

26. See, for example, Richard S. McCarroll, Samuel Gayden, and Jack Ginty to the Jewish Evangelization Department, October 1, 1928, containing a list of accusations against E. S. Greenbaum, archives of the Presbyterian Church in the U.S.A.

27. Louis Goldberg, former director of Jewish Studies and Jewish missionary training at the Moody Bible Institute and former president of the Hebrew Christian Alliance, interview with author, Chicago, February 1993.

CHAPTER TWELVE

1. Drury, *Presbyterian Panorama*, 79–80, 149–50, 164, 191; Evearitt, "Jewish-Christian Missions to Jews," 244–48.

2. Cf. Hutchison, *Errand to the World*, 112.

3. See articles in the mission's journal, *Our Jewish Neighbors*.

4. *Minutes of the General Assembly of the Presbyterian Church in the U.S.A.*, n.s., vol. 16, August 1916 (Philadelphia: Office of the General Assembly, 1916), 185–86.

5. Conning, *Our Jewish Neighbors*.

6. Ibid., esp. 40–50.

7. *Minutes of the General Assembly of the Presbyterian Church in the U.S.A.*, 3d ser., vol. 4, 1925, pt. 2, Board Reports (Philadelphia: Office of the General Assembly, 1925), 208–23.

8. Conning, *Jew at the Church Door*, 13.

9. On Presbyterian work among children and youth, see Thoma, *Esther*.

10. Detailed information on missions to the Jews: budgets, centers, expenditures, nature of activity, and numbers of Jews approached were provided annually in the Home Mission Reports to the General Assembly of the Presbyterian Church in the U.S.A. See such reports in the annual publications, *Minutes of the General Assembly of the Presbyterian Church in the U.S.A.* (Philadelphia: Office of the General Assembly, 1920–60).

11. This comes out strongly in Esther's biography, Thoma, *Esther*.

12. I owe thanks to Johanna Chernoff for providing me with the photograph as well as other valuable material relating to the history of the movement to evangelize the Jews and the rise of the Messianic Jewish movement in the 1930s to 1970s.

13. Thoma, *Esther*.

14. On the development of the relationship between Conning and Benedict, see Conning's reports at the Presbyterian Historical Society, group 127, box 15, folder 8.

15. See copies of Conning's letters promoting the book, such Conning to Rev. Howard V. Yergin, New York, at the Presbyterian Historical Society, group 127, box 15, folder 8.

16. *Who's Who in American Jewry* (1926), 42; *Central Conference of American Rabbis Year Book* 39 (1929), in which his name appears with that of other rabbis. After his conversion to Christianity, however, some Jewish spokesmen denied that he was ever a fully ordained rabbi. *Fiftieth Anniversary Temple Emmanu El of Lynbrook*, 8.

17. For example, Hoffman, "Jewry in Distress!," 261–62.

18. See also ibid.

19. Genizi, *American Apathy*.

20. See the files relating to the department's efforts in the Presbyterian Historical Society, group 127, box 15, folders 21–38.

21. "A Plan for German Refugee Relief," submitted October 15, 1938, quoted in Genizi, "Missionary Work among Holocaust Refugees," 336–42.

22. On details of such advocacies, see, for example, Neil, *History of Christian Missions*, 171–72; Hutchison, *Errand to the World*, 63.

23. Ross, "Perverse Witness to the Holocaust," 127–39.

24. See Conning's and Hoffman's correspondence with some directors of the missionary centers, for example, with Aaron Kligerman or David Bronstein, at the Presbyterian Historical Society, group 127, box 15, folder 4.

25. See details of the activity of such congregations, in the Presbyterian Historical Society, such as that related to Jewish evangelization in the metropolitan area of Philadelphia, which includes a list of a committee established to support the work in Philadelphia. Group 127, box 15, folder 14.

26. Hutchison, *Errand to the World*, esp. 15–42, 62–90.

27. *Minutes of the General Assembly of the Presbyterian Church in the U.S.A.*, 3d ser., vol. 10 (Philadelphia: Office of the General Assembly, 1931), pt. 2:47.

28. Bronstein, *Peniel Portrait*.

29. Thoma, *Esther*, 94–95, 133.

30. See, for example, Newman "Looking Back Twenty-five Years," 24. Newman was a Presbyterian minister for a number of years.

31. See Bronstein, *Peniel Portrait*.

32. See Bronstein's tract on Passover, *Jewish Passover and the Christian Communion*.

33. Esther Bronstein brings forth this issue as the major argument for building a Jewish congregation, Thoma, *Esther.*

34. Rausch, *Messianic Judaism,* 87.

35. Cf. Kraut, "Towards the Establishment of the National Conference of Christian and Jews," 388–412; Kraut, "Wary Collaboration," 193–230.

36. Cf. Conway, "Protestant Missions to the Jews," 127–46, esp. 134–44.

37. Kraut, "Wary Collaboration," 200.

38. Ibid.

39. Glazer, *American Judaism,* 106–28; Herberg, *Protestant, Catholic, Jew.*

40. Merson, "Minister, the Rabbi and Their House of God," 27, 36–37.

41. Rice, "Reinhold Niebuhr and Judaism," 101–46; Feldman, "Reinhold Niebuhr and the Jews," 293–302.

42. See yearly reports of the Missions Department in the yearly publications of the Presbyterian Church in the U.S.A., *Minutes of the General Assembly of the Presbyterian Church in the U.S.A.* (Philadelphia: Office of the General Assembly, 1946–60).

43. On the ecumenical-evangelical debate, see Hutchison, *Errand to the World,* 177–83.

44. *Minutes of the General Assembly of the Presbyterian Church in the U.S.A.* (Philadelphia: Office of the General Assembly, 1946–60).

45. See "A Theological Understanding of the Relationship between Christians and Jews," adopted by the General Assembly of the Presbyterian Church in the U.S.A. in June 1987, in *Theology of the Churches and the Jewish People,* 105–20.

CHAPTER THIRTEEN

1. Eichhorn, *Evangelizing the American Jew,* 165.

2. Such lists appeared monthly in the pages of *Jewish Era.*

3. See the pages of *Jewish Era* and the *A.M.F. Monthly,* which reported regularly on the mission's workers and branches.

4. On the character of the mission in its early decades, see Warnock, "To the Jew First," 73–147.

5. Lindberg, *Witnessing to Jews,* 10.

6. Ibid.

7. *Jewish Era* 47 (1937): 48–49.

8. See list of missionaries published in the pages of *Jewish Era* and *A.M.F. Monthly.*

9. Based on interviews with veterans of the mission.

10. Lindberg, *Witnessing to Jews,* 17.

11. Ibid.

12. Ibid., 49.

13. Ibid., 53–58, 76–82.

14. Prof. Paul Haik, interview with author, Chicago, May 24, 1995. I am indebted to Prof. Haik for discussing with me his father's career as a missionary to the Jews.

15. The booklet was published in both English and Hebrew.

16. See Blum's periodical accounts of his work in the pages of the *A.M.F. Monthly,* including letters he received from listeners. The AMF also published appeals for financing

the broadcasts, for which it paid the Monaco Trans-World radio fifty-four dollars for each broadcast.

17. Eichhorn, *Evangelizing the American Jew*, 78.

CHAPTER FOURTEEN

1. See Greenberg, *Holy Land in American Religious Thought*, 113–40.

2. Cf. Schmidgall, "American Holiness Churches."

3. For example, Rausch, *Zionism within Early American Fundamentalism*; Ariel, *On Behalf of Israel*.

4. On the British policy toward the Christian churches, see Colbi, *History of the Christian Presence in the Holy Land*, 143–62.

5. Malachy, *American Fundamentalism and Israel*, 45–46.

6. Ibid.

7. For example, Talbot and Orr, *New Nation of Israel and the Word of God*; DeHaan, *Jew and Palestine in Prophecy*; Hull, *Fall and Rise of Israel*; Davis, *God's Guiding Hand*; Walvoord, *Israel in Prophecy*.

8. In *Chosen People* 55 (November 1949): 16–17; Sevener, *Rabbi's Vision*, 162–76.

9. Davis, *Sowing God's Word in Israel Today*, 7.

10. See, for example, Carpenter and Shenk, *Earthen Vessels*, esp. 155–234.

11. On Israeli policy in its early years toward the Christian churches, see Colbi, *History of Christian Presence in the Holy Land*, 163–84. Weiner, *Wild Goats of Ein Gedi*, esp. 12–15, 29–111. Cf. also Zeldin, "Catholics and Protestants in Jerusalem."

12. For example, Minerbi, *Vatican and Zionism*.

13. During the 1948 war David Ben-Gurion, Israel's first prime minister, sent a telegram to the Israeli army officers ordering them to use severe, indeed draconian, measures to ensure the security and well-being of Christian institutions. See Israel State Archives, Jerusalem, Case 2397, folder 3, document H/A/15092. See also a declaration regarding religious freedom, adopted by the Provisional Government, May 23, 1948, eight days after the establishment of the state. See Recording of Provisional Government Meetings, p. 28, Israel State Archives.

14. See the Hebrew daily *Davar*, March 27, 1964. On the incident as well as the entire atmosphere under which missions operated in Israel, see Osterley, *Church in Israel*. Osterley's account is written from a distinct Protestant missionary point of view.

15. Cf. Henry, "Christian Witness in Israel," pt. 1:22–23. Henry complains about the quota system. For the various ways missionaries used to gain residence in Israel during that period, see, for example, Glora Ulysses of the International Missionary Council to George Sadler of the Foreign Mission Board of the Southern Baptist Convention, November 12, 1954. The letter, along with many of Lindsey's papers from the 1950s and 1960s, was given by him to Kim Jin-Hae, a Ph.D. student at the Hebrew University during the early and mid-1990s, for use in his work on a dissertation on Lindsey, the Baptists, and the Jerusalem School of New Testament Studies. Copies of the entire collection are also in the possession of Yaakov Ariel.

16. Sevener, *Rabbi's Vision*, 172.

17. On the transition that took place in Israel during its early years, see, for example, Pilowsky, *Transition from "Yishuv" to State*.

18. *Chosen People* 61 (May 1956): 11.

19. Cf. Weiner, *Wild Goats of Ein Gedi*, 63.

20. The Department of Christian Affairs at the Ministry of Religion distributed in the late 1950s and early 1960s "restricted" documents listing Protestant evangelical agencies in the country and their staff. The figures indicated more than 280 official staff members of evangelical churches and missionary stations. There were many missionaries working privately outside the recognized agencies, and missions hired, at times, local residents as well as employing temporary residents with no legal status. There were, of course, many nonevangelical Christian missionaries working in the country. See such a list on the mid-1950s in container 5827/d, file 29/1/100, Israel State Archives.

21. *Chosen People* 61 (April 1956): 8–9.

22. *Chosen People* 61 (May 1956): 11. Cf. also Henry, "Christian Witness in Israel," pt. 2:17–21.

23. *Chosen People* 58 (October 1952): 1.

24. Sevener, *Rabbi's Vision*, 164.

25. Ibid.

26. Ibid., 168–69.

27. Cf. Friedman, *The Haredi (Ultra Orthodox) Society*, 98.

28. "Sticks and Stones," 41.

29. A letter of Haim Wardi of the Department for Christian Affairs, the Ministry of Religious Affairs, February 27, 1953, Israel State Archives, container 5817/19, file 29/1/100.

30. Michelson, *Jews and Palestine in Light of Prophecy*.

31. In a letter in *Hatsophe*, November 17, 1961.

32. A copy in the possession of Yaakov Ariel.

33. A copy in Israel State Archives, container 5818/1, file 29/1/100.

34. See letters of officials of the various government agencies to the Ministry of Religious Affairs: for example, a letter of Walter Eitan, director general of the Ministry of Foreign Affairs, of May 26, 1952; a letter of J. L. Benor, director general of the Ministry of Education, container 5817/19, file 29/1/100, Israel State Archives. See also a letter of Avraham Biran, district officer for Jerusalem at the Ministry of Interior Affairs, container 5818 G, file 29/1/101.

35. This emerges clearly from his correspondence with other government agencies, such as the police or the Ministry of Interior Affairs (see note 34 above).

36. For example, Saul Colbi's letter of May 1953 to Histadrut HaMercaz, allocating one hundred pounds for rescuing Jewish children from missionary institutions, or his letter to the Committee for Fighting Alien Education of December 2, 1953, container 5817/19 G, file 29/1/100, Israel State Archives.

37. See *Missionary Enterprise and the Israeli Court System*.

38. On Robert Lindsey's life and work, see the special issue dedicated to him of *Jerusalem Perspective* 32 (May/June 1991).

39. Robert Lindsey to Dr. Goerner of the Southern Baptist Mission Department, April 16, 1960, in Lindsey's personal papers (copy in Yaakov Ariel's collection).

40. See one of Lindsey's early summaries of his theory, "Summary of Conclusions of

Research into the Synoptic Relationship," 2, 7. Lindsey's books on the topic include *A Hebrew Translation of the Gospel of Mark* and *A New Approach to the Synoptic Gospel*.

41. See, for example, Flusser, *Jewish Sources in Early Christianity*.

42. Shavit, *New Hebrew Nation*.

43. *Hakvutza Ha Cnaanit*.

44. Uri Avneri makes that claim in his book *Milhemet Hayom Hasheve*, 145–80.

45. Klatzker, "Israeli Civil Religion," 3:135–52.

46. Svi Rin to author, July 30, 1996.

47. See Robert Lindsey to Lillian E. Williams, September 28, 1959, in Lindsey's personal papers, and "Baptist Cites Israeli Discord," 8. See also Baker, "Baptists' Golden Jubilee," typed manuscript, copy in the Israel file in the archives of the Southern Baptist Convention, Richmond, Virginia.

48. Klatzker, "Israeli Civil Religion," 143.

49. A copy is in Lindsey's personal papers.

50. See correspondence between the Department of Christian Churches in the Ministry of Religious Affairs and the Department of Custom and Exercise of May 1953, container G5809, file 29/1/32, Israel State Archives.

51. Cf. Weiner, *Wild Goats of Ein Gedi*, 70.

52. On the American Council for Judaism, see Halperin, *Political World of American Zionism*, 86–92, 301–9, 351–52; Kolsky, *Jews against Zionism*.

53. See such correspondence in Lindsey's personal papers, for example, Elmer Berger's letters to Lindsey, July 22, 1953, and January 20, 1954; Lindsey's response, August 11, 1953.

54. Lindsey to Elmer Berger, May 30, 1953, in Lindsey's personal papers.

55. See "Memorandum: The Missionary Means of Operations in the Country," Central Zionist Archives, Jerusalem, Jerusalem Section 575, file 5345.

56. For example, Lud, "Kriat Am Adonai Al-pi Habrit Hachadsha," 4–5. See also Lindsey, "Salvation and the Jews," 20–47.

57. Lindsey, "Jews and the Christian Hope." See also Zeldin, "Catholics and Protestants in Jerusalem," 230–36.

58. For example, Lindsey's report to the Thirteenth Annual Conference of the United Christian Council in Israel UCCI), October 28–30, 1969, p. 3, at UCCI Archives, Church of the Nazarene, Jerusalem.

59. Lindsey, "Jews and Christian Hope."

60. For example, talk before the annual conference of the United Christian Council in Israel, November 14, 1958, Jerusalem. Quoted by Zeldin, "Catholics and Protestants in Jerusalem," 230.

61. This theme repeats itself in Lindsey's correspondence.

62. On the nature of the Baptist activity in Israel during the period, see, for example, Report of the Executive Committee, summary of meetings for the years 1958–59, compiled by Baptist activists in Israel, copy in the possession of Yaakov Ariel; Baker, "Baptists' Golden Jubilee."

63. Lindsey, *Munachim Meshichiim Notzriim*. The editorial work on the publication began in 1963.

64. Ilan, "Megaresh Hashedim Holech Habayta," 25–27. On the charismatic nature and practices of Baptist congregations in Israel, see Lanier, "Renewal of the Church in Israel"

(manuscript in Yaakov Ariel's private collection), which describes healing as a common practice among Baptists in Israel. Lanier was a missionary in Israel in the 1960s and 1970s.

65. See, for example, letters back and forth from Lindsey to the board in Richmond, Virginia, in Lindsey's personal papers.

66. Cf. Weiner, *Wild Goats of Ein Gedi*, 69–70; see also "Editorial," *Ha Boker*, May 4, 1962; Uri Kesari's article in *Ha Aretz*, October 26, 1961; Ben Ari, "Baptists Believe in Freedom of Religion"; and Stern, "Tragedy within a Tragedy."

67. For example, in the 1970s the Israeli Hebrew daily *Ha Aretz* carried a series, "A Week in the Life of One Person," in which noted public figures were asked to describe their week. Lindsey was one of the people asked by *Ha Aretz* to provide one of the articles.

68. See, for example, Benor to the Ministry of Religious Affairs, container 5817/19, file 29/1/100, Israel State Archives.

69. On Aimee Semple McPherson and the Foursquare Gospel Church, see Blumhofer, *Aimee Semple McPherson*.

70. See in Hull's articles, for example, "Letter from Zion Apostolic Mission to UNSCOP," 71.

71. For example, *A Voice in Jerusalem* 16 (October 1949): 13.

72. Hull, *Struggle for a Soul*.

73. Ibid., 159.

74. Malachy, *American Fundamentalism and Israel*, 105.

75. Ibid.

76. The Reverend Charles Kopp, interview with author, Jerusalem, January 1994.

77. Pragai, *Faith and Fulfillment*. This book was published by Pragai, who was a senior Israeli official, upon his retirement. He was the head of the Department for Christian Churches at the Israeli Foreign Ministry for many years. The book is dedicated to the theme of Christian supporters of Israel. In it Pragai makes no mention of the different theological motivations for Christian interest in Israel and fails to differentiate between various types of motivations such as between liberal and conservative Protestants.

78. On Oral Roberts's life and work, see Harrell, *Oral Roberts*.

79. Ibid., 136–37.

80. Ibid.

81. On the Pentecostal conference, see Malachy, *American Fundamentalism and Israel*, 106–11.

82. "Ambassador Lawson . . . had much advice to offer and much of it we accepted." In Kligerman, "Destination Israel," 154. I owe thanks to Robert Winer, M.D., for informing me of the existence of this source.

83. Menahem Benhayim, former secretary of the Messianic Jewish Alliance in Israel, estimated that in the early 1960s there were no more than three hundred Jewish members of evangelical congregations in the country. This included those converted outside Israel. In an interview with the author, Jerusalem, July 1994.

84. Michelson, *Out of Darkness into Light*, 6.

85. "Minutes of the Conference on Personal Status held by the United Christian Council in Israel. Personal Status Committee at Stella Carmel, Isafia, April 14–15, 1964," manuscript, p. 12, UCCI Archives.

86. Cf. Levitt, *Underground Church of Jerusalem*. Cf. also Henry, *Confessions of a Theologian*, 233.

87. Kligerman, "Destination Israel"; Levitt, *Underground Church of Jerusalem*, 95.

88. Ellison, "Christian Missions and Israel," 26.

89. Cf. Weiner, *Wild Goats of Ein Gedi*, 67.

90. Davis, *Sowing God's Word in Israel Today*, 45.

91. Ibid., 43–45.

CHAPTER FIFTEEN

1. Newman, *Enrichment of the Church*, 5–6.

2. See a description of such crypto-Jews in Wolff, *In Pharaoh's Army*; Gordon, *Shadow Man*.

3. Newman, *Enrichment of the Church*.

4. See, for example, Bronstein, *Peniel Portrait*.

5. Rambo, *Understanding Religious Conversion*, 66–75.

6. See Ariel, "From Judaism to Christianity," 123–29.

7. See the American Board of Missions to the Jews's special booklet (at the Chosen People Ministries) presenting employees who had been refugees from Nazi Europe.

8. A letter in the archives of the Presbyterian Historical Society, group 127, box 15, folder 3.

9. Ibid.

10. See, for example, Menahem Benhayim, "Messianic Movement in Israel—A Personal Perspective," 21–22.

11. See Ariel, "From Judaism to Christianity."

12. Sherman, *Escape from Jesus*.

13. Koser, *Come and Get It!*.

14. Cawelti, *Adventure Mystery and Romance*; Taylor, "Conversion and Cognition," 5–22; Beckford, "Accounting for Conversion," 249–62.

15. Pascal, *Design and Truth in Autobiography*.

16. For example, Wolff, *In Pharaoh's Army*; Gordon, *Shadow Man*.

17. Cf. Schechter, "American Jews in Liberal Protestant and Neo-Humanist Religious Institutions."

18. Cf. Glock and Stark, *Christian Beliefs and Anti-Semitism*.

19. Such incidents were noted by such different autobiographies as those of Joseph Cohn (*I Have Fought a Good Fight*) and Shlomo Sherman (*Escape from Jesus*).

20. Thoma, *Esther*, 94–95.

21. *Hebrew Christian Alliance Quarterly* 15 (1930).

22. Ibid.

23. See *Here Is the Story behind All These Smiling Faces*.

24. Bronstein, *Peniel Portrait*; Thoma, *Esther*.

25. Thoma, *Esther*; Sherman, *Escape from Jesus*.

26. Cf. Sherman, *Escape from Jesus*. Sherman emphasizes the absolute commitment of the group to middle-class behavior and style.

27. Sobel, *Hebrew Christianity*.

28. Sherman, *Escape from Jesus*, 74.

29. Newman, "Looking Back Twenty-five Years," 24.

30. Ibid.

31. See, for example, eulogies to Max Reich. Max Reich's file at the Moody Bible Institute archive.

32. "Our Purpose," stated on inner cover of the *Hebrew Christian Alliance Quarterly* 16 (April–June 1931).

33. See such lists in the pages of the *Hebrew Christian Alliance Quarterly*.

34. Cf. Sobel, "Tools of Legitimation," 241–50; Nerel, "Messianic Jews and the Modern Zionist Movement," 75–84. Sobel is suspicious of the Hebrew Christian motivation, while Nerel, who writes from within the movement, takes an apologetic line.

35. For example, "Present Situation in Palestine," 59; "We Might Unite with Our Jewish Brethren in Their Protest"; "Jewish Palestine Still Developing," 5; "Happenings in Israel," 28–31; and "Israel's Tenth Anniversary," 17–21.

36. "Zionism and Hebrew Christianity," 43.

37. John L. Zacker to Louis Lipsky, October 29, 1921, published by Winer, *The Calling*, 113.

38. Zacker to Lipsky, January 26, 1922, in Winer, *The Calling*, 115.

39. Ibid., 113.

40. Zacker to Lipsky, October 29, 1921, and January 26, 1922, and Lipsky's answers of November 22, 1921, and February 17, 1922. See also Emmanuel Greenbaum to Stephen S. Wise, September 15, 1933, published by Winer, *The Calling*, 113–17.

41. Newman, "There Is a Prince and Great Man Fallen This Day in Israel," 4–8.

CHAPTER SIXTEEN

1. Neill, *History of Christian Missions*, 331–32.

2. Presentations as well as information on both conferences were published in London in a volume entitled *The Christian Approach to the Jews Being a Report of Conferences on the Subject Held at Budapest and Warsaw in April 1927* (hereafter cited as *Christian Approach to the Jews*).

3. Black, "Jews and the Gentile," 1–17.

4. *Christian Approach to the Jews*, 18–20, 41–42.

5. Ibid., 24–26.

6. Ibid., 41–42.

7. Ibid., 100.

8. Ibid., 99–100.

9. *Christians and Jews*.

10. On John Mott and his missionary and ecumenical career, see Hopkins, *John R. Mott*.

11. Newman, *Why I Became a Lutheran*, 7.

12. See *Christians and Jews*.

13. See, for example, the presentations of Conrad Hoffmann and Henry Einspruch in ibid.

14. See a typewritten manuscript of the report at the World Mission Library, Union Theological Seminary, New York. I am thankful to the library for providing me with a microfilm copy of the report.

15. On Pentecostalism and its early development, see Synan, *Holiness-Pentecostal Movement in the United States*; Dayton, *Theological Roots of Pentecostalism*.

16. This is evident in its lists of supporters and budget for 1948–49. A copy in the collection of Yaakov Ariel.

17. On the Home Mission Council and its involvement with the efforts to evangelize the Jews, see Handy, *We Witness Together*, esp. 92–93, 140–43, 204–5.

18. "First Assembly of the WCC, Amsterdam, Holland, 1948, The Christian Approach to the Jews," in Croner, *Stepping Stones*, 69–72.

19. Ibid., 72–85.

20. Piper, Jocz, and Floreen, *Church Meets Judaism*, vii–viii.

21. Participants reached agreement on the following:

1. In our theology undergirding all mission concern, is the principle that the Gospel is for all men without distinction. . . .

2. We recognize that the evangelization of the Jews is a matter of Christian conscience and commitment, and that as instruments of the Holy Spirit we must persistently evangelize. . . .

3. It is our conviction that the time is right for a more intensive effort at the evangelization of the Jews.

4. The Christian Church must be made aware of the fact that its spiritual heritage is from the Jews, rooted in God's work within the old covenant, climaxed in Christ Jesus, a Jew, and communicated to us through the early Christian community which was Jewish.

5. We express regret over our neglect of our mission to Israel.
Ibid., 70–71.

22. Cf. Hutchison, *Errand to the World*, 177–82.

23. On the World Parliament of Religions, see Markus Braybrooke, *Pilgrimage of Hope*, 1–39.

24. See, for example, Holmes, *Judaism and Christianity*.

25. Kraut, "Wary Collaboration," 193–230.

26. Ibid., 210.

27. On Niebuhr and his attitude toward Jews, the idea of missionizing them, and the Zionist movement, see Niebuhr, "Rapprochement between Jews and Christians," 9–11. Niebuhr, "Jews after the War." See also Rice, "Reinhold Niebuhr and Judaism," 101–46; Feldman, "Reinhold Niebuhr and the Jews," 293–302; Fox, *Reinhold Niebuhr*; Feldman, "American Protestant Theologians on the Frontier of Jewish-Christian Relations," 363–85; Naveh, "Hebraic Foundation of Christian Faith, According to Reinhold Niebuhr," 37–56.

28. Littell, *Crucifixion of the Jews*; Eckardt, *Elder and Younger Brother*; Van Buren, *Discerning the Way*.

29. On the council and its attitude toward Jews, see Gilbert, *Vatican Council and the Jews*.

30. See such declarations as Croner, *Stepping Stones*, and *Theology of the Churches and the Jewish People*.

31. On the debates within the Lutheran churches, for example, see Gilbert, "New Trends in the Protestant Mission to the Jew," 51–56.

32. Lieske, *Witnessing to the Jewish People*, esp. 11–17, 46–48.

CHAPTER SEVENTEEN

1. Cf. Svonkin, *Jews against Prejudice*.

2. See the collection of documents of the Jewish Community Relations Committee of Cincinnati at the American Jewish Archives, microfilm no. 524.

3. Dinnerstein, *Anti-Semitism in America*, 78–149.

4. Herberg, *Protestant, Catholic, Jew.*

5. Lebeson, "Zionism Comes to Chicago," 165.

6. Eichhorn, "History of Christian Attempts to Convert the Jews."

7. Eisen, "Christian Missions to the Jews," 31–66.

8. Blumstock, "Evangelization of the Jews."

9. Small collections SC 2476, American Jewish Archives.

10. See, for example, the information provided by David Cooper of the Bible Institute of Los Angeles in an attachment to a letter of December 19, 1928, sent by Lenore Goldman Levin of the Jewish Aid Society, Los Angeles, to S. M. Neches. Small Collections SC 2476, American Jewish Archives.

11. Nissen Gross to Erwin Oreck, March 29, 1944, in the Jewish Community Relations Council of Minnesota Papers, P445, box 7—Appelman, Hyman J., at the Minnesota Historical Society. Gross could not know that Appelman broke away from Riley. See "Hyman Appelman Comes to Town," 8.

12. In a letter to Joseph Papo, Duluth Committee, Minnesota Jewish Council, April 5, 1944, in the Jewish Community Relations Council of Minnesota Papers, P445, box 7—Appelman, Hyman J., Minnesota Historical Society.

CHAPTER EIGHTEEN

1. On the new religious atmosphere of the era, see Roof, *Generation of Seekers*; Ellwood, *The Sixties Spiritual Awakening.* Cf. Bellah, Madsen, Sullivan, Swidler, and Tipton, *Habits of the Heart.*

2. Cf. Finke and Starck, *Churching of America*, esp. 237–75.

3. Sweet, "Modernization of Protestant Religion in America," 19–41.

4. On the Vietnam Era and its atmosphere, see Capps, *Unfinished War*; Clecak, *America's Quest for the Ideal Self*; Gitlin, *The Sixties*; O'Brien, *Dream Time.*

5. On the percentage of Jews in New Religious Movements, see, for example, Lucas, *Odyssey of a New Religion*; Eller, *Living In the Lap of the Goddess.*

6. See, for example, Linzer, *Torah and Dharmah*; Kamenetz, *Jew in the Lotus.*

7. On the changing realities of American Jewry in the last generation, see Bershtel and Graubard, *Saving Remnants*; Dershowitz, *Vanishing American Jew*; Wertheimer, *People Divided.*

8. On the new Jewish awareness that was created during the period, see Biale, Galchinsky, and Heschel, *Insider/Outsider.*

9. Cf. Glazer, *Ethnic Dilemmas.*

10. Ariel, "American Fundamentalists and the Establishment of a Jewish State," 288–309.

11. On the survey, see Ianniello, "Release for the Press."

12. On American Christian attitudes toward Israel during the period, see Pawlikowski, *What Are They Saying about Christian Jewish Relations?*, 109–28; and Rausch, "American Christians and Israel," 41–81; Banki, *Christian Responses to the Yom Kippur War.*

CHAPTER NINETEEN

1. For example, Palms, "Jews for Jesus," 7–9. Kaufman, "Jews for Jesus," 37.

2. Hineni, meaning "here I am" in Hebrew, refers to Isaiah 6:8. It conveys the self-understanding of the group as dedicated to promoting the word of God. "Whom shall I send and who will go for us? Then said I, Here I am send me."

3. On the place of the Jews in American premillennialist thought, see Ariel, *On Behalf of Israel*.

4. For example, Eichhorn, *Evangelizing the American Jew*, 172–76.

5. On Moishe Rosen's life and early career, see Lipson, *Jews for Jesus*, 54–60, and Rosen's autobiographical account, Rosen and Proctor, *Jews for Jesus*, 15–55.

6. Cf. Alinsky, *Rules for Radicals*; on Saul Alinsky and his teaching, see Horwitt, *Let Them Call Me Rebel*.

7. Rosen and Proctor, *Jews for Jesus*, 59.

8. Ibid.

9. Zaretsky and Leone, *Religious Movements in Contemporary America*; Roof, *Generation of Seekers*; Ellwood, *The Sixties Spiritual Awakening*.

10. On Jewish involvement in such groups, see Linzer, *Torah and Dharma*; Kamenetz, *Jew in the Lotus*.

11. Rosen and Rosen, *Share the New Life*, 29–31.

12. See ibid. This basic claim repeats itself throughout the book. Following the Israeli Yom Kippur War (1973), Rosen had a discussion on that topic with Menahem Benhayim, a leader of the Christian messianic Jewish community in Israel. Benhayim referred to the death of a medic in the war while saving the life of another soldier and voiced his opinion that the medic was saved because in his self-sacrificing deed he followed the example of Jesus Christ. Rosen did not agree and insisted that only the born-agains were saved. Menahem Benhayim, interview with author, Jerusalem, July 1994.

13. On such evangelists and groups, see Streiber, *Jesus Trip*.

14. Cf. photographs of Jews for Jesus, demonstrating or distributing leaflets and dressed in denim and with long hair, with those of other such groups, for example, Miller, "Jews as 'Jesus Freaks' "; Streiber, *Jesus Trip*, 30.

15. See, for example, the advertisement "Jews for Jesus Answers" in the *News York Times*, Sunday, June 27, 1976, which attempts to overcome possible Jewish objections and inhibitions vis-à-vis the group's Christian evangelical message.

16. Rosen and Proctor, *Jews for Jesus*, 23.

17. Rosen and Rosen, *Share the New Life*, 23, 28.

18. Rausch, *Messianic Judaism*, 89–91; Pruter, *Jewish Christians in the United States*, ix.

19. Johanna Chernoff, David Chernoff, and Robert Winer, M.D., activists and leaders in the Messianic Jewish movement in the 1970s, interviews with author, Philadelphia, December 9, 1994.

20. Ibid.

21. See Sevener, *Rabbi's Vision*, 417–20.

22. Glock and Stark, *Christian Beliefs and Anti-Semitism*; Ianniello, "Release for the Press."

23. Willoughby, "Breakthrough for Messianic Judaism?," 16–19.

24. See Eichhorn, *Evangelizing the American Jew*, 188. Cf. also Sevener, *Rabbi's Vision*, 296.

25. See, for example, Rosen and Proctor, *Jews for Jesus*, 1–2.

26. Rosen, *Jesus for Jews*, 185–200, particularly 199–200.

27. Rosen, *Sayings of Chairman Moishe*, 38–39.

28. Ibid., 22–23.

29. Ibid., 104–5.

30. See the biographical accounts in Rosen, *Jesus for Jews*, 82, 141–42, 198, 211, 239; cf. also Lipson, *Jews for Jesus*, 26–60.

31. Rosen, *Jesus for Jews*; Lipson, *Jews for Jesus*.

32. Rosen, *Jesus for Jews*, 199–200.

33. Lipson, *Jews for Jesus*, 50.

34. Rosen, *Jesus for Jews*, 139.

35. Ibid., 196.

36. Cf. Rosen and Proctor, *Jews for Jesus*, 78–81, 85, 114, 117, 119; Rosen, *Jesus for Jews*, 184–200, 231–41.

37. On the demographics of Jewish conversion to Christianity in America, see Goldstein, "Profile of American Jewry," 90.

38. On the ideology of the House of Love and Prayer, see writings and sayings of Shlomo Carlebach, for example, Carlebach, "In the Palace of the King," a record (New York: Vanguard Records, 1965); Carlebach, "Secrets of the Deepest Depths," a videocassette (Berkley, Calif.: Ain Sof Productions, 1987); Carlebach, "A Melava Malka," a record (Jerusalem: Noam, 1995). Cf. also Korenbrot, *Return to Modiim*; Carlebach and Mesinai, *Shlomo's Stories*; Mandelbaum, *Holy Brother*; Serkez, *Holy Beggars' Banquet*.

39. Lipson, *Jews for Jesus*, 32–54.

40. See, for example, Rosen, *Jesus for Jews*, 242–76; Roth, *They Thought for Themselves*, 85–100, 127–43.

41. Rambo, *Understanding Religious Conversion*, 108–13.

42. Goldstein, "Profile of American Jewry," 90.

43. Lipson, *Jews for Jesus*, 27–28.

44. Eichhorn, *Evangelizing the American Jew*, 172–76.

45. Cf. Danziger, *Returning to Tradition*; Prell, *Prayer and Community*.

46. On the number of Jews joining other religions, see Goldstein, "Profile of American Jewry," 90.

47. See, for example, Hopkins, "Jews for Jesus Give Mission 'Bad Name,' " 2.

48. See Jews for Jesus doctrinal statement: Lipson, *Jews for Jesus*, 182–83.

49. Rausch, *Communities in Conflict*, 128–29.

50. Rausch, *Messianic Judaism*, 89, 159, 202.

51. On criticism, see, for example, Hopkins "Jews for Jesus Give Mission 'Bad Name,' " 2; on denial of membership, see minutes of the February 1975 meeting of the Fellowship of Christian Testimonies to the Jews, Pennsauken, New Jersey, in the Official Secretary's Book of the FCTJ, formerly in the possession of the AMF-International, Lynwood, Illinois.

52. Cf. Herberg, *Protestant, Catholic, Jew*.

53. In March 1972, the Northern California Board of Rabbis circulated a letter to Hillel houses and Jewish communities advising against such invitations. Cf. Rausch, *Communities in Conflict*, 126.

54. In Eisenberg, *Smashing the Idols*, 41–48.

55. Cf. Cox, "Deep Structures in the Study of New Religions," 122–30.

56. In Eisenberg, *Smashing the Idols*, 178.

57. Fisch, *Jews for Nothing*, 28–29.

58. In Eisenberg, *Smashing the Idols*, 162.

59. Rosen and Proctor, *Jews for Jesus*, 12–13.

60. Ibid., 114.

61. See, for example, Fisch, *Jews for Nothing*, 21–71.

62. On the Jewish reaction to Key 73, see Rausch, *Communities in Conflict*, 114–21.

63. Graham, "Billy Graham on Key 73," 625.

64. See, for example, the pamphlet *What Evangelical Christians Should Know about Jews for Jesus*.

65. The organization's international posts are listed in *Lausanne Consultation on Jewish Evangelism: International Networking Directory 1992*.

66. On American missions towering over the missionary field in the latter decades of the twentieth century, see, for example, essays by Richard V. Pierard, Allen V. Koop, and Charles E. Van Engen in Carpenter and Shenk, *Earthen Vessels*, 155–234.

67. Cf. Moore, *Selling God*, 238–55.

68. Cf. *Lausanne Consultation on Jewish Evangelism: International Networking Directory 1992*, 6; Hogg, "Role of American Protestantism in World Mission," 368–402.

69. *Messianic Resource Catalog*, vol. 11, no. 1 (San Francisco: Purple Pomegranate Productions, 1996); *Messianic Resource: Price List* (San Francisco: Purple Pomegranate Productions, a division of Jews for Jesus, 1997).

70. *Messianic Resource Catalog*, vol. 11, no. 1, 14–19.

71. Ibid., 9.

CHAPTER TWENTY

1. On such eighteenth- and nineteenth-century missions and the new spirit and some of the methods they introduced, see, for example, Tuchman, *Bible and Sword*, 175–207; Crombie, *For the Love of Zion*, 1–163.

2. See Winer, *The Calling*.

3. For an interesting discussion of Jewish Christian hymnology before the rise of the modern movement of Messianic Judaism, see Nerel, "Messianic Jews in Eretz, Israel," 248–66.

4. Kai Kjaer-Hansen, *Joseph Rabinowitz and the Messianic Movement*.

5. Rausch, *Arno C. Gaebelein*, 19–52; Ariel, *On Behalf of Israel*, 99–108.

6. Cf. Newman, "Looking Back Twenty Five-years," 24.

7. Ariel, "Eschatology, Evangelism, and Dialogue," 29–41.

8. See Cohn, *I Have Fought a Good Fight*.

9. Cf. Rausch, *Messianic Judaism*, 11–85.

10. This comes across very clearly in the writings of Messianic Jews who emphasize the new, independent spirit of their movement. See, for example, Schiffman, *Return of the Remnant*.

11. For example, Stern, *Messianic Jewish Manifesto*, 74–76.

12. See, for example, Schiffman, *Return of the Remnant*.

13. Rohold, "Messianic Judaism," 8–11; Rausch, *Messianic Judaism*, 32–43.

14. For example, Lindsey, *Christian Terms in Hebrew*.

15. In 1949, Joseph Cohn, the director of the American Board of Missions to the Jews, introduced the term into the missionary Yiddish literature the mission was circulating. He had to explain the term and its meaning. See "Wer Is a Meshichi," in the Yiddish section of the *Shepherd of Israel* 31 (June 1949).

16. Much of the information on Martin Chernoff and the early beginnings of the Messianic movement in Cincinnati was provided by Johanna Chernoff in an interview in Philadelphia, October 27, 1995.

17. See letters of appreciation sent to Johanna Chernoff by the president and executive director of Glen Manor, home of the Jewish aged, January 10, 1965. See also her name in the *National Council of Jewish Women, Cincinnati Section Yearbooks*, 1965–66 and 1967–68; a letter of appreciation from the Jewish Family Service Bureau of December 1, 1966; and a letter from Alvin M. Loeb, thanking Mrs. Chernoff for writing a biographical sketch for the *Glen Manor News*. In line with the manners of the age, the letter addressed Johannah as Mrs. Martin Chernoff. Copies in the possession of Yaakov Ariel.

18. Johanna Chernoff attributed the change of attitude during the 1970s to the effect of "antimissionary agitators."

19. I am thankful to Michael Wolf, the Messianic rabbi of Beth Messiah Congregation, Cincinnati, and his wife, Rachel, as well as to Joe Finkelstein himself, for the information on "Fink's Zoo."

20. Cf. Harris-Shapiro, "Syncretism or Struggle," 44.

21. This came up, for example, in interviews with David Chernoff, rabbi of Beth Yeshua in Philadelphia, Philadelphia, October 1995, and with Harold Sevener, president emeritus of the Chosen People Ministries, in an interview in Chapel Hill in 1995. See also Klayman, "Messianic Zionism," 3–8.

22. See, for example, Stern, *Messianic Jewish Manifesto*, 99–119.

23. See the brochure of the program Beth Yeshua prepared for the Israeli Day of Independence, 1991. "Yom Haatzmaut: Day of Independence," Congregation Beth Yeshua 5751, 1991. A copy in the possession of Yaakov Ariel.

24. See the yearly advertisements of the Messiah Conferences, in Yaakov Ariel's collection.

25. See the brochure *The Chalutzim Day School of Philadelphia*, in Yaakov Ariel's collection.

26. See, for example, *Magnify and Sanctify His Name*; *Messianic Congregation Peniel, Songbook*.

27. On the Bar Mitzvah in American Jewish life, see Joselit, *Wonders of America*, 89–133.

28. I am thankful to Richard and Sherry Heller for inviting me to their son Eli Robert's Messianic Jewish Bar Mitzvah.

29. "Do Messianic Jews Proselytize?" 68–69.

30. See Brotman, *Training Manual on How to Share the Messiah*.

31. Cf. Harding, "Convicted by the Holy Spirit," 167–81. For an interesting discussion of the role of language in the process of conversion, see also Stromberg, *Language and Self-Transformation*.

32. Cf. Ammerman, *Bible Believers*.

33. Cf. Feher, *Passing over Easter*, 94–97.

34. For example, Feinberg, *Prophetic Truth Unfolding Today*; Feinberg, *Prophecy and the Seventies*; Goldberg, *Turbulence over the Middle East*, a book based on a series of articles he published in 1968–69 in the *Moody Monthly*.

35. On the trend among the previous generation to downplay and eradicate Jewish attributes, see Calvin Trillin's autobiography, *Messages from My Father*.

36. A famous book that gave expression to as well as enhanced the trend was Alex Haley's *Roots*, which became an international best-seller and a movie.

37. Cf. Danzger, *Returning to Tradition*.

38. Cf. Glazer, *Ethnic Dilemmas*, 17.

39. I am thankful to the Reverend William Currie, former president of the now defunct FCTJ, for sharing with me his experiences and insights regarding this organization.

40. See minutes of the February 1975 meeting of the Fellowship of Christian Testimonies to the Jews, Pennsauken, New Jersey, in the Official Secretary's Book of the FCTJ, in the possession of the AMF-International, Lynwood, Illinois. This source, together with the entire collection of the FCTJ material, was later given to the Billy Graham Center in Wheaton, Illinois. I am thankful to the Reverends William Currie and Wes Taber for allowing me access to the material.

41. The Reverend William Currie, interview with author, Chicago, May 20, 1995; Dr. Louis Goldberg, interview with author, Chicago, May 21, 1995.

42. Cf. Rausch, *Messianic Judaism*, ix–xviii. See also *Orthodox Messianic Judaism*.

43. On similar fears among members of the older generation of Hebrew Christians, see Rausch, "Hebrew Christian Renaissance and Early Conflict with Messianic Judaism," 67–79.

44. See below in chapter 21.

45. Minutes of the Annual Meeting of the FCTJ, October 17, 1975.

46. Quoted in Sevener, *Rabbi's Vision*, 419.

47. I am indebted to Louis Goldberg, who, in a series of talks during the 1980s and 1990s, shared his experiences and insights with me.

48. The author viewed the April 1975 correspondence between Rosenthal and Goldberg when it was still in Goldberg's possession. It is now collected with Goldberg's personal papers at the Jews for Jesus archive, San Francisco.

49. Hutchens, "Case for Messianic Judaism," preface.

50. Marsden, *Reforming Fundamentalism*.

51. Willoughby, "Breakthrough for Messianic Judaism?," 16–19.

52. Plowman, "Turning On to Jeshua," 34–39; Henry, "Jews Find the Messiah," 28–29.

53. Rausch, *Messianic Judaism*.

54. Rausch, "Messianic Jewish Congregational Movement," 928–29.

55. See, for example, *Theology of the Churches and the Jewish People*.

56. Ariel, "Protestant Attitudes to Jews and Judaism during the Last Fifty Years," 334–39.

57. For example, Lacocque, "Key 73, Judaism, and the Tragedy of Triumphalism," 629–31.

58. Cf. Rausch, *Messianic Judaism*, 244–45.

59. In the mid-1990s, two organizations of Messianic Jewish congregations previously divided along charismatic/noncharismatic lines decided to unite, a major sign that the tensions between the two groups were easing and that the Messianic Jewish identity often takes precedence over the divisions between charismatics and noncharismatics.

60. See *Sheelot ve Teshuvot*, 17–18; "Frequently Asked Questions about Messianic Judaism," Covenant and Love Messianic Outreach. http://www.teshuvah.com/tomj/index.html; March 21, 1995.

61. On B'nai Noah, see Kaplan, *Radical Religion in America*, 100–126.

62. See, for example, Hutchens, "Case for Messianic Judaism."

63. On such groups, see, for example, Walsh, *Key to Charismatic Renewal in the Catholic Church*, or the Website http://www.cwo.com/pentrack/catholic/index.html.

64. *Insight* [an in-house journal of the American Board of Missions to the Jews] (June 1976): 3.

65. Goldberg, "Some of Their Best Friends Are Jews," 42–44.

66. Cf. Rambo, *Understanding Religious Conversion*, 108–13.

67. Sevener, *Rabbi's Vision*, 420–21, 453–56.

68. See "The American Board of Missions to the Jews Response to the Grace Community Church Position Paper entitled, 'The American Messianic Synagogue Movement: Deficiencies, Mistakes, and Errors in Light of the Scriptures.'" I am thankful to Dr. Louis Goldberg for providing me with a copy of the document.

69. Sevener, *Rabbi's Vision*, 453–54.

70. Ibid., 454–55.

71. I owe thanks to a number of friends who have invited me to visit their congregations in northern Chicago, among them Kroy Ellis, Rivka Katzir, and Derrel Simms.

72. Cf. Balmer, *Mine Eyes Have Seen the Glory*, 17.

73. See the congregation's brochure, "Olive Tree Congregation," copy in Yaakov Ariel's collection. Among other things, it states in an apologetic tone: "You will notice a genuine Jewish 'flavor' to our worship. . . . The Jewish roots of our faith in Messiah Jesus are important to us. . . . But you don't have to be Jewish to be here!" The brochure ends with a declaration of the community's obligation to evangelizing. "We are committed to sharing the Good News of the atonement Messiah Yeshua has provided, for the sin of all men. We want to communicate with both Jewish and Gentile people, whether it's across the street or around the world!"

74. Sevener, *Rabbi's Vision*, 454.

75. Cf. Harris-Shapiro, "Syncretism or Struggle," 141.

76. See "Elohai Notzeir," in *Congregation Tiferet Israel*, August 20, 1993, 2.

77. See, for example, Lipson, *Passover Haggadah*; Tavalin, *Kol Hesed Messianic Haggadah*; Sevener, *Passover Haggadah for Biblical Jews and Christians*.

78. Lipson, *Passover Haggadah*, 66.

79. Ibid., 23.

80. For example, Young, *Jesus and His Jewish Parables*.

81. See, for example, *One Hundred Years of Blessing*, 31.

82. Schiffman, *Return of the Remnant*.

83. Cf. ibid., 126, and Goldstein, "Profile of American Jewry," 124–28.

84. On non-Jews versus Jews in Messianic congregations, see Feher, *Passing over Easter*.

85. Cf. Kohn, "Dual Membership and Sectarian Status," 159.

86. Cf. Rausch, *Messianic Judaism*, 167.

87. For example, ibid., 145–62.

88. Fruchtenbaum, *Hebrew Christianity*.

89. Ibid., 98.

90. "An Interchange on Hebrew Christian/Messianic Jewish Congregation," app. 3, in Fruchtenbaum, *Israelology*, 917–49.

91. Stern, *Messianic Jewish Manifesto*.

92. Ibid., 12.

93. Juster, *Jewish Roots*, 111.

94. Ibid., vii.

95. Fischer and Bronstein, *Siddur for Messianic Jews*.

96. Fischer, "Development of a Professional Competencies Program."

97. Another guide for prospective evangelists promoting a Messianic Jewish language is Rubin, *You Bring the Bagels, I'll Bring the Gospel*.

98. Stern, *Messianic Jewish Manifesto*, 4.

CHAPTER TWENTY-ONE

1. See, for example, Sarna, "American Jewish Response to Nineteenth-Century Christian Missions," 35–51.

2. Cf. Herberg, *Protestant, Catholic, Jew*.

3. A number of those declarations were reprinted in *Theology of the Churches and the Jewish People*.

4. See Ariel, "In the Shadow of the Millennium," 435–50.

5. Ibid.

6. For example, Goldberg, *Our Jewish Friends*; Fruchtenbaum, *Jesus Was a Jew*; Fischer, *Olive Tree Connection*.

7. Cf. Rausch, *Communities in Conflict: Evangelicals and Jews*, 6, 84–85.

8. For example, Eichhorn, *Evangelizing the American Jew*.

9. "Jews for Jesus Is New Freak Group."

10. In March 1972, the Northern California Board of Rabbis issued a statement warning against this practice. Cf. Rausch, *Communities in Conflict*, 126.

11. Mach, "Their Mission," 45.

12. For example, in articles collected by Eisenberg, *Smashing the Idols*; Kelly, *Cults and the Jewish Community*.

13. Gittelsohn, "Jews for Jesus," reprinted in Eisenberg, *Smashing the Idols*, 171.

14. Ibid., 172.

15. Cox, "Deep Structures in the Study of New Religions," 122–30.

16. Cf. Rudin, "Cults and Missionaries." Rudin's article reads as if it were written to demonstrate Cox's paradigm.

17. Cf. Wiesel, *All Rivers Run to the Sea*, 238–42.

18. Wiesel, "Missionary Menace," reprinted in Eisenberg, *Smashing the Idols*, 162.

19. Daum, "You Are the Target," 5.

20. Kanter, "They're Playing Our Song," reprinted in Eisenberg, *Smashing the Idols*, 174–85.

21. Fisch, *Jews for Nothing*, 28–29.

22. Resolution adopted at the General Assembly of the Union of American Hebrew Congregations, November 1977.

23. Eisenberg, *Smashing the Idols*, xv.

24. Schwartz, "Cults and the Vulnerability of Jewish Youth," reprinted in Eisenberg, *Smashing the Idols*, 4.

25. Fisch, *Jews for Nothing*, 12–13.

26. "Chabad Encounters Witnesses," 1, 3.

27. Lieff, "Emes Leader Keeps Promise at Grand Central," 2. See also a leaflet distributed by Emes. All copies of the leaflets and brochures cited here and in the following notes are in Yaakov Ariel's collection.

28. Beth Shifra Institution, leaflet.

29. See Yad L'Achim Wall Calendar, distributed to Orthodox synagogues worldwide, copy in Yaakov Ariel's collection.

30. The information on Golding is taken from his own brochures and leaflets. See, for example, the leaflet "About the Institute."

31. "Anti-Semitism in the New Testament," 12.

32. See the leaflet "$10,000 Reward." The leaflet invites the reader to contact, for further information, Shmuel Golding at P.O. Box 13099, Jerusalem; copy in Yaakov Ariel's collection.

33. Golding, *Guide to the Misled*.

34. Menahem Benhayim, former head of the Messianic Jewish Alliance, interview with author, Israel, September 1993.

35. Freed, "Torah Dispute."

36. See "Beth Yeshua's Bid Meets Resistance," 1; "Messianic Jews Zoning Opposed in Merion," 18A; "Messianic Jews Fight for a Home"; Loyd, "Love Thy Neighbor?," 1B–2B. I am indebted to Johanna Chernoff for providing me with copies of the articles, as well as with other sources on this topic.

37. See J. E. Rahming, Postal Inspector, Philadelphia Division, to Richard Wiedus, Office Manager, Messianic Ministries, Inc., July 12, 1979, copy in the possession of Yaakov Ariel.

38. Copy in the possession of Yaakov Ariel.

39. For example, Rausch, *Messianic Judaism*, 202, 208, 233.

40. Bonnie Fechter, Executive Director, Jewish Defense League, Pennsylvania and South Jersey, in a letter of March 1, 1976, copy in Yaakov Ariel's collection. See also a letter of February 1979, thanking Johanna Chernoff for her contribution to the Jewish Defense League.

41. See a copy of a leaflet of December 1979, in Yaakov Ariel's collection.

42. Rosen and Proctor, *Jews for Jesus*, 56.

43. Ibid., 1–2.

44. Sevener, "From the President," 2.

45. "Profile of an Anti Missionary," 5.

46. See Malamed, "How to Answer Street Missionaries," 49–51.

47. Ibid., 49.

48. On the complex aspects of the conversion process, in which theological arguments play a very small part, see Rambo, *Understanding Religious Conversion*.

49. Goldberg, *Jewish Christian Response*.

50. Kaplan, *Real Messiah?*, 2.

51. Siegel, "How Local Jewish Groups Respond to Threat," 47.

52. "Report of Activities, 1987."

53. A letter sent by the Task Force on Missionaries and Cults, December 16, 1987, copy in Yaakov Ariel's collection.

54. See Leavey, "Why I Embraced Then Rejected Messianic Judaism."

55. Rottenberg, "Should There Be a Christian Witness to the Jews?," 352–56.

56. Littell, "Why a Christian Authority Opposes Misisonaries," 17; Lacoque, "Key 73, Judaism, and the Tragedy of Triumphalism," 629–31; Rylaarsdam, "Mission to Christians," 17–18; Stendahl, "Limits of Christian Mission," 19.

57. For example, Henry, "Christian Missions Must Continue," 16.

58. Cf. Ariel, "American Fundamentalists and the Emergence of a Jewish State," 303–9.

59. Cf. Ariel, "Christian Fundamentalist's Vision of the Middle East," 363–97.

60. On Key 73 and the Jewish reaction to it, see Rausch, *Communities in Conflict*, 111–21.

61. Graham, "Billy Graham on Key 73," 625.

62. Eckstein, *What Christians Should Know about Jews and Judaism*, 299.

63. Even articles dealing with Christian fundamentalism ignored the missionary aspect. See, for example, Neuhaus, "What the Fundamentalists Want," 41–46.

64. Eichhorn, *Evangelizing the American Jew.*

65. Ibid., 185–95.

66. Sobel, *Hebrew Christianity.*

67. Goldscheider and Zuckerman, *Transformation of the Jews*, 185.

68. Fein, *Where Are We?*; Herzberg, "End of American Jewish History."

69. Cf. Goldstein, "Profile of American Jewry," 77–143.

70. Edelstein, "Jews Who Chose Jesus," 30–39; Beiser, "For the Love of Jesus," 26–31.

CHAPTER TWENTY-TWO

1. "Communications Card"; Bratman, *Training Manual On How to Share the Messiah.*

2. Cf. Masuzawa, "Culture," 70–93.

3. See Kohn, *I Have Fought a Good Fight!.*

4. Cf., for example, Davis, *Road to Carmel.*

5. Beit-Hallahmi, *Despair and Deliverance.*

6. Lindsey, *Christian Terms in Hebrew.*

7. For example, *One Hundred Years of Blessing*, 30.

8. Cf. Beit-Hallahmi, *Despair and Deliverance.*

9. Kjaer-Hansen, "Jerusalem March and the Name of Jesus," 3–4.

10. Cf. *The Dahaf Report on Israeli Public Opinion Concerning Messianic Jewish Aliyah*, translated into English by Amikam Tavor; comments by David H. Stern (Jerusalem: David H. Stern, 1988).

11. See the autobiographies of Israeli converts to Christianity: Zeidan, *Messiah Now*; Hoekendyk, *Twelve Jews Discover Messiah*; Damkani, *Why Me?.*

12. Cf. also Viswanathan, *Outside the Fold.*

13. On Jewish Orthodox attitudes toward Messianic Jews, see chapter 21. On Messianic Jewish attitudes toward Orthodox Judaism, see, for example, "Habad Movement as a Mission Movement," 4–6; "Boom in Jewish Conversions in Israel," 3.

14. Cf. Smith, *American Evangelicalism.*

15. Cf. Stern, *Messianic Jewish Manifesto*, 220–21.

16. Benhayim, "Messianic Movement in Israel—A Personal Perspective," 4–34.

17. Ibid., 30.

18. See, for example, audiotape of a 1980 radio program "The Promise of Tomorrow," produced by the American Board of Missions to the Jews, Accession #82–97, Billy Graham Center.

19. See, for example, the brochure "See Israel through Jewish Eyes, conducted by Harold and Grace Sevener," Chosen People Ministries, November 1991, copy in Yaakov Ariel's collection.

20. Cf. Ariel, "Christian Fundamentalist Vision of the Middle East," 363–97.

21. *Mishkan* 12 (January 1990); the volume was dedicated to condemning the ICEJ.

22. Cf. Osterley, *Church in Israel*.

23. Cf. Benhayim, "The Messianic Movement in Israel—A Personal Perspective," 24.

24. Ben-Simon, "Doing Something for Judaism," 1–2.

25. It takes three rounds of voting to pass a law in the Israeli parliament.

26. See, for example, e-mails sent by 100320-1324@compuserve.com and a Website: http://www.dlorio.com/Jerusalem-gate/news.htm. Also, see a letter circulated through the Internet by Noam Hendren, Baruch Maoz, and Marvin Kramer of March 1997.

27. In the letter circulated by Hendren, Maoz, and Kramer.

28. Cf. such letters at http://sites.goshen.net/messiah/congregational.html.

29. Kai Kjaer-Hansen, "Editorial," *Mishkan* 28 (1998): 1.

30. Ariel, "Christian Fundamentalist Vision of the Middle East," 389–90.

31. Cf. William Packard, *Evangelism in America: From Tents to T.V.* (New York: Paragon House, 1988).

32. Cf. Ammerman, "Fundamentalists Proselytizing Jews."

33. Cf. Damkani, *Why Me?*.

34. Kjaer-Hansen, "Evangelization on the Sea Front," 8–9; Damkani, *Why Me?*, see especially the photographs between pp. 51 and 53. Concerning El-Al flights, see, for example, "Kol Simcha Sound of Joy: Israel Tour, First Time in the Land," videotape (Joshua's Movies Production, 1991).

35. "Open to the Message," 30.

36. Cf. Davidman, *Tradition in a Rootless World*.

37. Burkett, *Right Women*. Cf. also Griffith, *God's Daughters*.

38. Cf. Bendroth, *Fundamentalism and Gender*.

39. Beaver, *American Protestant Women in World Missions*.

40. Cf. Synan, *Holiness Pentecostal Movement in the United States*.

41. Levitt, *Corned Beef, Knishes, and Christ*, 135; Levitt, *Zola's Millennial Catalog*.

42. On the history, nature, and scope of the Lausanne Consultation on Jewish Evangelism, see "The Lausanne Covenant," 570–76; *Thailand Report on the Jewish People*; *Lausanne Consultation on Jewish Evangelism: International Networking Directory 1992*. On the Lausanne Congresses, see Yates, *Christian Mission in the Twentieth Century*.

43. Cf. *LCJE Bulletin* 29 (August 1992). The issue was dedicated to articles on Japanese activity.

Bibliography

PRIMARY SOURCES

Archival Material

Sources used for this work are located at the following archives:

The American Jewish Archives, Cincinnati, Ohio
AMF-International, Lansing, Illinois
Archives of the Southern Baptist Convention, Richmond, Virginia
The Billy Graham Center, Wheaton, Illinois
Central Zionist Archives, Jerusalem
The Chosen People Ministries, Charlotte, North Carolina
Israel State Archives, Jerusalem
Jews for Jesus, San Francisco
Minnesota Historical Society, Minneapolis, Minnesota
The Moody Bible Institute, Chicago
Presbyterian Historical Society, Philadelphia
Union Theological Seminary, New York

Periodicals

Al Hamishmar
A.M.F. Monthly
American Hebrew
American Hebrew Christian
American Israelite
Bible News Flashes
Biblical Polemics
Central Conference of American Rabbis Year
    Book
Century Magazine
Chabad Times
Chosen People
Christian Century
Christianity Today
Christian Workers Magazine
Cincinnati Enquirer
Commentary
Davar
Emanu-EL
Face to Face: An Interreligious Bulletin
Glory of Israel

Good News
Haaretz
Haboker
Hatsophe
Hayahad
Hebrew Christian
Hebrew Christian Alliance Quarterly
Holy Beggar's Gazette
Home Missions
Immanuel's Witness
Insight
International Review of Missions
Israelite
Jerusalem in Perspective
Jerusalem Report
Jewish Era
Jewish Exponent
Jewish Hope
Jewish Mission Magazine
Jewish Post and Opinion
Jewish Press

Jewish Week
Journal of the General Convention of the
Protestant Episcopal Church in the
United States of America
Keeping Posted
Kol Hair
Lausanne Consultation on Jewish
Evangelism
LCJE Bulletin
Maariv
Main Line Times
Menorah
Messianic Outreach
Messianic Resource Catalog
Mishkan
Missionary Review of the World
Moment

Moody Bible Institute Bulletin
Moody Bible Institute Monthly
New York Review of Books
New York Times
Norman Oklahoma Transcript
Our Hope
Our Jewish Neighbors
The People, the Land and the Book
Prayer and Work for Israel
Salvation
Scattered Nation
Shepherd of Israel
Truth
A Voice in Jerusalem
Watchman Examiner
Kol Yavneh

Books and Articles

Alinsky, Saul. *Rules for Radicals: A Practical Primer for Realistic Radicals*. New York: Random House, 1971.

Angel, Bernhard. "The Day of Atonement." *Jewish Era* 2 (1893): 225–28.

———. "Mistakes." *Hebrew Christian* 9 (March 1894): 2–3.

———. "Report of Work during 1891." *Jewish Era* 2 (1892): 19.

"Anti-Semitism in the New Testament." *Biblical Polemics* 1 (May 1988): 12.

Appelman, Hyman J. "A Suffering People." In *Israel's Restoration*, edited by John W. Bradbury. New York: Iversen-Ford, n.d. [c. 1952].

Avodat Y'Shua. San Francisco: Purple Pomegranate Productions, 1991.

Bacon, Alexander S. *The Strange Story of Dr. Cohn and Mr. Joszovics*. New York: by the author, 1918.

Baker, Dwight L. "Baptists' Golden Jubilee: Fifty Years in Palestine-Israel." Typed manuscript in the archives of the Southern Baptist Convention, Richmond, Virginia.

"Baptist Cites Israeli Discord." *Norman Oklahoma Transcript*, June 24, 1960.

Baron, David. "Messianic Judaism or Judaising Christianity." *Scattered Nation* (October 1911). Reprinted as a booklet, Chicago: American Messianic Fellowship, 1974.

Beiser, Vince. "For the Love of Jesus." *Jerusalem Report*, January 26, 1995, 26–31.

Ben Ari, Gideon. "The Baptists Believe in Freedom of Religion." *Maariv*, September 21, 1961.

Benedict, George. *Christ Finds a Rabbi*. Philadelphia: Bethlehem Presbyterian Church, 1932.

Benhayim, Menahem. "The Messianic Movement in Israel—A Personal Perspective." *Mishkan* 28 (1998): 14–34.

Ben-Simon, Daniel. "Doing Something for Judaism." *Ha'aretz*, December 18, 1997, English ed., 1–2.

Bernstein, A. *Some Jewish Witnesses for Christ*. London: Operative Jewish Christian Institution, 1909.

Bernstein, Elias. *The Ways of God: Some Recollection of the Life of Elias Bernstein*. Los
    Angeles: Bible Institute of Los Angeles, 1927.

"Beth Yeshua's Bid Meets Resistance." *Main Line Times*, October 25, 1979, 1.

Birnbaum, Solomon. "Preaching to Jews at Atlantic City." *Moody Bible Institute Monthly* 30
    (1929–30): 199.

Black, James. "The Jews and the Gentile: A Story of Despair and Hope." In *The Christian
    Approach to the Jews Being a Report of Conferences on the Subject Held at Budapest and
    Warsaw in April 1927*. London: Edinburgh House Press, 1927.

Blackstone, William E. *The Heart of the Jewish Problem*. Chicago: Chicago Hebrew
    Mission, 1905.

——. "Jerusalem." *Jewish Era* 1 (1892): 67–71.

——. *Jesus Is Coming*. [1878]. 3d ed. Los Angeles: Bible House, 1908.

——. "Letter." *Jewish Era* 24 (1915): 75.

——. *The Millennium*. Chicago: Fleming H. Revell, 1904.

"Boom in Jewish Conversions in Israel." *LCJE Bulletin* 26 (November 1991): 3.

Bradbury, John W., ed. *Light for the World's Darkness*. New York: Loizeaux Brothers, 1944.

——. "The New State of Israel: An Historical Miracle." In *Israel's Restoration*. New York:
    Iversen-Ford Associates, n.d.

——, ed. *Israel's Restoration*. New York: Iversen-Ford Associates, n.d.

Bronstein, David. *The Jewish Passover and the Christian Communion*. Chicago: by the
    author, 1941.

——. *Peniel Portrait*. Chicago: D. Cameron Peck, 1943.

Bronstein, Esther. *Esther*. Edited by Janet Thoma. Elgin, Ill.: David C. Cook, 1982.

Brookes, James H. *Maranatha, or the Lord Cometh*. St. Louis: Edward Bredell, 1874.

——. "Work among the Jews." *Truth* 20 (1894): 15–16.

Brooks, Keith L. *Lies Have Wings: "Cohn Uncovered" or Riley Unmasked—Which?*
    Brooklyn: American Board of Missions to the Jews, n.d.

Brotman, Manny. *A Training Manual on How to Share the Messiah*. Bethesda, Md.:
    Messianic Jewish Movement International, 1977.

"Builders of Israel or Anti missionaries." *Prayer and Work for Israel* 7 (1916): 7–10.

Burrell, David J. "Signs of the Times." In *Christ and Glory, Addresses Delivered at the New
    York Prophetic Conference Carnegie Hall*, edited by Arno C. Gaebelein. New York:
    Publication Office Our Hope, n.d.

Cahan, Abraham. "The Apostate of Chego-Chegg." *Century Magazine* 59 (1899): 94–105.

——. *The Imported Bridegroom and Other Stories of the New York Ghetto*. Mineola, N.Y.:
    Dover Publications, 1970.

Carlebach, Shlomo, and Susan Yael Mesinai. *Shlomo's Stories*. Northvale, N.J.: Jason
    Aaronson, 1994.

Cast, David T. "The Story of the Conversion of a Young Jewess." *Jewish Era* 46 (1936): 71.

Catalog of Moody Bible Institute. 1948–49.

"Chabad Encounters Witnesses." *Chabad Times* (August 1979): 1, 3.

Chafer, Lewis S. "The Coming Destruction of Ecclesiastical and Political Babylon." In *Light
    for the World's Darkness*, edited by John W. Bradbury. New York: Loizeaux Brothers,
    1944.

——. "An Introduction to Eschatology." In *Israel's Restoration*, edited by John W. Bradbury.
    New York: Iversen-Ford Associates, n.d.

Chalmers, M. "The Blood Accusation." *Prayer and Work for Israel* 10 (1919): 57–59.

The Christian Approach to the Jews Being a Report of Conferences on the Subject Held at Budapest and Warsaw in April 1927. London: Edinburgh House Press, 1927.

Christians and Jews: Report of the Atlantic City Conference on the Christian Approach to the Jews. Atlantic Jews, Atlantic City, New Jersey, May 12–15, 1931. New York: International Missionary Council, 1931.

Cohen, Abe, Rachel, Sarah, and Esther. "More Jewish Than Ever—We've Found the Messiah." *Christianity Today*, February 1, 1974, 11–17.

Cohen, Rose. *Out of the Shadow*. Ithaca, N.Y.: Cornell University Press, 1995.

Cohn, Esther. "Talks with Girls and Boys." *Chosen People* 12 (May 1907): 5–6.

Cohn, Joseph H. *I Have Fought a Good Fight*. New York: American Board of Missions to the Jews, 1957.

——. *I Have Loved Jacob*. Orangeburg, N.Y.: American Board of Missions to the Jews, 1948.

——. "Russian Envoy Comes to Israel," *Shepherd of Israel* 30 (January 1949): 1–4.

——. *A Tomorrow for the Jews: Must We Leave the Jews Alone in This Age?* New York: American Board of Missions to the Jews, n.d.

——. *Will They Psychoanalyze God?* New York: American Board of Missions to the Jews, n.d.

Cohn, Leopold. "Announcement." *Chosen People* 2 (November 1896): 7.

——. *Behold the Virgin*. Brooklyn, N.Y.: Brooklyn Mission, 1908.

——. *Behold the Virgin Shall Conceive and Bear a Son*. Brooklyn, N.Y.: American Board of Missions to the Jews, n.d.

——. "A Believer's Meeting." *Chosen People* 6 (February 1900): 4.

——. *The Broken Matzo*. Brooklyn, N.Y.: Brooklyn Mission, 1908.

——. *The Chosen People Question Box*. New York: American Board of Missions to the Jews, 1938.

——. "The Christian Duty to the Jews." *Chosen People* 1 (February 1896): 4–5.

——. "Daughters of Zion Class," *Jewish Era* 12 (1903): 32.

——. "Editorial." *Chosen People* 22 (January 1917): 3–4.

——. "Gathering of Christian Jews." *Chosen People* 4 (February 1899): 3.

——. *Jewish Holidays and Their Significance*. Brooklyn, N.Y.: American Board of Missions to the Jews, n.d.

——. "Mr. Needleman." *Chosen People* 10 (April 1905): 7.

——. *A Modern Missionary to an Ancient People*. Brooklyn, N.Y.: Brooklyn Mission, 1908.

——. "The Possibilities." *Chosen People* 10 (November 1904): 1.

——. "Questions and Answers." *Chosen People* 28 (March 1923): 15.

——. "Reasons for the Immediate Evangelization of the Jews." *Chosen People* 4 (April 1899): 7.

——. "Salutation." *Chosen People* 6 (February 1900): 1.

——. "Salutation." *Chosen People* 22 (March 1917): 4–5.

——. *To Both Houses of Israel*. Brooklyn, N.Y.: Beth Sar Shalom, n.d.

——. *What Is His Son's Name?*. Brooklyn, N.Y.: American Board of Mission to the Jews, n.d.

Communications Card. Washington D.C.: Messianic Jewish Movement International, 1973.

Conning, John S. *The Jew at the Church Door*. New York: Board of National Missions, 1938.

——. *Our Jewish Neighbors: An Essay in Understanding*. New York: Fleming H. Revell, 1927.

Cooper, David L. *Why Evangelize Israel in This Generation and How*. New York: Biblical Research Society, 1887.

Croner, Helga, ed. *Stepping Stones to Further Jewish-Christian Relations*. London: Stimulus Book, 1977.

Damkani, Yaakov. *Why Me?* (in Hebrew). Tel Aviv: Kochav Hayom, 1993.

Das Neu Testament. Chicago: Distribution Fund, n.d.

Daum, Annette. "You Are the Target." *Keeping Posted* 32 (February 1987): 5.

Davis, David. *The Road to Carmel: A Couple's Dramatic Journey from Broadway to Mount Carmel*. Haifa: House of Victory, 1997.

Davis, George T. B. *God's Guiding Hand*. Philadelphia: Million Testaments Campaigns, 1962.

———. *Sowing God's Word in Israel Today*. Philadelphia: Million Testaments Campaigns, 1953.

DeHaan, M. R. *The Jew and Palestine in Prophecy*. Grand Rapids, Mich.: Zondervan, 1950.

Denman, F. L. "The Second Coming of Our Lord and Its Relation to the Jews." *Jewish Era* 21 (1912): 1–6.

Dennis, James S., Harlan P. Beach, and Charles H. Fahs, eds. *World Atlas of Christian Missions*. New York: Student Voluntary Movement for Foreign Missions, 1911.

Deutsch, Gerhard. "Has Reform Judaism Stimulated Apostasy." *American Hebrew* 95 (July 17, 1914): 307.

"Do Messianic Jews Proselytize?" *IRC Report* 4 (Winter 1993): 68–69.

Douglas, C. G. *Herman Warszawiak "The Little Messianic Prophet," or Two Years Labour among the Refugee Jews of New York*. Edinburgh: Andrew Elliott, 1892.

"Dr. Max I. Reich, Moody Bible Institute Teacher, Wrote Religious Books." *New York Times*, August 12, 1945.

"Dr. Max Isaac Reich." *Chicago Sun*, August 13, 1945.

Dushaw, Amos I. "Hebrew Christian Literature." *The People, the Land and the Book* 5 (January 1905): 34–35.

———. *Proselytes of the Ghetto*. New Brunswick, N.J.: J. Heidingsfeld, 1909.

———. *The Rivals: A Tragedy of the New York Ghetto*. London: Arthur H. Stockwell, n.d.

———. *When Mr. Thompson Got to Heaven*. New York: by the author, 1932.

Dushkin, Alexander M. *Jewish Education in New York City*. New York: Bureau of Jewish Education, 1918.

Eckardt, Roy A. *Elder and Younger Brother: The Encounter of Jews and Christians*. New York: Scribner's, 1967.

Eckstein, Yechiel. *What Christians Should Know about Jews and Judaism*. Waco, Tex.: Word Books, 1984.

Edelstein, Alan. "Jews Who Chose Jesus." *Moment* 19 (August 1994): 30–39.

"Editorial." *Ha Boker*, May 4, 1962.

Eerdman, William J. "The Structure and Book of Isaiah and Part II. 40–66: A Prediction of Jewish History during the Times of the Gentiles." In *Addresses of the International Prophetic Conference Held December 10–15, 1901, in the Clarendon Street Baptist Church, Boston, Mass*, edited by William J. Eerdman. Boston: Watchword and Truth, n.d.

Einspruch, Henry. "Christ, Christians, and the Jews." *Missionary Review of the World* 56 (March 1933): 151–52.

———. "Literature for the Christian Approach to the Jews." In *Christians and Jews: Report of the Atlantic City Conference on the Christian Approach to the Jews, Atlantic City, New Jersey, May 12–15, 1931*. New York: International Missionary Council, 1931.

———. *The Man with the Book*. Baltimore: Lederer Foundation, 1976.

——. *Raisins and Almonds*. Baltimore: Lederer Foundation, 1965.

——. *When Jews Face Christ*. Brooklyn: American Board of Missions to the Jews, 1939.

Eisenberg, Gary D., ed. *Smashing the Idols: A Jewish Inquiry into the Cult Phenomenon*. Northvale, N.J.: Jason Aronson, 1988.

Ellinger, M. "Editorial." *Menorah* 14 (May 1893): 320–23.

Ellison, H. L. "Christian Missions and Israel." *Hebrew Christian* 26 (Spring 1953): 26.

Fein, Leonard. *Where Are We?: The Inner Life of America's Jews*. New York: Harper and Row, 1988.

Feinberg, Charles L. *Prophecy and the Seventies*. Chicago: Moody Press, 1971.

——, ed. *Prophetic Truth Unfolding Today*. New York: Fleming H. Revell, 1968.

Felsenthal, Bernhard. *Why Do the Jews Not Accept Jesus as Their Messiah?* Chicago: Bloch and Newman, 1893.

Fiftieth Anniversary Temple Emmanu El of Lynbrook. N.p., n.d.

"The First Annual Report." *Jewish Era* 1 (1889): 7.

Fisch, Dov Aharoni. *Jews for Nothing: On Cults, Intermarriage, and Assimilation*. New York: Feldheim Publishers, 1984.

Fischer, John. "The Development of a Professional Competencies Program as a First Stage in a Yeshiva Curriculum for Training Messianic Jewish Leaders." Ph.D. diss., University of South Florida, 1987.

——. *The Olive Tree Connection: Sharing Messiah with Israel*. Palm Harbor, Fla.: Menorah Ministries, 1983.

Fischer, John, and David Bronstein. *Siddur for Messianic Jews*. Palm Harbor, Fla.: Menorah Ministries, 1988.

The Four-Fold Gospel. New York: Christian Alliance Publication, 1925.

Freed, Kenneth. "Torah Dispute." *Los Angeles Times*, March 1, 1980.

Freuder, Samuel. *My Return to Judaism*. New York: Bloch Publishing Co., 1924.

Fruchtenbaum, Arnold G. *Hebrew Christianity: Its Theology, History, and Philosophy*. Grand Rapids, Mich.: Baker Book House, 1974.

——. *Israelology: The Missing Link in Systematic Theology*. Tustin, Calif.: Ariel Ministries, 1983.

——. *Jesus Was a Jew*. Tustin, Calif.: Ariel Ministries, 1981.

Fuchs, Daniel. *How to Reach the Jew for Christ*. Grand Rapids, Mich.: Zondervan, 1943.

——. *Is Sputnik Another Tower of Babel?* New York: American Board of Missions to the Jews, n.d.

The Fundamentals: A Testimony to the Truth. 12 vols. Chicago: Testimony Publishing Co., 1910–15.

Gaebelein, Arno C. "Aspects of Jewish Power in the United States." *Our Hope* 29 (1922): 103.

——. "The Capture of Jerusalem and the Glorius Future of That City," In *Christ and Glory, Addresses Delivered at the New York Prophetic Conference Carnegie Hall*, edited by Arno C. Gaebelein. New York: Publication Office Our Hope, n.d.

——. *The Conflict of the Ages*. New York: Our Hope, 1933.

——. *Half a Century: The Autobiography of a Servant*. New York: Our Hope, 1930.

——. *Hath God Cast Away His People?* New York: Gospel Publishing House, 1905.

——. "Herman Warszawiak's Method of Getting Crowds to Hear the Gospel." *Our Hope* 2 (1895): 2–5.

——. "How the Hope of Israel Became Undenominational." *Our Hope* 4 (1897): 3–5.

——. *The Jewish Question*. New York: Gospel Publishing House, 1905; New York: Our Hope, 1912.

——. *The Messiah and His People Israel*. New York: Hope of Israel, 1898.

——. "The Same Old Accusation." *Our Hope* 30 (1924): 556.

——. "A Short Review of Our Mission and the Principles of the Hope of Israel Movement." *Our Hope* 6 (1899): 68–71.

——, ed. *Christ and Glory, Addresses Delivered at the New York Prophetic Conference Carnegie Hall*. New York: Publication Office Our Hope, n.d.

Gartenhaus, Jacob. *How to Win the Jews*. Atlanta: Baptist Home Mission Board, n.d.

——. *Unto His Own*. London: International Board of Jewish Missions, 1965.

——. *Winning Jews to Christ*. Grand Rapids, Mich.: Zondervan, 1963.

Gidney, W. T. *The History of the London Society for Promoting Christianity amongst the Jews from 1809 to 1908*. London: London Society for Promoting Christianity amongst the Jews, 1908.

Gittelsohn, Ronald B. "Jews for Jesus: Are They Real?" In *Smashing the Idols: A Jewish Inquiry into the Cult Phenomenon*, edited by Gary Eisenberg. Northvale, N.J.: Jason Aronson, 1988.

Goldberg, Jeffrey. "Some of Their Best Friends Are Jews." *New York Times Magazine*, March 16, 1997, 42–44.

Goldberg, Louis. *A Jewish Christian Response*. San Francisco: Jews for Jesus, 1986.

——. "The Messianic Jew." *Christianity Today*, February 1, 1974, 6–11.

——. *Our Jewish Friends*. Neptune, N.J.: Loizeaux Brothers, 1977.

——. *Turbulence over the Middle East*. Neptune, N.J.: Loizeaux Brothers, 1982.

Golding, Shmuel. "Anti-Semitism in the New Testament." *Biblical Polemics* 1 (May 1988): 12.

——. *A Guide to the Misled*. Jerusalem: Jerusalem Institute of Biblical Polemics, 1983.

Goldstein, John L. *All the Doors Were Opened*. London: Mildmay Mission to the Jews, 1950.

Gordon, Arthur H. "The House of the Prince of Peace." *Watchman Examiner*, February 10, 1927, 184.

——. "Machlins Will Celebrate Two Anniversaries." *Buffalo Post*, September 2, 1935.

Gordon, Mary. *The Shadow Man: A Daughter's Search for Her Father*. New York: Random House, 1996.

Graham, Billy. "Billy Graham on Key 73." *Christianity Today*, March 16, 1973, 625.

——. *World Aflame*. Garden City, N.Y.: Doubleday and Co., 1965.

Gray, James M. *Great Epochs of Sacred History*. New York: Fleming H. Revell, 1910.

——. *A Textbook on Prophecy*. New York: Fleming H. Revell, 1918.

"The Habad Movement as a Mission Movement." *LCJE Bulletin* 29 (August 1992): 4–6.

Hanson, C. M. *These Also I Must Bring*. Minneapolis: Augsburg Publishing House, 1964.

"Happenings in Israel." *Hebrew Christian Alliance Quarterly* 34 (Summer 1948): 28–31.

Hart, Lewis A. *A Jewish Reply to Christian Evangelists*. New York: Bloch and Publishing Co., 1906.

Hellyer, H. L. *From the Rabbis to Christ, or In Quest of the Truth*. Philadelphia: Westminster Press, 1911.

Henry, Carl F. H. "Christian Missions Must Continue." *Face to Face: An Interreligious Bulletin* 3–4 (Fall/Winter 1977): 16.

——. "The Christian Witness in Israel." Pt. 1, *Christianity Today*, July 31, 1961, 22–23.

——. "The Christian Witness in Israel." Pt. 2, *Christianity Today*, August 28, 1961, 17–21.

——. *Confessions of a Theologian*. Waco, Tex.: Word Books, 1986.

——. "Jews Find the Messiah." *Christianity Today*, April 13, 1973, 28–29.

Here Is the Story behind All These Smiling Faces. New York: Beth Sar Shalom Fellowship, n.d.

Herzberg, Arthur. "End of American Jewish History." *New York Review of Books* 36 (November 23, 1989): 26–30.

Heydt, Henry J. *The Chosen People Question Box II*. Englewood Cliffs, N.J.: American Board of Missions to the Jews, 1976.

——. *Studies in Jewish Evangelism*. New York: American Board of Missions to the Jews, 1951.

Hinz, O. F. "Some Discouragements in Jewish Mission Work." *Prayer and Work for Israel* 9 (1918): 183–84.

Hoekendyk, Ben. *Twelve Jews Discover Messiah: A Fascinating Insight into What God Is Doing in Israel Today*. Eastbourne, England: Kingsway Publications, 1992.

Hoffman, Conrad. "Jewry in Distress! What of It?" *Missionary Review of the World* 61 (June 1938): 261–62.

——. *To Be a Non-Aryan in Germany*. New York: Department of Jewish Evangelization of the Presbyterian Church in the USA, 1939.

Holmes, John Haynes. *Judaism and Christianity*. New York: Community Pulpit, 1928.

"The Home Going of Max Reich." *Jewish Mission Magazine* (September 1945).

Hopkins, Oz. "Jews for Jesus Give Mission 'Bad Name.' " *Oregon Journal*, July 27, 1973, 2.

Huisjen, Albert. *The Home Front of Jewish Missions*. Grand Rapids, Mich.: Baker Book House, 1962.

——. *Talking about Jesus to a Jewish Neighbor*. Grand Rapids, Mich.: Baker Book House, 1964.

Hull, William L. *The Fall and Rise of Israel*. Grand Rapids, Mich.: Zondervan, 1954.

——. "Letter from Zion Apostolic Mission to UNSCOP." *Pentecost in Jerusalem* 13 (July 1947): 71.

——. *A Struggle for a Soul*. New York: Doubleday, 1963.

"Hyman Appelman Comes to Town." *Bible News Flashes* 5 (August 1944): 8.

Ianniello, Lynne. "Release for the Press." Anti-Defamation League, New York, January 8, 1986.

Ilan, Shachar. "Megaresh Hashedim Holech Habayta" [The exorcist goes home]. *Kol Hair*, January 9, 1987, 25–27.

Ironside, Harry A. "Fulfilled Prophecy Concerning the Jew." In *Israel's Restoration*, edited by John W. Bradbury. New York: Iverson-Ford, n.d.

"Israel's Tenth Anniversary." *American Hebrew Christian* 44 (Summer 1958): 17–21.

Jacobs, Hyman. *Nationalism and Religion*. Jerusalem: privately published, 1927.

"Jesus Saves." *Jewish Era* (April 15, 1908): 77–78.

"Jewish Bill against Missionaries." *American Hebrew* 89 (May 19, 1911): 87.

"Jewish Ordinances." *Hebrew Christian Alliance Quarterly* 2 (1917): 23–36.

"Jewish Palestine Still Developing." *Hebrew Christian Alliance Quarterly* 19 (April 1934): 5.

"Jews for Jesus Answers." *New York Times*, Sunday, June 27, 1976.

"Jews for Jesus Is New Freak Group." *Jewish Post and Opinion*, May 14, 1971.

"Jews Mob a Mission." *American Hebrew* 89 (September 1911): 531.

"Jews Warned against Missionaries." *American Hebrew* 92, no. 6 (December 6, 1912): 182.

Juster, Daniel. *Jewish Roots: A Foundation of Biblical Theology for Messianic Judaism*. Rockville, MD.: Davar Publishing, 1986.

Kanter, Shamai. "They're Playing Our Song." In *Smashing the Idols: A Jewish Inquiry into the Cult Phenomenon*, edited by Gary Eisenberg. Northvale, N.J.: Jason Aronson, 1988.

Kaplan, Aryeh. *The Real Messiah?: A Jewish Response to Missionaries*. New York: National Conference of Synagogue Youth, 1976.

Kaufman, Ben. "Jews for Jesus." *Cincinnati Enquirer*, February 10, 1973, 37.

Kelly, Aidan A., ed. *Cults and the Jewish Community*. New York: Garland Publishing, 1990.

Kjaer-Hansen, Kai. "Evangelization on the Sea Front." *LCJE Bulletin* 38 (November 1994): 8–9.

———. "The Jerusalem March and the Name of Jesus." *LCJE Bulletin* 38 (November 1994): 3–4.

Klayman, Elliot. "Messianic Zionism: God's Plan for Israel." *Messianic Outreach* 7 (Summer 1998): 3–8.

Kligerman, Aaron J. *Sharing Christ with Our Jewish Neighbors*. Cleveland: Bible House, 1946.

Kligerman, Aaron J., and Nate Schaiff. "Destination Israel." *American Hebrew Christian* 42 (Fall 1956): 9–11.

———. *The Gospel and the Jew*. Baltimore: King Brothers, n.d.

Korenbrot, Israel. *Return to Modiim*. Jerusalem: Gefen, 1985.

Koser, Hilda. *Come and Get It!* Orlando, Fla.: Golden Rule Book Press, 1987.

Kuldell, A. R. *Some Hindrances in Jewish Missions and How to Remove Them*. Columbus, Ohio: Lutheran Book Concern, 1903.

Kyle, Joseph, and William S. Miller, eds. *Addresses on the Second Coming of the Lord Delivered at the Prophetic Conference*, Allegheny, Pa., December 3–6, 1895. Pittsburgh: W. W. Waters, n.d.

Lacocque, Andre. "Key 73, Judaism, and the Tragedy of Triumphalism." *Christian Century*, May 30, 1973, 629–31.

Lanier, Chandler. "The Renewal of the Church in Israel." Unpublished manuscript in Yaakov Ariel's possession.

Lausanne Consultation on Jewish Evangelism: International Networking Directory 1992. Lystrup, Denmark: LCJE, 1992.

"The Lausanne Covenant." *International Review of Missions* 63 (October 1974): 570–76.

Leavey, Larry. "Why I Embraced Then Rejected Messianic Judaism." Press release, September 11, 1995.

Levi, Mark J. *Christianity: The Flower and Fruit of Judaism*. Washington, D.C.: Christian League of Jewish Friendship, 1923.

Levitt, Zola. *Corned Beef, Knishes, and Christ*. Wheaton, Ill.: Tyndale House Publishers, 1975.

———. *The Underground Church of Jerusalem*. Nashville: T. Nelson, 1978.

———. *Zola's Millennial Catalog*. Dallas: Zola Levitt Ministries, n.d.

Levy, Joel. Letter to James Gray. *Moody Bible Institute Monthly* 22 (March 1922): 854.

Lieff, Julius. "Emes Leader Keeps Promise at Grand Central." *Jewish Press*, June 26, 1987, 2.

Lieske, Bruce J. *Witnessing to the Jewish People*. St. Louis, Mo.: Board for Evangelism, the Lutheran Church—Missouri Synod, 1975.

Lindberg, Milton B. *The Jew and Modern Israel in Light of Prophecy*. Chicago: Moody Press, 1930.

———. *Witnessing to Jews: A Handbook of Practical Aids*. Chicago: Chicago Hebrew Mission, 1948.

Lindsey, Albert. "The Church and the Jews: What the Church Will Have to Do for the Jew in the Post War Period." In *Light for the World's Darkness*, edited by John W. Bradbury. New York: Loizeaux Brothers, 1944.

Lindsey, Hal. *The Late Great Planet Earth*. Grand Rapids, Mich.: Zondervan, 1971.

Lindsey, Robert. *A Hebrew Translation of the Gospel of Mark*. Jerusalem: Dugit Publishing House, n.d.

———. "The Jews and the Christian Hope." Typewritten manuscript in Lindsey's personal papers.

———. *A New Approach to the Synoptic Gospel*. Jerusalem: Dugit Publishing House, 1971.

———. "Salvation and the Jews." *International Review of Missions* 61 (January 1972): 20–47.

———. "Summary of Conclusions of Research into the Synoptic Relationship." *Hayahad* 3 (November/December 1963): 2, 7.

———, ed. *Munachim Meshichiim Notzriim*. Jerusalem: United Christian Council in Israel, 1976. Published in English as *Christian Terms in Hebrew*. Jerusalem: United Christian Council in Israel, 1976.

Lipson, Eric Peter. *Passover Haggadah: A Messianic Celebration*. San Francisco: JFJ Publications, 1986.

Littell, Franklin H. "Why a Christian Authority Opposes Missionaries." *Jewish Week*, April 8, 1983, 17.

Loyd, Linda. "Love Thy Neighbor?" *Philadelphia Inquirer*, April 19, 1981, 1B–2B.

Lud, Reuven. "Kriat Am Adonai Al-pi Habrit Hachadasha" [The nation of God, according to the New Testament]. *Hayahad* 25 (April 1963): 4–5.

Mach, Michael. "Their Mission: Converting Jews." *Jewish Exponent*, January 29, 1982, 45.

Machlin, A. B. "A Leaf from a Missionary's Diary." In *Israel's Restoration*, edited by John W. Bradbury. New York: Iversen-Ford, n.d.

"Magnify and Sanctify His Name." *Hebrew Christian Alliance Quarterly* 15 (1930).

Magnify and Sanctify His Name. Vancouver: Zion Messianic Fellowship, 1987.

Malamed, Gad. "How to Answer Street Missionaries." *Kol Yavneh* 4, no. 5 (1977). Also published in *Jewish Digest* 23 (February 1977): 49–51.

Mandelbaum, Yitta Halberstam. *Holy Brother: Inspiring Stories and Enchanted Tales about Rabbi Shlomo Carlebach*. Northvale, N.J.: Jason Aaronson, 1997.

Marshal, Louis. "On Christian Missions to the Jews." *American Hebrew* 125 (1929): 201–2.

Merson, Ben. "The Minister, the Rabbi, and Their House of God." *Collier's*, February 17, 1951, 27, 36–37.

Messianic Congregation Peniel, Songbook. Tiberias, Israel: Peniel Fellowship, n.d.

"Messianic Jews Fight for a Home." *Philadelphia Inquirer*, November 6, 1979.

"Messianic Jews Zoning Opposed in Merion." *Philadelphia Bulletin*, October 22, 1979, 18A.

Metshnick, Charles. "The Meshumod." *Jewish Era* 21 (1912): 74–78.

Meyer, Louis. "Directory of Protestant Jewish Missionary Societies." *Jewish Era* 23 (1913): 114–22.

———. *Eminent Hebrew Christians of the Nineteenth Century*. New York: Edwin Mellen Press, 1982.

———. "German Jewish Missions from 1517 to 1800." *Jewish Era* 22 (1913): 136–41.

———. "Protestant Missions to the Jews." *Missionary Review of the World* 25 (December 1902): 910–11.

Michelson, Arthur U. *From Judaism and Law to Christ and Grace*. Los Angeles: Jewish Hope Publishing House, 1934.

———. *The Jewish Passover and the Lord's Supper*. Los Angeles: Jewish Hope Publishing House, 1936.

———. *The Jews and Palestine in Light of Prophecy*. Los Angeles: Jewish Hope Publishing House, n.d.

———. *Out of Darkness into Light*. Los Angeles: Jewish Hope Publishing House, n.d.

Miller, Lindsay. "Jews as 'Jesus Freaks.'" *New York Post*, September 2, 1972.

Minutes of the First Hebrew-Christian Conference of the United States. Pittsburgh: n.p., 1903.

The Missionary Enterprise and the Israeli Court System: Jewish Children and the Legal System. Jerusalem: Keren Yeladenu, n.d.

"Missionary Work in New York." *Menorah* 12 (November 1906): 250–51.

Muntz, J. Palmer. "The Jew in History and Destiny." In *Israel's Restoration*, edited by John W. Bradbury. New York: Iversen-Ford, n.d.

———. Pamphlet. Buffalo, N.Y.: privately published, 1944.

Needleman, Samuel. "My Conversion." *Chosen People* 6 (December 1900): 3–4.

Neuhaus, Richard John. "What the Fundamentalists Want." *Commentary* 79 (May 1985): 41–46.

Newitz, Alexander. "The Story of My Conversion." *Chosen People* 3 (February 1904): 3–4.

Newman, Elias. *The Enrichment of the Church and the Results of Jewish Missions*. Minneapolis: Zion Society for Israel, 1933.

———. *The Fundamentalists' Resuscitation of the Antisemitic Protocol Forgery*. Minneapolis: Augsburg Publishing House, 1934.

———. *The Jewish Peril and the Hidden Hand*. N.p.: Elias Newman, 1933.

———. "The Late Rev. Joel Levy." *Moody Bible Institute Monthly* 22 (August 1922): 1147.

———. "Looking Back Twenty-five Years." *Hebrew Christian Alliance Quarterly* 25 (Summer 1940): 24.

———. "The Place of the Moody Bible Institute in Jewish Evangelization." *Moody Bible Institute Monthly* 24 (December 1923): 176–77.

———. "There Is a Prince and Great Man Fallen This Day in Israel." *Hebrew Christian Alliance Quarterly* 16 (1931): 4–8.

———. *Why I Became a Lutheran*. Minneapolis: Zion Society for Israel, 1933.

Niebuhr, Reinhold. "Jews after the War." *Nation*, February 21, 1942, 214–16; February 28, 1942, 253–55.

———. "The Rapprochement between Jews and Christians." *Christian Century*, January 7, 1926, 9–11.

North American Protestant Foreign Mission Agencies. New York: Missionary Research Library, 1962.

"Notes from Our Mission." *Our Hope* 1 (1894): 24.

"Open Letter to Bishop Greer." *American Hebrew* 99 (December 27, 1916): 881.

"Open to the Message." *Jerusalem Report*, January 26, 1995, 30.

Orthodox Messianic Judaism. Odessa, Tex.: House of Yahweh, n.d.

Osterley, Per. *The Church in Israel*. Lund, Sweden: Gleerup, 1970.

"Our Purpose." *Hebrew Christian Alliance Quarterly* 16 (April–June 1931): inner cover.

Padington, P. *Twenty-five Wonderful Years: 1889–1914*. New York: Christian Alliance Publishing, 1914.

Palms, Roger. "Jews for Jesus." *Home Missions* 44 (January 1973): 7–9.

Pawlikowski, John T. *What Are They Saying about Christian Jewish Relations?* New York: Paulist Press, 1980.

Pearlstein, M. B. "Physician's Report." *Chosen People* 9 (March 1904): 8.

Peltz, Jacob. *Christian Modernism and Reform Judaism in League against Jewish Evangelization.* Chicago: Hebrew Christian Alliance of America, 1933.

Pettingill, William L., J. R. Schafter, and J. D. Adams, eds. *Light on Prophecy: A Coordinated Constructive Teaching being the Proceedings and Addresses at the Philadelphia Prophetic Conference, May 28–30, 1918.* New York: Christian Herald Bible House, 1918.

Pfefer, Joseph N. "We Salute the Rev. Nathan J. Stone." *American Hebrew Christian* 50 (Summer 1965): 19–20.

Piper, Otto, Jakob Jocz, and Harold Floreen. *The Church Meets Judaism.* Minneapolis: Augsburg Publishing House, 1960.

Plowman, Edward E. "Turning On to Jeshua." *Christianity Today*, December 17, 1971, 34–39.

"Present Situation in Palestine." *Hebrew Christian Alliance Quarterly* 4 (April 1922): 59.

"Profile of an Anti Missionary." *Chosen People* 93 (June 1987): 5.

"Question Column." *Chosen People* 14 (April 1909): 7.

Rabinowitz, Joseph. *Jesus of Nazareth, the King of the Jews.* Translated by Arno C. Gaebelein. New York: Hope of Israel, 1898.

"Raiding the Missionaries," *American Hebrew* 89 (September 1911): 617.

Reich, Max I. "Israel." *Hebrew Christian Alliance Quarterly* 6 (1922): 45.

———. *The Messianic Hope of Israel.* Grand Rapids, Mich.: William B. Eerdmans, 1940.

———. *Sketches of Messianic Prophecy in the Book of Isaiah.* Chicago: Bible Institute Colportage Association, 1922.

———. *Sweet Singer of Israel.* Chicago: Moody Press, 1948.

"Report of Activities, 1987." Task Force on Missionaries and Cults. New York, 1987.

"Report of Dr. F. Charles." *Jewish Era* (January 1902): 33.

Reuben, Maurice. "The Conversion of Maurice Reuben." *Glory of Israel* 1 (1903): 16–17.

Riley, William B. "The Last Times." In *Christ and Glory, Addresses Delivered at the New York Prophetic Conference Carnegie Hall*, edited by Arno C Gaebelein. New York: Publication Office Our Hope, 1919.

———. *Wanted—A World Leader!* Minneapolis: by the author, n.d.

Rohold, S. B. "Messianic Judaism." *Prayer and Work for Israel* (January 1918): 8–11, 32–43.

———. *The War and the Jews.* Cincinnati: Standard Publishing Co., 1917.

Rosen, Moishe. *The Sayings of Chairman Moishe.* Carol Stream, Ill.: Creation House, 1974.

Rosen, Moishe, and William Proctor. *Jews for Jesus.* Old Tappan, N.J.: Fleming H. Revell, 1974.

Rosen, Moishe, and Ceil Rosen. *Share the New Life with a Jew.* Chicago: Moody Press, 1976.

Rosen, Ruth, ed. *Jesus for Jews.* San Francisco: A Messianic Jewish Perspective, 1987.

Roth, Sid. *They Thought for Themselves.* Brunswick, G.A.: MV Press, 1996.

Rottenberg, Isaac C. "Should There Be a Christian Witness to the Jews?" *Christian Century*, April 1, 1977, 352–56.

Rounds, Tryphena. "Liberal Judaism." *Jewish Era* 19 (1910): 69–70.

———. "The Pale of Settlement." *Jewish Era* 5 (1895): 94–96.

———. "Reformed Judaism—a Failure." *Jewish Era* 6 (1907): 74–75.

Rubin, Barry. *You Bring the Bagels, I'll Bring the Gospel*. Old Tappan, N.J.: Chosen Books, 1989.

Rudin, Marcia R. "Cults and Missionaries." *Encyclopedia Judaica, Year Book 1986–1987*: 80–90.

Rylaarsdam, J. Coert. "Mission to Christians." *Face to Face: An Interreligious Bulletin* 3–4 (Fall/Winter 1977): 17–18.

Schiffman, Michael. *Return of the Remnant: The Rebirth of Messianic Judaism*. Baltimore: Lederer Publications, 1992.

Schwartz, Lita Linzer. "Cults and the Vulnerability of Jewish Youth." In *Smashing the Idols: A Jewish Inquiry into the Cult Phenomenon*, edited by Gary Eisenberg. Northvale, N.J.: Jason Aronson, 1988.

Scofield, C. I. *Addresses on Prophecy*. New York: Our Hope, 1910.

Segal, Benjamin J., ed. *The Missionary at the Door—Our Uniqueness*. New York: Youth Commission, United Synagogue of America, 1983.

Seiss, Joseph A. "Who Are the 144,000?" *Glory of Israel* 1 (1903): 10.

Serkez, Kalman, ed. *The Holy Beggars' Banquet*. Northvale, N.J.: Jason Aaronson, 1988.

Sevener, Harold. "From the President." *Chosen People* 93 (June 1987): 2.

——. *A Rabbi's Vision: A Century of Proclaiming Messiah: A History of Chosen People Ministries, Inc.* Charlotte, N.C.: Chosen People Ministries, 1994.

——, ed. *Passover Haggadah for Biblical Jews and Christians*. Orangeburg, N.Y.: Chosen People Publications, n.d.

"Several Members of the Y.W.H.A. Brooklyn Form an Anti-Missionary League to Combat the Work of Christian Missions (to Convert Jews) in Their Area." *American Hebrew* 91 (September 27, 1912): 617.

Sheelot ve Teshuvot. Rischon Letsion, Israel: Hagafen Publishing House, 1986.

Sherburne, Mary C. "Our Mission Hall." *Chosen People* 1 (February 1896): 5.

——. "Our Schools." *Chosen People* 2 (October 1896): 5.

Sherman, Shlomo. *Escape from Jesus*. New York: Decalogue Books, 1983.

Siegel, Burt. "How Local Jewish Groups Respond to Threat." *Jewish Exponent*, January 29, 1982, 47.

Sigal, Gerald. *The Jew and the Christian Missionary: A Jewish Response to Missionary Christianity*. New York: Ktav Publishing House, 1981.

Silberman, Charles. *A Certain People: American Jews and Their Lives Today*. New York: Summit Books, 1985.

Silverman, Lawrence M. *What to Say When a Missionary Comes to Your Door*. Plymouth, Mass.: Plymouth Lodge–B'nai B'rith, n.d.

Simon, Abraham. "Conversion." *Emanu-EL*, April 24, 1896, 7.

Simpson, Albert B. *The Gospel of the Kingdom*. New York: Christian Alliance Publication, 1890.

"The Sixth Annual Conference of the Chicago Hebrew Mission." *Jewish Era* 12 (1903): 174.

Sola Mendes, F. de. "Missionary Work in New York," *Menorah* 12 (November 1906).

Starr, Jacob. "Report of J. R. Lewek." *Jewish Era* (January 1902): 31–32.

——. "The Story of the Life and Conversion of Jacob Starr." *Immanuel's Witness* 2 (1900): 156–57.

"Stealing Jewish Children," *American Hebrew* 78 (October 16, 1903): 705–6.

Steiner, Edward A. *From Alien to Citizen*. New York: Fleming H. Revell, 1914.

Stendahl, Krister. "Limits of Christian Mission." *Face to Face: An Interreligious Bulletin* 3–4 (Fall/Winter 1977): 19.

Stern, David. *The Jewish New Testament*. Jerusalem: Jewish New Testament Publications, 1990.

——. *Messianic Jewish Manifesto*. Jerusalem: Jewish New Testament Publications, 1988.

Stern, Gabriel. "A Tragedy within a Tragedy." *Al Ha Mishmar*, September 27, 1961.

"Sticks and Stones." *Newsweek*, July, 24, 1961, 41.

Stone, Nathan J. *Names of God in the Old Testament*. Chicago: Moody Press, 1944.

Strack, Herman L., ed. *Yearbook of Evangelical Missions among the Jews*. 2 vols. Leipzig: J. C. Hinrichs'sche Buchhandlung, 1906.

Strober, Gerald. "My Life as a Christian." *Commentary* 73 (June 1982): 38.

Stroeter, Ernest F. "A Misapprehension Corrected." *Our Hope* 2 (1895): 55–58.

——. "The Second Coming of Christ In Relation to Israel." *Addresses on the Second Coming of the Lord Delivered at the Prophetic Conference, Allegheny, Pa., December 3–6 1895,* edited by Joseph Kyle and William S. Miller. Pittsburgh: W. W. Waters, n.d.

Talbot, Louis T., and William W. Orr. *The New Nation of Israel and the Word of God*. Los Angeles: Bible Institute of Los Angeles, 1948.

Tannenbaum, Marc H., Marvin R. Wilson, and A. James Rudin, eds. *Evangelicals and Jews in Conversation*. Grand Rapids, Mich.: Baker Book House, 1978.

Tavalin, Ron. *Kol Hesed Messianic Haggadah*. N.p.: Dogwood Press, 1993.

The Thailand Report on the Jewish People. Wheaton, Ill.: Lausanne Committee for World Evangelization, 1980.

The Theology of the Churches and the Jewish People: Statements by the World Council of Churches and Its Member Churches. Geneva: World Council of Churches, 1988.

Thompson, Albert E. *A Century of Jewish Missions*. Chicago: Fleming H. Revell, 1902.

——. *The Life of A. B. Simpson*. New York: Christian Alliance Publication Co., 1920.

Torrey, Reuben A. "The Blessed Hope." In *Christ and Glory, Addresses Delivered at the New York Prophetic Conference Carnegie Hall*, edited by Arno C. Gaebelein. New York: Publication Office Our Hope, 1919.

——. *The Return of the Lord Jesus*. Los Angeles: Bible Institute of Los Angles, 1913.

Trillin, Calvin. *Messages from My Father*. New York: Farrar, Straus, and Giroux, 1966.

Twenty Second Annual Report of the Society for Promoting Christianity amongst the Jews. New York: Church Society for Promoting Christianity Amongst the Jews, 1900.

Van Buren, Paul M. *Discerning the Way: A Theology of the Jewish Christian Realities*. New York: Seabury Press, 1980.

Vester, Bertha Spafford. *Our Jerusalem*. Garden City, N.Y.: Doubleday, 1950.

Walsh, Vincent M. *A Key to Charismatic Renewal in the Catholic Church*. St. Meinard, Ind.: Abbey Press, 1974.

Walvoord, John. *Israel in Prophecy*. Grand Rapids, Mich.: Zondervan, 1962.

"Want to Drive Out Missionaries?" *American Hebrew* 92 (January 31, 1913): 399.

"We Have Not Lost Our Hope: A National Hebrew Messianic Song." *Hebrew Christian Alliance Quarterly* 1 (1917).

Weiss, Louis. *Some Burning Questions: An Exegetical Treatise on Christianizing of Judaism*. Columbus, Ohio: by the author, 1893.

"We Might Unite with Our Jewish Brethren in Their Protest." *Hebrew Christian Alliance Quarterly* 19 (April 1934): 5.

"Wer Is a Meshichi." *Shepherd of Israel* 31 (June 1949).

Wertheimer, Max. *From Rabbinism to Christ: The Story of My Life.* Ada, Ohio: Wertheimer Publications, 1934.

West, Nathaniel, "Prophecy and Israel." In *Prophetic Studies of the International Prophetic Conference, Chicago, Ill., November 1886*, edited by George C. Needham. Chicago: Fleming H. Revell, 1886.

"West Side Organization to Oppose Missionaries." *American Hebrew* 95 (June 19, 1914): 219.

What Evangelical Christians Should Know about Jews for Jesus. San Francisco: Jews for Jesus, n.d.

White, Aidine. "The Gospel to the Jews: A Neglected Work." *Glory of Israel* 15 (1917): 56–59.

Why We Resign from the American Board of Missions to the Jews. Chicago: American Association for Jewish Evangelism, 1944.

Wiesel, Elie. *All Rivers Run to the Sea: Memories.* New York: Alfred A. Knopf, 1995.

——. "The Missionary Menace." In *Smashing the Idols: A Jewish Inquiry into the Cult Phenomenon*, edited by Gary Eisenberg. Northvale, N.J.: Jason Aronson, 1988.

Wilkinson, Samuel. "The Moral Defensibility of Some of the Methods Employed in Jewish Missions." In *Yearbook of the Evangelical Missions among the Jews*, vol. 1, edited by Hermann L. Strack. Leipzig: J. C. Hinrich'sche Buchhandlung, 1906.

"Williamsburg Mission to the Jews: Abstract of the Report of the Committee of Investigation." *Christian Workers Magazine* 17 (November 1916): 191–92.

Willoughby, William. "A Breakthrough for Messianic Judaism?" *Moody Monthly* 72 (March 1972): 16–19.

Wise, Isaac M. *A Defense of Judaism versus Proselytizing Christianity.* Cincinnati: American Israelite, 1889.

Wolff, Tobias. *In Pharaoh's Army.* New York: Vintage Books, 1994.

"Working against Missions." *American Hebrew* 92 (December 27, 1912): 264.

Young, Brad H. *Jesus and His Jewish Parables: Rediscovering the Roots of Jesus' Teaching.* New York: Paulist Press, 1989.

Zeidan, David. *Messiah Now: Ten True Stories from Modern Israel of Men and Women Who Met Yeshua.* Carlisle, England: OM Publishing, 1992.

"Zionism and Hebrew Christianity." *Hebrew Christian Alliance Quarterly* 6 (April 1922): 43.

"The Zionist Movement." *Jewish Era* 10 (1901): 96.

SECONDARY SOURCES

Allison, Joel. "Religious Conversion: Regression and Progression in Adolescent Experience." *Journal for the Scientific Study of Religion* 8 (1969): 23–38.

Ammerman, Nancy Tatom. *Bible Believers: Fundamentalists in the Modern World.* New Brunswick, N.J.: Rutgers University Press, 1997.

——. "Fundamentalists Proselytizing Jews: Incivility in Preparation for the Rapture." In *Pushing the Faith: Proselytism and Civility in a Pluralistic World*, edited by Martin E. Marty and Frederick E. Greenspahn, 109–22. New York: Corssroad, 1988.

Appel, John J. "Christian Science and the Jews." *Jewish Social Studies* 31 (1969): 100–121.

Ariel, Yaakov. "American Dispensationalists and Jerusalem, 1870–1918." In *With Eyes toward Zion*, vol. 5, edited by Moshe Davis and Yehoshua Ben Arieh. New York: Praeger, 1997.

———. "An American Evangelist and the Jews: Dwight L. Moody and His Attitudes toward the Jewish People." *Immanuel* 22–23 (1989): 41–49.

———. "American Fundamentalists and the Emergence of a Jewish State." In *New Dimensions in American Religious History*, edited by Jay P. Dolan and James P. Wind, 303–9. Grand Rapids, Mich.: William B. Eerdmans, 1993.

———. "An American Initiative for a Jewish State: William Blackstone and the Petition of 1891." *Studies in Zionism* 10 (1989): 125–38.

———. "A Christian Fundamentalist Vision of the Middle East: Jan Willem van der Hoeven and the International Christian Embassy." In *Spokesmen for the Despised: Fundamentalist Leader of the Middle East*, edited by R. Scott Appleby. Chicago: University of Chicago Press, 1997.

———. "Eschatology, Evangelism, and Dialogue: The Presbyterian Mission to the Jews, 1920–1960." *American Presbyterians: The Journal of Presbyterian History* 75 (Spring 1997): 29–41.

———. "From Judaism to Christianity: Autobiographies of Jewish Converts to Christianity in the Twentieth Century." *Proceedings of the Eleventh World Congress of Jewish Studies*. Jerusalem: World Union of Jewish Studies, 1994, Division B, Volume 2: 122–129. [In Hebrew].

———. "In the Shadow of the Millennium: American Fundamentalists and the Jewish People." *Studies in Church History* 29 (1992): 435–50.

———. "A Neglected Chapter in the History of Christian Zionism in America: William Blackstone and the Petition of 1916." *Studies in Contemporary Jewry* 7 (1991): 87–102.

———. *On Behalf of Israel: American Fundamentalist Attitudes toward Jews, Judaism, and Zionism, 1865–1945*. New York: Carlson Publishing, 1991.

———. "Protestant Attitudes to Jews and Judaism during the Last Fifty Years." In *Terms of Survival: The Jewish World since 1945*, edited by Robert S. Wistrich. London: Routledge, 1995.

Avneri, Uri. *Milhemet Hayom Hasheve* [The Seventh-Day War]. Tel Aviv: Yam Suf, 1968.

Balmer, Randall. *Mine Eyes Have Seen the Glory*. New York: Oxford University Press, 1989.

Banki, Judith H. *Christian Responses to the Yom Kippur War*. New York: American Jewish Committee, 1974.

Bass, Clarence B. *Background to Dispensationalism*. Grand Rapids, Mich.: William B. Eerdmans, 1960.

Beaver, R. Pierce. *American Protestant Women in World Missions: History of the First Feminist Movement in North America*. Grand Rapids, Mich.: William B. Eerdmans, 1968.

Beckford, James A. "Accounting for Conversion." *British Journal of Sociology* 29 (1978): 249–62.

Beit-Hallahmi, Benjamin. *Despair and Deliverance*. Albany: State University of New York Press, 1992.

Bellah, Robert, Richard Madsen, William M. Sullivan, Ann Swidler, and Steven M. Tipton. *Habits of the Heart: Individualism and Commitment in American Life*. New York: Harper and Row, 1985.

Bellow, Saul. *Mr. Sammler's Planet*. New York: Viking, 1970.

Bendroth, Margaret Lamberts. *Fundamentalism and Gender*. New Haven: Yale University Press, 1993.

Berlin, George L. *Defending the Faith: Nineteenth-Century American Jewish Writings on Christianity and Jesus*. Albany: State University of New York Press, 1989.

Bershtel, Sara, and Allen Graubard. *Saving Remnants: Feeling Jewish in America*. Berkeley: University of California Press, 1993.

Biale, David, Michael Galchinsky, and Susannah Heschel, eds. *Insider/Outsider: American Jews and Multiculturalism*. Berkeley: University of California Press, 1998.

Blumhofer, Edith. *Aimee Semple McPherson: Everybody's Sister*. Grand Rapids, Mich.: William B. Eerdmans, 1994.

Blumstock, Robert. "The Evangelization of the Jews: Study in Interfaith Relations." Ph.D. diss., University of Oregon, 1964.

Braybrooke, Markus. *Pilgrimage of Hope*. New York: Crossroad, 1992.

Burkett, Elinor. *The Right Women: A Journey through the Heart of Conservative America*. New York: Scribner's, 1997.

Capps, Walter. *The Unfinished War: Vietnam and the American Conscience*. Boston: Beacon Press, 1982.

Carpenter, Joel A., and Wilber R. Shenk, eds. *Earthen Vessels: American Evangelicals and Foreign Missions, 1880–1980*. Grand Rapids, Mich.: William B. Eerdmans, 1990.

Cawelti, John G. *Adventure Mystery and Romance: Formula Stories as Art and Popular Culture*. Chicago: University of Chicago Press, 1976.

Clark, Christopher M. *The Politics of Conversion*. Oxford: Clarendon Press, 1995.

Clecak, Peter. *America's Quest for the Ideal Self: Dissent and Fulfillment in the Sixties and Seventies*. New York: Oxford University Press, 1983.

Cohen, Jeremy. *The Friars and the Jews*. Ithaca, N.Y.: Cornell University Press, 1982.

Colbi, Saul. *A History of the Christian Presence in the Holy Land*. Lanham, Md.: University Press of America, 1988.

Conway, John S. "Protestant Missions to the Jews, 1810–1980: Ecclesiastical Imperialism or Theological Aberration?" *Holocaust and Genocide Studies* 1 (1986): 127–46.

Cowan, Neil M., and Ruth Schwartz Cowan. *Our Parents' Lives: The Americanization of Eastern European Jews*. New York: Basic Books, 1989.

Cox, Harvey. "Deep Structures in the Study of New Religions." In *Understanding the New Religions*, edited by Jacob Needleman and George Baker. New York: Seabury Press, 1978.

Crombie, Kelvin. *For the Love of Zion*. London: Hodder and Stoughton, 1991.

Danziger, Herbert M. *Returning to Tradition: The Contemporary Revival of Orthodox Judaism*. New Haven: Yale University Press, 1989.

Davidman, Lynn. *Tradition in a Rootless World: Women Turn to Orthodox Judaism*. Berkeley: University of California Press, 1991.

Davis, Allen F. *American Heroine: The Life and Legend of Jane Addams*. New York: Oxford University Press, 1973.

Davis, Moshe, and Yehoshua Ben Arieh, eds. *With Eyes toward Zion*. Vol. 5. New York: Praeger, 1997.

Dayton, Donald W. *Theological Roots of Pentecostalism*. Grand Rapids, Mich.: Francis Asbury Press, 1987.

Dershowitz, Alan M. *The Vanishing American Jew*. New York: Little, Brown, 1997.

Dinnerstein, Leonard. *Anti-Semitism in America*. New York: Oxford University Press, 1994.

Dolan, Jay. *Catholic Revivalism: The American Experience, 1830–1900*. Notre Dame, Ind.: University of Notre Dame Press, 1978.

Drury, Clifford Merrill. *Presbyterian Panorama*. Philadelphia: Presbyterian Church in the U.S.A., 1952.

Ehlert, Arnold D. *A Bibliographic History of Dispensationalism*. Grand Rapids, Mich.: Baker Book House, 1965.

Eichhorn, David. *Evangelizing the American Jew*. New York: Jonathan David, 1978.

——. "A History of Christian Attempts to Convert the Jews in the United States and Canada." Ph.D. diss., Hebrew Union College, 1938.

Eisen, Max. "Christian Missions to the Jews in North America and Great Britain." *Jewish Social Studies* 10 (1948): 31–72.

Elgvin, Torleif, ed. *Israel and Yeshua*. Jerusalem: Caspari Center, 1993.

Eller, Cynthia. *Living in the Lap of the Goddess: The Feminist Spirituality Movement in America*. New York: Crossroad, 1993.

Ellwood, Robert S. *The Sixties Spiritual Awakening*. New Brunswick, N.J.: Rutgers University Press, 1994.

Endelman, Todd M., ed. *Jewish Apostasy in the Modern World*. New York: Holmes and Meier, 1987.

Epperson, Steven. *Mormons and Jews: Early Mormon Theologies of Israel*. Salt Lake City: Signature Books, 1992.

Evearitt, Daniel J. "Jewish-Christian Missions to Jews, 1820–1935." Ph.D. diss., Drew University, 1988.

Feher, Shoshanah. *Passing over Easter: Constructing the Boundaries of Messianic Judaism*. Walnut Creek, Calif.: Altamira Press, 1998.

Feldman, Egal. "American Protestant Theologians on the Frontier of Jewish-Christian Relations, 1922–1982." In *Anti-Semitism in American History*, edited by David A. Gerber. Urbana: University of Illinois Press, 1986.

——. *Dual Destinies: The Jewish Encounter with Protestant America*. Urbana: University of Illinois Press, 1990.

——. "Reinhold Niebuhr and the Jews." *Jewish Social Studies* 46 (Summer/Fall 1984): 292–302.

Finke, Roger, and Rodney Starck. *The Churching of America, 1776–1990*. New Brunswick, N.J.: Rutgers University Press.

Fishman, Sylvia Barack. *A Breath of Life: Feminism in the American Jewish Community*. Hanover, N.H.: University Press of New England, 1995.

Flusser, David. *Jewish Sources in Early Christianity: Studies and Essays*. Tel Aviv: Sifriat Poalim, 1979.

Fox, Richard Wrightman. *Reinhold Niebuhr: A Biography*. New York: Pantheon Books, 1985.

Fried, Louis. "Jacob Riis and the Jews: The Ambivalent Quest for Community." *American Studies* 20 (Winter 1979): 5–24.

Friedman, Menachem. *The Haredi (Ultra Orthodox) Society—Sources, Trends, and Processes*. Jerusalem: Jerusalem Institute for Israel Studies, 1991.

Geldbach, Erich. *Christlich Versammlung und Heilgeschichte Bei John Nelson Darby*. Wuppertal, Germany: Theologischer Verlag Rolf Brockhaus, 1971.

Genizi, Haim. *American Apathy: The Plight of Christian Refugees from Nazism*. Ramat Gan, Israel: Bar Ilan University Press, 1983.

——. "Missionary Work among Holocaust Refugees." *Bar Ilan University Year Book* (in Hebrew) 16–17 (1979): 336–42.

Gerber, David A., ed. *Anti-Semitism in American History*. Urbana: University of Illinois Press, 1986.

Getz, Gene A. *MBI: The Story of the Moody Bible Institute*. Chicago: Moody Press, 1969.

Gidney, W. T. *The History of the London Society for Promoting Christianity amongst the Jews from 1809 to 1908*. London: London Society for Promoting Christianity amongst the Jews, 1908.

Gilbert, Arthur. "New Trends in the Protestant Mission to the Jew." *Conservative Judaism* 19 (Spring 1965): 51–56.

——. *The Vatican Council and the Jews*. Cleveland: World Publishing Co., 1968.

Gitlin, Todd. *The Sixties: Years of Hope, Days of Rage*. New York: Bantam, 1987.

Glazer, Nathan. *American Judaism*. Chicago: University of Chicago Press, 1972.

——. *Ethnic Dilemmas, 1964–1982*. Cambridge: Harvard University Press, 1983.

Glock, Charles Y., and Rodney Stark, *Christian Beliefs and Anti-Semitism*. New York: Harper and Row, 1966.

Goldscheider, Calvin, and Alan Zuckerman. *The Transformation of the Jews*. Chicago: University of Chicago Press, 1984.

Goldstein, Sidney. "Profile of American Jewry: Insights from the 1990 National Jewish Population Survey." *American Jewish Year Book* 92. Philadelphia: Jewish Publication Society, 1992.

Goren, Arthur A. *New York Jews and the Quest for Community*. New York: Columbia University Press, 1970.

Greenberg, Gershon. *The Holy Land in American Religious Thought, 1620–1948*. Lanham, Md.: University Press of America, 1994.

Griffith, R. Marie. *God's Daughters: Evangelical Women and the Power of Submission*. Berkeley: University of California Press, 1997.

Gurock, Jeffrey S. "Jacob A. Riis: Christian Friend or Missionary Foe." *American Jewish History* 71 (September 1981): 29–48.

——. "Jewish Communal Divisiveness in Response to Christian Influences on the Lower East Side, 1900–1910." In *Jewish Apostasy in the Modern World*, edited by Todd M. Endelman. New York: Holmes and Meier, 1987.

Hagner, Donald H. *The Jewish Reclamation of Jesus*. Grand Rapids, Mich.: Academie Books, 1984.

Hakvutza Ha Cnaanit: Sifrut Ve Edeologia [The Canaanite group: Literature and ideology]. Tel Aviv: Everyman's University, 1987.

Hales, Peter B. *Silver Cities: The Photography of American Urbanization, 1839–1915*. Philadelphia: Temple University Press, 1984.

Halperin, Samuel. *The Political World of American Zionism*. Detroit: Wayne State University Press, 1961.

Handy, Robert T. *A Christian America: Protestant Hopes and Historical Realities*. New York: Oxford University Press, 1981.

——. *We Witness Together*. New York: Friendship Press, 1956.

Harding, Susan F. "Convicted by the Holy Spirit: The Rhetoric of Fundamentalist Baptist Conversion." *American Ethnologist* 14 (1987): 167–81.

Harrell, David E. *Oral Roberts: An American Life*. Bloomington: Indiana University Press, 1985.

Harris-Shapiro, Carol. "Syncretism or Struggle: The Case of Messianic Judaism." Ph.D. diss., Temple University, 1992.

Hartzfeld, David F., and Charles Nienkirchen, eds. *The Birth of a Vision*. Alberta, Canada: Buena Book Services, 1987.

Herberg, Will. *Protestant, Catholic, Jew*. New York: Anchor Books, 1960.

Hogg, Richie. "The Role of American Protestantism in World Mission." In *American Missions in Bicentennial Perspective*, edited by R. Pierce Beaver. South Pasadena, Calif.: William Carey Library, 1977.

Hopkins, Howard. *John R. Mott, 1865–1955: A Biography*. Grand Rapids, Mich.: William B. Eerdmans, 1979.

Horwitt, Sanford D. *Let Them Call Me Rebel: Saul Alinsky—His Life and Legacy*. New York: Alfred A. Knopf, 1989.

Howe, Irving. *World of Our Fathers: The Journey of the East European Jews to America and the Life They Found and Made*. New York: Alfred A. Knopf, 1976.

Hutchens, James. "A Case for Messianic Judaism." Ph.D. diss., Fuller Theological Seminary, 1974.

——. "Messianic Judaism: A Progress Report." *Missiology* 7 (1977): 285–99.

Hutchison, William R. *Errand to the World: American Protestant Thought and Foreign Missions*. Chicago: University of Chicago Press, 1987.

——. *The Modernist Impulse in American Protestantism*. New York: Oxford University Press, 1982.

——, ed. *Between the Times: The Travail of the Protestant Establishment in America, 1900–1960*. Cambridge: Cambridge University Press, 1989.

Hyman, Paula E. *Gender and Assimilation in Modern Jewish History: The Roles and Representations of Women*. Seattle: University of Washington Press, 1995.

James, J. W., ed. *Women in American Religion*. Philadelphia: University of Pennsylvania Press, 1980.

Joselit, Jenna Weissman. *The Wonders of America*. New York: Hill and Wang, 1994.

Kamenetz, Roger. *The Jew in the Lotus: A Poet's Rediscovery of Jewish Identity in Buddhist India*. New York: HarperCollins, 1994.

Kjaer-Hansen, Kai. *Joseph Rabinowitz and the Messianic Movement*. Grand Rapids, Mich.: William B. Eerdmans, 1995.

Kaplan, Jeffrey. *Radical Religion in America: Millennarian Movements from the Far Right to the Children of Noah*. Syracuse, N.Y.: Syracuse University Press, 1997.

Kaplan, Marion A. *The Making of the Jewish Middle Class*. New York: Oxford University Press, 1991.

Kelly, Aidan A., ed. *Cults and the Jewish Community*. New York: Garland Publishing, 1990.

Klatzker, David. "Israeli Civil Religion and Jewish Christian Relations: The Case of the Baptists." In *Jewish Civilization: Essays and Studies*, vol. 3, edited by Ronald A. Brauner. Philadelphia: Reconstructionist Rabbinical College, 1985.

Klausner, Samuel Z. "How to Think about Mass Religious Conversion: Toward an

Explanation of the Conversion of American Jews to Christianity." *Contemporary Jewry* 18 (1997): 76–129.

Kohn, Rachel. "Dual Membership and Sectarian Status: The Case of a Hebrew Christian." *Studies in Religion* 12, no. 2 (1983): 159.

Kolsky, Thomas A. *Jews against Zionism: The American Council for Judaism*. Philadelphia: Temple University Press, 1990.

Kraut, Benny. "Towards the Establishment of the National Conference of Christians and Jews: The Tenuous Road to Religious Goodwill in the 1920s." *American Jewish History* 77 (March 1988): 388–412.

——. "A Wary Collaboration: Jews, Catholics, and the Protestant Goodwill Movement." In *Between the Times: The Travail of the Protestant Establishment in America, 1900–1960*, edited by William R. Hutchison. Cambridge: Cambridge University Press, 1989.

Lane, James B. *Jacob A. Riis and the American City*. Port Washington, N.Y.: Kennikat Press, 1974.

Lebeson, Anita Libman. "Zionism Comes to Chicago." In *Early History of Zionism in America*, edited by Isidore S. Meyer. New York: American Jewish Historical Society and Theodor Herzl Foundation, 1958.

Linzer, Judith. *Torah and Dharma: Jewish Seekers in Eastern Religions*. Northvale, N.J.: Jason Aronson, 1996.

Lipson, Juliene G. *Jews for Jesus: An Anthropological Study*. New York: AMS Press, 1990.

Littell, Franklin H. "Amsterdam and Its Absentees." *Journal of Ecumenical Studies* 16 (1979): 111–12.

——. *The Crucifixion of the Jews*. New York: Harper and Row, 1975.

Lofland, John, and Norman Skonvod. "Conversion Motifs." *Journal for the Scientific Study of Religion* 20 (1981): 373–85.

Lofland, John, and Rodney Stark. "Becoming a World-Saver: A Theory of Conversion to a Deviant Perspective." *American Sociological Review* 30 (1965): 865–75.

Lucas, Phillip C. *The Odyssey of a New Religion: The Holy Order of MANS from New Age to Orthodoxy*. Bloomington: Indiana University Press, 1995.

MacPherson, Dave. *The Incredible Cover Up: The True Story of the Pre-Tribulation Rapture*. Plainfield, N.J.: Omega Publications, 1975.

Malachy, Yona. *American Fundamentalism and Israel*. Jerusalem: Institute of Contemporary Jewry, Hebrew University of Jerusalem, 1978.

Marsden, George M. *Fundamentalism and American Culture*. New York: Oxford University Press, 1982.

——. *Reforming Fundamentalism: Fuller Seminary and the New Evangelicalism*. Grand Rapids, Mich.: William B. Eerdmans, 1987.

Marty, Martin E. *Modern American Religion*. Vol. 1, *The Irony of It All*. Chicago: University of Chicago Press, 1987.

——. *Modern American Religion*. Vol. 2, *The Noise of Conflict, 1919–1941*. Chicago: University of Chicago Press, 1991.

Masuzawa, Tomoko. "Culture." In *Critical Terms for Religious Studies*, edited by Mark C. Taylor. Chicago: University of Chicago Press, 1998.

McLoughlin, William. *Revivals, Awakenings, and Reform*. Chicago: University of Chicago Press, 1978.

Merkley, Paul C. *The Politics of Christian Zionism, 1891–1948*. London: Frank Cass, 1998.

Meyer, Isidore S., ed. *Early History of Zionism in America*. New York: American Jewish Historical Society and Theodor Herzl Foundation, 1958.

Meyer, Michael. *Response to Modernity: A History of the Reform Movement in Judaism*. New York: Oxford University Press, 1988.

Minerbi, Sergio I. *The Vatican and Zionism*. New York: Oxford University Press, 1990.

Moore, R. Laurence. *Selling God: American Religion in the Marketplace of Culture*. New York: Oxford University Press, 1994.

Naveh, Eyal. "The Hebraic Foundation of Christian Faith, According to Reinhold Niebuhr." *Judaism* 41 (Winter 1992): 37–56.

Needleman, Jacob, and George Baker, eds. *Understanding the New Religions*. New York: Seabury Press, 1978.

Neill, Stephen. *A History of Christianity in India*. 2 vols. Cambridge: Cambridge University Press, 1985.

———. *A History of Christian Missions*. Harmondsworth, England: Penguin Books, 1979.

Nerel, Gershon. "Messianic Jews and the Modern Zionist Movement." In *Israel and Yeshua*, edited by Torleif Elgvin. Jerusalem: Caspari Center, 1993.

———. "Messianic Jews in Eretz Israel (1917–1967): Trends and Changes in Shaping Self-Identity." Ph.D. diss., Hebrew University of Jerusalem, 1996.

Niklaus, Robert L., John S. Sawin, and Samuel J. Stoesz. *All for Jesus: God at Work in the Christian and Missionary Alliance over One Hundred Years*. Camp Hill, Pa.: Christian Publications, 1986.

Numbers, Ronald L., and Jonathan M. Butler. *The Disappointed: Millerism and Millenarianism in the Nineteenth Century*. Bloomington: Indiana University Press, 1987.

O'Brien, Geoffrey. *Dream Time: Chapters from the Sixties*. New York: Viking, 1998.

One Hundred Years of Blessing, 1887–1997: The Centennial History of the American Messianic Fellowship. Lansing, Ill.: American Messianic Fellowship, 1987.

Ozick, Cynthia. *The Pagan Rabbi and Other Stories*. Syracuse, N.Y.: Syracuse University Press, 1971.

Pascal, R. *Design and Truth in Autobiography*. Cambridge: Harvard University Press, 1960.

Pilowsky, Varda, ed. *Transition from "Yishuv" to State*. Haifa: University of Haifa, 1988.

Praeger, Leonard. *Yiddish Culture in Britain*. Frankfurt-am-Main: Peter Lang, 1990.

Pragai, Michael. *Faith and Fulfillment*. London: Mitchel, 1985.

Prell, Riv Ellen. *Prayer and Community: The Havura Movement in American Judaism*. Detroit: Wayne State University Press, 1989.

Pruter, Karl. *Jewish Christians in the United States: A Bibliography*. New York: Garland Publishing, 1987.

Pyles, Franklin Arthur. "The Missionary Eschatology of A. B. Simpson." In *The Birth of a Vision*, edited by David F. Hartzfeld and Charles Nienkirchen. Alberta, Canada: Buena Book Services, 1987.

Rambo, Lewis. "The Psychology of Conversion." In *Handbook of Religious Conversion*, edited by H. Newton Malony and Samuel Southard. Birmingham, Ala.: Religious Education Press, 1992.

———. *Understanding Religious Conversion*. New Haven: Yale University Press, 1993.

Rausch, David. *Arno C. Gaebelein, 1861–1945: Irenic Fundamentalist and Scholar*. Lewiston, N.Y.: Edwin Mellen Press, 1983.

——. *Communities in Conflict: Evangelicals and Jews.* Philadelphia: Trinity Press International, 1991.

——. "Hebrew Christian Renaissance and Early Conflict with Messianic Judaism." *Fides et Historia* 15 (Spring/Summer 1983): 67–79.

——. "The Messianic Jewish Congregational Movement." *Christian Century*, September 15–22, 1982, 926–29.

——. *Messianic Judaism: Its History, Theology, and Polity.* New York: Edwin Mellen Press, 1982.

——. *Zionism within Early American Fundamentalism, 1878–1918.* New York: Edwin Mellen Press, 1978.

Rice, Dan. "Reinhold Niebuhr and Judaism." *Journal of the American Academhy of Religion* 45 (March 1977): 101–46.

Ricks, Eldin. "Zionism and the Mormon Church." In *Herzl Year Book* 5, edited by Raphael Patai. New York: Herzl Press, 1963.

Rischin, Moses. *The Promised City: New York Jews, 1870–1914.* Cambridge: Harvard University Press, 1978.

Rockaway, Robert A. *Words of the Uprooted: Jewish Immigrants in Early Twentieth Century America.* Ithaca, N.Y.: Cornell University Press, 1998.

Roof, Wade Clark. *A Generation of Seekers: The Spiritual Journeys of the Baby Boom Generation.* San Francisco: Harper San Francisco, 1993.

Rosenbloom, Joseph R. *Conversion to Judaism: From the Biblical Period to the Present.* Cincinnati: Hebrew Union College Press, 1978.

Ross, Robert W. "Perverse Witness to the Holocaust: Christian Missions and Missionaries." In *Holocaust Studies Annual*, vol. 2, *The Churches' Response to the Holocaust*, edited by Jack Fischel and Sanford Pinsker. Greenwood, Fla.: Penkeville Publishing Co., 1986.

Ruether, Rosemary Radford. *Faith and Fratricide: The Theological Roots of Anti-Semitism.* New York: Seabury Press, 1974.

Sandeen, Ernest. *The Roots of Fundamentalism: British and American Millenarianism, 1800–1930.* Grand Rapids, Mich.: Baker Book House, 1978.

Sarna, Jonathan D. "The American Jewish Response to Nineteenth-Century Christian Missions." *Journal of American History* 68 (1981): 35–51.

——. "The Impact of Nineteenth-Century Christian Missionaries on American Jews." In *Jewish Apostasy in the Modern World*, edited by Todd Endelman. New York: Holmes and Meier, 1987.

Schechter, Philip E. "American Jews in Liberal Protestant and Neo-Humanist Religious Institutions: Study in the Patterns of Assimilation." Rabbinical thesis, Hebrew Union College—Jewish Istitution of Religion, 1960.

Schmidgall, Paul. "American Holiness Churches in the Holy Land, 1890–1990: Mission to Jews, Arabs and Armenians." Ph.D. diss., Hebrew University of Jerusalem, 1996.

Schwartz, P. Z. *Schem Hagdolim.* Brooklyn, N.Y.: "Jerusalem" Publishing, 1959.

Sconvod, Norman. "Conversion Motifs." *Journal for the Scientific Study of Religion* 20 (1981).

Scult, Mel. *Millennial Expectations and Jewish Liberties.* Leiden, the Netherlands: E. J. Brill, 1978.

Shavit, Yaacov. *MeIvri Ad Cnaani* [From Hebrew to Canaanite]. Tel Aviv: Domino Press, 1984.

——. *The New Hebrew Nation*. London: Frank Cass, 1989.

Shipps, Jan. *The Mormon Tradition*. Urbana: University of Illinois Press, 1979.

Shulman, Abraham. "Boulevard Isaac Bashevis Singer in the Heart of New York." *Midstream* 41 (November 1995): 38–40.

Smalley, William F. "Alliance Mission in Palestine, Arab Lands, and Israel, 1890–1970." Manuscript, New York, 1971. A copy in the Christian and Missionary Alliance House, the Prophets Street, Jerusalem.

——. *Translation as Mission: Bible Translation in the Modern Missionary Movement*. Macon, Ga.: Mercer University Press, 1991.

Smith, Christian. *American Evangelicalism: Embattled and Thriving*. Chicago: University of Chicago Press, 1998.

Sobel, B. Z. *Hebrew Christianity: The Thirteenth Tribe*. New York: John Wiley & Sons, 1974.

——. "The Tools of Legitimation: Zionism and the Hebrew Christian Movement." *Jewish Journal of Sociology* 10 (1968): 241–50.

Sorin, Gerald A. *The Jewish People in America*. Vol 3, *A Time for Building: The Third Migration, 1880–1920*. Baltimore: Johns Hopkins University Press, 1992.

Stark, Rodney, and William Sims Bainbridge, "Networks of Faith: Interpersonal Bonds and Recruitments to Cults." *American Journal of Sociology* 85 (1980): 1376–95.

Streiber, Lowell D. *The Jesus Trip: Advent of the Jesus Freaks*. New York: Abingdon, 1971.

Stromberg, Peter G. "The Impression Point: Synthesis of Symbol and Self." *Ethos: Journal of the Society for Psychological Anthropology* 13 (Spring 1985): 56–74.

——. *Language and Self-Transformation: A Study of the Christian Conversion Narrative*. Cambridge: Cambridge University Press, 1993.

Svonkin, Stuart. *Jews against Prejudice: American Jews and the Fight for Civil Liberties*. New York: Columbia University Press, 1997.

Sweet, Leonard I. "The Modernization of Protestant Religion in America." In *Altered Landscapes: Christianity in America 1935–1985*, edited by David W. Lotz. Grand Rapids, Mich.: William B. Eerdmans, 1989.

Synan, Vinson. *The Holiness-Pentecostal Movement in the United States*. Grand Rapids, Mich.: William B. Eerdmans, 1971.

Talmage, Frank E., ed., *Disputation and Dialogue: Reading in the Jewish-Christian Encounter*. New York: Ktav Publishing House, 1975.

Taylor, Bryan. "Conversion and Cognition." *Social Compass* 23 (1976): 5–22.

Toon, Peter, ed., *Puritans, the Millennium, and the Future of Israel: Puritan Eschatology, 1600–1660*. London: James Clarke, 1970.

Trollinger, William V. *God's Empire: William Bell Riley and Midwestern Fundamentalism*. Madison: University of Wisconsin Press, 1990.

Tuchman, Barbara. *Bible and Sword*. London: Macmillan, 1983.

Tucker, Ruth A., and Walter Liefeld. *Daughters of the Church: Women and Ministry from New Testament Times to the Present*. Grand Rapids, Mich.: Zondervan, 1987.

Tuerk, Richard. "Jacob Riis and the Jews." *New York Historical Society Quarterly* 63 (July 1979): 179–201.

Ullman, Chana. *The Transformed Self*. New York: Plenum Press, 1989.

Urofsky, Melvin I. *American Zionism from Herzl to the Holocaust*. Garden City, N.Y.: Doubleday, 1975.

Viswanathan, Gauri. *Outside the Fold: Conversion, Modernity, and Belief*. Princeton: Princeton University Press, 1998.

Voss, Carl Hermann, and David A. Rausch. "American Christians and Israel, 1948–1988." *American Jewish Archives* 50 (April 1988): 41–81.

Warnock, James. "This Year They More Nearly Approached Us Than Ever: A Response of the Protestant Episcopal Church to Jewish Immigration." *Fides et Historia* 22 (1990): 43.

———. "To the Jew First: The Evangelical Mission to Jewish Immigrants, 1885–1915." Ph.D. diss., University of Washington, 1989.

Weber, Timothy P. *Living in the Shadow of the Second Coming: American Premillennialism, 1875–1982*. Grand Rapids, Mich.: Zondervan, 1983.

Weiner, *The Wild Goats of Ein Gedi*. Garden City, N.Y.: Doubleday, 1961.

Welter, B. "She Hath Done What She Could: Protestant Women's Missionary Careers in the Nineteenth Century." In *Women in American Religion*, edited by J. W. James. Philadelphia: University of Pennsylvania Press, 1980.

Wertheimer, Jack. *A People Divided: Judaism in Contemporary America*. Hanover, N.H.: University Press of New England, 1997.

Winer, Robert I. *The Calling: The History of the Messianic Jewish Alliance of America, 1915–1990*. Wynnewood, Pa.: Messianic Jewish Alliance of America, 1990.

Yates, Timothy. *Christian Mission in the Twentieth Century*. Cambridge: Cambridge University Press, 1994.

Zaretsky, Irving I., and Mark P. Leone, eds. *Religious Movements in Contemporary America*. Princeton: Princeton University Press, 1974.

Zeldin, Gavriel. "Catholics and Protestants in Jerusalem and the 'Return of Jews to Zion,' 1948–1988." Ph.D. diss., Hebrew University of Jerusalem, 1992.

Index

Home Mission Council, 180

Hope of Israel (New York), 9, 13, 14, 16, 18–20, 24, 69, 220

House of Love and Prayer, 209–11

Howe, C. F., 26

Huisjen, Albert, 83–84

Hull, William, 156–59

Hull House (Chicago), 26. *See also*, Addams, Jane

Huntley, Frances, 30, 101

Hutchens, James, 238

Immanuel's Witness, 15

Immigrants, Jewish: in America, 3, 9, 12, 31, 39, 45, 67, 68, 121, 125, 137, 190, 196; from Eastern Europe, 12, 55–56, 67–68, 72–73, 102, 138, 146, 161, 163; from Germany, 12; from Russia, 256; second generation, 3, 166, 170, 288; third generation, 4, 146, 205, 211
— in Israel: from Ethiopia, 273; from former Soviet Union, 266, 273–74, 281; from Middle East, 146, 161, 163; from North Africa, 149, 161, 163

India, 74, 75

Indianapolis, Ind., 136

Interdenominational missions, 1, 12, 86, 175

Interfaith: activity, 128; dialogue, 4, 133, 134, 182, 185, 213, 239, 252–53, 264

Intermarriage, 46, 49, 196, 247, 268

International Board of Jewish Missions, 86

International Christian Embassy (Jerusalem), 276

International Hebrew Christian Alliance, 162, 163, 172

International Messianic Fellowship of Chattanooga, Tennessee, 137

International Missionary Council, 175, 177, 178, 180, 181; Committee on the Christian Approach to the Jews, 175, 178–80

Internet technology, 217, 279–80

Ironside, Harry, 105, 116

Isaiah, Book of, 16, 261

Israel, State of, 100, 110, 117, 131, 140, 141, 223, 227, 229, 230, 266; government and

officials of, 144, 145, 146, 150, 158, 159, 162, 214, 271, 276–79; Ministry of Religious Affairs, 150, 153, 159; missionary work in, 116, 141, 143–64, 271–72; pro-Israel activity in, 276; society in, 156, 160, 271–75; tours to, 276. *See also* Land of Israel

Israelites of the New Covenant (Kishinev), 19

Israel's Restoration (Bradbury), 116

Issues: A Messianic Jewish Perspective, 217

Jabotinsky Order Medal, 265, 275

Jacobs, Hayman, 141

Jaffa, 35, 144, 147

Japan, 284, 286

Jehovah's Witnesses, 195

Jeremiah, Book of, 10

Jerusalem, 35–36, 144, 147, 153, 157

Jerusalem Institute of Biblical Polemics, 257

Jerusalem Report, 268

Jerusalem School of New Testament Studies, 151

Jesuits, 207

Jesus, 31, 43, 85, 210, 227, 228, 232, 233, 234, 241, 246, 249, 262; Second Coming of, 2, 10, 12, 13, 218, 265

"Jesus movement," 213

"Jesus People," 202

Jewish Agency, Department of Social Services of (Palestine), 188

"Jewish Believers," 229

Jewish Christians, 120, 123, 160, 162, 231; conferences of, 48; congregations of, 125, 130, 131, 132, 174, 205–6, 243, 249, 273, 288; and Zionism, 99, 174

Jewish-Christian relationship 2, 5, 84, 123, 130, 132, 143, 176, 207, 215, 239, 264

Jewish Community Centers (JCCs), 125

Jewish Community Relations Council of New York, Task Force on Missionaries and Cults, 264

Jewish Defense League (JDL), 214, 258, 259

Jewish Era, 15, 16, 25, 26, 97

Missions: advertising by, 101, 107, 217; aid offered by, 2, 3, 23, 25, 43–44, 55, 64, 161–62; attitudes of toward Jews, 56, 84, 289; broadcasting by, 101, 107, 118, 141, 275; conferences of, 70, 175–78, 181, 285–86; and Jewish holidays, 15, 131; and Jewish symbols, 16; reputations of, 69–76; tracts and journals of, 12, 24, 73, 279–80; new vocabulary of, 270–72; use of Internet technology by, 217, 279–80; and women, 25–23, 35, 41, 107, 127, 138, 200, 203, 209, 282, 283; and Zionism, 12–13. *See also* American Association for Jewish Evangelism; American Baptists; American Board of Missions to the Jews; American Messianic Fellowship; Buffalo Hebrew Christian Mission; Chicago Hebrew Mission; Chosen People Ministries; Christian and Missionary Alliance; Cleveland Hebrew Mission; Friends of Israel; Hope of Israel; Jews for Jesus; Lederer Foundation; Lutherans; Methodist Episcopal Church; Mildmay Mission to the Jews; Million Testaments Campaign; Missionaries; Presbyterian Church in the U.S.A., Southern Baptists

Missouri Synod, 184

Modernists (Protestant), 79–80, 82

Moment, 268

Monophisite churches, 36

Moody, Dwight, 26, 28, 34, 45, 93

Moody Bible Institute, 28, 32, 33, 50, 85, 86, 92–101, 108, 114, 115, 116, 120, 127, 135, 172, 236–38, 262

Moody Memorial Church (Chicago), 105, 116

Moody Monthly, 93, 236, 238

Moon, Sun Myung, 202, 254. *See also* Unification Church

Mormons, 2, 10

Mott, John R., 177

Muntz, J. Palmer, 115, 117

Muskegon, Mich., 136

Muslims, 35, 36, 182, 255

Musrara, Israel, 149, 162

Nadler, Sam, 218

Nathan, Dorothy, 189

National Conference of Synagogue Youth, 263

National Council of Christians and Jews, 182

National Council of Churches, 183–84

National Jewish Demographic Survey, 267–68

National Lutheran Council, Department for the Christian Approach to the Jewish People, 181

National Religious Jewish Students' Association, 261

Native Americans, 129, 229, 206, 241, 242

Nativist movements, 186, 252

Nazi persecution of Jews, 30, 106, 128, 129, 157–58; reaction of missions to, 109–10, 128–30

Needleman, Samuel, 30, 44

Neo-Orthodox (Christian) theology, 183

Netanyahu, Benjamin, 278

Newark, N.J., 126

"New Christian music," 227

New Covenant Mission (Pittsburgh), 17, 93

New Jersey, 170

Newman, Elias, 82, 112, 171, 189

New Orleans, La., 135

New Testament, 33, 58, 65, 88, 89, 90, 91, 92, 99, 103, 150, 246, 249, 257–58, 262; modern Hebrew translation of, 150–51; Yiddish translation of, 88–92

New York, N.Y., 12, 22, 27, 32, 61, 63, 69, 70, 106, 119, 178, 202, 212, 256, 264, 280; Lower East Side, 9, 19, 36, 39, 43, 47, 58, 64–65, 70, 126, 220; West Side, 62. *See also* Brooklyn, N.Y.

New York Mission and Tract Society, 70

Niebuhr, Reinhold, 132–33, 182

Northeastern Bible School, 202

Northern Baptist Theological Seminary, 99, 141

Northwestern School of the Bible, 112

Norwegian Zion Mission to the Jews, 108

Nyack, N.Y., 35

premillennialist Christian view of, 12–13, 173, 183, 227, 289–90; view of by missionaries, 12–13, 25, 97, 103, 140–41, 154, 156, 158, 174, 227, 288–90; and missionaries, 63–64, 187

Lamar Cecil, *Wilhelm II: Prince and Emperor, 1859–1900* (1989).

Carolyn Merchant, *Ecological Revolutions: Nature, Gender, and Science in New England* (1989).

Gladys Engel Lang and Kurt Lang, *Etched in Memory: The Building and Survival of Artistic Reputation* (1990).

Howard Jones, *Union in Peril: The Crisis over British Intervention in the Civil War* (1992).

Robert L. Dorman, *Revolt of the Provinces: The Regionalist Movement in America* (1993).

Peter N. Stearns, *Meaning Over Memory: Recasting the Teaching of Culture and History* (1993).

Thomas Wolfe, *The Good Child's River,* edited with an introduction by Suzanne Stutman (1994).

Warren A. Nord, *Religion and American Education: Rethinking a National Dilemma* (1995).

David E. Whisnant, *Rascally Signs in Sacred Places: The Politics of Culture in Nicaragua* (1995).

Lamar Cecil, *Wilhelm II: Emperor and Exile, 1900–1941* (1996).

Jonathan Hartlyn, *The Struggle for Democratic Politics in the Dominican Republic* (1998).

Louis A. Pérez Jr., *On Becoming Cuban: Identity, Nationality, and Culture* (1999).

Yaakov Ariel, *Evangelizing the Chosen People: Missions to the Jews in America, 1880–2000* (2000)